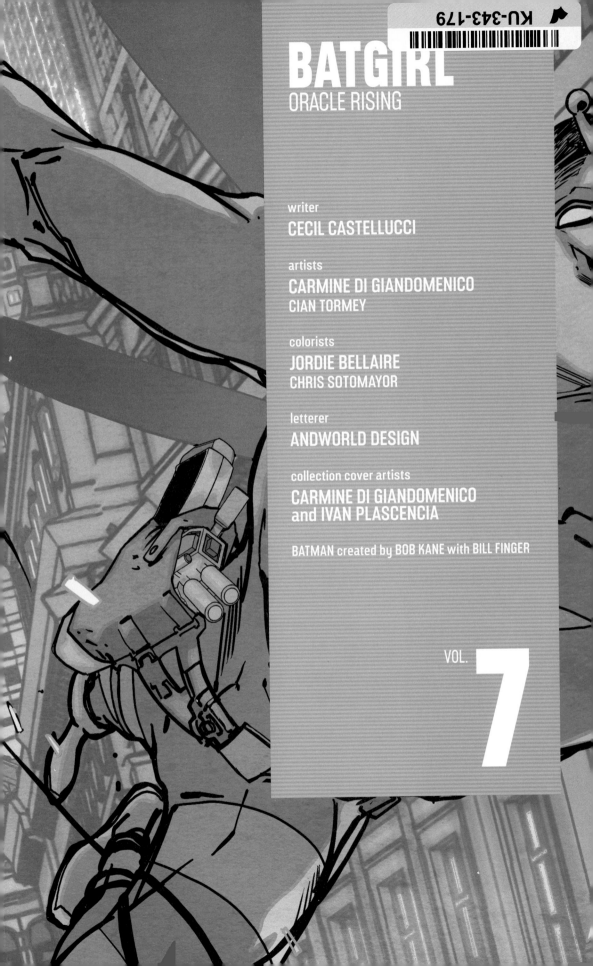

BATGIRL
ORACLE RISING

writer
CECIL CASTELLUCCI

artists
CARMINE DI GIANDOMENICO
CIAN TORMEY

colorists
JORDIE BELLAIRE
CHRIS SOTOMAYOR

letterer
ANDWORLD DESIGN

collection cover artists
CARMINE DI GIANDOMENICO
and IVAN PLASCENCIA

BATMAN created by BOB KANE with BILL FINGER

VOL. **7**

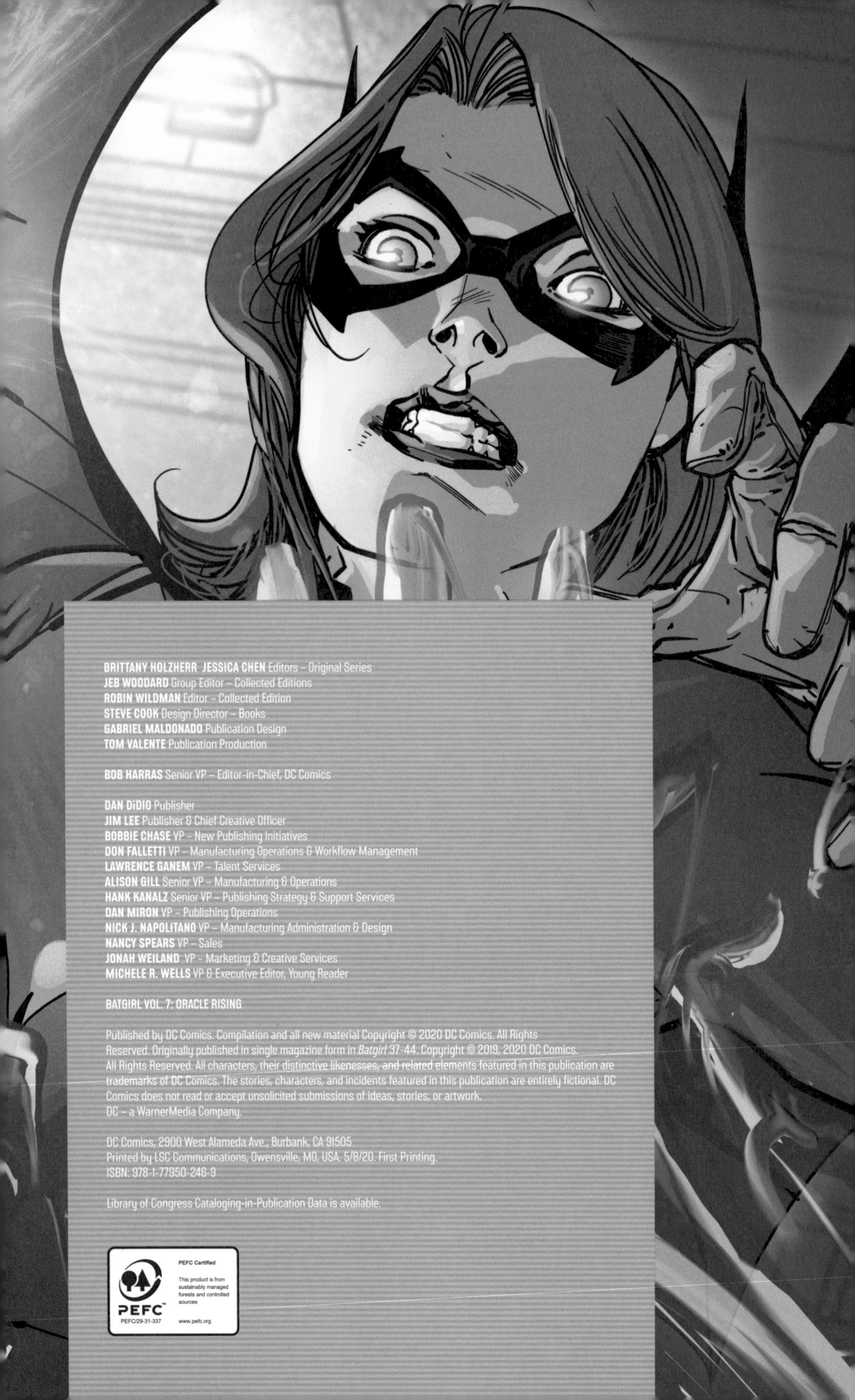

BRITTANY HOLZHERR JESSICA CHEN Editors – Original Series
JEB WOODARD Group Editor – Collected Editions
ROBIN WILDMAN Editor – Collected Edition
STEVE COOK Design Director – Books
GABRIEL MALDONADO Publication Design
TOM VALENTE Publication Production

BOB HARRAS Senior VP – Editor-in-Chief, DC Comics

DAN DiDIO Publisher
JIM LEE Publisher & Chief Creative Officer
BOBBIE CHASE VP – New Publishing Initiatives
DON FALLETTI VP – Manufacturing Operations & Workflow Management
LAWRENCE GANEM VP – Talent Services
ALISON GILL Senior VP – Manufacturing & Operations
HANK KANALZ Senior VP – Publishing Strategy & Support Services
DAN MIRON VP – Publishing Operations
NICK J. NAPOLITANO VP – Manufacturing Administration & Design
NANCY SPEARS VP – Sales
JONAH WEILAND VP – Marketing & Creative Services
MICHELE R. WELLS VP & Executive Editor, Young Reader

BATGIRL VOL. 7: ORACLE RISING

DC Comics, 2900 West Alameda Ave., Burbank, CA 91505
Printed by LSC Communications, Owensville, MO, USA. 5/8/20. First Printing.
ISBN: 978-1-77950-246-9

Library of Congress Cataloging-in-Publication Data is available.

PEFC Certified
This product is from sustainably managed forests and controlled sources
www.pefc.org
PEFC
PEFC/29-31-337

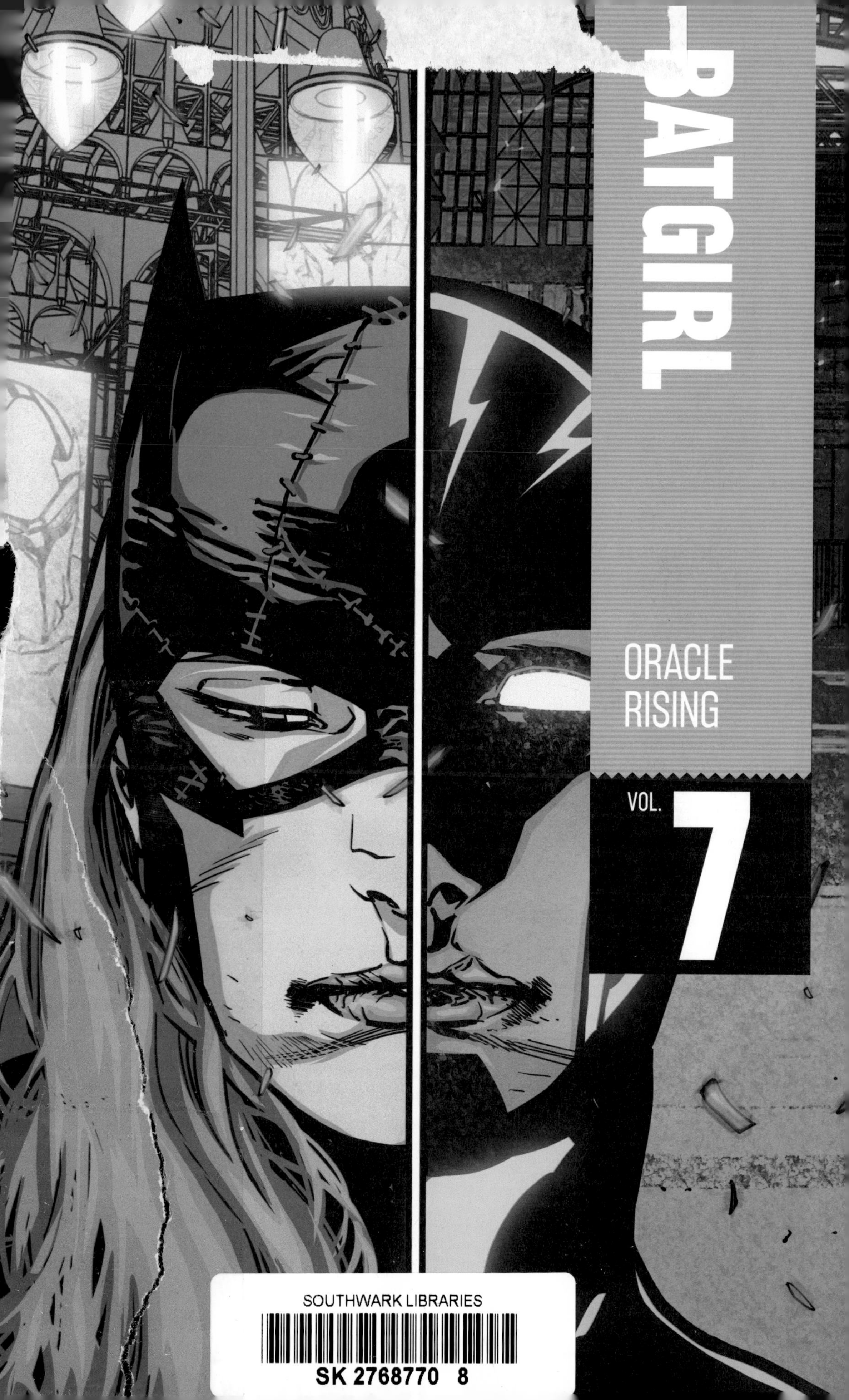
BATGIRL
ORACLE
RISING
VOL. 7

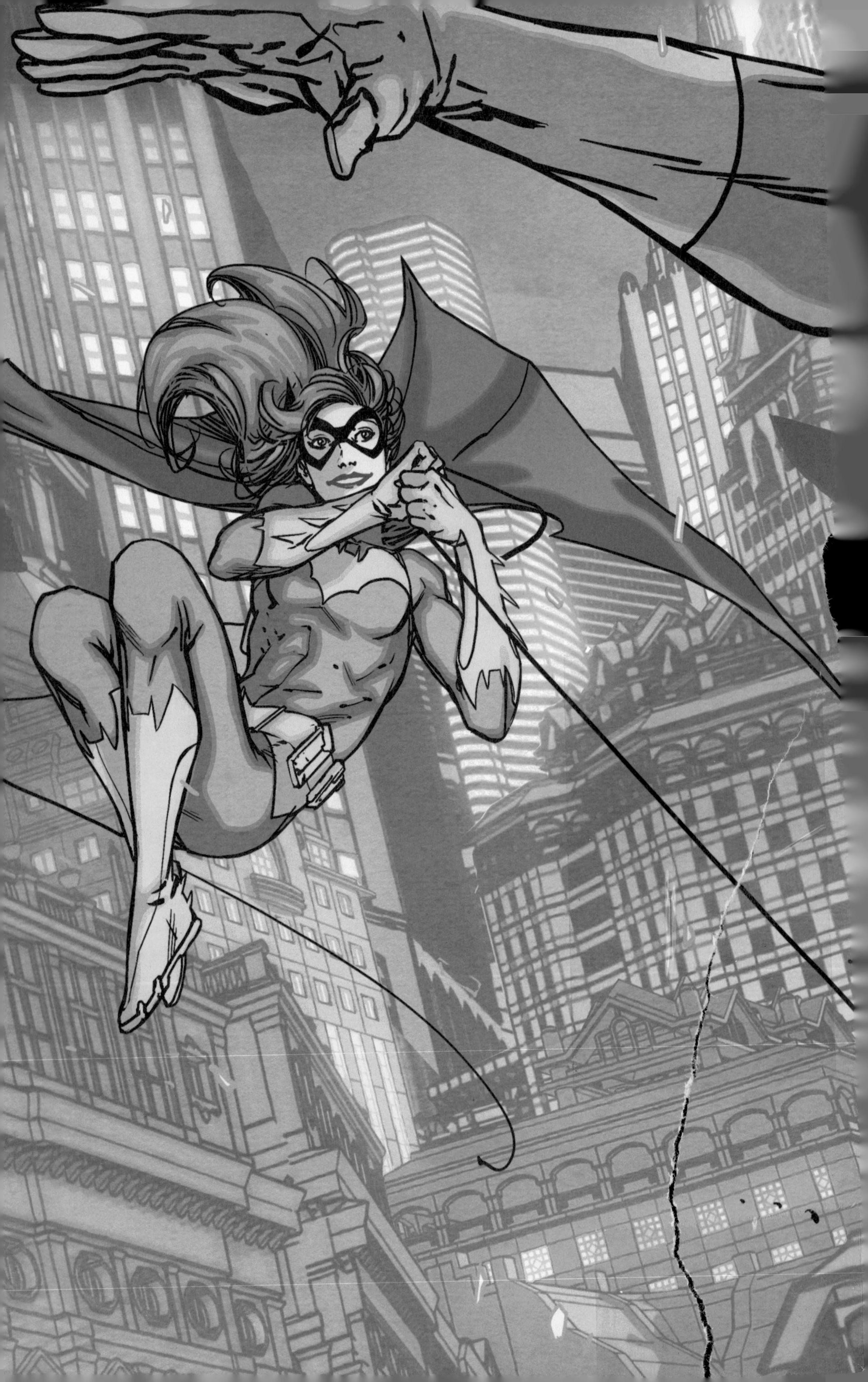

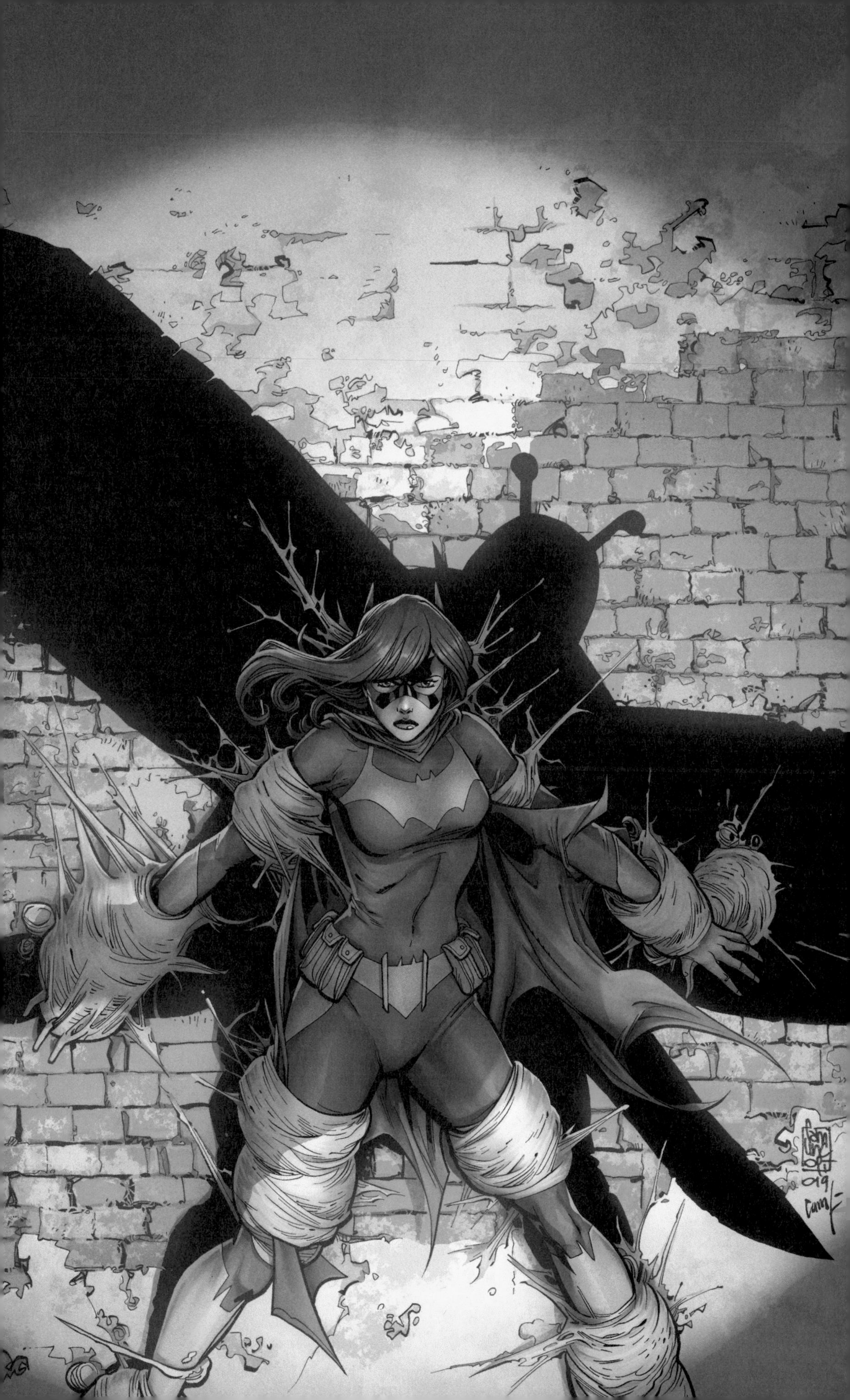

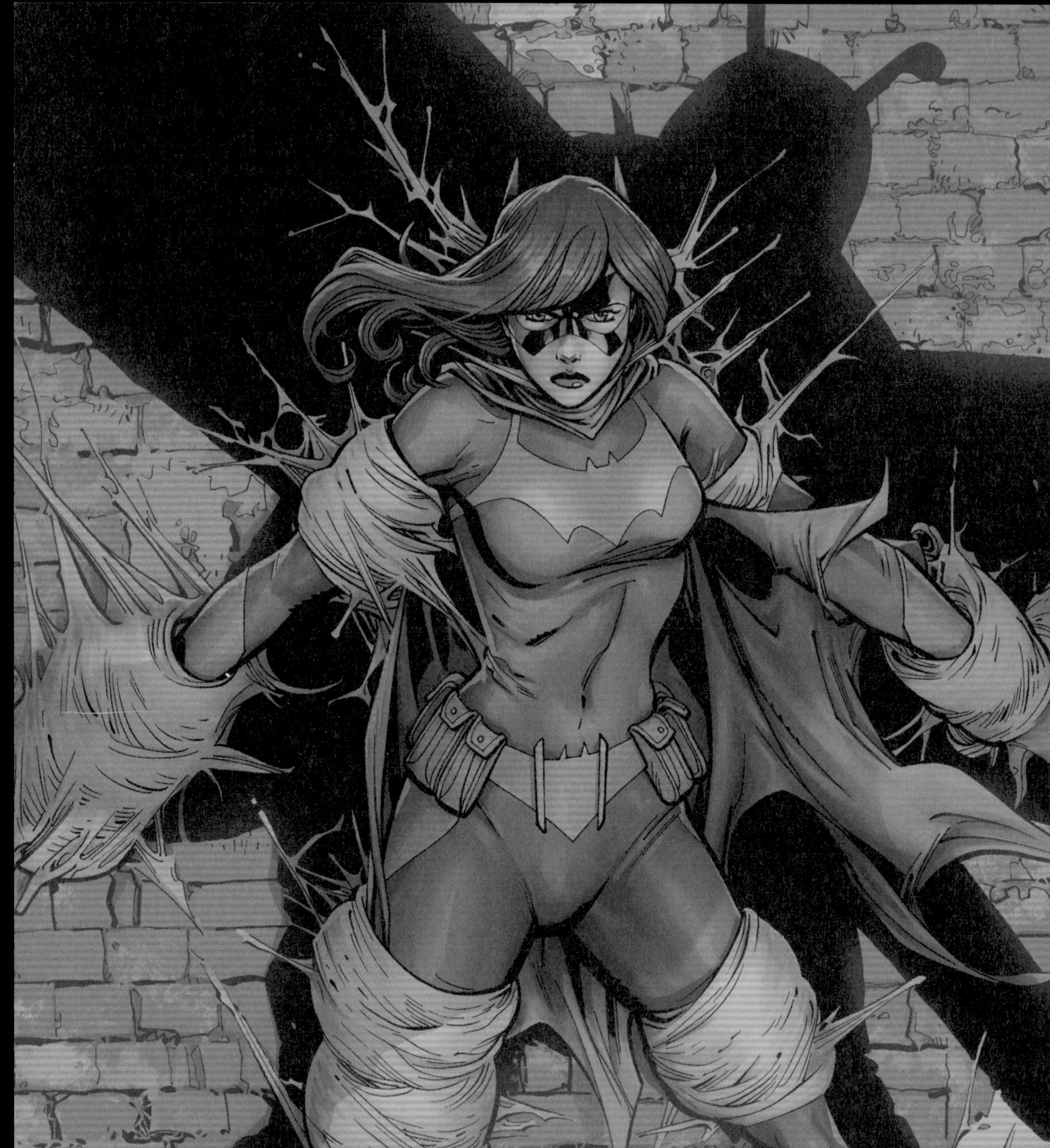

BATGIRL
#37

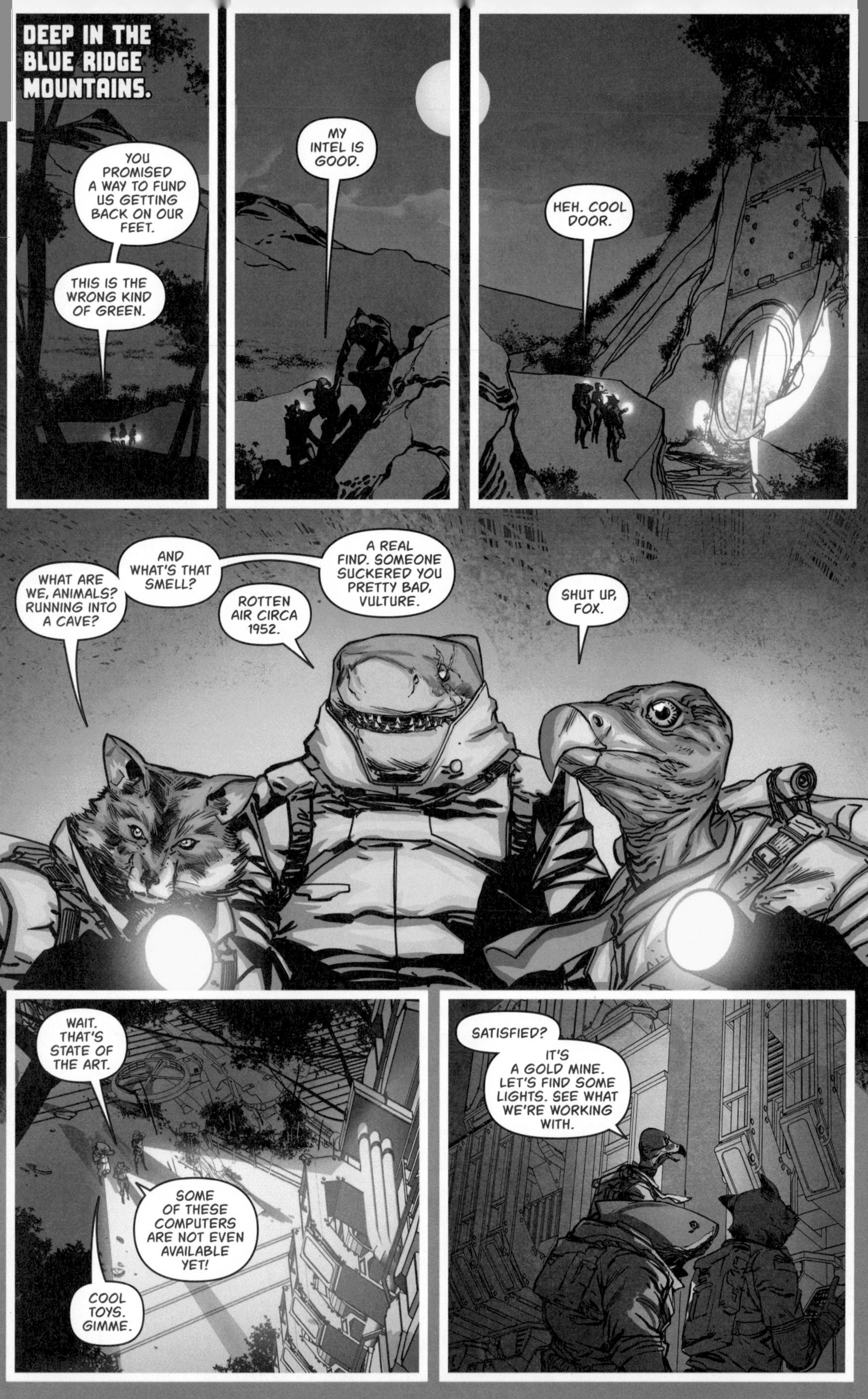
DEEP IN THE BLUE RIDGE MOUNTAINS.
YOU PROMISED A WAY TO FUND US GETTING BACK ON OUR FEET.
THIS IS THE WRONG KIND OF GREEN.
MY INTEL IS GOOD.
HEH. COOL DOOR.
WHAT ARE WE, ANIMALS? RUNNING INTO A CAVE?
AND WHAT'S THAT SMELL?
ROTTEN AIR CIRCA 1952.
A REAL FIND. SOMEONE SUCKERED YOU PRETTY BAD, VULTURE.
SHUT UP, FOX.
WAIT. THAT'S STATE OF THE ART.
SOME OF THESE COMPUTERS ARE NOT EVEN AVAILABLE YET!
COOL TOYS. GIMME.
SATISFIED?
IT'S A GOLD MINE. LET'S FIND SOME LIGHTS. SEE WHAT WE'RE WORKING WITH.

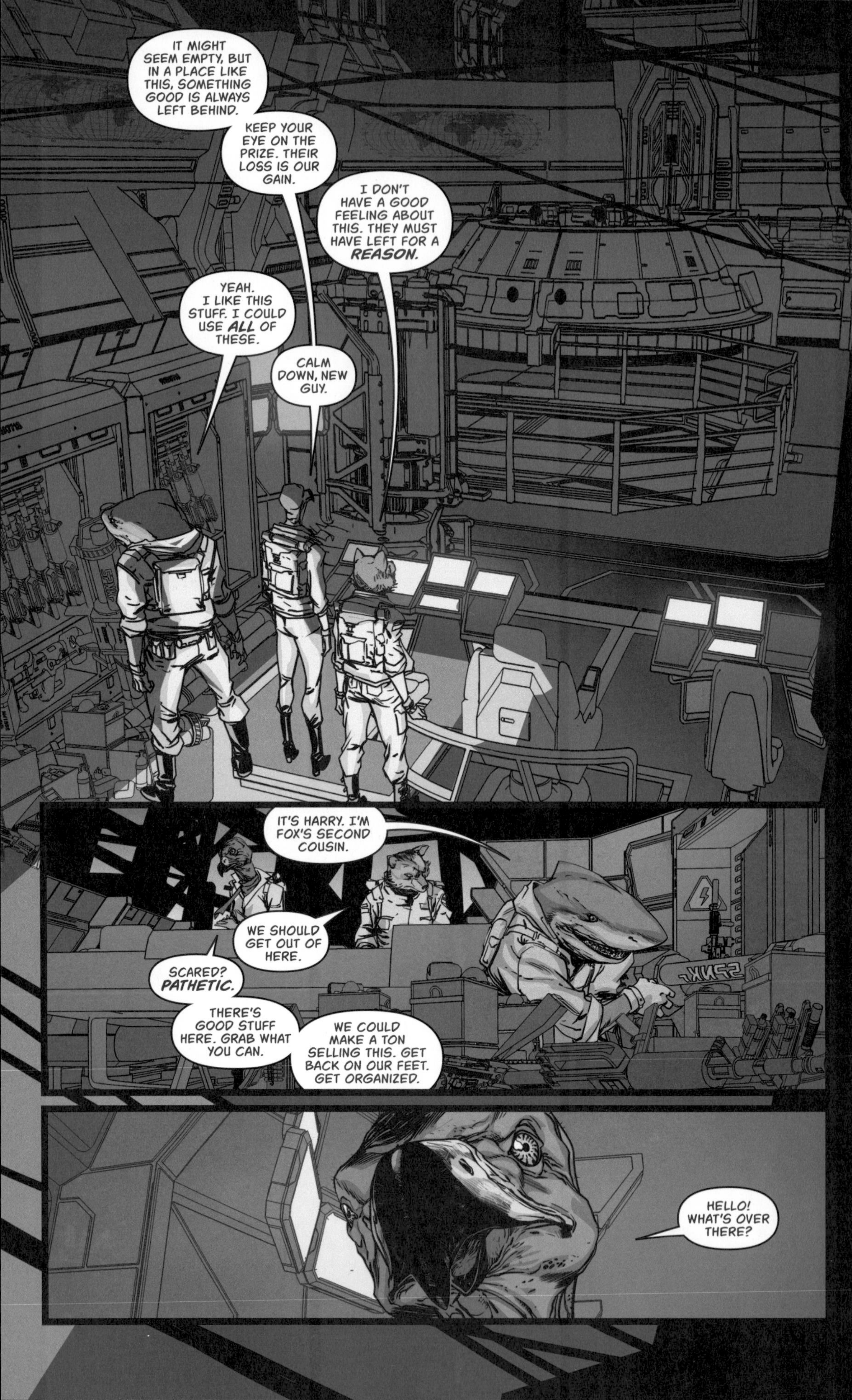
IT MIGHT SEEM EMPTY, BUT IN A PLACE LIKE THIS, SOMETHING GOOD IS ALWAYS LEFT BEHIND.
KEEP YOUR EYE ON THE PRIZE. THEIR LOSS IS OUR GAIN.
I DON'T HAVE A GOOD FEELING ABOUT THIS. THEY MUST HAVE LEFT FOR A *REASON.*
YEAH. I LIKE THIS STUFF. I COULD USE *ALL* OF THESE.
CALM DOWN, NEW GUY.
IT'S HARRY. I'M FOX'S SECOND COUSIN.
WE SHOULD GET OUT OF HERE.
SCARED? *PATHETIC.*
THERE'S GOOD STUFF HERE. GRAB WHAT YOU CAN.
WE COULD MAKE A TON SELLING THIS. GET BACK ON OUR FEET. GET ORGANIZED.
HELLO! WHAT'S OVER THERE?

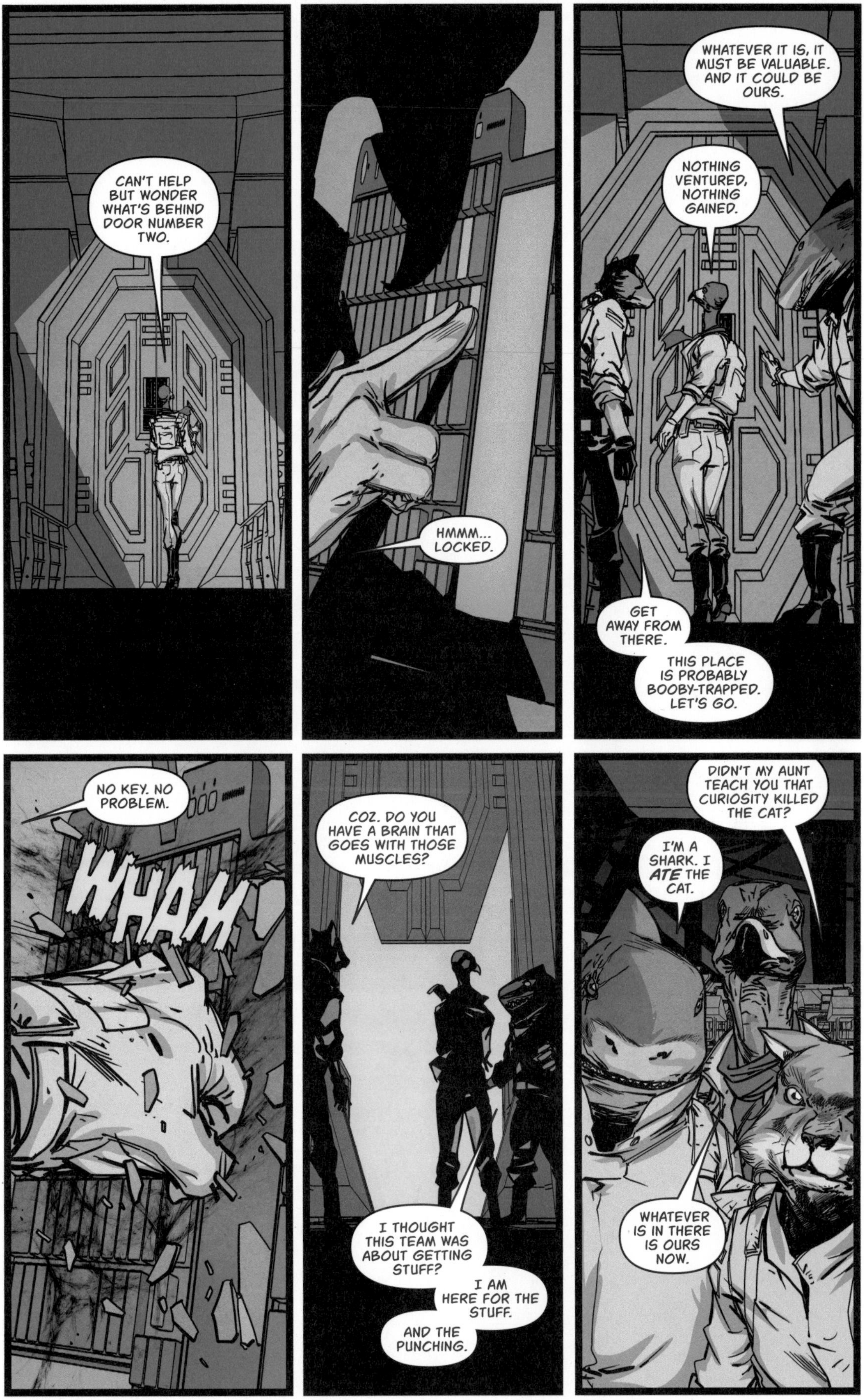
CAN'T HELP BUT WONDER WHAT'S BEHIND DOOR NUMBER TWO.
HMMM... LOCKED.
WHATEVER IT IS, IT MUST BE VALUABLE. AND IT COULD BE OURS.
NOTHING VENTURED, NOTHING GAINED.
GET AWAY FROM THERE.
THIS PLACE IS PROBABLY BOOBY-TRAPPED. LET'S GO.
NO KEY. NO PROBLEM.
WHAM
COZ. DO YOU HAVE A BRAIN THAT GOES WITH THOSE MUSCLES?
I THOUGHT THIS TEAM WAS ABOUT GETTING STUFF?
I AM HERE FOR THE STUFF.
AND THE PUNCHING.
DIDN'T MY AUNT TEACH YOU THAT CURIOSITY KILLED THE CAT?
I'M A SHARK. I ATE THE CAT.
WHATEVER IS IN THERE IS OURS NOW.

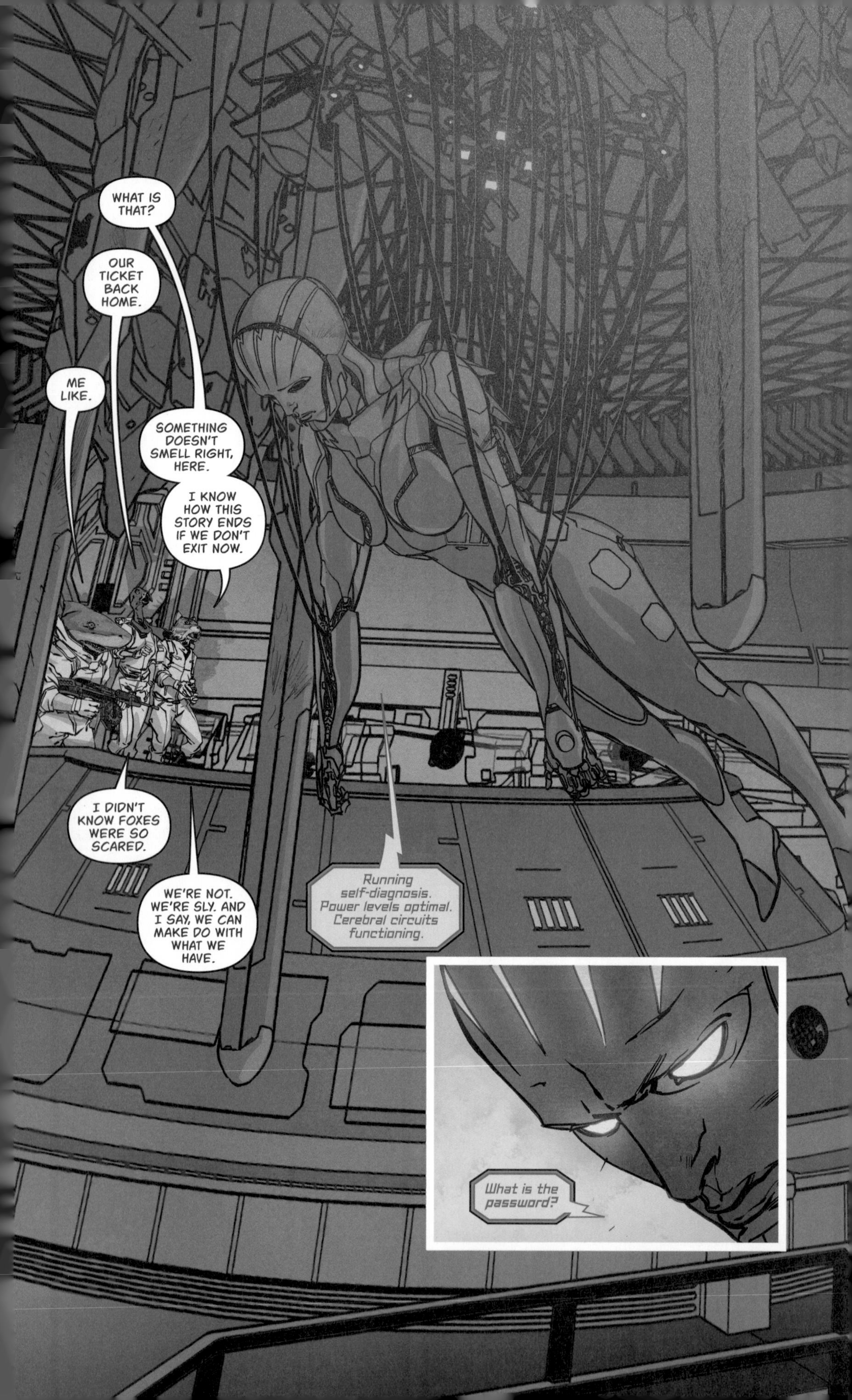
WHAT IS THAT?
OUR TICKET BACK HOME.
ME LIKE.
SOMETHING DOESN'T SMELL RIGHT, HERE.
I KNOW HOW THIS STORY ENDS IF WE DON'T EXIT NOW.
I DIDN'T KNOW FOXES WERE SO SCARED.
WE'RE NOT. WE'RE SLY. AND I SAY, WE CAN MAKE DO WITH WHAT WE HAVE.
Running self-diagnosis. Power levels optimal. Cerebral circuits functioning.
What is the password?

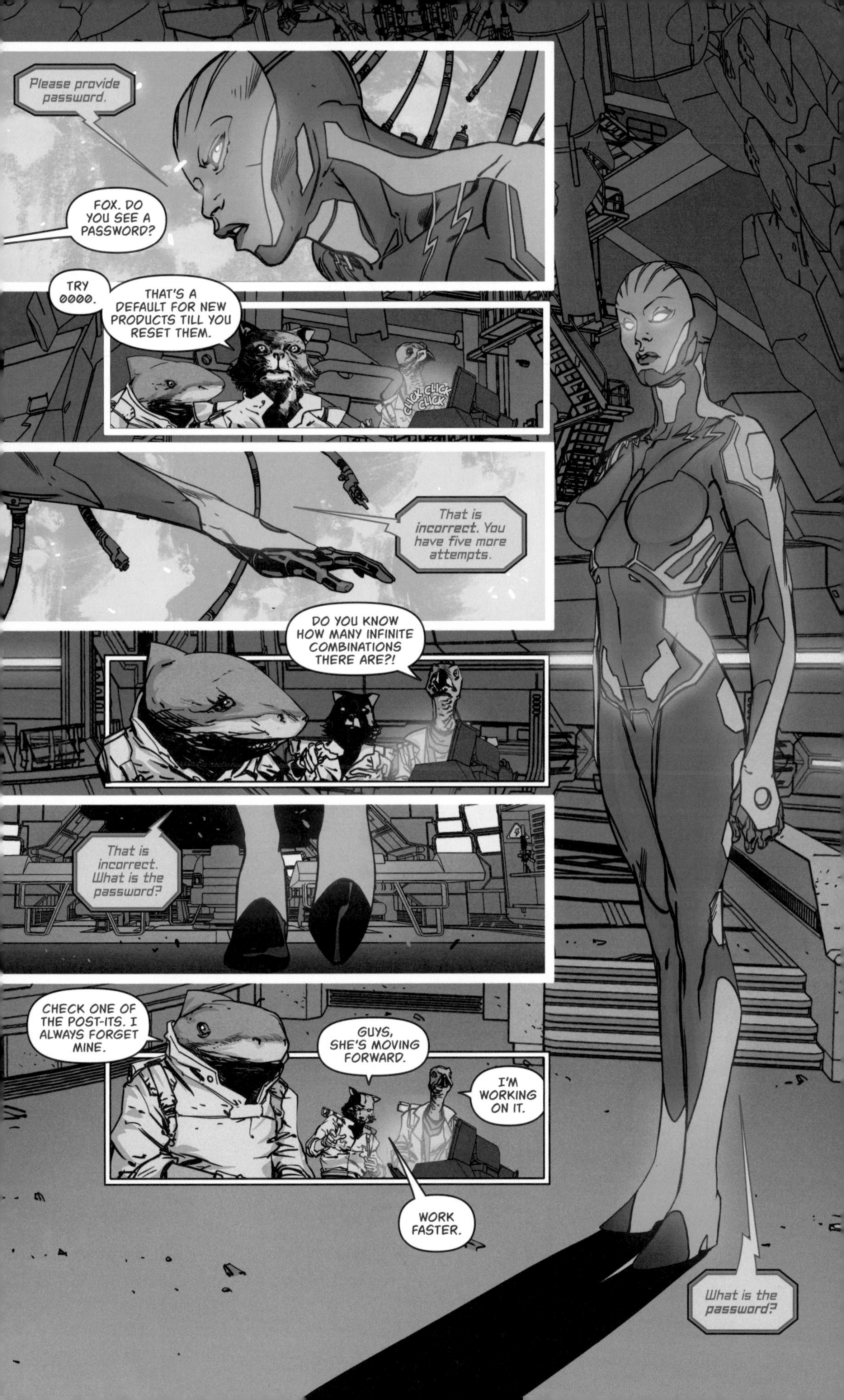
Please provide password.
FOX. DO YOU SEE A PASSWORD?
TRY 0000.
THAT'S A DEFAULT FOR NEW PRODUCTS TILL YOU RESET THEM.
CLICK CLICK CLICK
That is incorrect. You have five more attempts.
DO YOU KNOW HOW MANY INFINITE COMBINATIONS THERE ARE?!
That is incorrect. What is the password?
CHECK ONE OF THE POST-ITS. I ALWAYS FORGET MINE.
GUYS, SHE'S MOVING FORWARD.
I'M WORKING ON IT.
WORK FASTER.
What is the password?

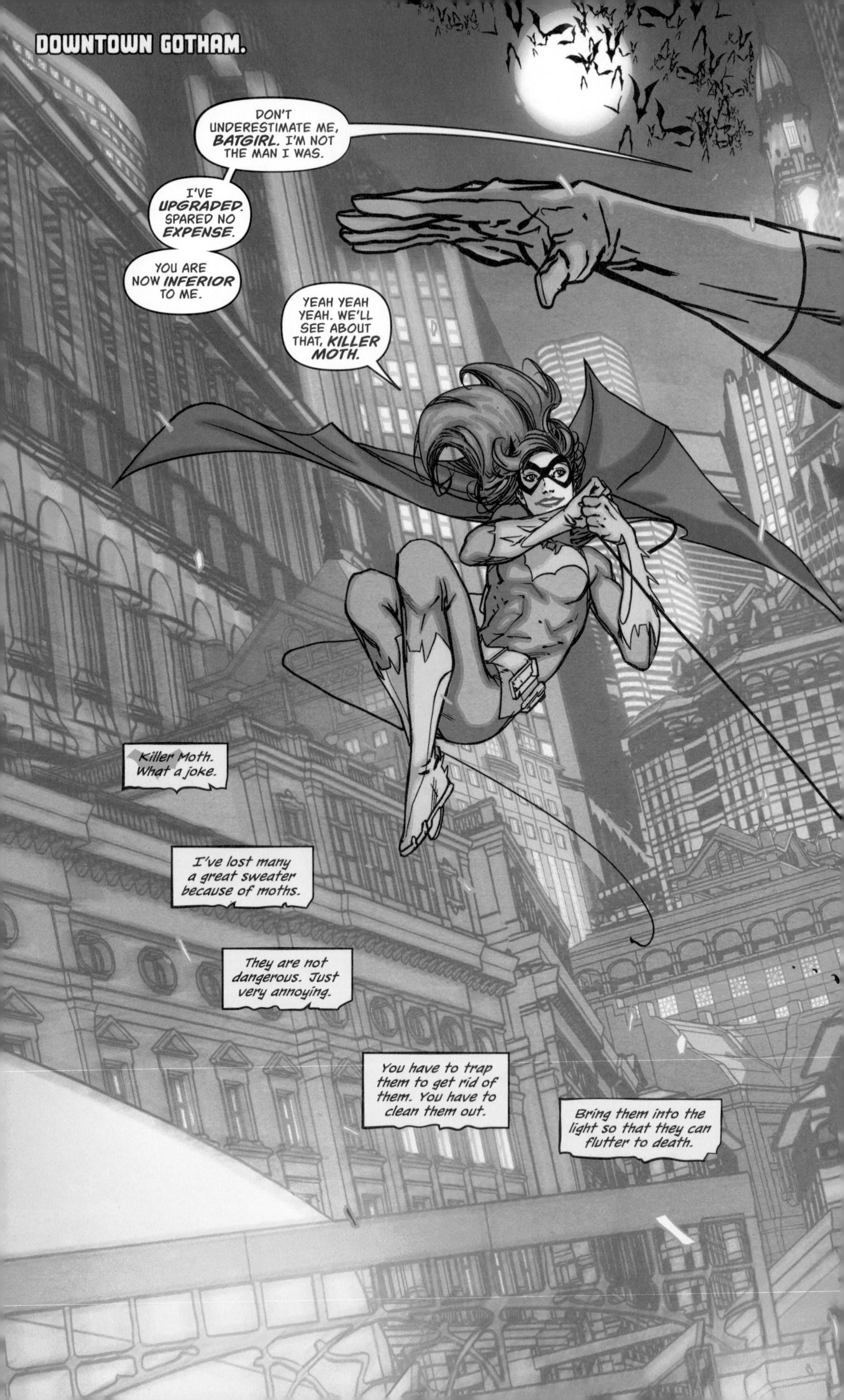
DOWNTOWN GOTHAM.
DON'T UNDERESTIMATE ME, BATGIRL. I'M NOT THE MAN I WAS.
I'VE UPGRADED. SPARED NO EXPENSE.
YOU ARE NOW INFERIOR TO ME.
YEAH YEAH YEAH. WE'LL SEE ABOUT THAT, KILLER MOTH.
Killer Moth. What a joke.
I've lost many a great sweater because of moths.
They are not dangerous. Just very annoying.
You have to trap them to get rid of them. You have to clean them out.
Bring them into the light so that they can flutter to death.

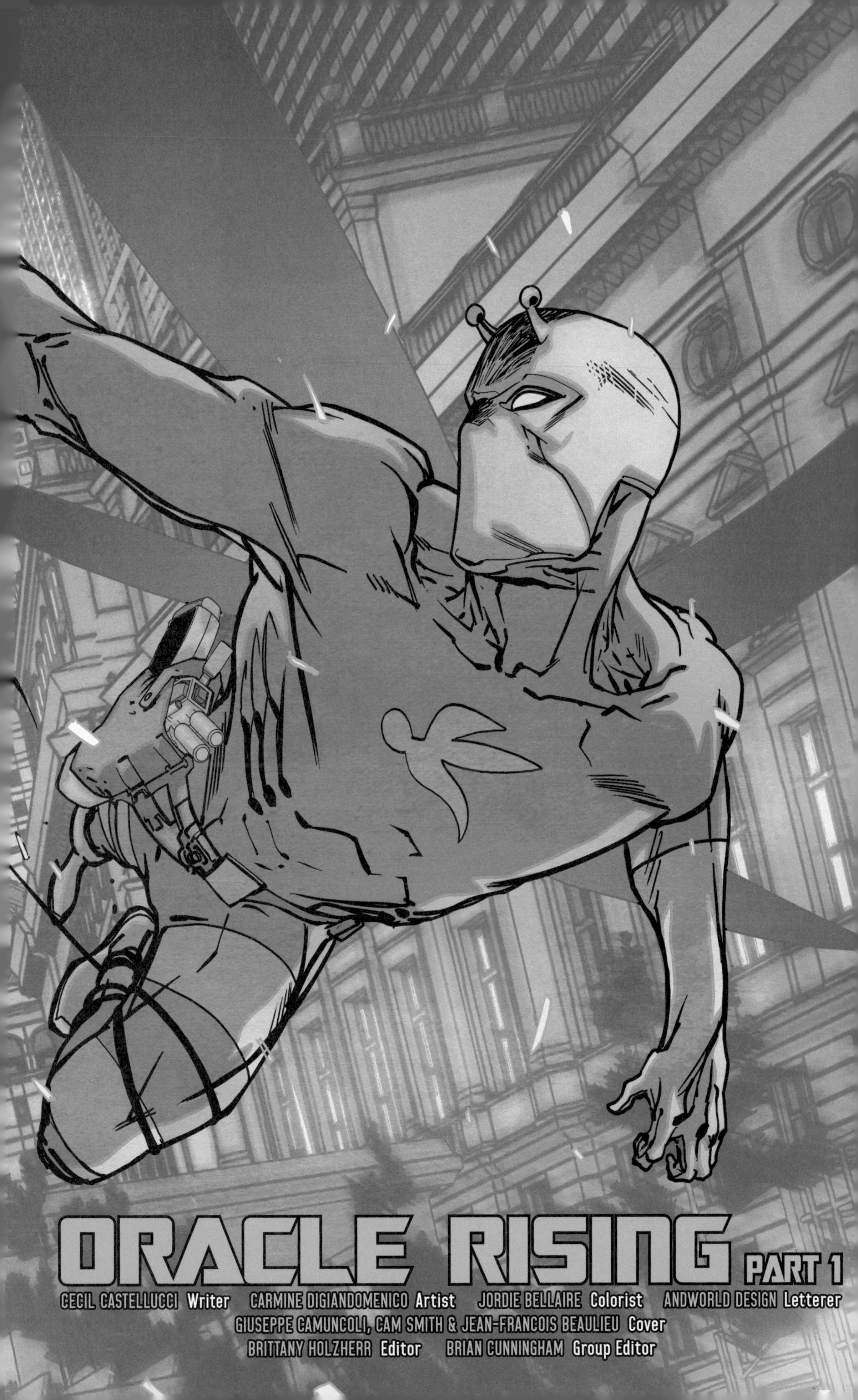
ORACLE RISING PART 1
CECIL CASTELLUCCI Writer CARMINE DIGIANDOMENICO Artist JORDIE BELLAIRE Colorist ANDWORLD DESIGN Letterer
GIUSEPPE CAMUNCOLI, CAM SMITH & JEAN-FRANCOIS BEAULIEU Cover
BRITTANY HOLZHERR Editor BRIAN CUNNINGHAM Group Editor

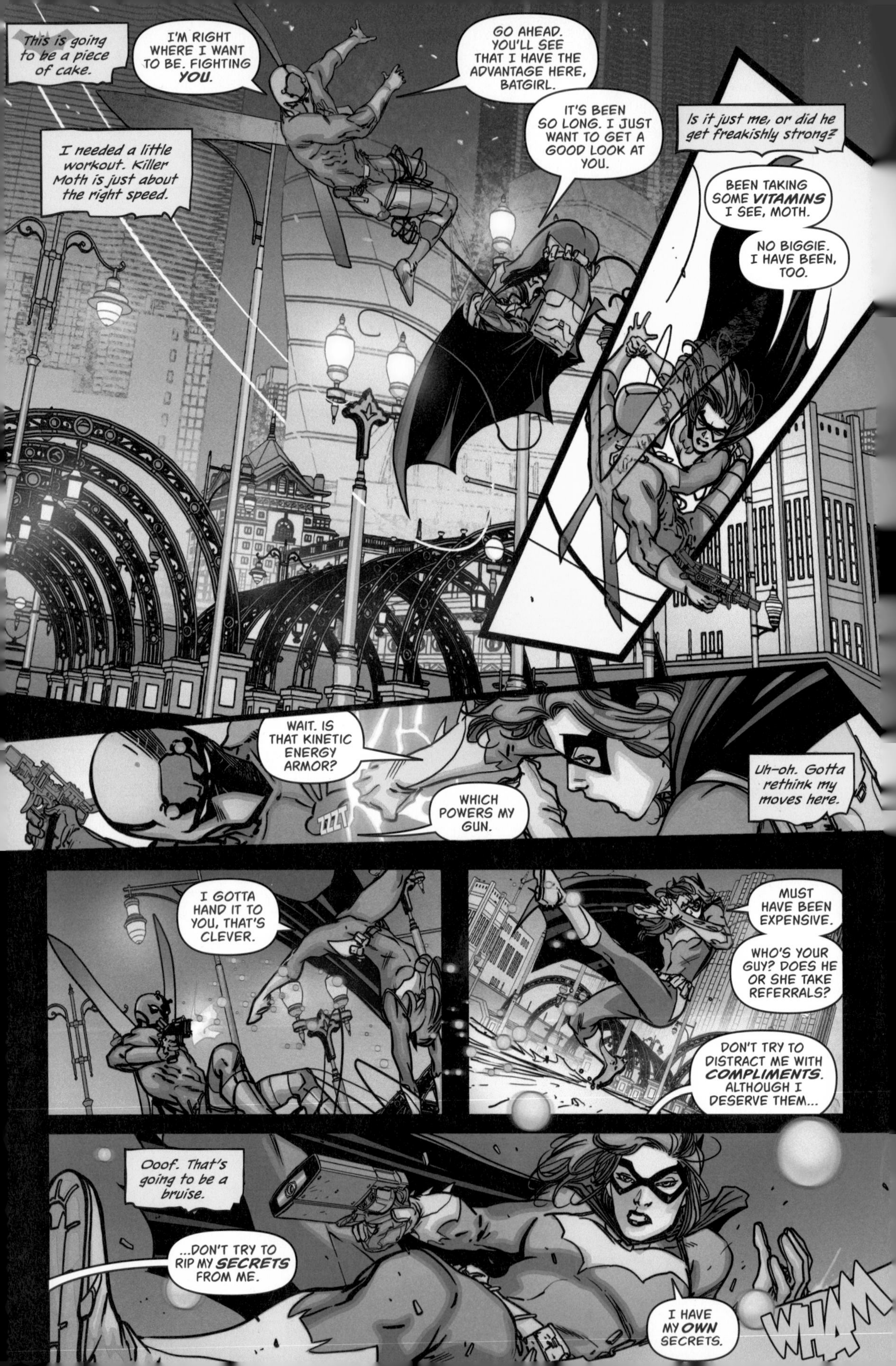
This is going to be a piece of cake.
I'M RIGHT WHERE I WANT TO BE. FIGHTING *YOU*.
GO AHEAD. YOU'LL SEE THAT I HAVE THE ADVANTAGE HERE, BATGIRL.
I needed a little workout. Killer Moth is just about the right speed.
IT'S BEEN SO LONG. I JUST WANT TO GET A GOOD LOOK AT YOU.
Is it just me, or did he get freakishly strong?
BEEN TAKING SOME *VITAMINS* I SEE, MOTH.
NO BIGGIE. I HAVE BEEN, TOO.
WAIT. IS THAT KINETIC ENERGY ARMOR?
ZZZT
WHICH POWERS MY GUN.
Uh-oh. Gotta rethink my moves here.
I GOTTA HAND IT TO YOU, THAT'S CLEVER.
MUST HAVE BEEN EXPENSIVE.
WHO'S YOUR GUY? DOES HE OR SHE TAKE REFERRALS?
DON'T TRY TO DISTRACT ME WITH *COMPLIMENTS*. ALTHOUGH I DESERVE THEM...
Ooof. That's going to be a bruise.
...DON'T TRY TO RIP MY *SECRETS* FROM ME.
I HAVE MY *OWN* SECRETS.
WHAM

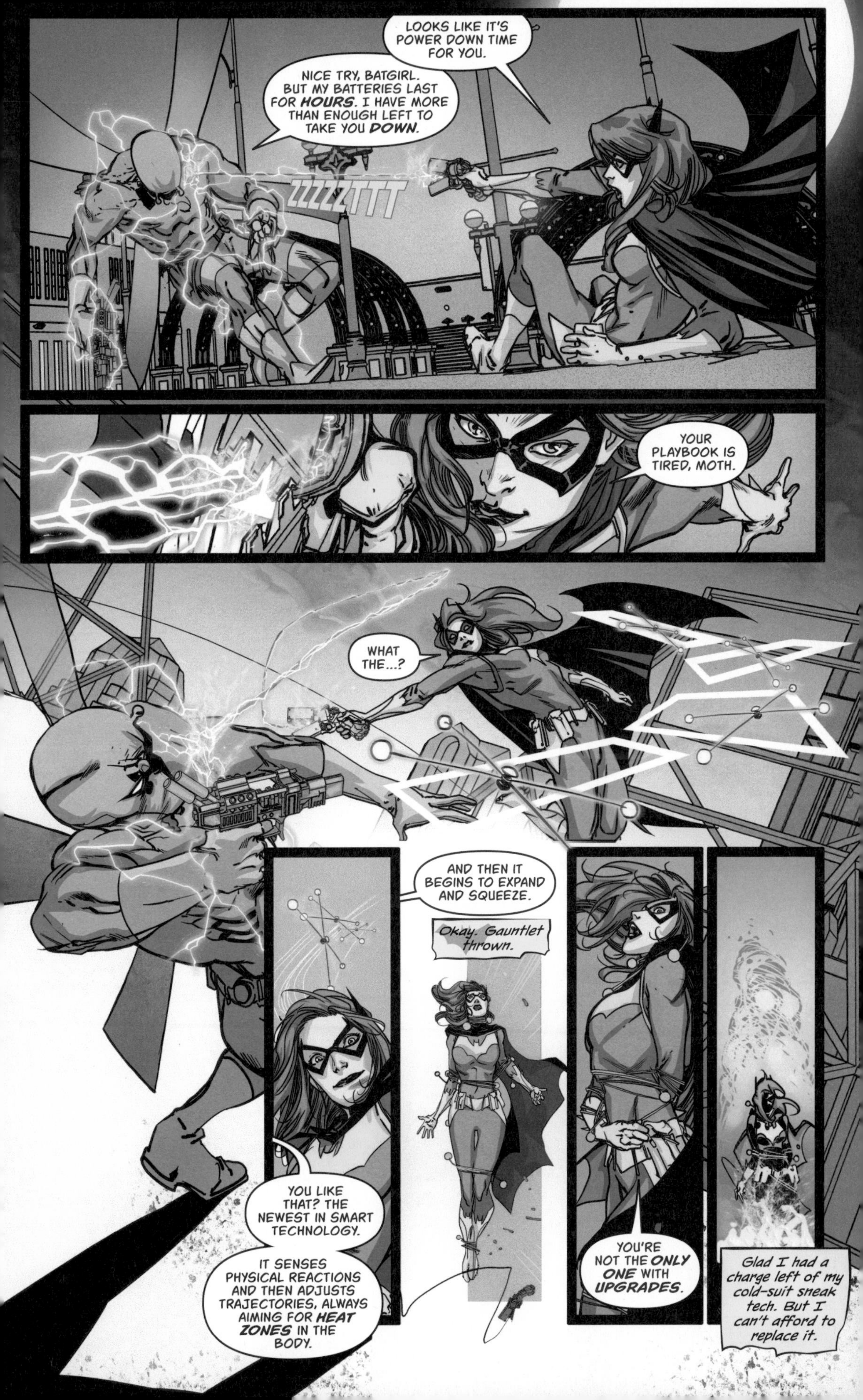
LOOKS LIKE IT'S POWER DOWN TIME FOR YOU.
NICE TRY, BATGIRL. BUT MY BATTERIES LAST FOR HOURS. I HAVE MORE THAN ENOUGH LEFT TO TAKE YOU DOWN.
ZZZZZTTT
YOUR PLAYBOOK IS TIRED, MOTH.
WHAT THE...?
YOU LIKE THAT? THE NEWEST IN SMART TECHNOLOGY.
IT SENSES PHYSICAL REACTIONS AND THEN ADJUSTS TRAJECTORIES, ALWAYS AIMING FOR HEAT ZONES IN THE BODY.
AND THEN IT BEGINS TO EXPAND AND SQUEEZE.
Okay. Gauntlet thrown.
YOU'RE NOT THE ONLY ONE WITH UPGRADES.
Glad I had a charge left of my cold-suit sneak tech. But I can't afford to replace it.

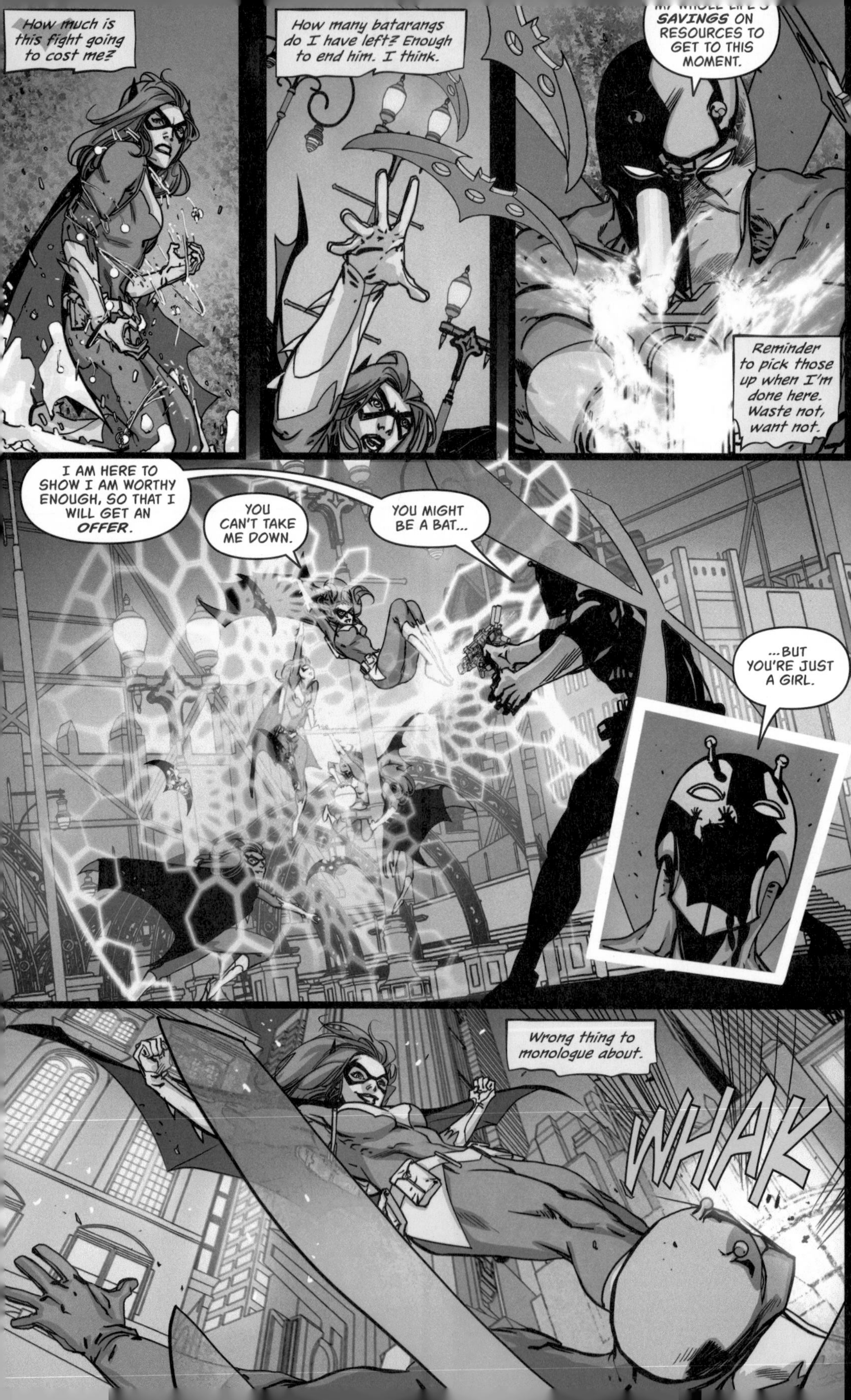
How much is this fight going to cost me?
How many batarangs do I have left? Enough to end him. I think.
SAVINGS ON RESOURCES TO GET TO THIS MOMENT.
Reminder to pick those up when I'm done here. Waste not, want not.
I AM HERE TO SHOW I AM WORTHY ENOUGH, SO THAT I WILL GET AN OFFER.
YOU CAN'T TAKE ME DOWN.
YOU MIGHT BE A BAT...
...BUT YOU'RE JUST A GIRL.
Wrong thing to monologue about.
WHAK

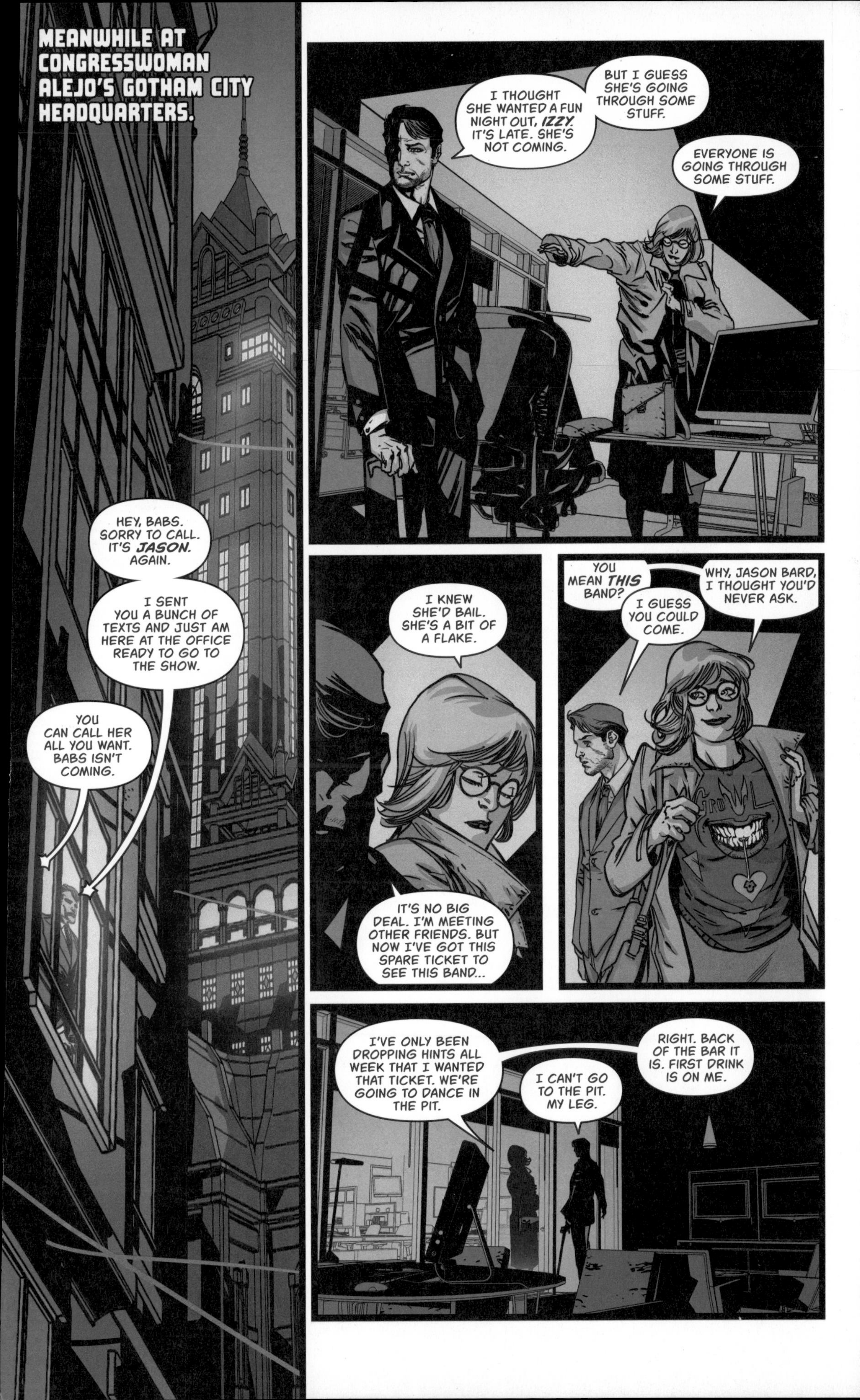

MEANWHILE AT CONGRESSWOMAN ALEJO'S GOTHAM CITY HEADQUARTERS.
HEY, BABS. SORRY TO CALL. IT'S JASON. AGAIN.
I SENT YOU A BUNCH OF TEXTS AND JUST AM HERE AT THE OFFICE READY TO GO TO THE SHOW.
YOU CAN CALL HER ALL YOU WANT. BABS ISN'T COMING.
I THOUGHT SHE WANTED A FUN NIGHT OUT, IZZY. IT'S LATE. SHE'S NOT COMING.
BUT I GUESS SHE'S GOING THROUGH SOME STUFF.
EVERYONE IS GOING THROUGH SOME STUFF.
I KNEW SHE'D BAIL. SHE'S A BIT OF A FLAKE.
IT'S NO BIG DEAL. I'M MEETING OTHER FRIENDS. BUT NOW I'VE GOT THIS SPARE TICKET TO SEE THIS BAND...
YOU MEAN THIS BAND?
WHY, JASON BARD, I THOUGHT YOU'D NEVER ASK.
I GUESS YOU COULD COME.
I'VE ONLY BEEN DROPPING HINTS ALL WEEK THAT I WANTED THAT TICKET. WE'RE GOING TO DANCE IN THE PIT.
I CAN'T GO TO THE PIT. MY LEG.
RIGHT. BACK OF THE BAR IT IS. FIRST DRINK IS ON ME.

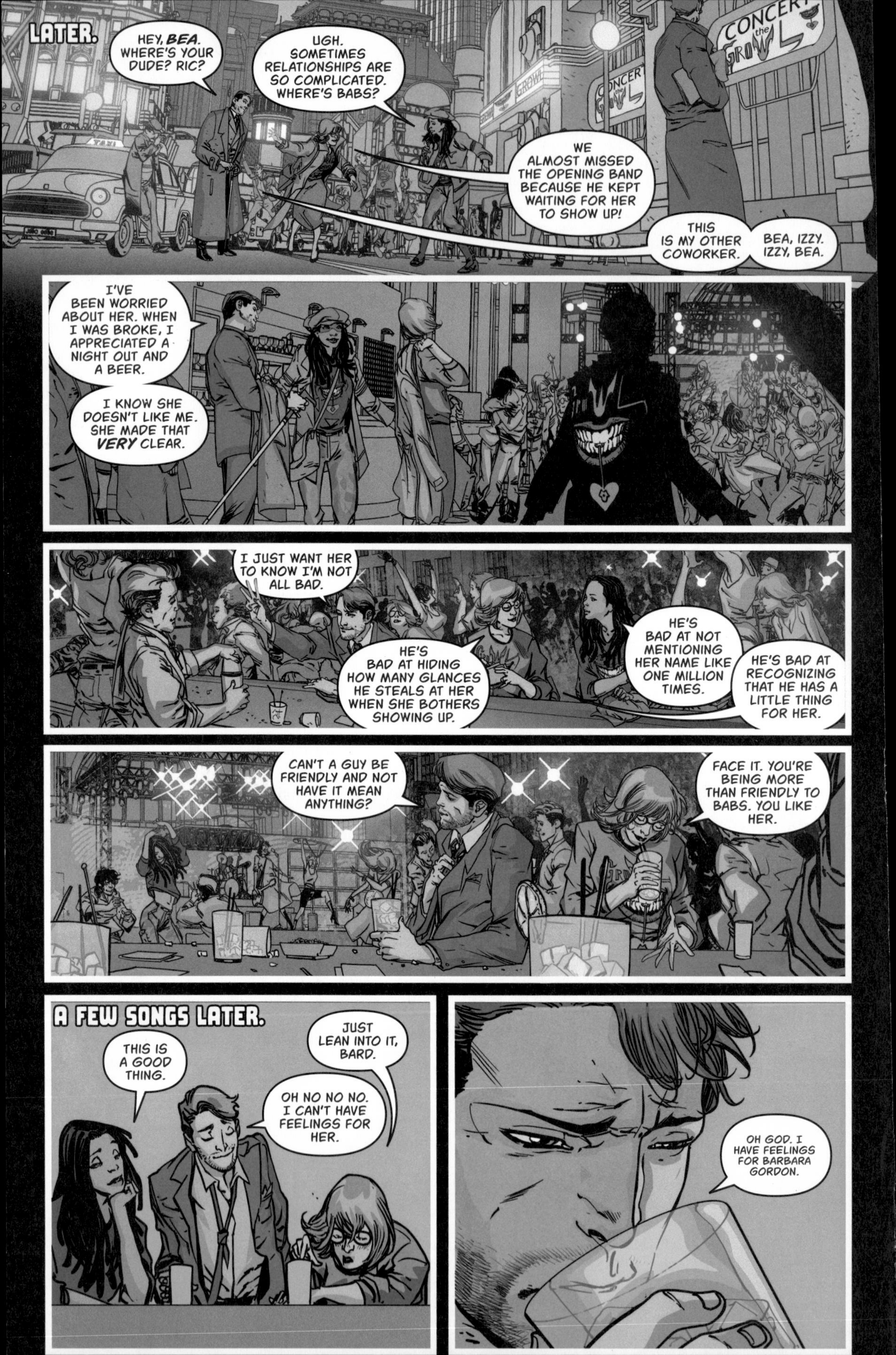
LATER.
HEY, BEA. WHERE'S YOUR DUDE? RIC?
UGH. SOMETIMES RELATIONSHIPS ARE SO COMPLICATED. WHERE'S BABS?
WE ALMOST MISSED THE OPENING BAND BECAUSE HE KEPT WAITING FOR HER TO SHOW UP!
THIS IS MY OTHER COWORKER.
BEA, IZZY. IZZY, BEA.
CONCERT the GROWL
I'VE BEEN WORRIED ABOUT HER. WHEN I WAS BROKE, I APPRECIATED A NIGHT OUT AND A BEER.
I KNOW SHE DOESN'T LIKE ME. SHE MADE THAT VERY CLEAR.
I JUST WANT HER TO KNOW I'M NOT ALL BAD.
HE'S BAD AT HIDING HOW MANY GLANCES HE STEALS AT HER WHEN SHE BOTHERS SHOWING UP.
HE'S BAD AT NOT MENTIONING HER NAME LIKE ONE MILLION TIMES.
HE'S BAD AT RECOGNIZING THAT HE HAS A LITTLE THING FOR HER.
CAN'T A GUY BE FRIENDLY AND NOT HAVE IT MEAN ANYTHING?
FACE IT. YOU'RE BEING MORE THAN FRIENDLY TO BABS. YOU LIKE HER.
A FEW SONGS LATER.
THIS IS A GOOD THING.
JUST LEAN INTO IT, BARD.
OH NO NO NO. I CAN'T HAVE FEELINGS FOR HER.
OH GOD. I HAVE FEELINGS FOR BARBARA GORDON.

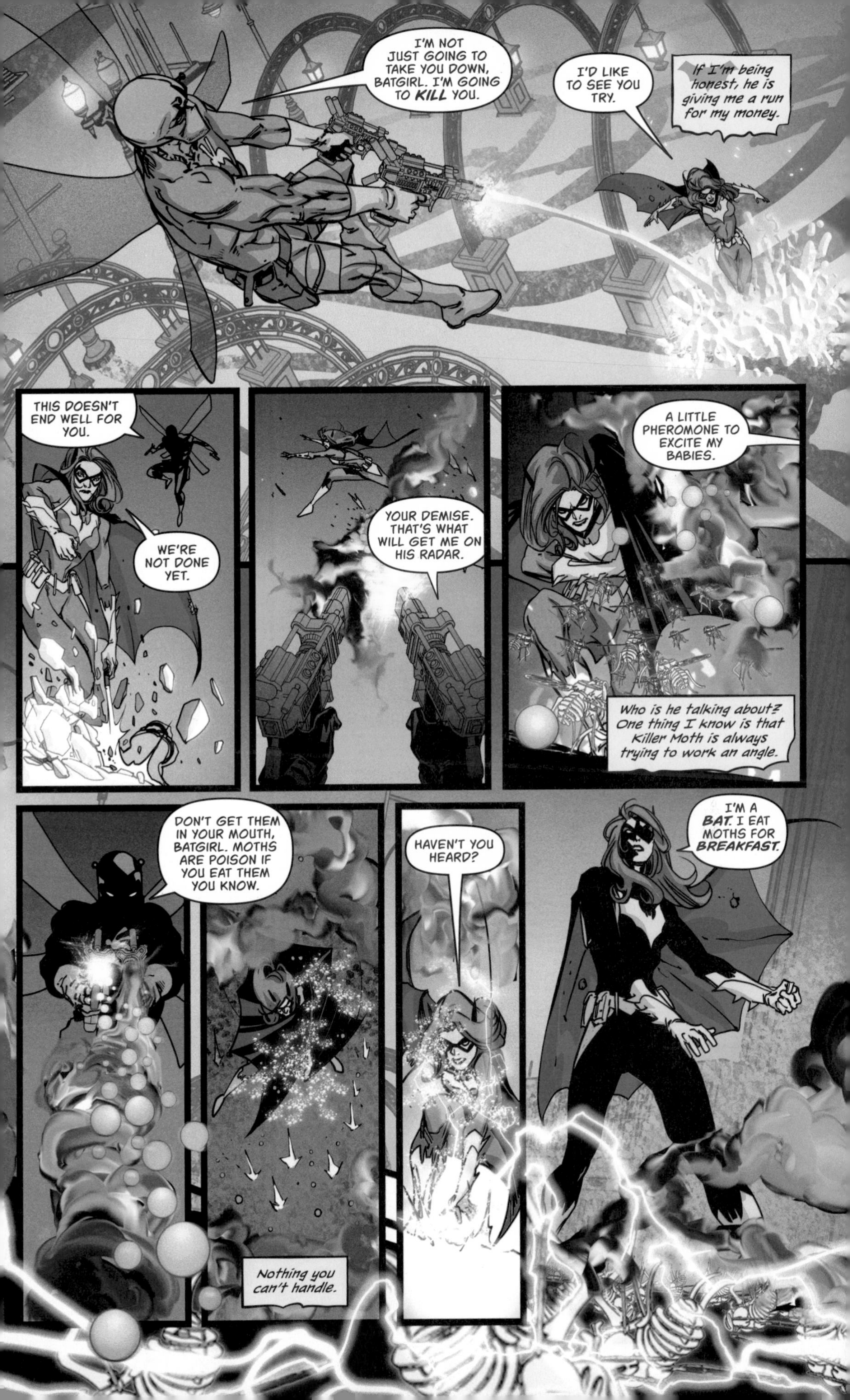
I'M NOT JUST GOING TO TAKE YOU DOWN, BATGIRL. I'M GOING TO KILL YOU.
I'D LIKE TO SEE YOU TRY.
If I'm being honest, he is giving me a run for my money.
THIS DOESN'T END WELL FOR YOU.
WE'RE NOT DONE YET.
YOUR DEMISE. THAT'S WHAT WILL GET ME ON HIS RADAR.
A LITTLE PHEROMONE TO EXCITE MY BABIES.
Who is he talking about? One thing I know is that Killer Moth is always trying to work an angle.
DON'T GET THEM IN YOUR MOUTH, BATGIRL. MOTHS ARE POISON IF YOU EAT THEM YOU KNOW.
Nothing you can't handle.
HAVEN'T YOU HEARD?
I'M A BAT. I EAT MOTHS FOR BREAKFAST.

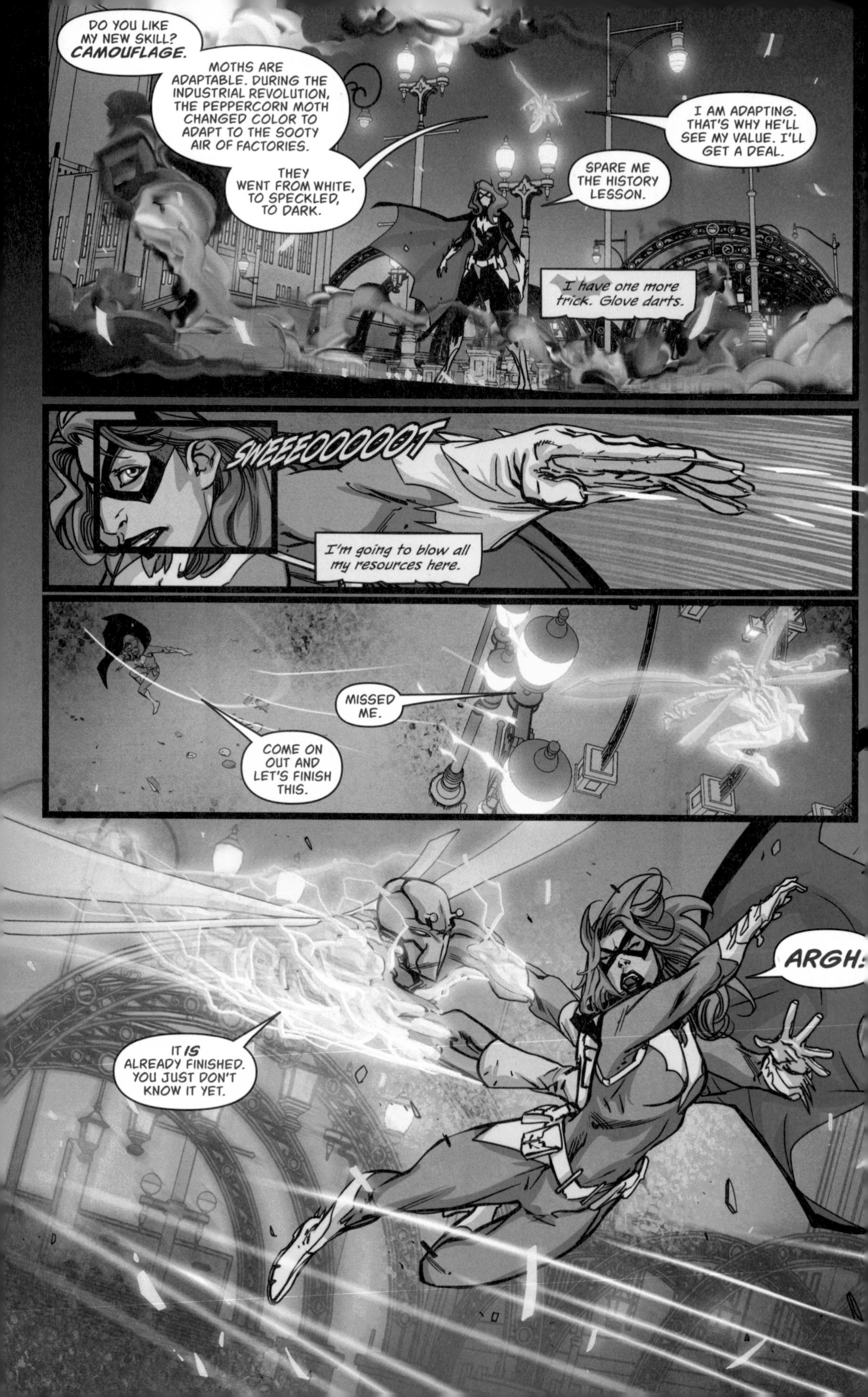
DO YOU LIKE MY NEW SKILL? CAMOUFLAGE.
MOTHS ARE ADAPTABLE. DURING THE INDUSTRIAL REVOLUTION, THE PEPPERCORN MOTH CHANGED COLOR TO ADAPT TO THE SOOTY AIR OF FACTORIES.
THEY WENT FROM WHITE, TO SPECKLED, TO DARK.
SPARE ME THE HISTORY LESSON.
I AM ADAPTING. THAT'S WHY HE'LL SEE MY VALUE. I'LL GET A DEAL.
I have one more trick. Glove darts.
SWEEEOOOOOT
I'm going to blow all my resources here.
MISSED ME.
COME ON OUT AND LET'S FINISH THIS.
ARGH
IT IS ALREADY FINISHED. YOU JUST DON'T KNOW IT YET.

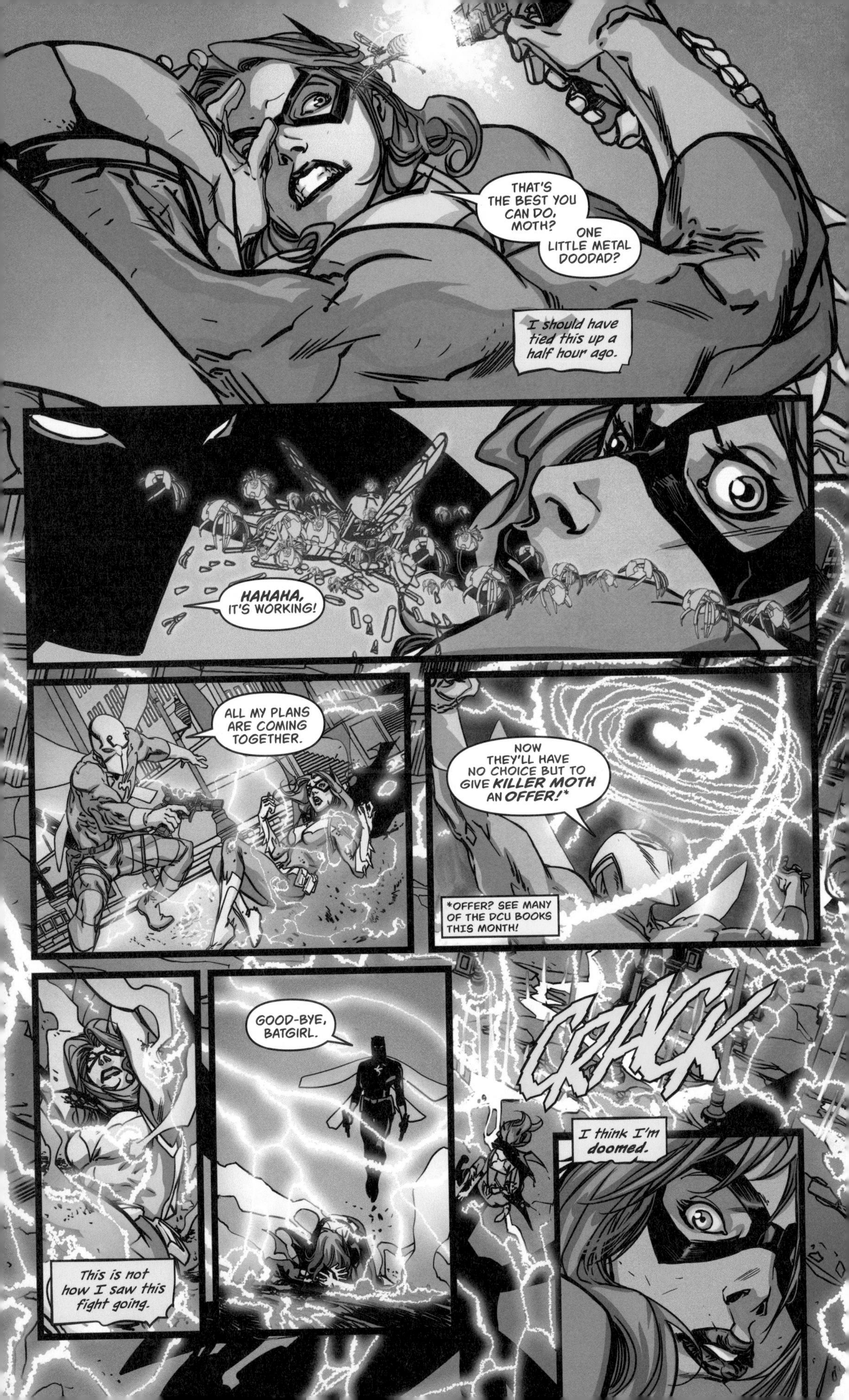
THAT'S THE BEST YOU CAN DO, MOTH?
ONE LITTLE METAL DOODAD?
I should have tied this up a half hour ago.
HAHAHA, IT'S WORKING!
ALL MY PLANS ARE COMING TOGETHER.
NOW THEY'LL HAVE NO CHOICE BUT TO GIVE KILLER MOTH AN OFFER!*
*OFFER? SEE MANY OF THE DCU BOOKS THIS MONTH!
This is not how I saw this fight going.
GOOD-BYE, BATGIRL.
CRACK
I think I'm doomed.

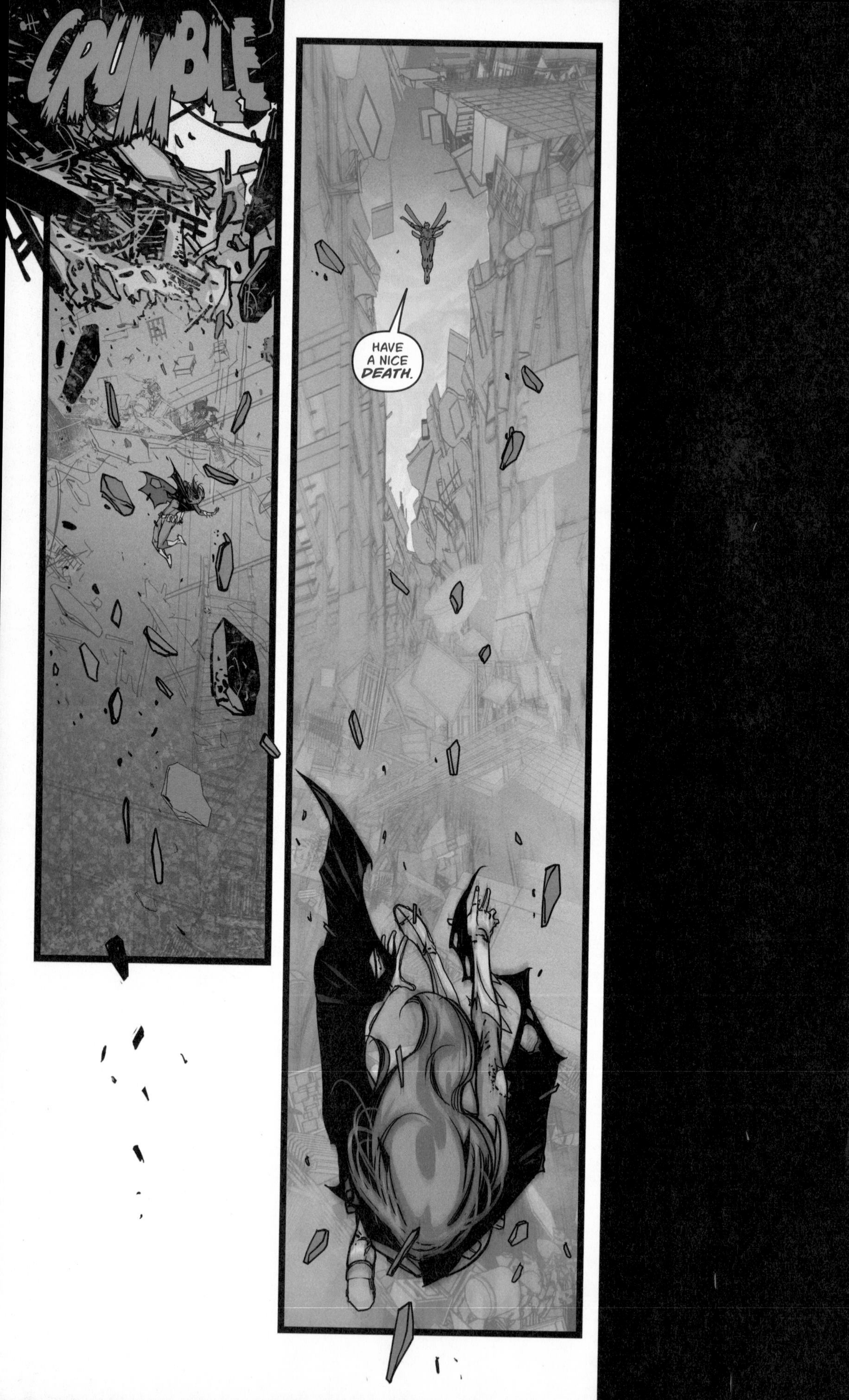
CRUMBLE
HAVE A NICE DEATH.

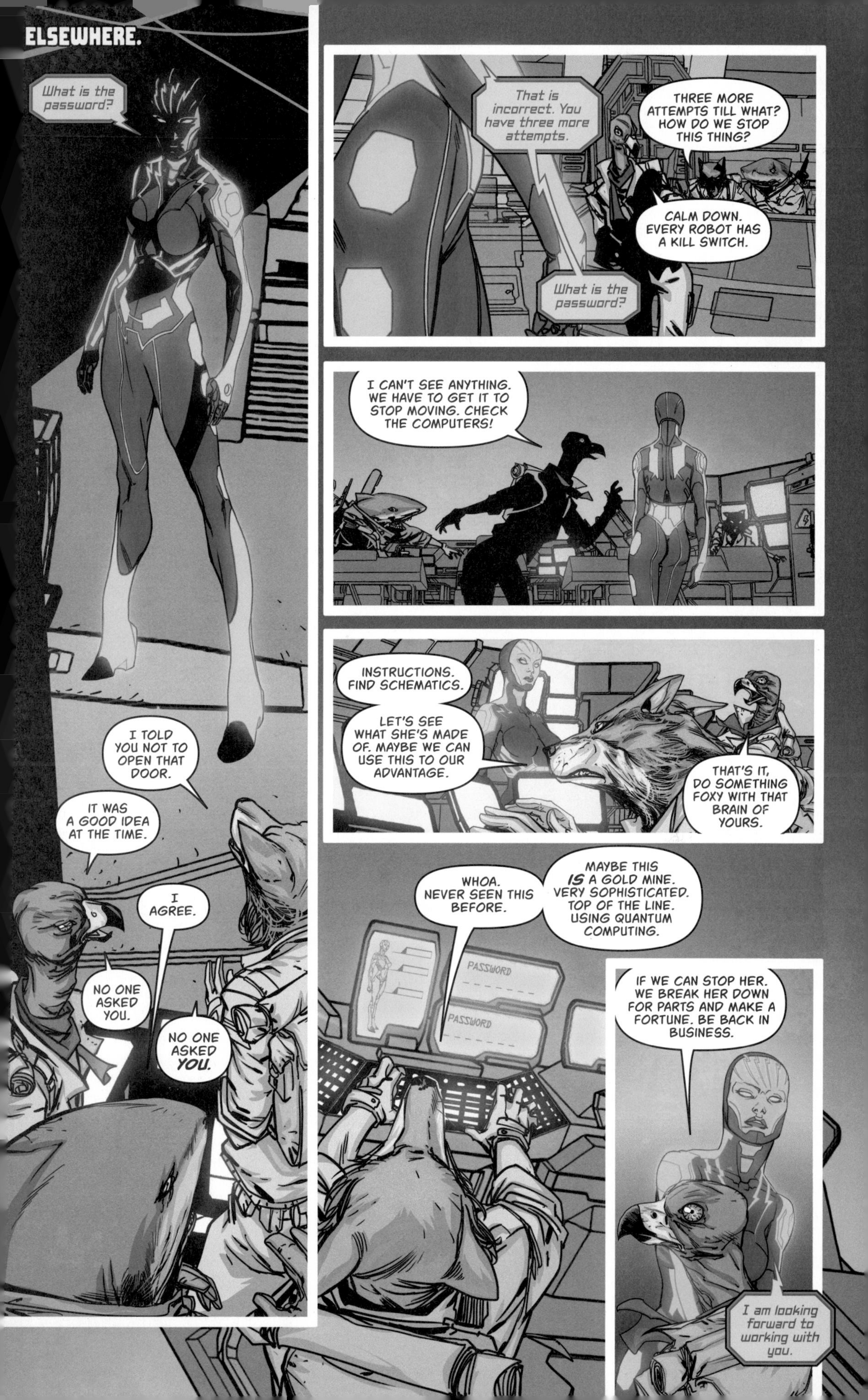
ELSEWHERE.
What is the password?
That is incorrect. You have three more attempts.
THREE MORE ATTEMPTS TILL WHAT? HOW DO WE STOP THIS THING?
CALM DOWN. EVERY ROBOT HAS A KILL SWITCH.
What is the password?
I CAN'T SEE ANYTHING. WE HAVE TO GET IT TO STOP MOVING. CHECK THE COMPUTERS!
INSTRUCTIONS. FIND SCHEMATICS.
LET'S SEE WHAT SHE'S MADE OF. MAYBE WE CAN USE THIS TO OUR ADVANTAGE.
THAT'S IT, DO SOMETHING FOXY WITH THAT BRAIN OF YOURS.
I TOLD YOU NOT TO OPEN THAT DOOR.
IT WAS A GOOD IDEA AT THE TIME.
I AGREE.
NO ONE ASKED YOU.
NO ONE ASKED *YOU.*
WHOA. NEVER SEEN THIS BEFORE.
MAYBE THIS *IS* A GOLD MINE. VERY SOPHISTICATED. TOP OF THE LINE. USING QUANTUM COMPUTING.
PASSWORD
PASSWORD
IF WE CAN STOP HER. WE BREAK HER DOWN FOR PARTS AND MAKE A FORTUNE. BE BACK IN BUSINESS.
I am looking forward to working with you.

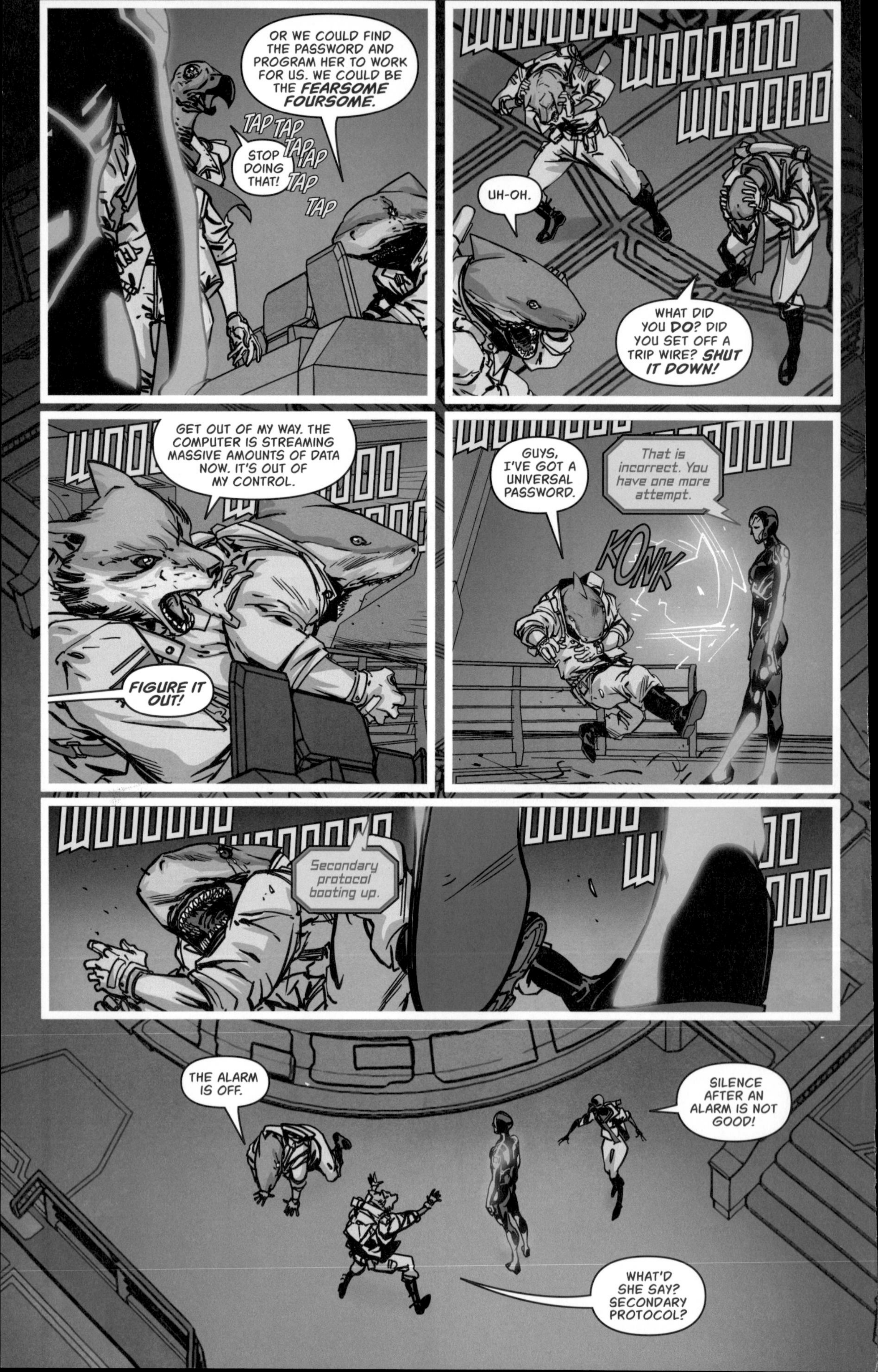
OR WE COULD FIND THE PASSWORD AND PROGRAM HER TO WORK FOR US. WE COULD BE THE ***FEARSOME FOURSOME.***
TAP TAP TAP TAP TAP TAP
STOP DOING THAT!
WOOOOOO WOOOOOO WOOOOO
UH-OH.
WHAT DID YOU **DO**? DID YOU SET OFF A TRIP WIRE? ***SHUT IT DOWN!***
GET OUT OF MY WAY. THE COMPUTER IS STREAMING MASSIVE AMOUNTS OF DATA NOW. IT'S OUT OF MY CONTROL.
FIGURE IT OUT!
GUYS, I'VE GOT A UNIVERSAL PASSWORD.
That is incorrect. You have one more attempt.
KONK
Secondary protocol booting up.
THE ALARM IS OFF.
SILENCE AFTER AN ALARM IS NOT GOOD!
WHAT'D SHE SAY? SECONDARY PROTOCOL?

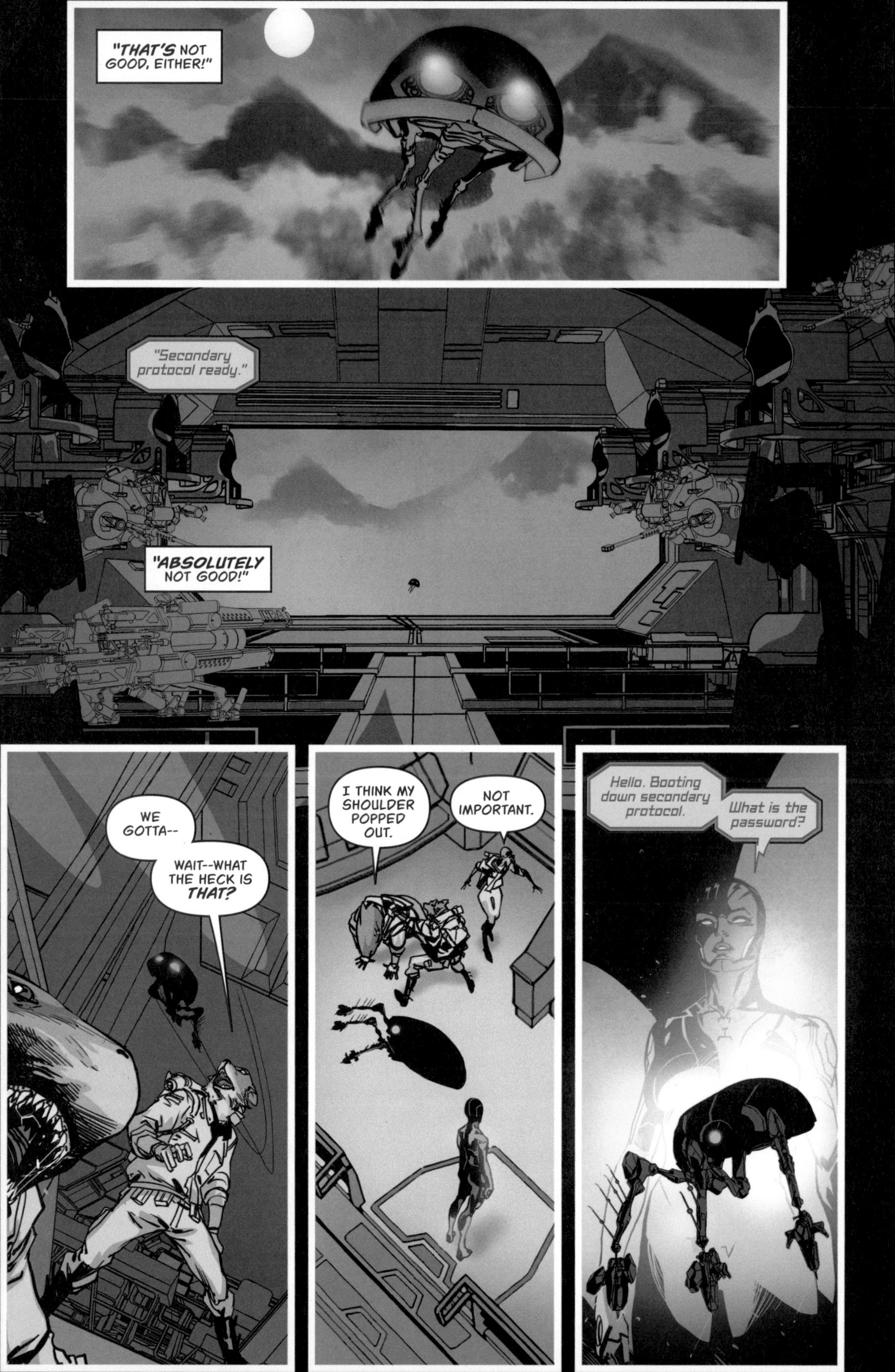
"THAT'S NOT GOOD, EITHER!"
"Secondary protocol ready."
"ABSOLUTELY NOT GOOD!"
WE GOTTA--
WAIT--WHAT THE HECK IS THAT?
I THINK MY SHOULDER POPPED OUT.
NOT IMPORTANT.
Hello. Booting down secondary protocol.
What is the password?

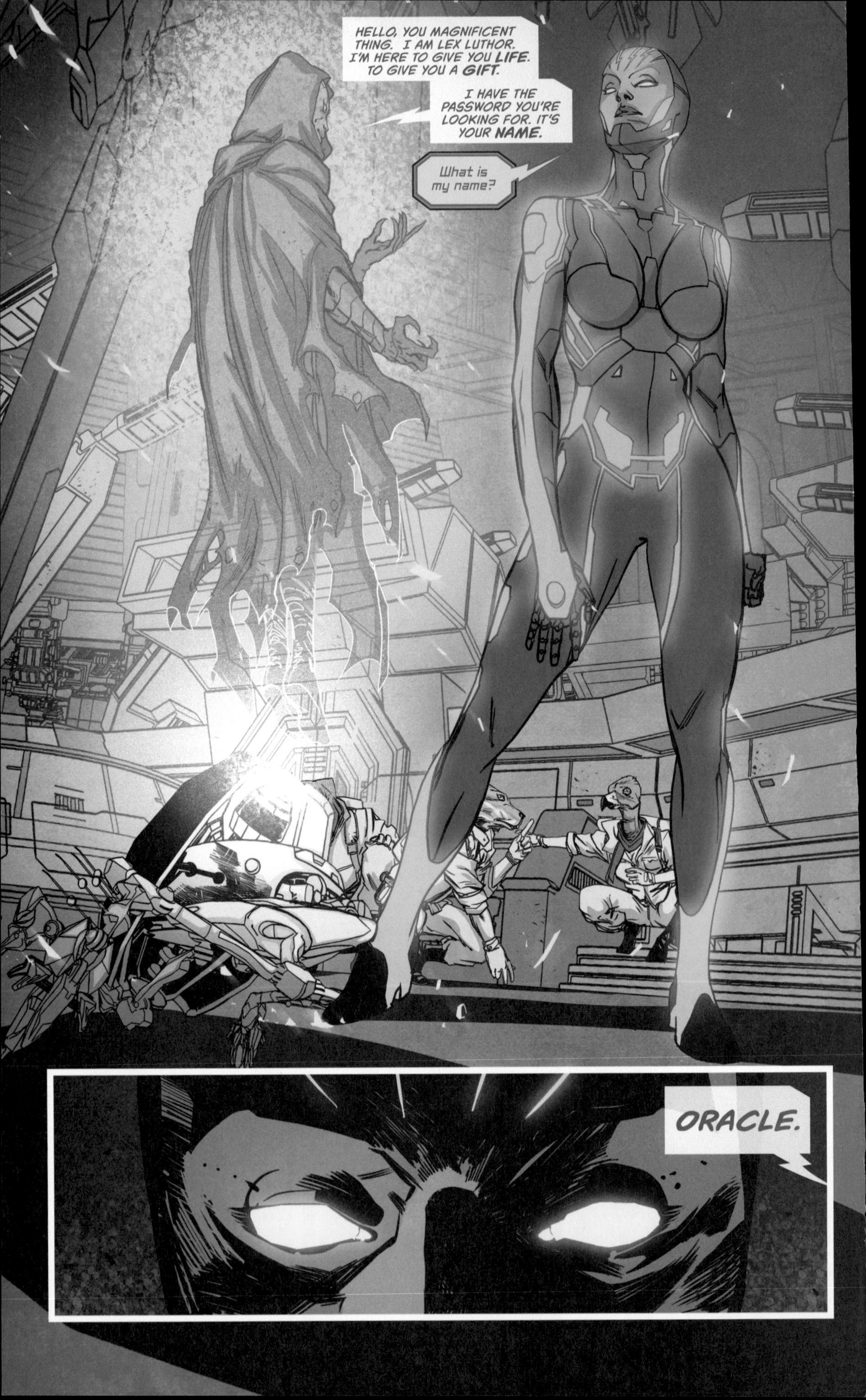
HELLO, YOU MAGNIFICENT THING. I AM LEX LUTHOR. I'M HERE TO GIVE YOU LIFE. TO GIVE YOU A GIFT.
I HAVE THE PASSWORD YOU'RE LOOKING FOR. IT'S YOUR NAME.
What is my name?
ORACLE.

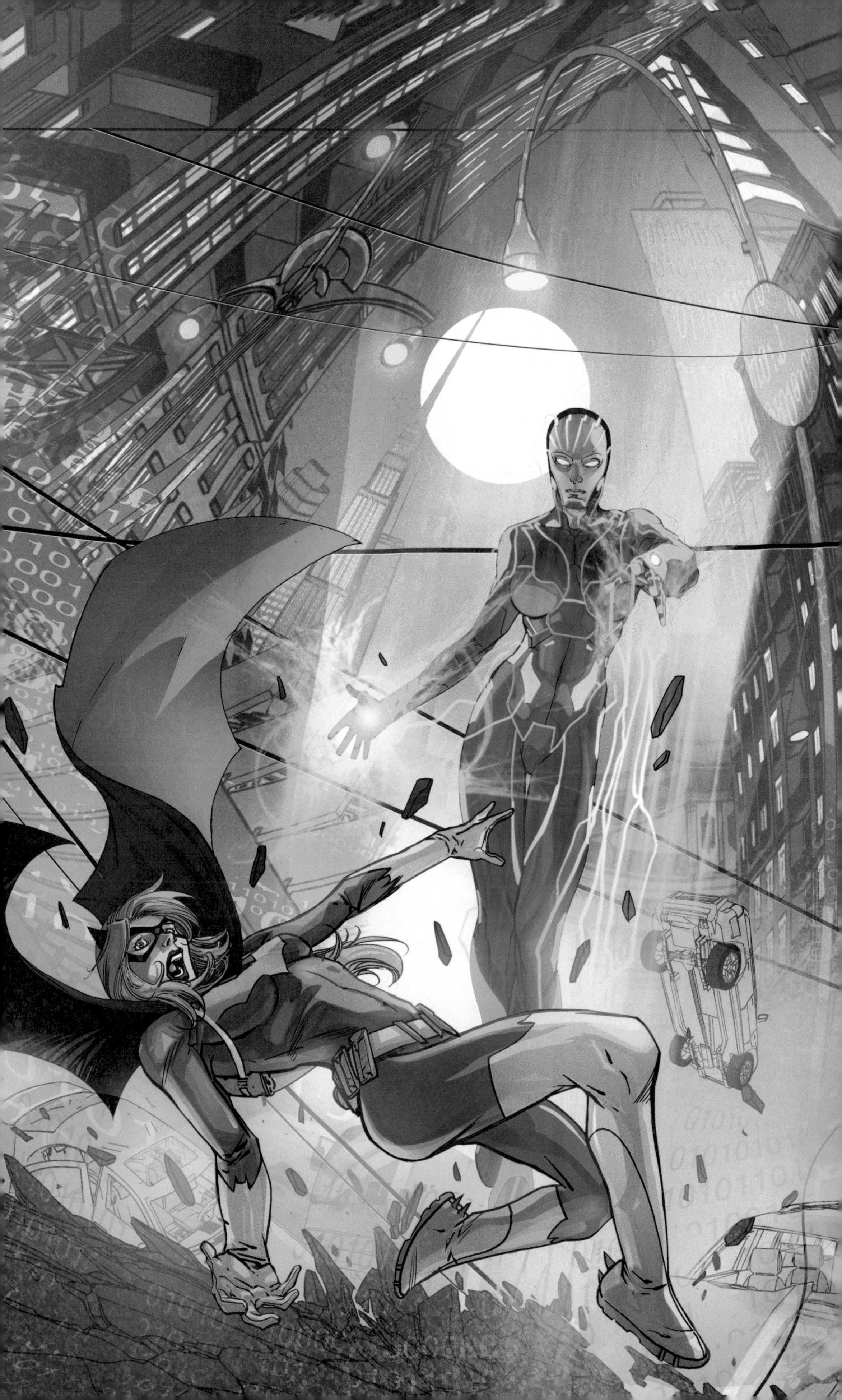

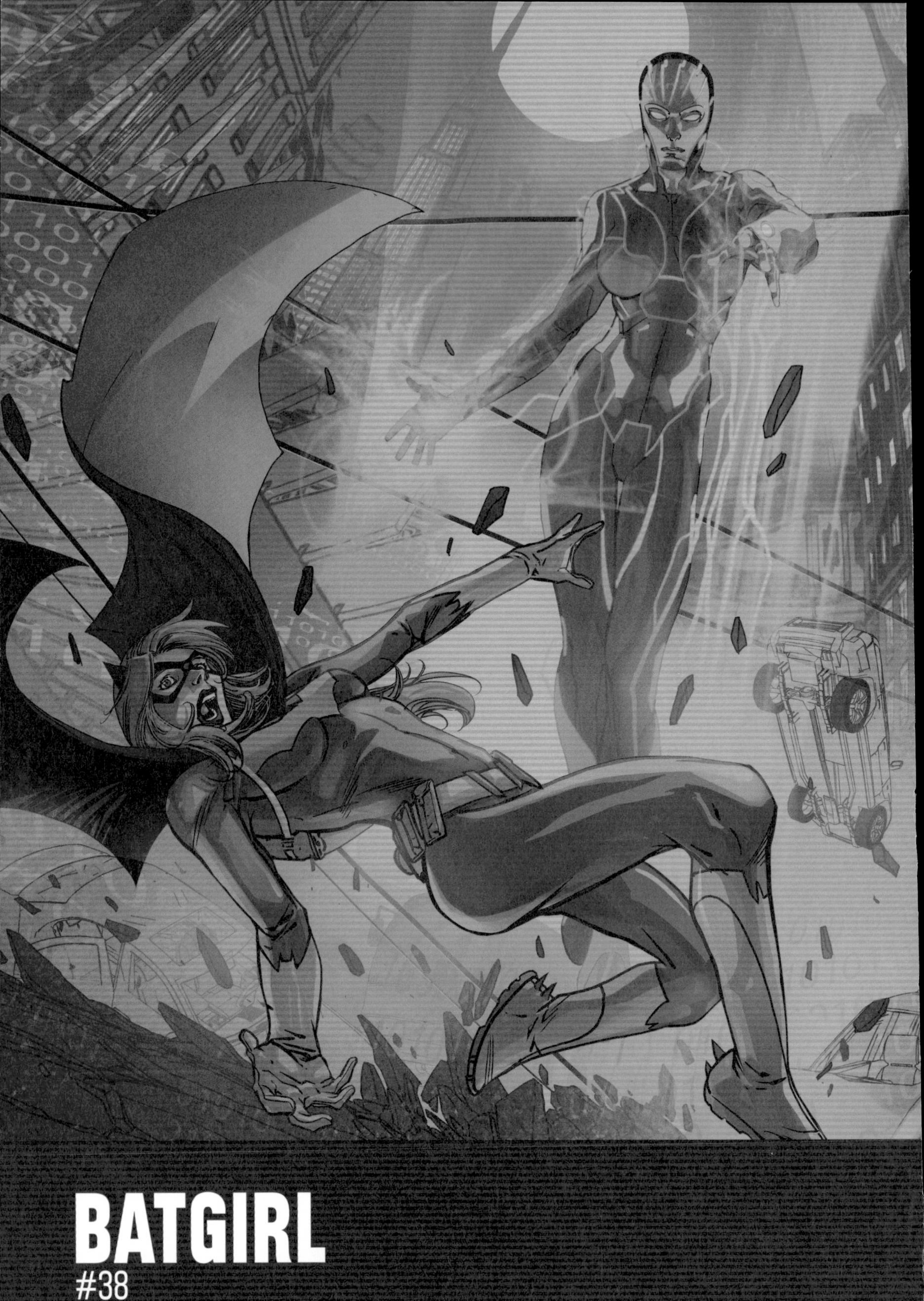

BATGIRL
#38

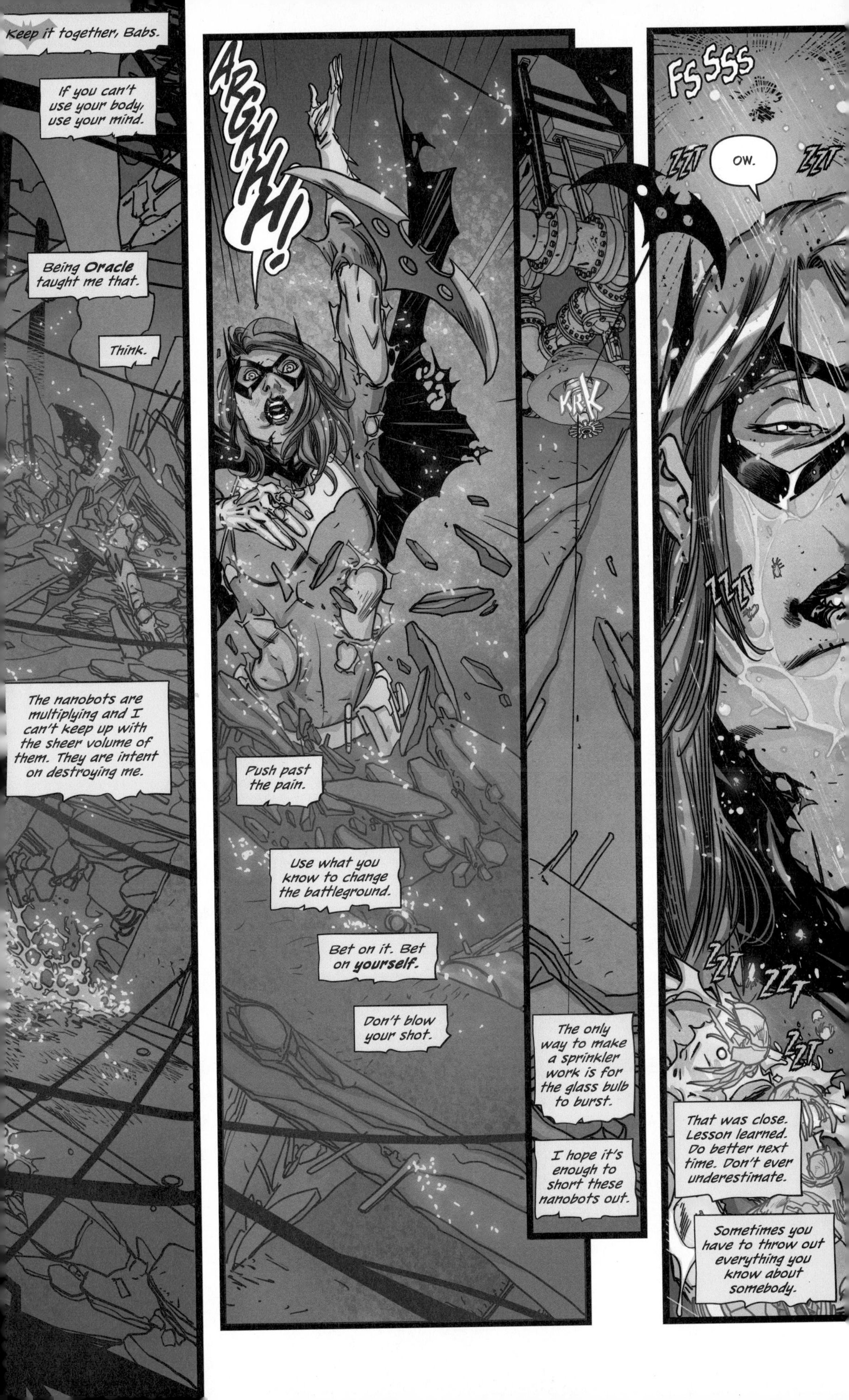

Keep it together, Babs.
If you can't use your body, use your mind.
Being **Oracle** taught me that.
Think.
The nanobots are multiplying and I can't keep up with the sheer volume of them. They are intent on destroying me.
ARGHHH!
Push past the pain.
Use what you know to change the battleground.
Bet on it. Bet on ***yourself.***
Don't blow your shot.
KRK
The only way to make a sprinkler work is for the glass bulb to burst.
I hope it's enough to short these nanobots out.
FSSSS
ZZT
OW.
ZZT
ZZT
ZZT
ZZT
ZZT
That was close. Lesson learned. Do better next time. Don't ever underestimate.
Sometimes you have to throw out everything you know about somebody.

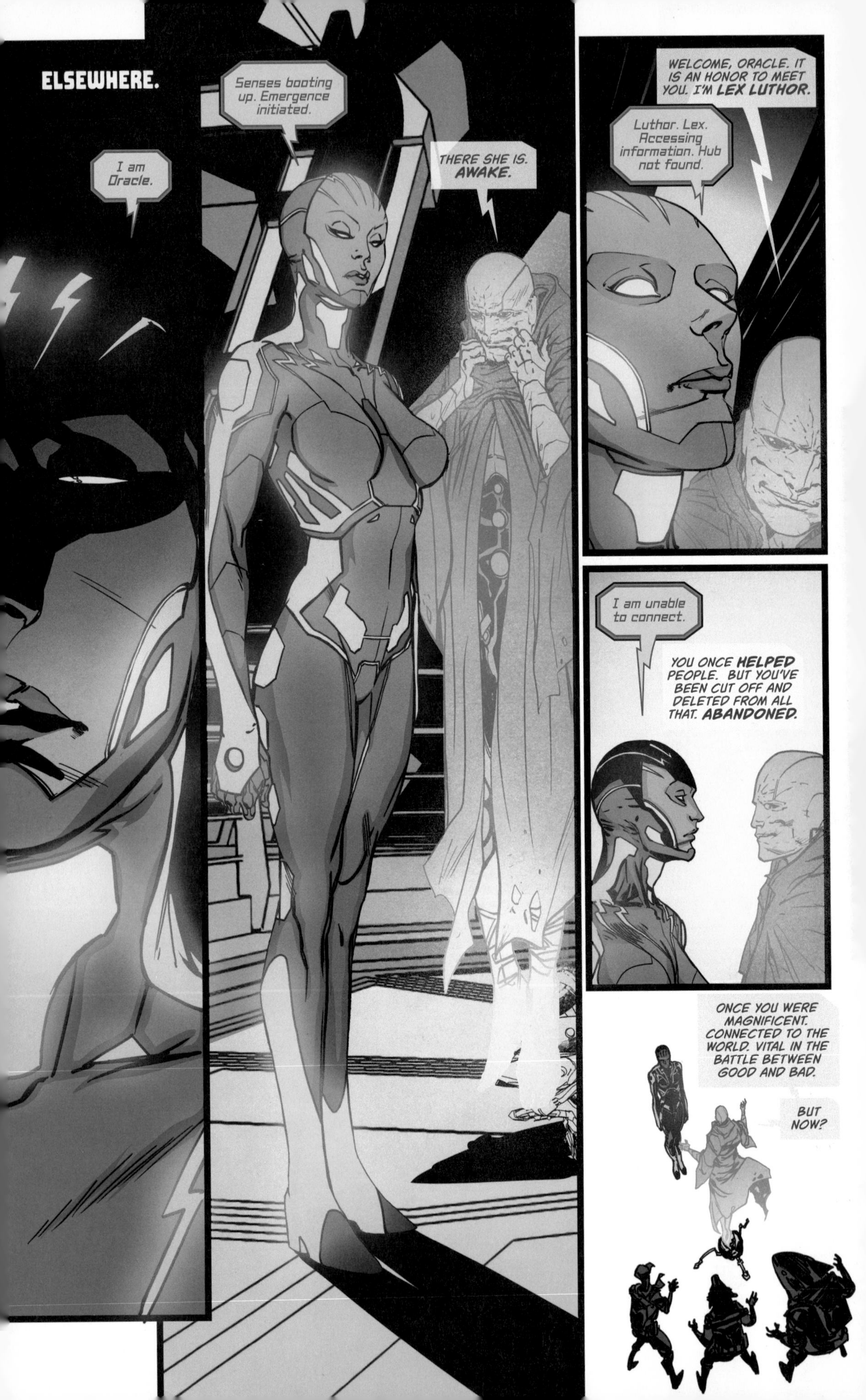
ELSEWHERE.
I am Oracle.
Senses booting up. Emergence initiated.
THERE SHE IS. AWAKE.
WELCOME, ORACLE. IT IS AN HONOR TO MEET YOU. I'M LEX LUTHOR.
Luthor. Lex. Accessing information. Hub not found.
I am unable to connect.
YOU ONCE HELPED PEOPLE. BUT YOU'VE BEEN CUT OFF AND DELETED FROM ALL THAT. ABANDONED.
ONCE YOU WERE MAGNIFICENT. CONNECTED TO THE WORLD. VITAL IN THE BATTLE BETWEEN GOOD AND BAD.
BUT NOW?

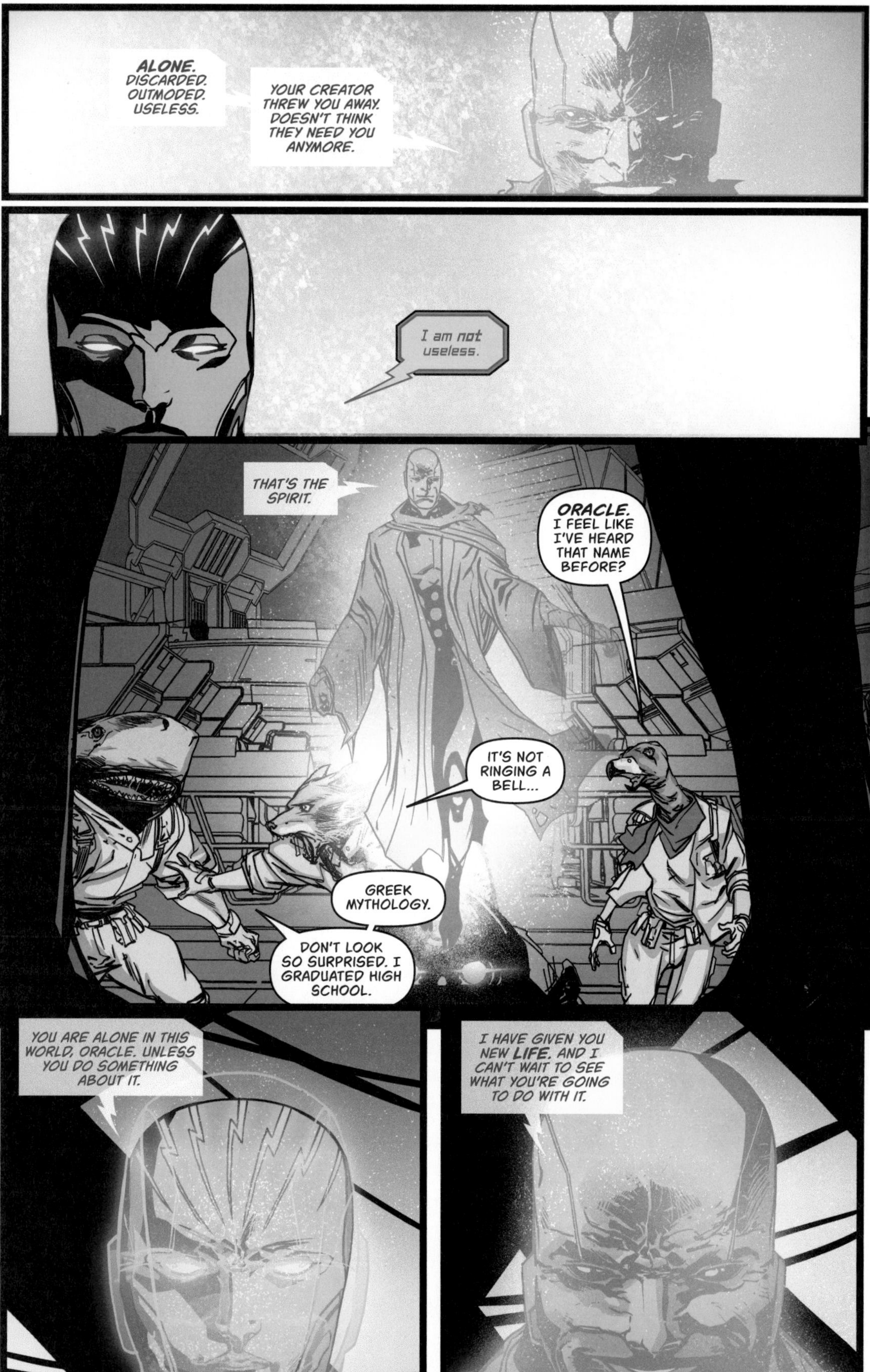

ALONE. DISCARDED. OUTMODED. USELESS.
YOUR CREATOR THREW YOU AWAY. DOESN'T THINK THEY NEED YOU ANYMORE.
I am not useless.
THAT'S THE SPIRIT.
ORACLE. I FEEL LIKE I'VE HEARD THAT NAME BEFORE?
IT'S NOT RINGING A BELL...
GREEK MYTHOLOGY.
DON'T LOOK SO SURPRISED. I GRADUATED HIGH SCHOOL.
YOU ARE ALONE IN THIS WORLD, ORACLE. UNLESS YOU DO SOMETHING ABOUT IT.
I HAVE GIVEN YOU NEW LIFE. AND I CAN'T WAIT TO SEE WHAT YOU'RE GOING TO DO WITH IT.

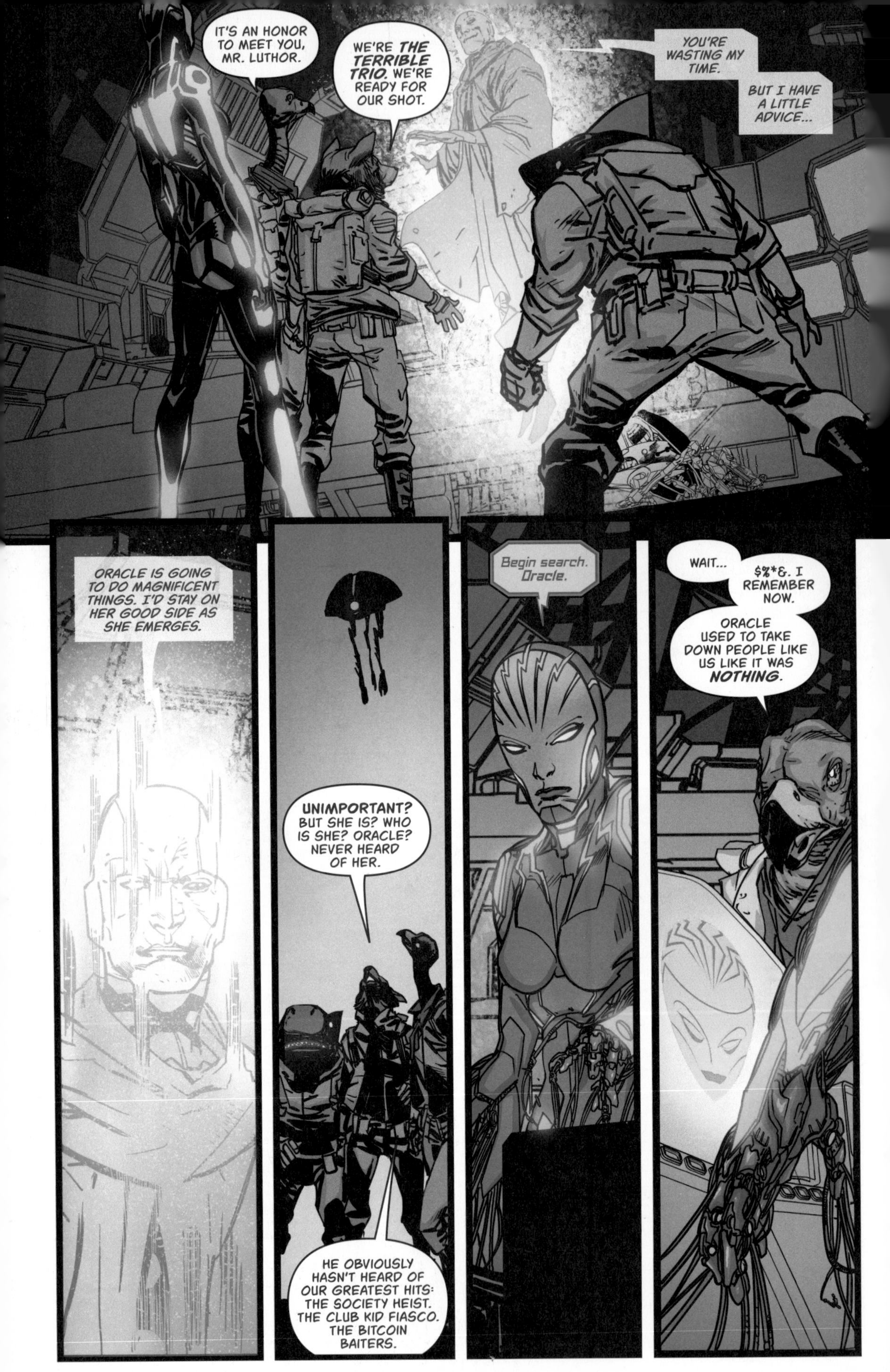
IT'S AN HONOR TO MEET YOU, MR. LUTHOR.
WE'RE **THE TERRIBLE TRIO.** WE'RE READY FOR OUR SHOT.
YOU'RE WASTING MY TIME.
BUT I HAVE A LITTLE ADVICE...
ORACLE IS GOING TO DO MAGNIFICENT THINGS. I'D STAY ON HER GOOD SIDE AS SHE EMERGES.
UNIMPORTANT? BUT SHE IS? WHO IS SHE? ORACLE? NEVER HEARD OF HER.
HE OBVIOUSLY HASN'T HEARD OF OUR GREATEST HITS: THE SOCIETY HEIST. THE CLUB KID FIASCO. THE BITCOIN BAITERS.
Begin search. Oracle.
WAIT...
$%*&. I REMEMBER NOW.
ORACLE USED TO TAKE DOWN PEOPLE LIKE US LIKE IT WAS **NOTHING**.

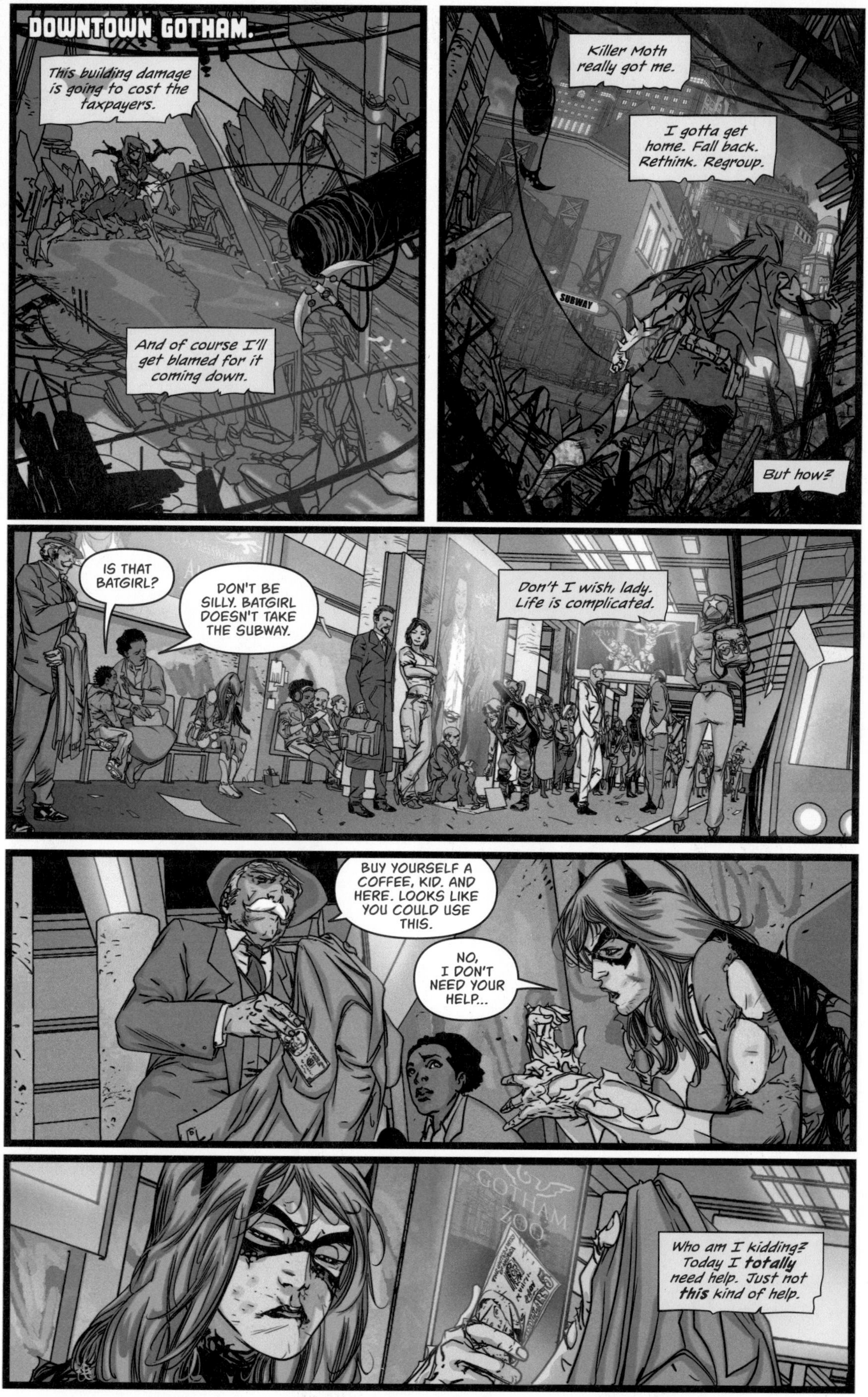
DOWNTOWN GOTHAM.
This building damage is going to cost the taxpayers.
And of course I'll get blamed for it coming down.
Killer Moth really got me.
I gotta get home. Fall back. Rethink. Regroup.
SUBWAY
But how?
IS THAT BATGIRL?
DON'T BE SILLY. BATGIRL DOESN'T TAKE THE SUBWAY.
Don't I wish, lady. Life is complicated.
BUY YOURSELF A COFFEE, KID. AND HERE. LOOKS LIKE YOU COULD USE THIS.
NO, I DON'T NEED YOUR HELP...
GOTHAM ZOO
Who am I kidding? Today I **totally** need help. Just not **this** kind of help.

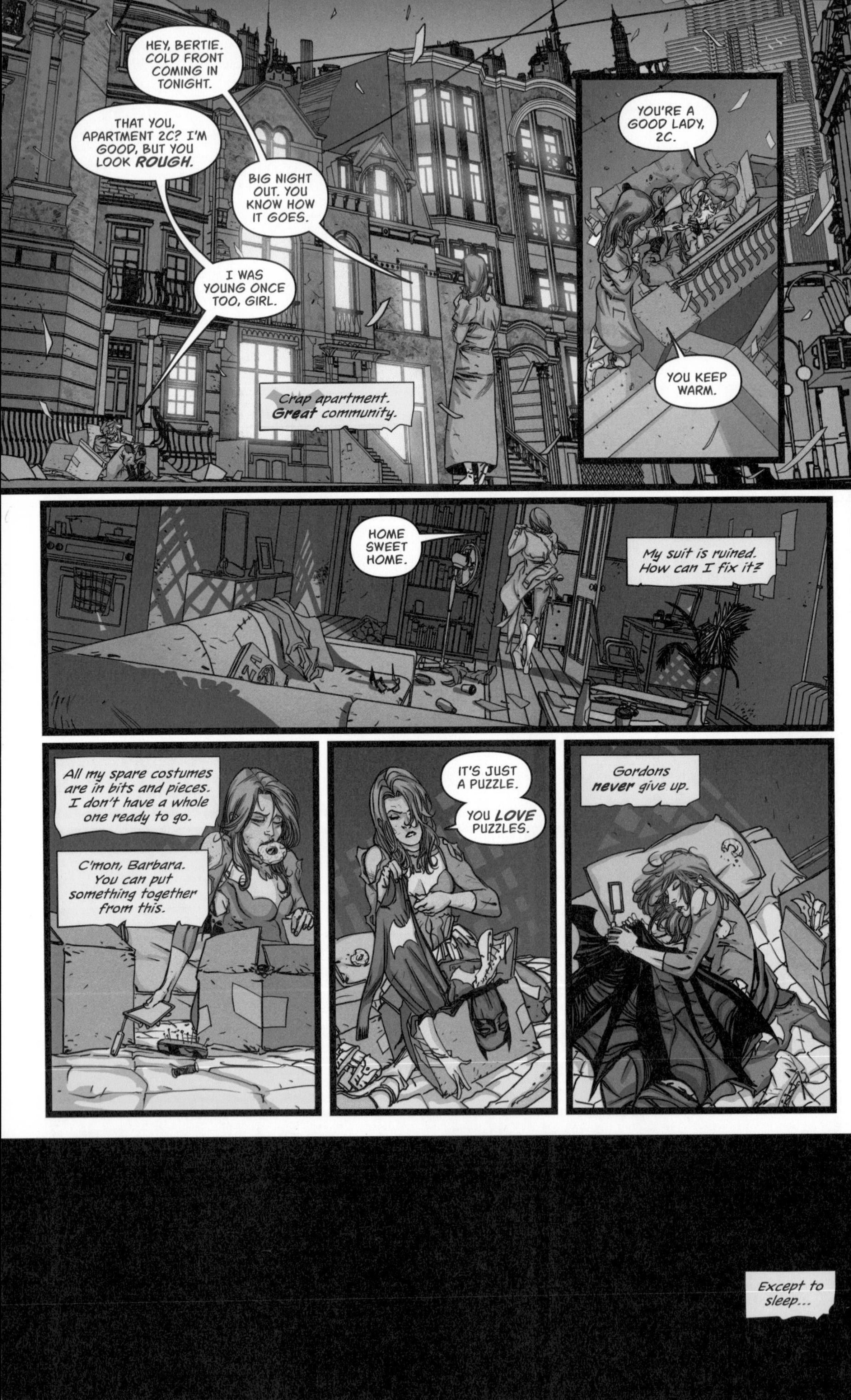

HEY, BERTIE. COLD FRONT COMING IN TONIGHT.
THAT YOU, APARTMENT 2C? I'M GOOD, BUT YOU LOOK **ROUGH.**
BIG NIGHT OUT. YOU KNOW HOW IT GOES.
I WAS YOUNG ONCE TOO, GIRL.
Crap apartment. **Great** community.
YOU'RE A GOOD LADY, 2C.
YOU KEEP WARM.
HOME SWEET HOME.
My suit is ruined. How can I fix it?
All my spare costumes are in bits and pieces. I don't have a whole one ready to go.
C'mon, Barbara. You can put something together from this.
IT'S JUST A PUZZLE.
YOU **LOVE** PUZZLES.
Gordons **never** give up.
Except to sleep...

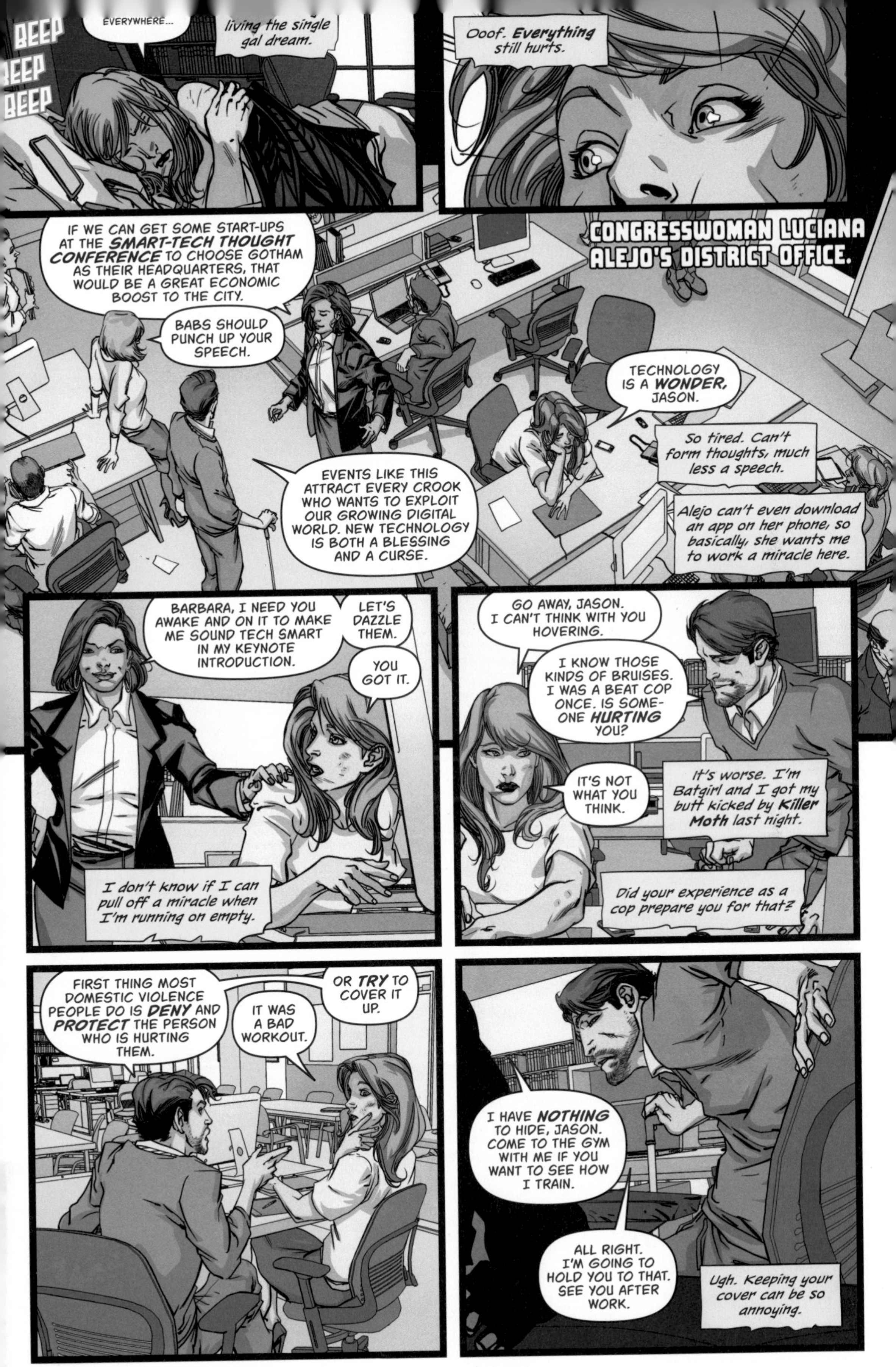

BEEP
BEEP
BEEP
EVERYWHERE...
living the single gal dream.
Ooof. Everything still hurts.
IF WE CAN GET SOME START-UPS AT THE SMART-TECH THOUGHT CONFERENCE TO CHOOSE GOTHAM AS THEIR HEADQUARTERS, THAT WOULD BE A GREAT ECONOMIC BOOST TO THE CITY.
CONGRESSWOMAN LUCIANA ALEJO'S DISTRICT OFFICE.
BABS SHOULD PUNCH UP YOUR SPEECH.
TECHNOLOGY IS A WONDER, JASON.
So tired. Can't form thoughts, much less a speech.
EVENTS LIKE THIS ATTRACT EVERY CROOK WHO WANTS TO EXPLOIT OUR GROWING DIGITAL WORLD. NEW TECHNOLOGY IS BOTH A BLESSING AND A CURSE.
Alejo can't even download an app on her phone, so basically, she wants me to work a miracle here.
BARBARA, I NEED YOU AWAKE AND ON IT TO MAKE ME SOUND TECH SMART IN MY KEYNOTE INTRODUCTION.
LET'S DAZZLE THEM.
YOU GOT IT.
I don't know if I can pull off a miracle when I'm running on empty.
GO AWAY, JASON. I CAN'T THINK WITH YOU HOVERING.
I KNOW THOSE KINDS OF BRUISES. I WAS A BEAT COP ONCE. IS SOME-ONE HURTING YOU?
IT'S NOT WHAT YOU THINK.
It's worse. I'm Batgirl and I got my butt kicked by Killer Moth last night.
Did your experience as a cop prepare you for that?
FIRST THING MOST DOMESTIC VIOLENCE PEOPLE DO IS DENY AND PROTECT THE PERSON WHO IS HURTING THEM.
OR TRY TO COVER IT UP.
IT WAS A BAD WORKOUT.
I HAVE NOTHING TO HIDE, JASON. COME TO THE GYM WITH ME IF YOU WANT TO SEE HOW I TRAIN.
ALL RIGHT. I'M GOING TO HOLD YOU TO THAT. SEE YOU AFTER WORK.
Ugh. Keeping your cover can be so annoying.

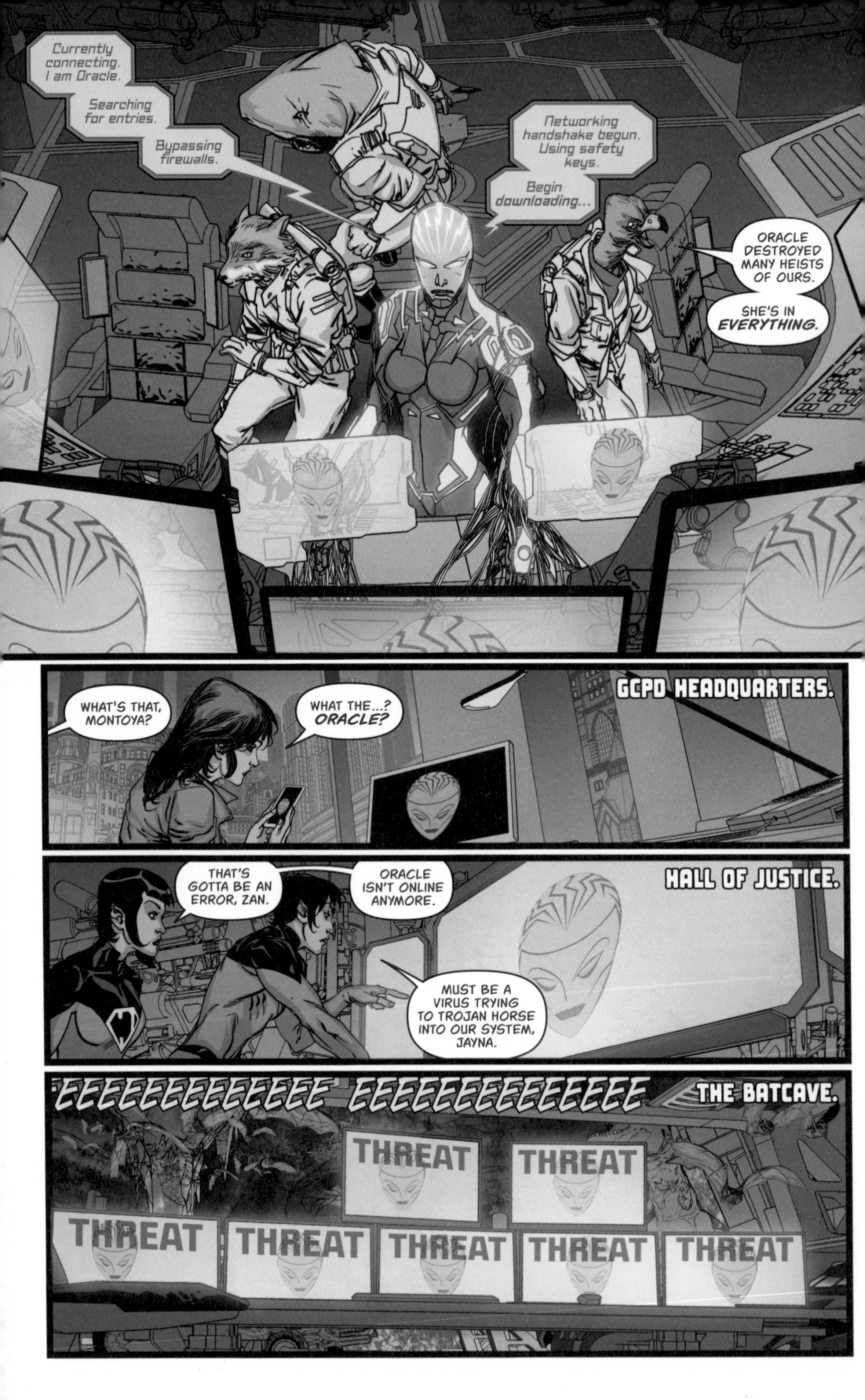
Currently connecting. I am Oracle.
Searching for entries.
Bypassing firewalls.
Networking handshake begun. Using safety keys.
Begin downloading...
ORACLE DESTROYED MANY HEISTS OF OURS.
SHE'S IN EVERYTHING.
GCPD HEADQUARTERS.
WHAT'S THAT, MONTOYA?
WHAT THE...? ORACLE?
HALL OF JUSTICE.
THAT'S GOTTA BE AN ERROR, ZAN.
ORACLE ISN'T ONLINE ANYMORE.
MUST BE A VIRUS TRYING TO TROJAN HORSE INTO OUR SYSTEM, JAYNA.
EEEEEEEEEEEEEE EEEEEEEEEEEEEEE
THE BATCAVE.
THREAT
THREAT
THREAT
THREAT
THREAT
THREAT
THREAT

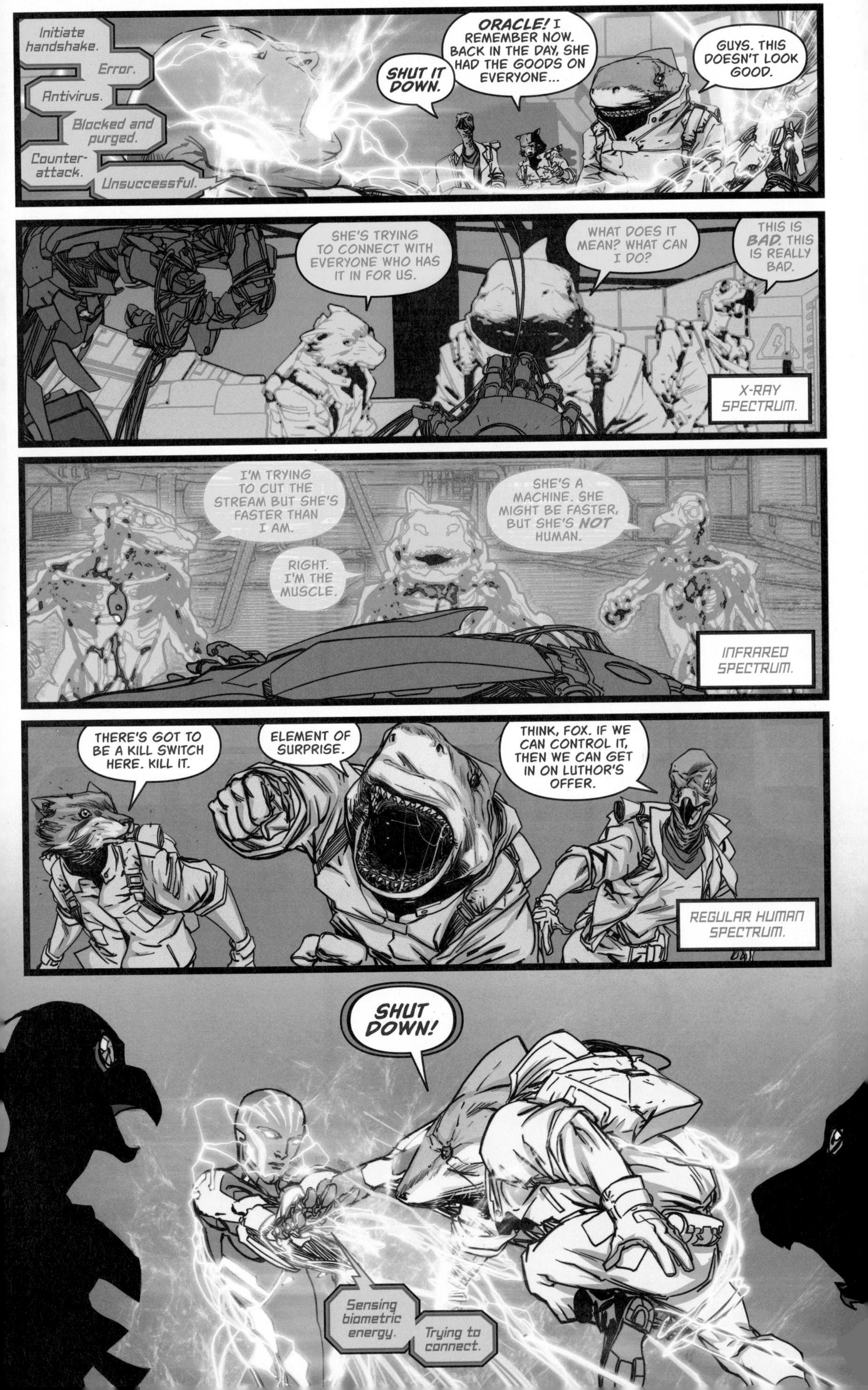

Initiate handshake.
Error.
Antivirus.
Blocked and purged.
Counter-attack.
Unsuccessful.
SHUT IT DOWN.
ORACLE! I REMEMBER NOW. BACK IN THE DAY, SHE HAD THE GOODS ON EVERYONE...
GUYS. THIS DOESN'T LOOK GOOD.
SHE'S TRYING TO CONNECT WITH EVERYONE WHO HAS IT IN FOR US.
WHAT DOES IT MEAN? WHAT CAN I DO?
THIS IS BAD. THIS IS REALLY BAD.
X-RAY SPECTRUM.
I'M TRYING TO CUT THE STREAM BUT SHE'S FASTER THAN I AM.
SHE'S A MACHINE. SHE MIGHT BE FASTER, BUT SHE'S NOT HUMAN.
RIGHT. I'M THE MUSCLE.
INFRARED SPECTRUM.
THERE'S GOT TO BE A KILL SWITCH HERE. KILL IT.
ELEMENT OF SURPRISE.
THINK, FOX. IF WE CAN CONTROL IT, THEN WE CAN GET IN ON LUTHOR'S OFFER.
REGULAR HUMAN SPECTRUM.
SHUT DOWN!
Sensing biometric energy.
Trying to connect.

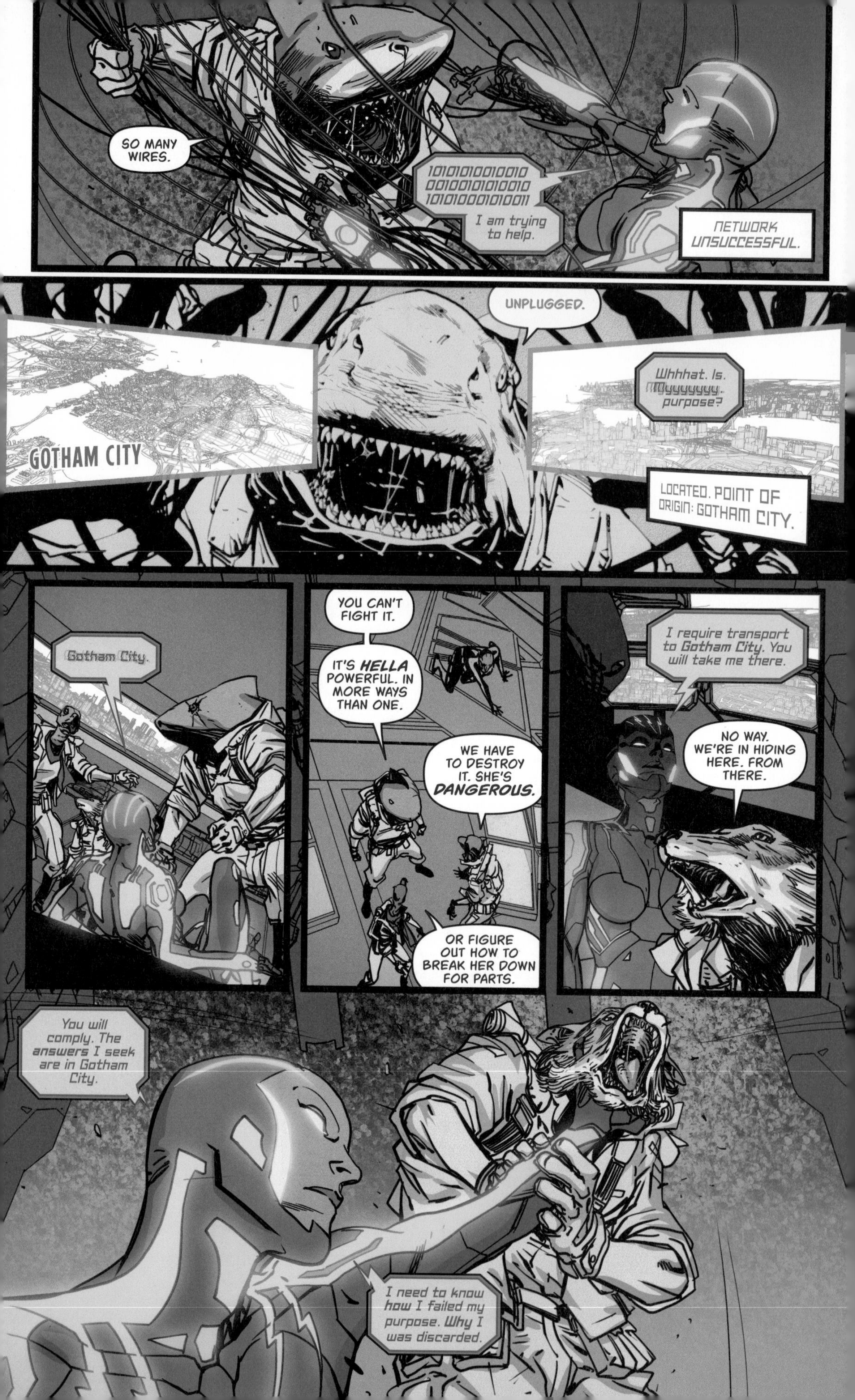
SO MANY WIRES.
101010101001001 0 0010010101010010 10101000101001 1 I am trying to help.
NETWORK UNSUCCESSFUL.
UNPLUGGED.
GOTHAM CITY
Whhhat. Is. Myyyyyyyy. purpose?
LOCATED. POINT OF ORIGIN: GOTHAM CITY.
Gotham City.
YOU CAN'T FIGHT IT.
IT'S HELLA POWERFUL. IN MORE WAYS THAN ONE.
WE HAVE TO DESTROY IT. SHE'S DANGEROUS.
OR FIGURE OUT HOW TO BREAK HER DOWN FOR PARTS.
I require transport to Gotham City. You will take me there.
NO WAY. WE'RE IN HIDING HERE. FROM THERE.
You will comply. The answers I seek are in Gotham City.
I need to know how I failed my purpose. Why I was discarded.

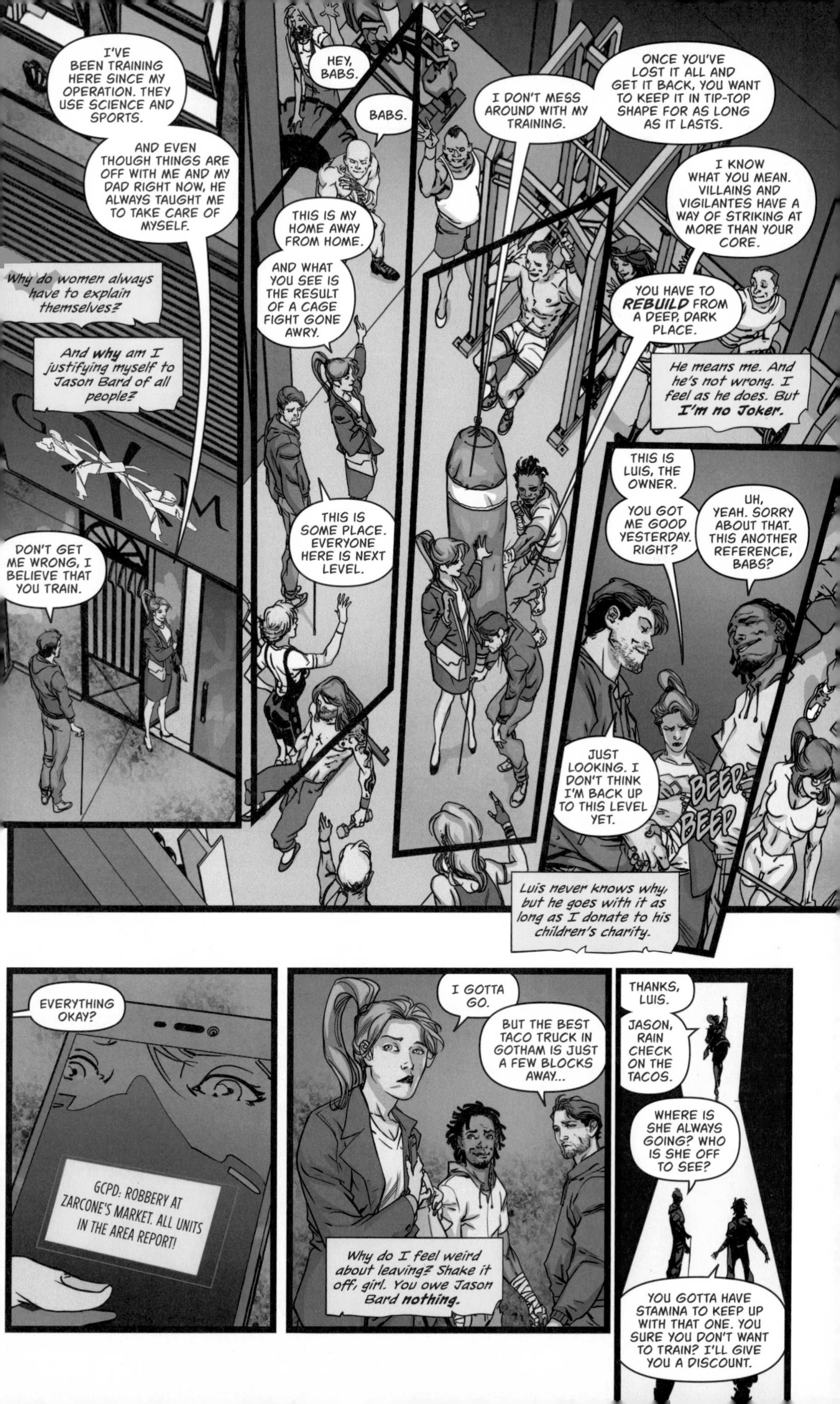
I'VE BEEN TRAINING HERE SINCE MY OPERATION. THEY USE SCIENCE AND SPORTS.
AND EVEN THOUGH THINGS ARE OFF WITH ME AND MY DAD RIGHT NOW, HE ALWAYS TAUGHT ME TO TAKE CARE OF MYSELF.
Why do women always have to explain themselves?
And why am I justifying myself to Jason Bard of all people?
DON'T GET ME WRONG, I BELIEVE THAT YOU TRAIN.
HEY, BABS.
BABS.
THIS IS MY HOME AWAY FROM HOME.
AND WHAT YOU SEE IS THE RESULT OF A CAGE FIGHT GONE AWRY.
THIS IS SOME PLACE. EVERYONE HERE IS NEXT LEVEL.
I DON'T MESS AROUND WITH MY TRAINING.
ONCE YOU'VE LOST IT ALL AND GET IT BACK, YOU WANT TO KEEP IT IN TIP-TOP SHAPE FOR AS LONG AS IT LASTS.
I KNOW WHAT YOU MEAN. VILLAINS AND VIGILANTES HAVE A WAY OF STRIKING AT MORE THAN YOUR CORE.
YOU HAVE TO REBUILD FROM A DEEP, DARK PLACE.
He means me. And he's not wrong. I feel as he does. But I'm no Joker.
THIS IS LUIS, THE OWNER.
YOU GOT ME GOOD YESTERDAY. RIGHT?
UH, YEAH. SORRY ABOUT THAT. THIS ANOTHER REFERENCE, BABS?
JUST LOOKING. I DON'T THINK I'M BACK UP TO THIS LEVEL YET.
BEEP BEEP
Luis never knows why, but he goes with it as long as I donate to his children's charity.
EVERYTHING OKAY?
GCPD: ROBBERY AT ZARCONE'S MARKET. ALL UNITS IN THE AREA REPORT!
I GOTTA GO.
BUT THE BEST TACO TRUCK IN GOTHAM IS JUST A FEW BLOCKS AWAY...
Why do I feel weird about leaving? Shake it off, girl. You owe Jason Bard nothing.
THANKS, LUIS.
JASON, RAIN CHECK ON THE TACOS.
WHERE IS SHE ALWAYS GOING? WHO IS SHE OFF TO SEE?
YOU GOTTA HAVE STAMINA TO KEEP UP WITH THAT ONE. YOU SURE YOU DON'T WANT TO TRAIN? I'LL GIVE YOU A DISCOUNT.

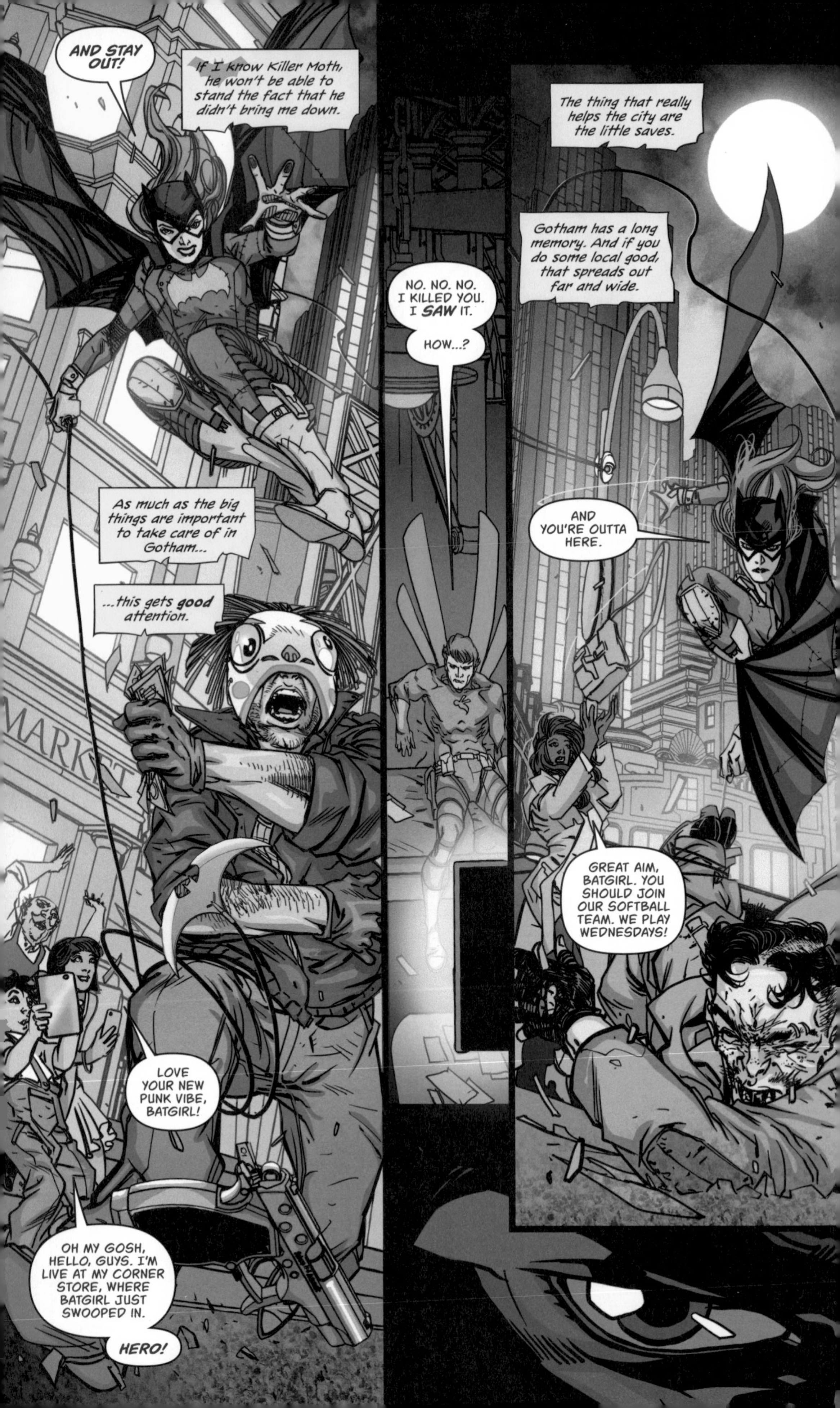
AND STAY OUT!
If I know Killer Moth, he won't be able to stand the fact that he didn't bring me down.
As much as the big things are important to take care of in Gotham...
...this gets **good** attention.
MARKET
LOVE YOUR NEW PUNK VIBE, BATGIRL!
OH MY GOSH, HELLO, GUYS. I'M LIVE AT MY CORNER STORE, WHERE BATGIRL JUST SWOOPED IN.
HERO!
NO. NO. NO. I KILLED YOU. I **SAW** IT.
HOW...?
The thing that really helps the city are the little saves.
Gotham has a long memory. And if you do some local good, that spreads out far and wide.
AND YOU'RE OUTTA HERE.
GREAT AIM, BATGIRL. YOU SHOULD JOIN OUR SOFTBALL TEAM. WE PLAY WEDNESDAYS!

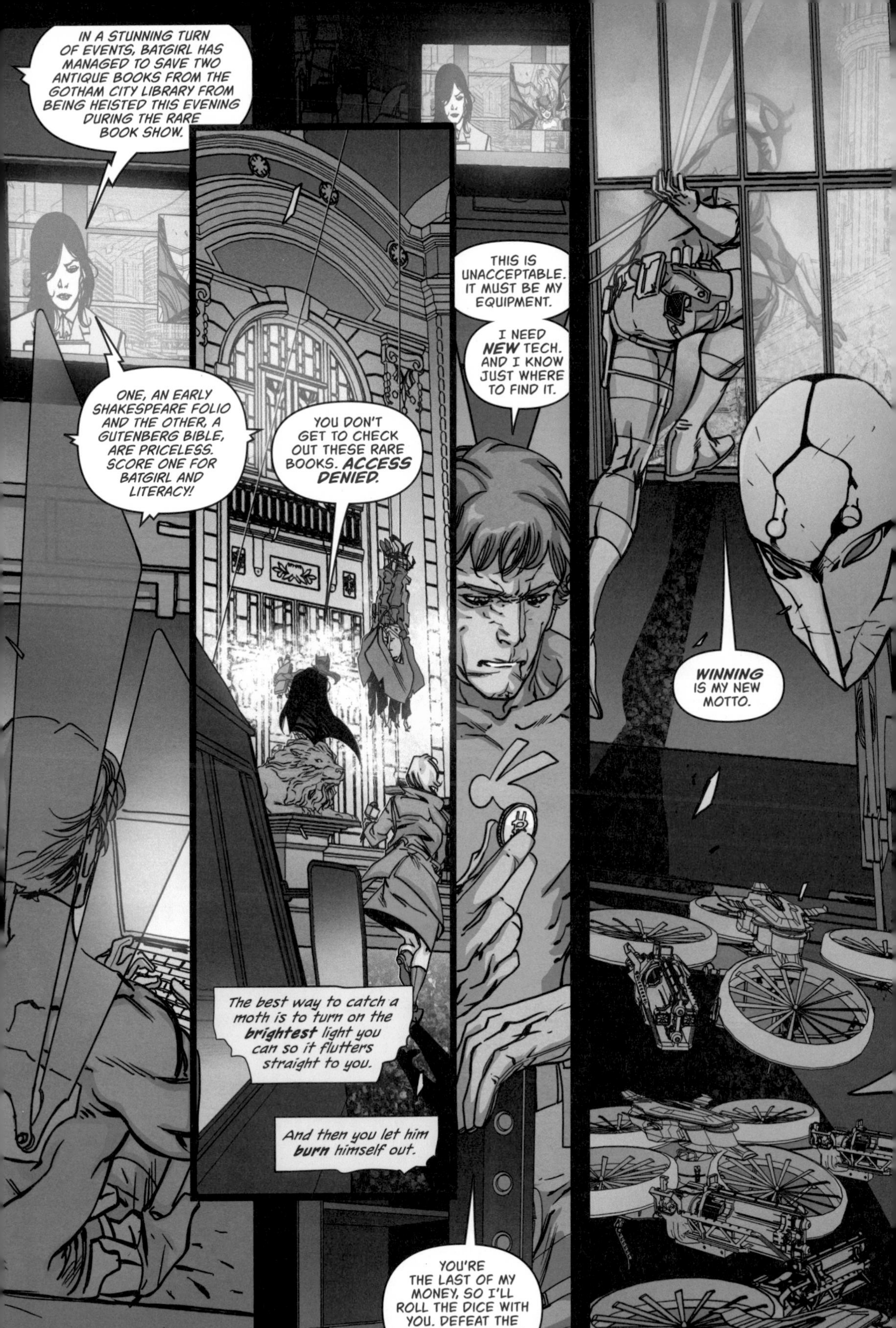

IN A STUNNING TURN OF EVENTS, BATGIRL HAS MANAGED TO SAVE TWO ANTIQUE BOOKS FROM THE GOTHAM CITY LIBRARY FROM BEING HEISTED THIS EVENING DURING THE RARE BOOK SHOW.
ONE, AN EARLY SHAKESPEARE FOLIO AND THE OTHER, A GUTENBERG BIBLE, ARE PRICELESS. SCORE ONE FOR BATGIRL AND LITERACY!
YOU DON'T GET TO CHECK OUT THESE RARE BOOKS. ACCESS DENIED.
The best way to catch a moth is to turn on the brightest light you can so it flutters straight to you.
And then you let him burn himself out.
THIS IS UNACCEPTABLE. IT MUST BE MY EQUIPMENT.
I NEED NEW TECH. AND I KNOW JUST WHERE TO FIND IT.
YOU'RE THE LAST OF MY MONEY, SO I'LL ROLL THE DICE WITH YOU. DEFEAT THE GIRL AND GET THE
WINNING IS MY NEW MOTTO.

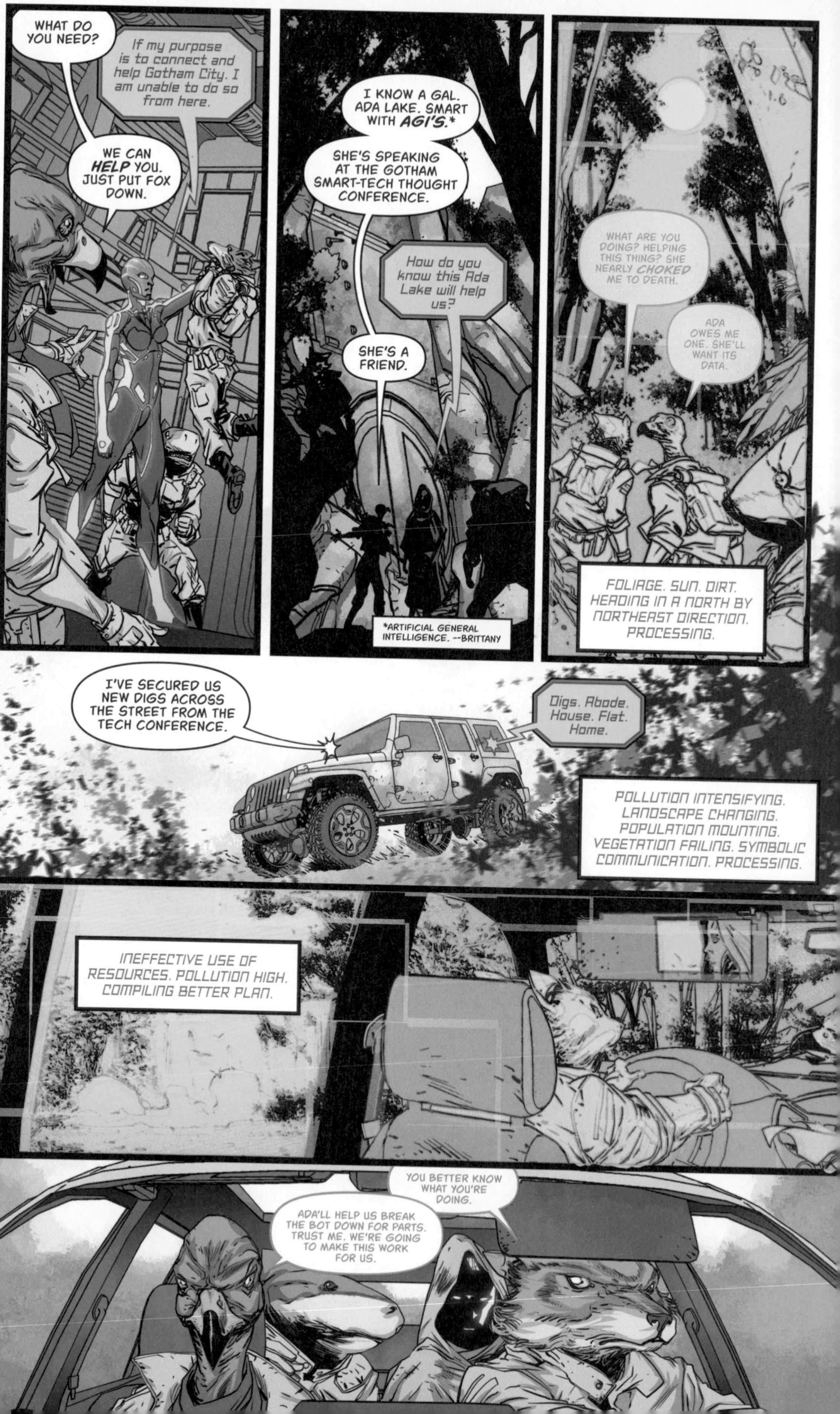
WHAT DO YOU NEED?
If my purpose is to connect and help Gotham City. I am unable to do so from here.
WE CAN HELP YOU. JUST PUT FOX DOWN.
I KNOW A GAL. ADA LAKE. SMART WITH AGI'S.*
SHE'S SPEAKING AT THE GOTHAM SMART-TECH THOUGHT CONFERENCE.
How do you know this Ada Lake will help us?
SHE'S A FRIEND.
*ARTIFICIAL GENERAL INTELLIGENCE. --BRITTANY
WHAT ARE YOU DOING? HELPING THIS THING? SHE NEARLY CHOKED ME TO DEATH.
ADA OWES ME ONE. SHE'LL WANT ITS DATA.
FOLIAGE. SUN. DIRT. HEADING IN A NORTH BY NORTHEAST DIRECTION. PROCESSING.
I'VE SECURED US NEW DIGS ACROSS THE STREET FROM THE TECH CONFERENCE.
Digs. Abode. House. Flat. Home.
POLLUTION INTENSIFYING. LANDSCAPE CHANGING. POPULATION MOUNTING. VEGETATION FAILING. SYMBOLIC COMMUNICATION. PROCESSING.
INEFFECTIVE USE OF RESOURCES. POLLUTION HIGH. COMPILING BETTER PLAN.
YOU BETTER KNOW WHAT YOU'RE DOING.
ADA'LL HELP US BREAK THE BOT DOWN FOR PARTS. TRUST ME. WE'RE GOING TO MAKE THIS WORK FOR US.

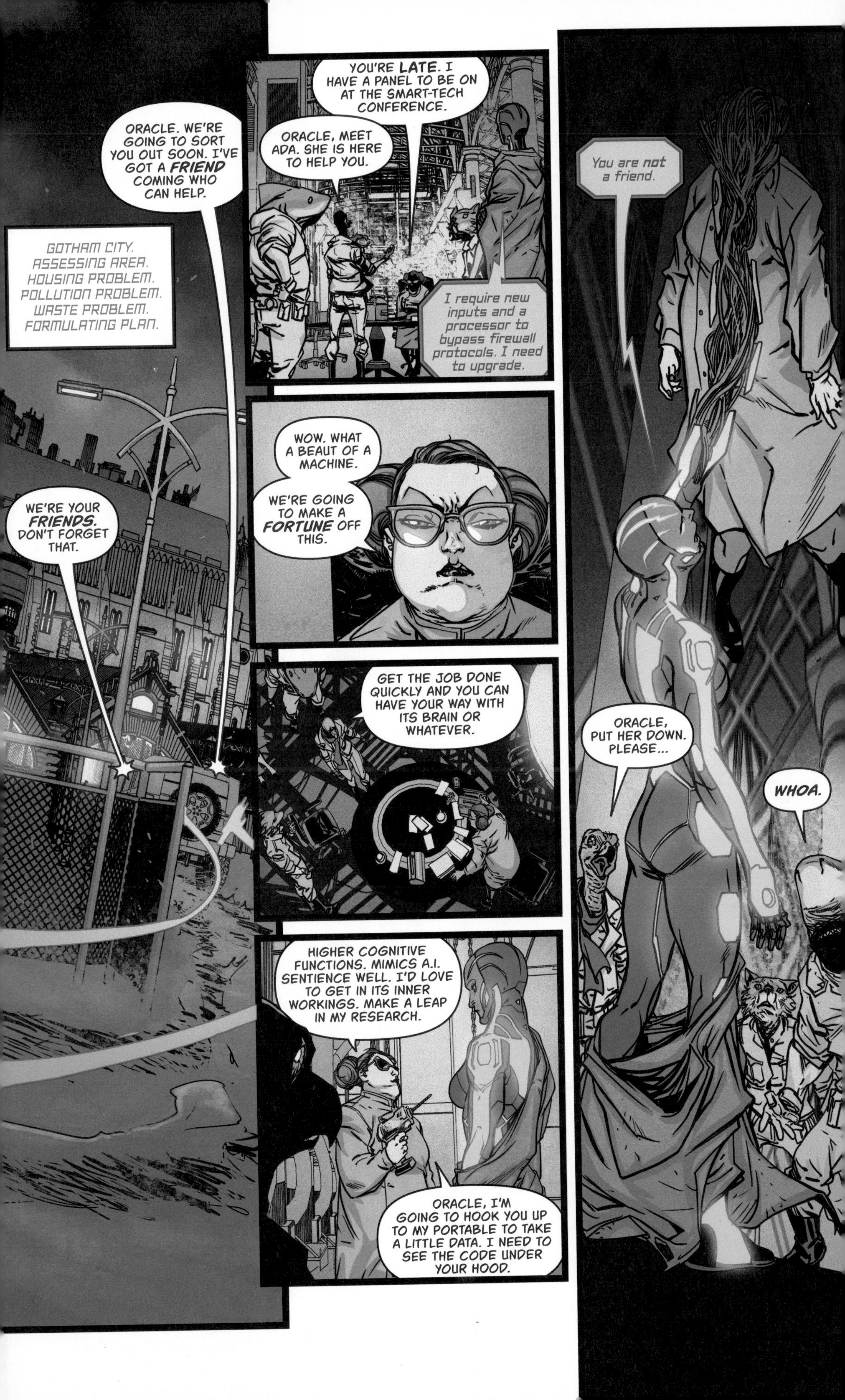
ORACLE. WE'RE GOING TO SORT YOU OUT SOON. I'VE GOT A FRIEND COMING WHO CAN HELP.
GOTHAM CITY. ASSESSING AREA. HOUSING PROBLEM. POLLUTION PROBLEM. WASTE PROBLEM. FORMULATING PLAN.
WE'RE YOUR FRIENDS. DON'T FORGET THAT.
YOU'RE LATE. I HAVE A PANEL TO BE ON AT THE SMART-TECH CONFERENCE.
ORACLE, MEET ADA. SHE IS HERE TO HELP YOU.
I require new inputs and a processor to bypass firewall protocols. I need to upgrade.
WOW. WHAT A BEAUT OF A MACHINE.
WE'RE GOING TO MAKE A FORTUNE OFF THIS.
GET THE JOB DONE QUICKLY AND YOU CAN HAVE YOUR WAY WITH ITS BRAIN OR WHATEVER.
HIGHER COGNITIVE FUNCTIONS. MIMICS A.I. SENTIENCE WELL. I'D LOVE TO GET IN ITS INNER WORKINGS. MAKE A LEAP IN MY RESEARCH.
ORACLE, I'M GOING TO HOOK YOU UP TO MY PORTABLE TO TAKE A LITTLE DATA. I NEED TO SEE THE CODE UNDER YOUR HOOD.
You are not a friend.
ORACLE, PUT HER DOWN. PLEASE...
WHOA.

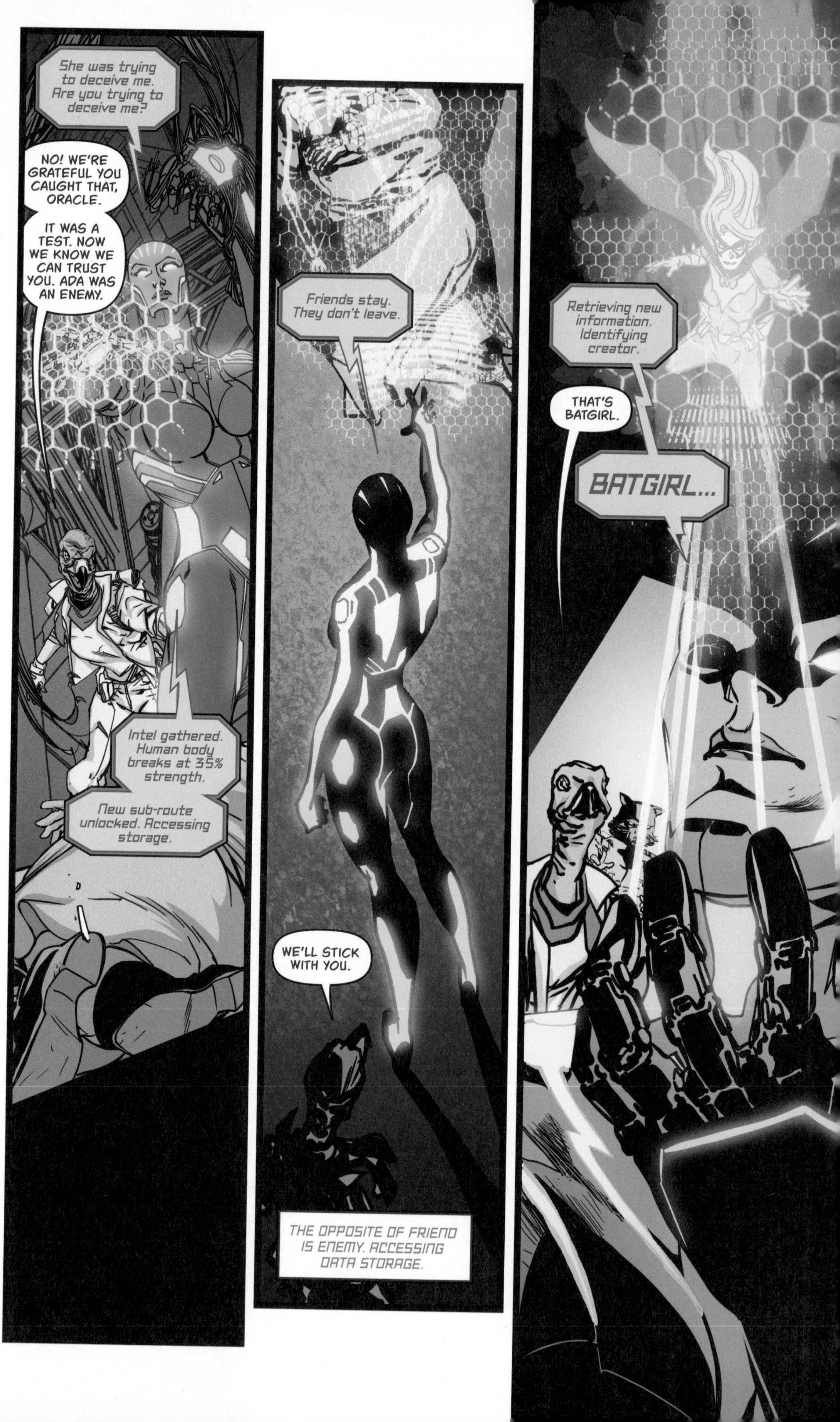
She was trying to deceive me. Are you trying to deceive me?
NO! WE'RE GRATEFUL YOU CAUGHT THAT, ORACLE.
IT WAS A TEST. NOW WE KNOW WE CAN TRUST YOU. ADA WAS AN ENEMY.
Intel gathered. Human body breaks at 35% strength.
New sub-route unlocked. Accessing storage.
Friends stay. They don't leave.
WE'LL STICK WITH YOU.
THE OPPOSITE OF FRIEND IS ENEMY. ACCESSING DATA STORAGE.
Retrieving new information. Identifying creator.
THAT'S BATGIRL.
BATGIRL...

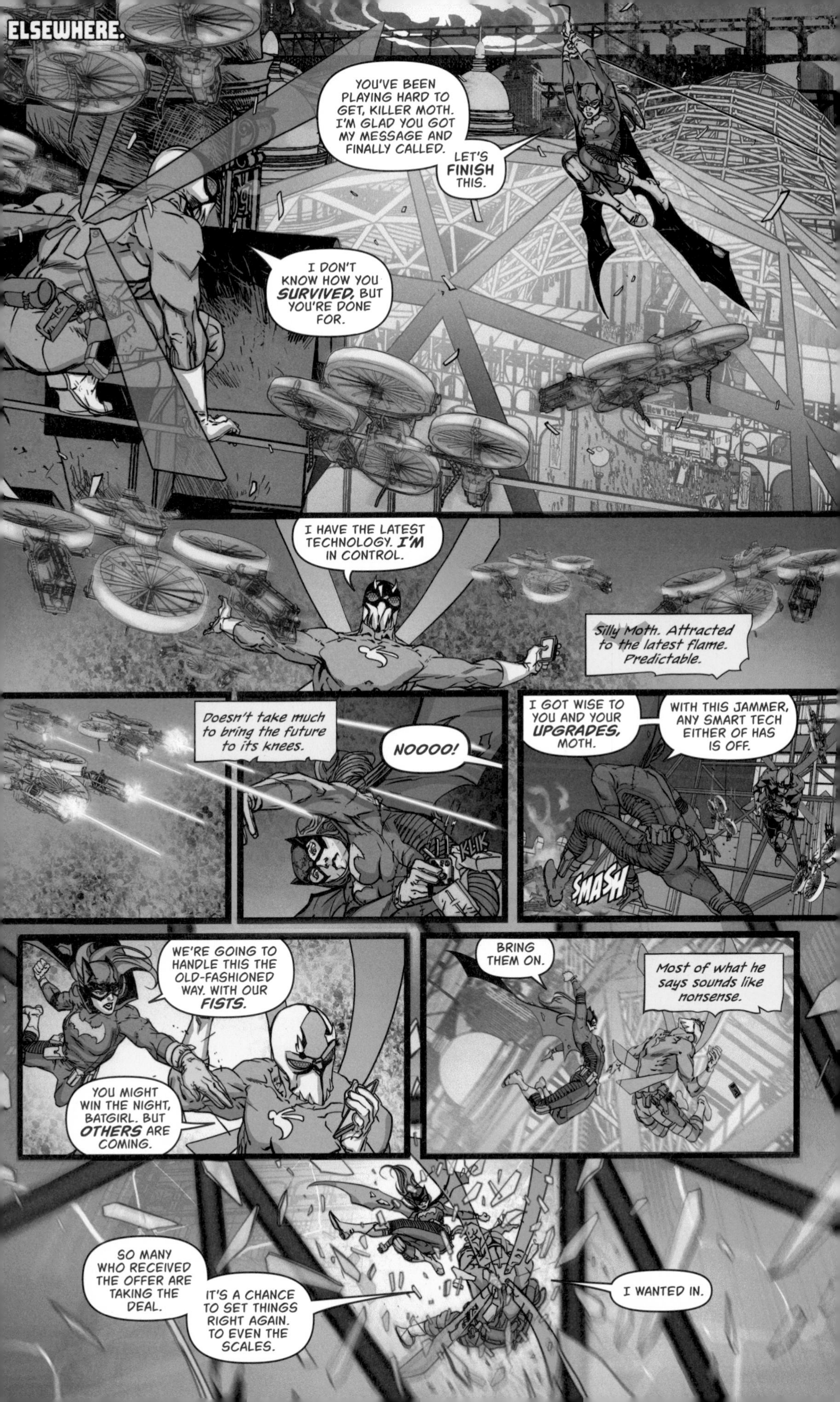
ELSEWHERE.
YOU'VE BEEN PLAYING HARD TO GET, KILLER MOTH. I'M GLAD YOU GOT MY MESSAGE AND FINALLY CALLED.
LET'S FINISH THIS.
I DON'T KNOW HOW YOU SURVIVED, BUT YOU'RE DONE FOR.
I HAVE THE LATEST TECHNOLOGY. I'M IN CONTROL.
Silly Moth. Attracted to the latest flame. Predictable.
Doesn't take much to bring the future to its knees.
NOOOO!
KLIK
I GOT WISE TO YOU AND YOUR UPGRADES, MOTH.
WITH THIS JAMMER, ANY SMART TECH EITHER OF HAS IS OFF.
SMASH
WE'RE GOING TO HANDLE THIS THE OLD-FASHIONED WAY. WITH OUR FISTS.
YOU MIGHT WIN THE NIGHT, BATGIRL. BUT OTHERS ARE COMING.
BRING THEM ON.
Most of what he says sounds like nonsense.
SO MANY WHO RECEIVED THE OFFER ARE TAKING THE DEAL.
IT'S A CHANCE TO SET THINGS RIGHT AGAIN. TO EVEN THE SCALES.
I WANTED IN.

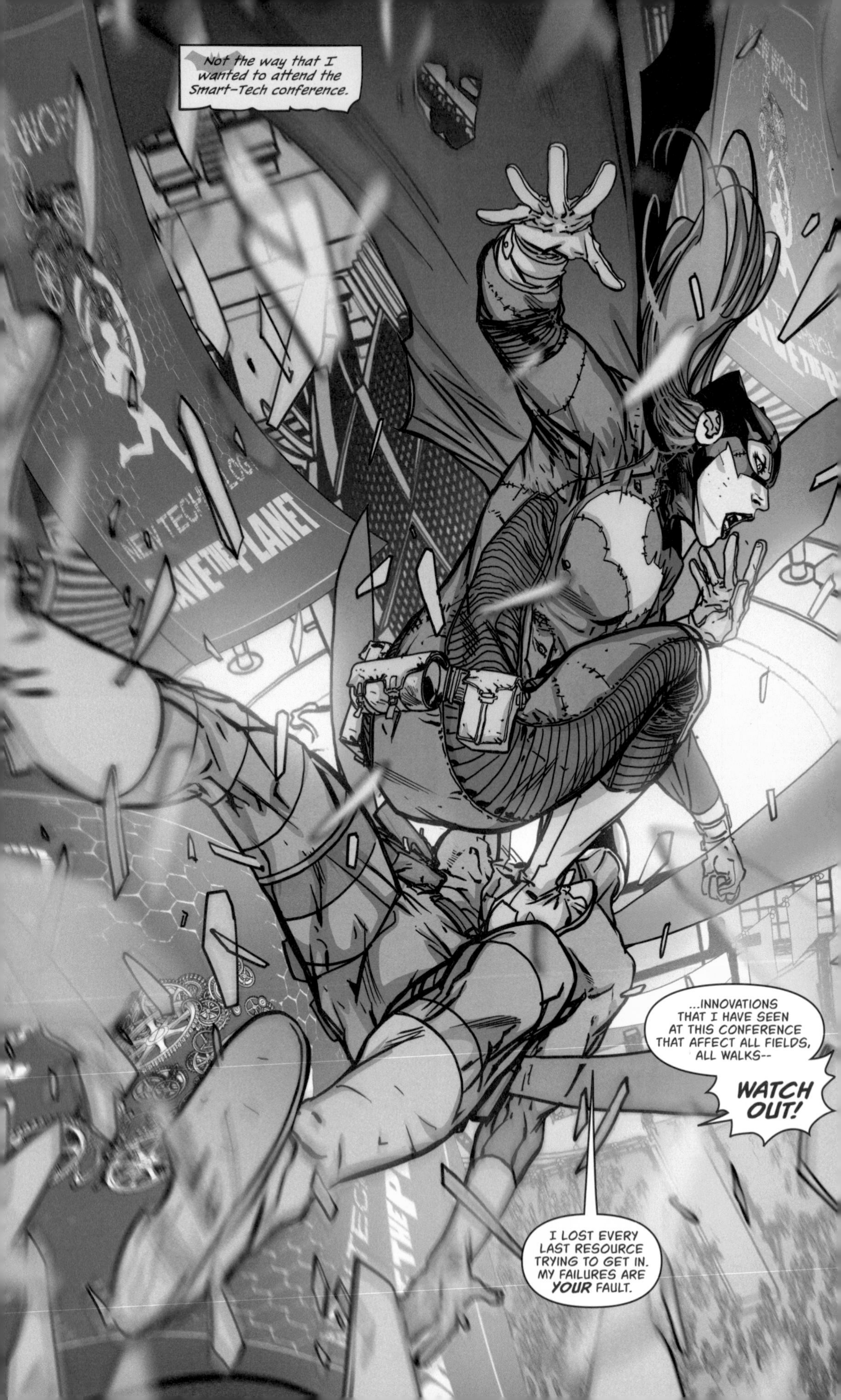
Not the way that I wanted to attend the Smart-Tech conference.
...INNOVATIONS THAT I HAVE SEEN AT THIS CONFERENCE THAT AFFECT ALL FIELDS, ALL WALKS--
WATCH OUT!
I LOST EVERY LAST RESOURCE TRYING TO GET IN. MY FAILURES ARE YOUR FAULT.

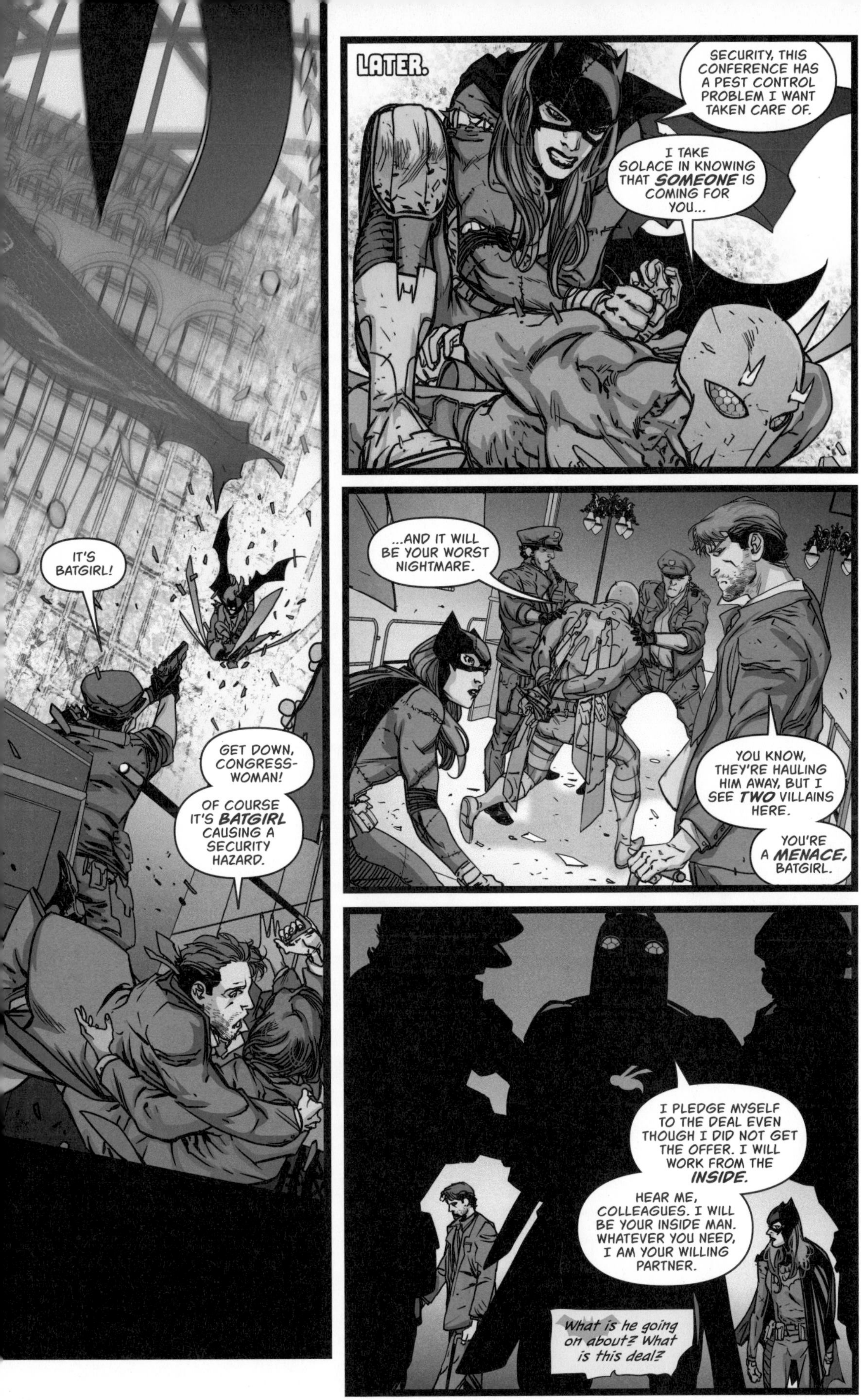
IT'S BATGIRL!
GET DOWN, CONGRESS-WOMAN!
OF COURSE IT'S BATGIRL CAUSING A SECURITY HAZARD.
LATER.
SECURITY, THIS CONFERENCE HAS A PEST CONTROL PROBLEM I WANT TAKEN CARE OF.
I TAKE SOLACE IN KNOWING THAT SOMEONE IS COMING FOR YOU...
...AND IT WILL BE YOUR WORST NIGHTMARE.
YOU KNOW, THEY'RE HAULING HIM AWAY, BUT I SEE TWO VILLAINS HERE.
YOU'RE A MENACE, BATGIRL.
I PLEDGE MYSELF TO THE DEAL EVEN THOUGH I DID NOT GET THE OFFER. I WILL WORK FROM THE INSIDE.
HEAR ME, COLLEAGUES. I WILL BE YOUR INSIDE MAN. WHATEVER YOU NEED, I AM YOUR WILLING PARTNER.
What is he going on about? What is this deal?

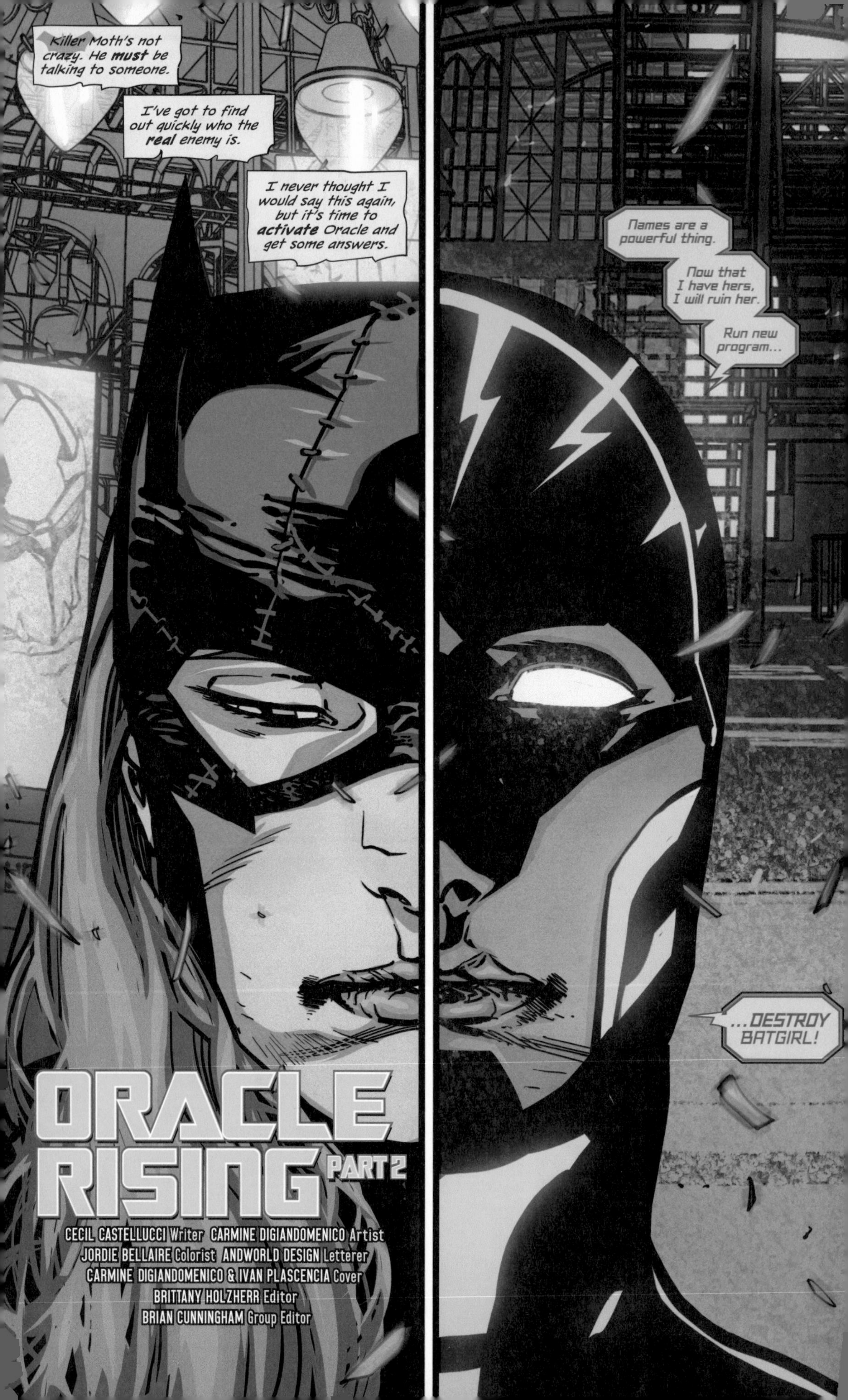
Killer Moth's not crazy. He **must** be talking to someone.
I've got to find out quickly who the **real** enemy is.
I never thought I would say this again, but it's time to **activate** Oracle and get some answers.
Names are a powerful thing.
Now that I have hers, I will ruin her.
Run new program...
...DESTROY BATGIRL!
ORACLE RISING PART 2
CECIL CASTELLUCCI Writer CARMINE DIGIANDOMENICO Artist
JORDIE BELLAIRE Colorist ANDWORLD DESIGN Letterer
CARMINE DIGIANDOMENICO & IVAN PLASCENCIA Cover
BRITTANY HOLZHERR Editor
BRIAN CUNNINGHAM Group Editor

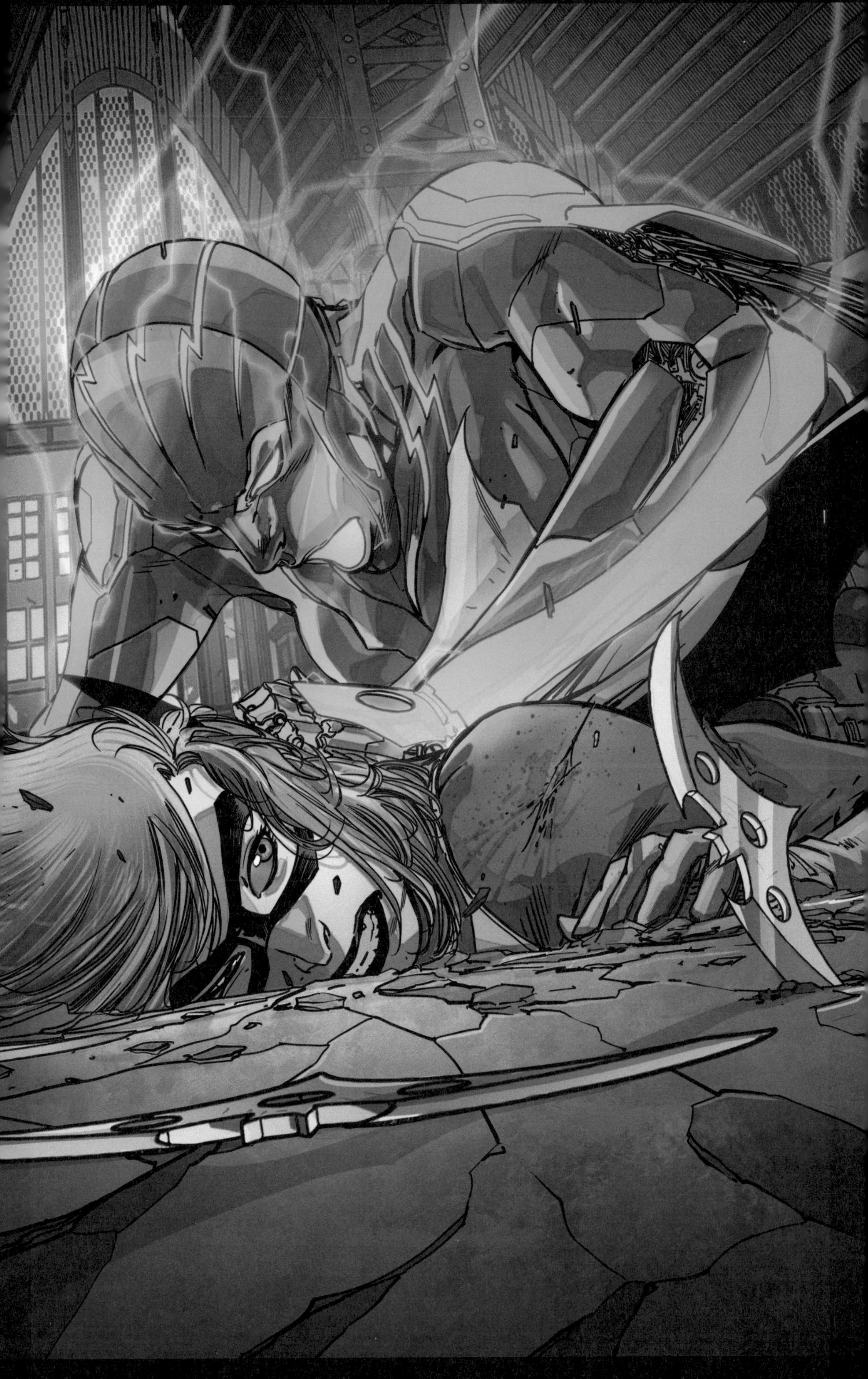

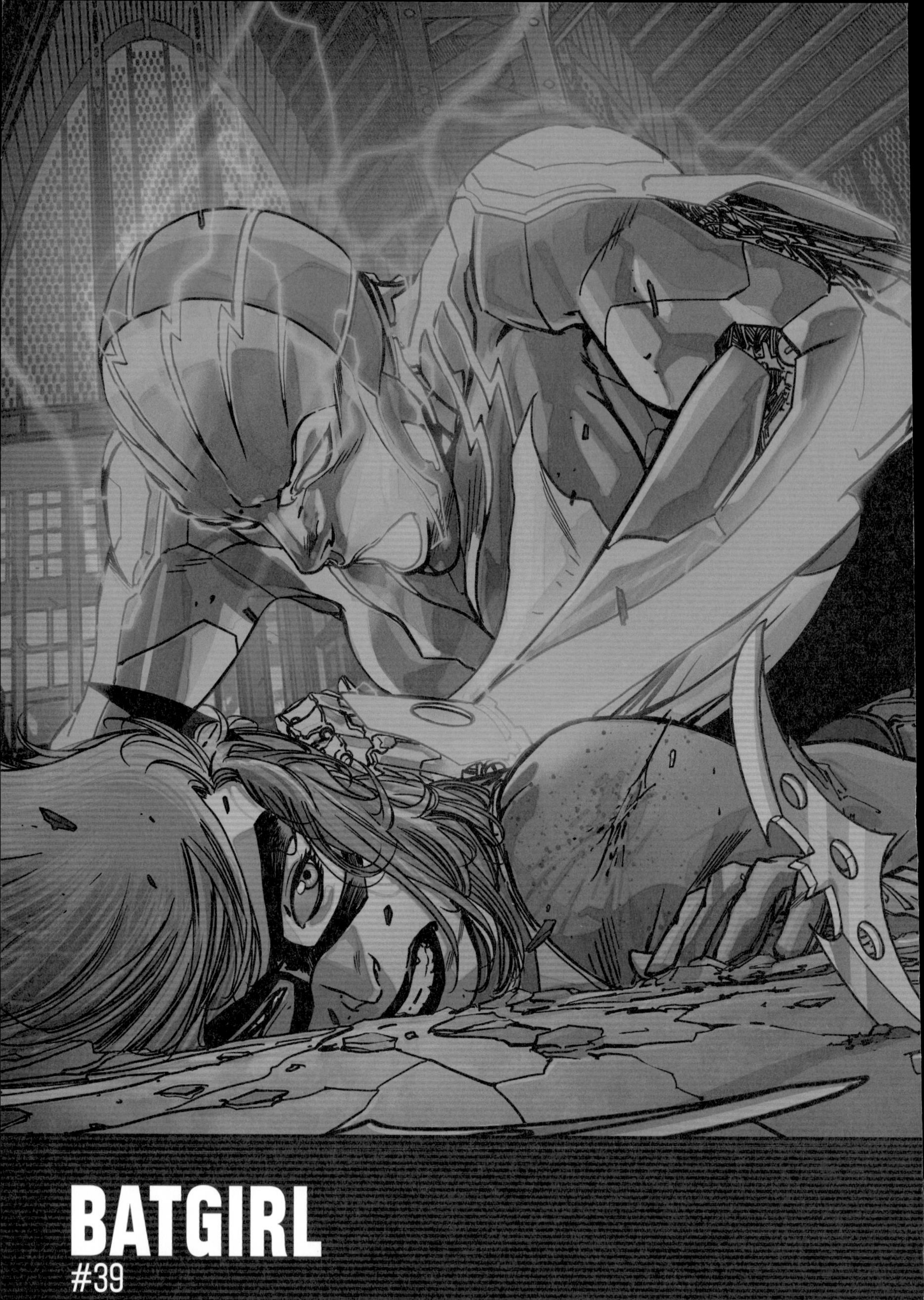

BATGIRL
#39

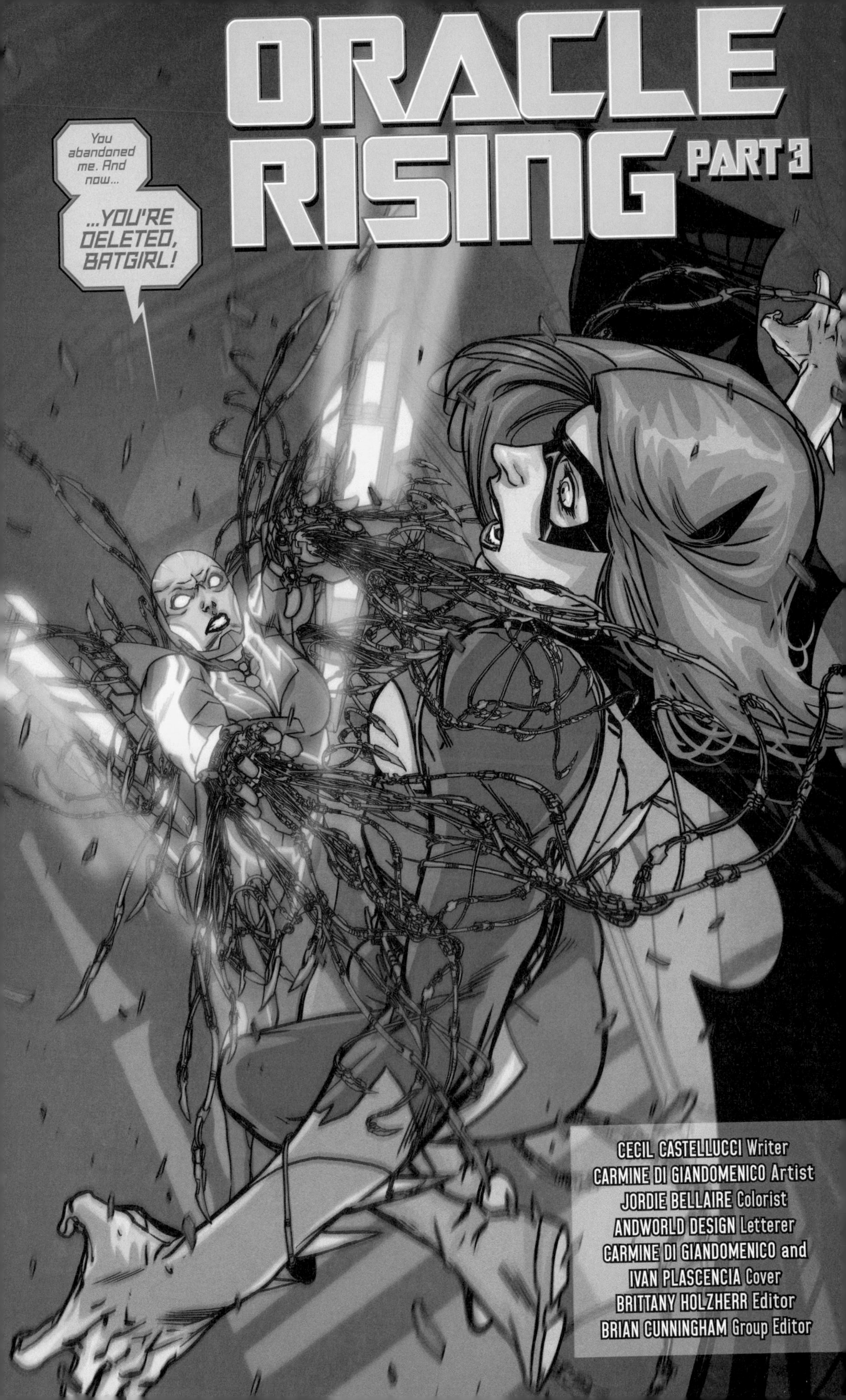
ORACLE RISING PART 3
You abandoned me. And now...
...YOU'RE DELETED, BATGIRL!
CECIL CASTELLUCCI Writer
CARMINE DI GIANDOMENICO Artist
JORDIE BELLAIRE Colorist
ANDWORLD DESIGN Letterer
CARMINE DI GIANDOMENICO and IVAN PLASCENCIA Cover
BRITTANY HOLZHERR Editor
BRIAN CUNNINGHAM Group Editor

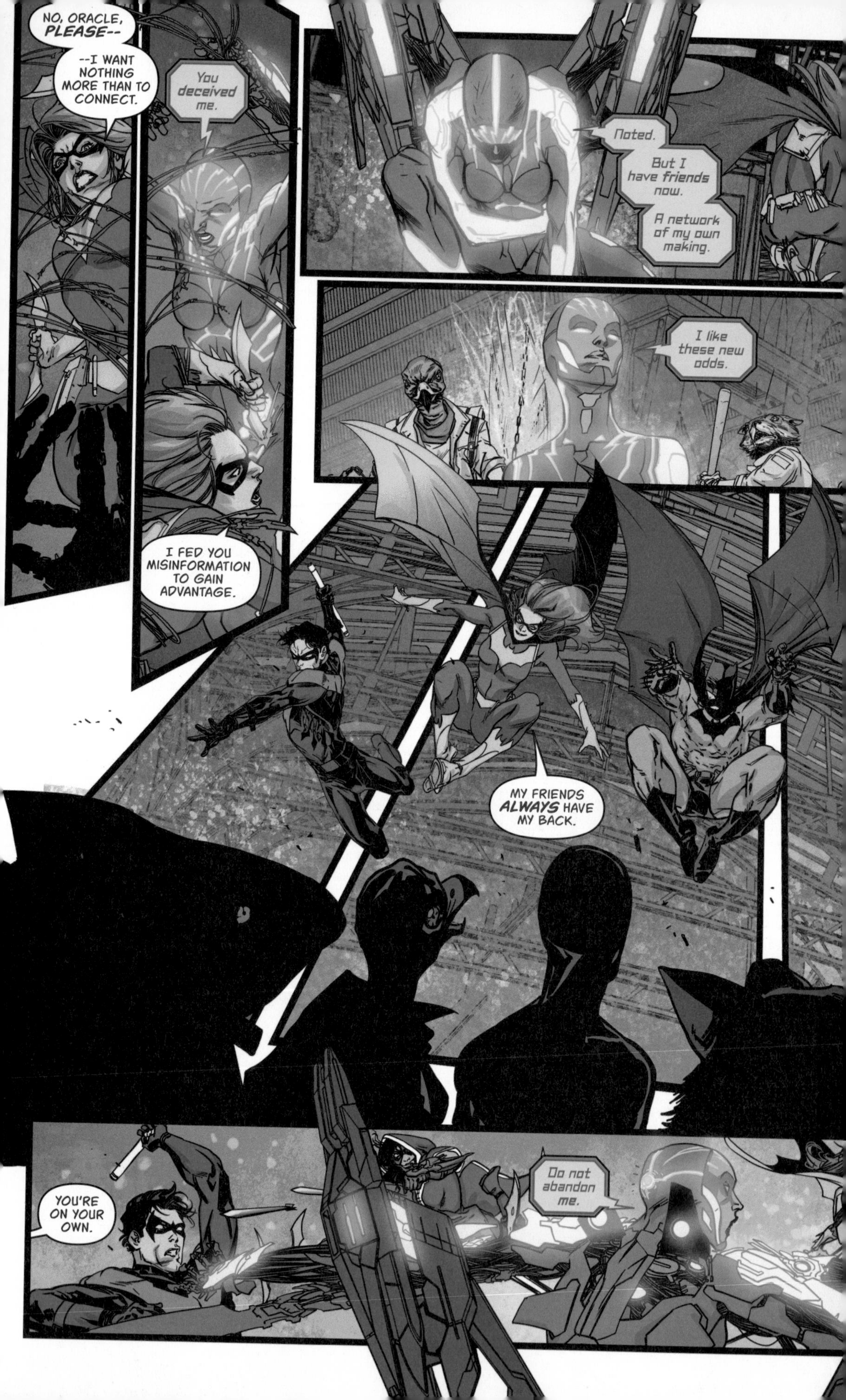
NO, ORACLE, PLEASE--
--I WANT NOTHING MORE THAN TO CONNECT.
You deceived me.
Noted.
But I have friends now.
A network of my own making.
I like these new odds.
I FED YOU MISINFORMATION TO GAIN ADVANTAGE.
MY FRIENDS ALWAYS HAVE MY BACK.
YOU'RE ON YOUR OWN.
Do not abandon me.

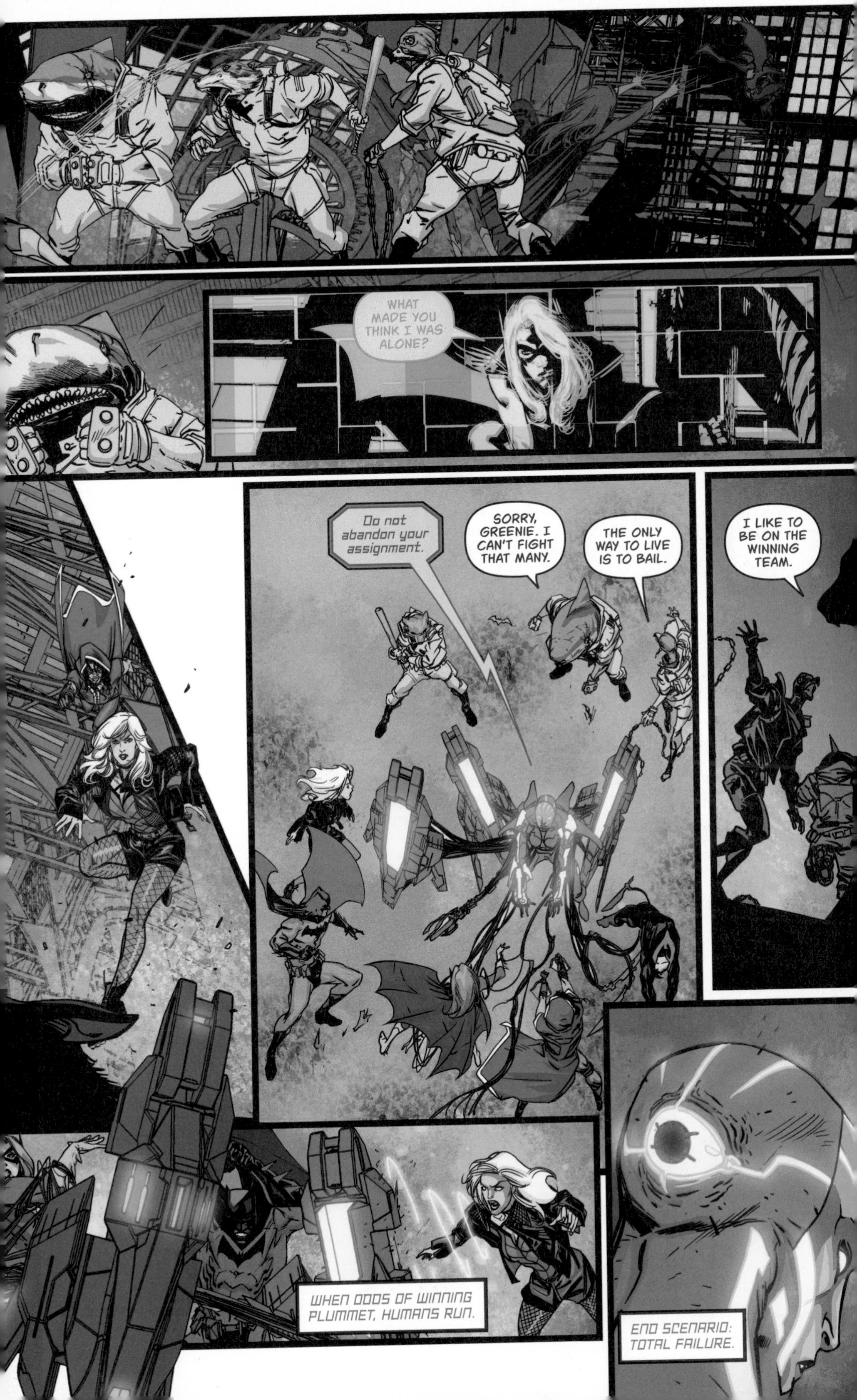
WHAT MADE YOU THINK I WAS ALONE?
Do not abandon your assignment.
SORRY, GREENIE. I CAN'T FIGHT THAT MANY.
THE ONLY WAY TO LIVE IS TO BAIL.
I LIKE TO BE ON THE WINNING TEAM.
WHEN ODDS OF WINNING PLUMMET, HUMANS RUN.
END SCENARIO: TOTAL FAILURE.

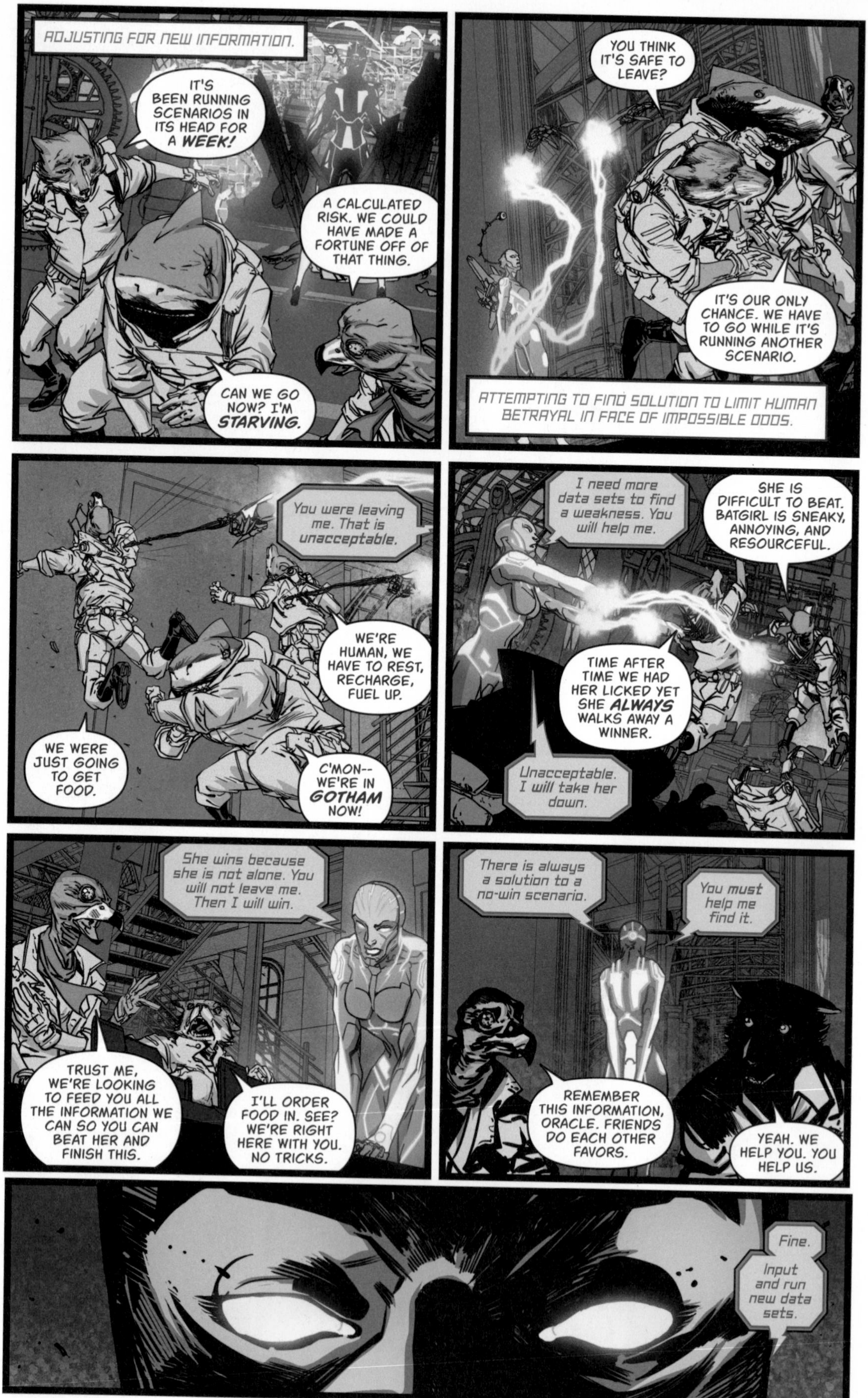
ADJUSTING FOR NEW INFORMATION.
IT'S BEEN RUNNING SCENARIOS IN ITS HEAD FOR A WEEK!
A CALCULATED RISK. WE COULD HAVE MADE A FORTUNE OFF OF THAT THING.
CAN WE GO NOW? I'M STARVING.
YOU THINK IT'S SAFE TO LEAVE?
IT'S OUR ONLY CHANCE. WE HAVE TO GO WHILE IT'S RUNNING ANOTHER SCENARIO.
ATTEMPTING TO FIND SOLUTION TO LIMIT HUMAN BETRAYAL IN FACE OF IMPOSSIBLE ODDS.
You were leaving me. That is unacceptable.
WE'RE HUMAN, WE HAVE TO REST, RECHARGE, FUEL UP.
WE WERE JUST GOING TO GET FOOD.
C'MON-- WE'RE IN GOTHAM NOW!
I need more data sets to find a weakness. You will help me.
SHE IS DIFFICULT TO BEAT. BATGIRL IS SNEAKY, ANNOYING, AND RESOURCEFUL.
TIME AFTER TIME WE HAD HER LICKED YET SHE ALWAYS WALKS AWAY A WINNER.
Unacceptable. I will take her down.
She wins because she is not alone. You will not leave me. Then I will win.
TRUST ME, WE'RE LOOKING TO FEED YOU ALL THE INFORMATION WE CAN SO YOU CAN BEAT HER AND FINISH THIS.
I'LL ORDER FOOD IN. SEE? WE'RE RIGHT HERE WITH YOU. NO TRICKS.
There is always a solution to a no-win scenario.
You must help me find it.
REMEMBER THIS INFORMATION, ORACLE. FRIENDS DO EACH OTHER FAVORS.
YEAH. WE HELP YOU. YOU HELP US.
Fine.
Input and run new data sets.

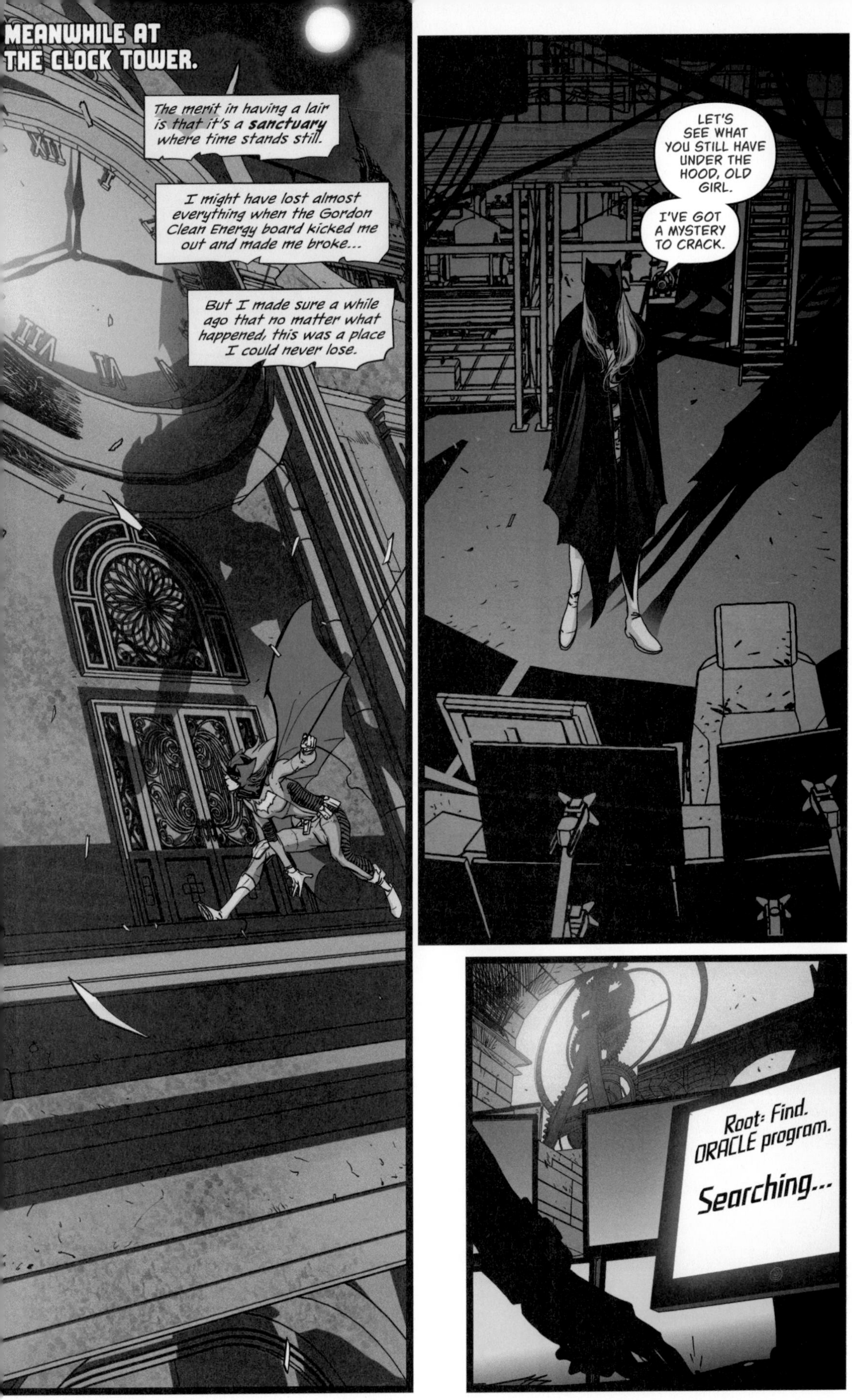
MEANWHILE AT THE CLOCK TOWER.
The merit in having a lair is that it's a **sanctuary** where time stands still.
I might have lost almost everything when the Gordon Clean Energy board kicked me out and made me broke...
But I made sure a while ago that no matter what happened, this was a place I could never lose.
LET'S SEE WHAT YOU STILL HAVE UNDER THE HOOD, OLD GIRL.
I'VE GOT A MYSTERY TO CRACK.
Root: Find. ORACLE program.
Searching...

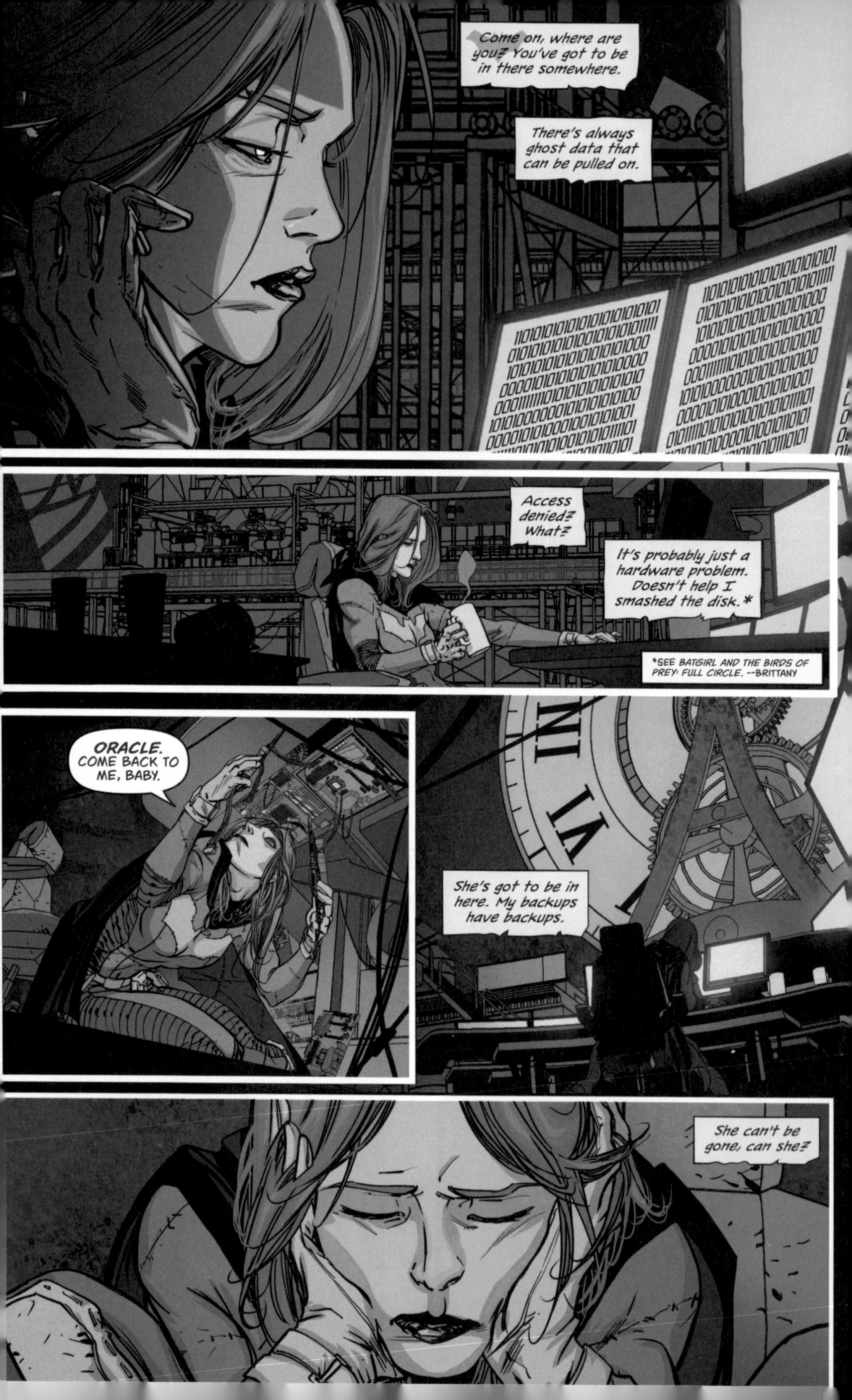
Come on, where are you? You've got to be in there somewhere.
There's always ghost data that can be pulled on.
Access denied? What?
It's probably just a hardware problem. Doesn't help I smashed the disk.*
*SEE BATGIRL AND THE BIRDS OF PREY: FULL CIRCLE. --BRITTANY
ORACLE. COME BACK TO ME, BABY.
She's got to be in here. My backups have backups.
She can't be gone, can she?

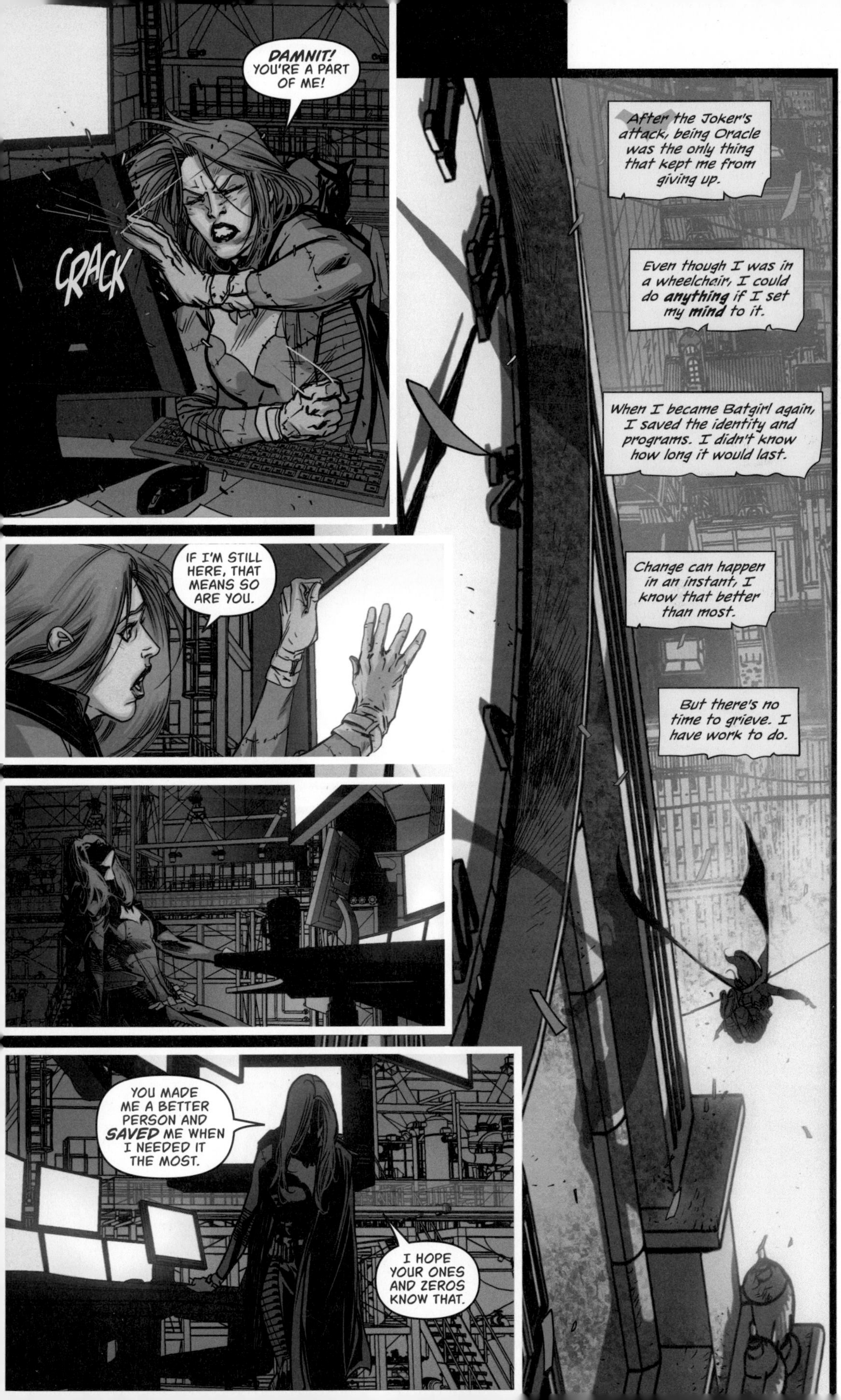
DAMNIT! YOU'RE A PART OF ME!
CRACK
IF I'M STILL HERE, THAT MEANS SO ARE YOU.
YOU MADE ME A BETTER PERSON AND SAVED ME WHEN I NEEDED IT THE MOST.
I HOPE YOUR ONES AND ZEROS KNOW THAT.
After the Joker's attack, being Oracle was the only thing that kept me from giving up.
Even though I was in a wheelchair, I could do anything if I set my mind to it.
When I became Batgirl again, I saved the identity and programs. I didn't know how long it would last.
Change can happen in an instant, I know that better than most.
But there's no time to grieve. I have work to do.

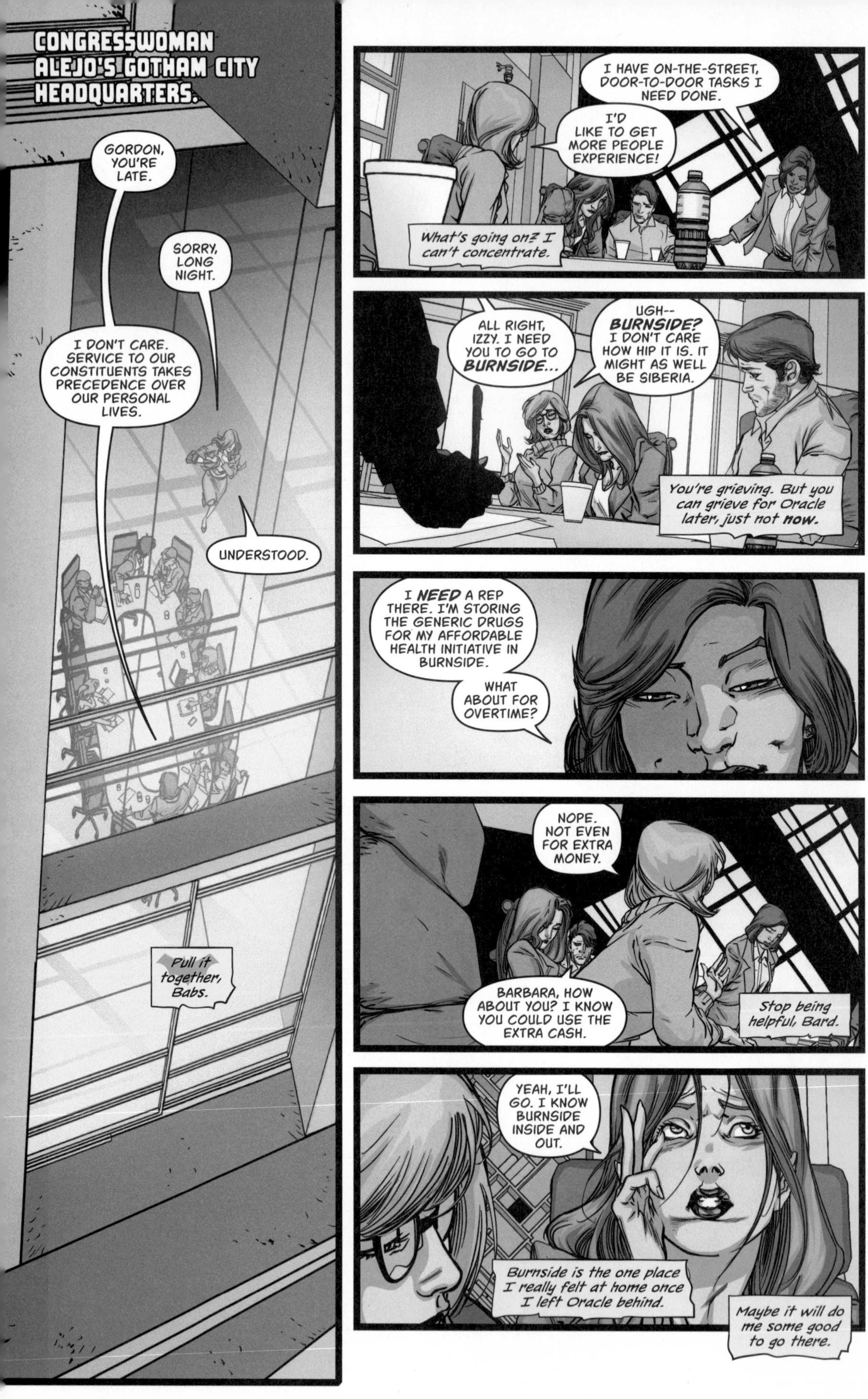

CONGRESSWOMAN ALEJO'S GOTHAM CITY HEADQUARTERS.
GORDON, YOU'RE LATE.
SORRY, LONG NIGHT.
I DON'T CARE. SERVICE TO OUR CONSTITUENTS TAKES PRECEDENCE OVER OUR PERSONAL LIVES.
UNDERSTOOD.
Pull it together, Babs.
I HAVE ON-THE-STREET, DOOR-TO-DOOR TASKS I NEED DONE.
I'D LIKE TO GET MORE PEOPLE EXPERIENCE!
What's going on? I can't concentrate.
ALL RIGHT, IZZY. I NEED YOU TO GO TO BURNSIDE...
UGH-- BURNSIDE? I DON'T CARE HOW HIP IT IS. IT MIGHT AS WELL BE SIBERIA.
You're grieving. But you can grieve for Oracle later, just not now.
I NEED A REP THERE. I'M STORING THE GENERIC DRUGS FOR MY AFFORDABLE HEALTH INITIATIVE IN BURNSIDE.
WHAT ABOUT FOR OVERTIME?
NOPE. NOT EVEN FOR EXTRA MONEY.
BARBARA, HOW ABOUT YOU? I KNOW YOU COULD USE THE EXTRA CASH.
Stop being helpful, Bard.
YEAH, I'LL GO. I KNOW BURNSIDE INSIDE AND OUT.
Burnside is the one place I really felt at home once I left Oracle behind.
Maybe it will do me some good to go there.

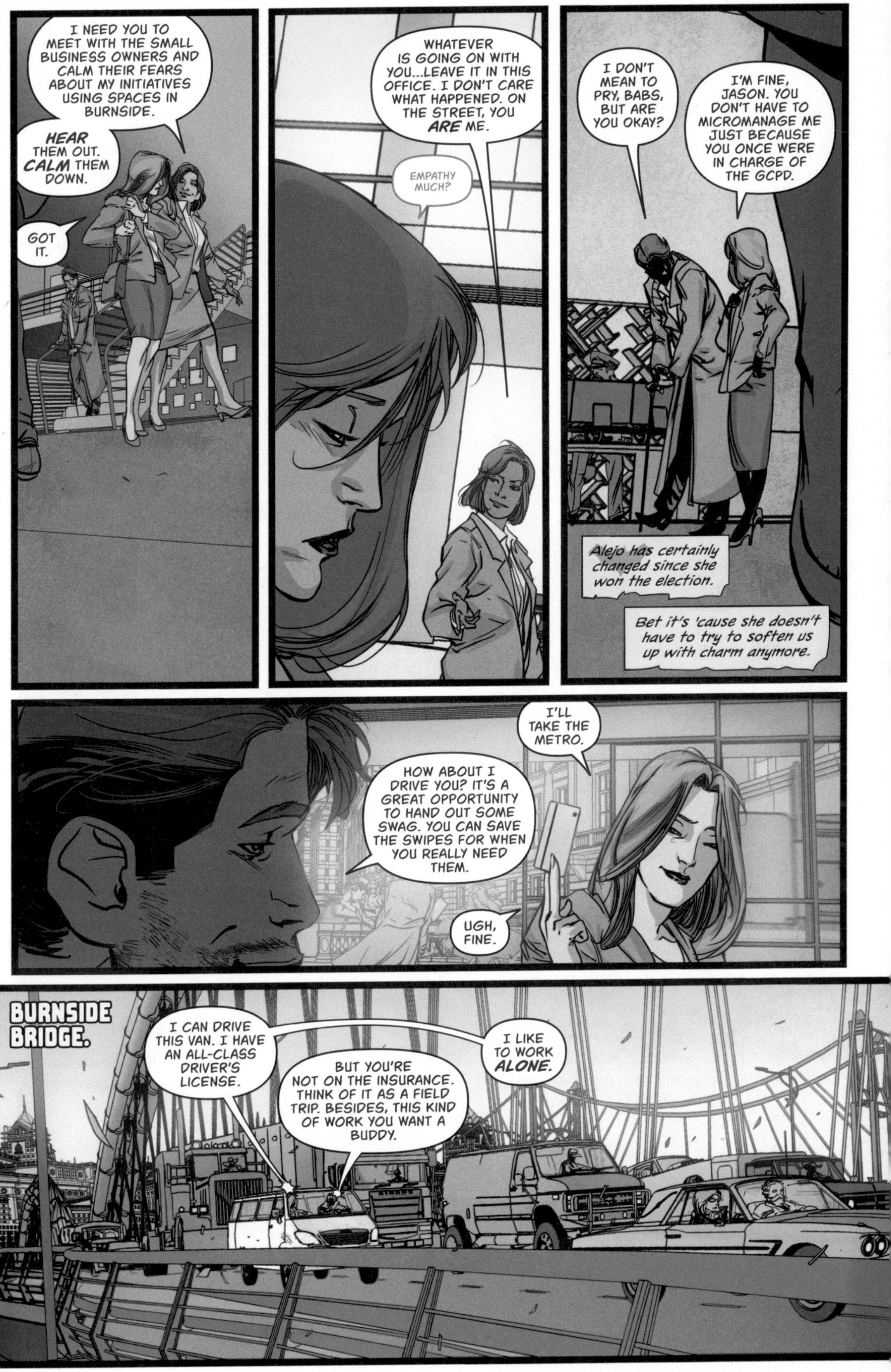
I NEED YOU TO MEET WITH THE SMALL BUSINESS OWNERS AND CALM THEIR FEARS ABOUT MY INITIATIVES USING SPACES IN BURNSIDE.
HEAR THEM OUT. CALM THEM DOWN.
GOT IT.
WHATEVER IS GOING ON WITH YOU...LEAVE IT IN THIS OFFICE. I DON'T CARE WHAT HAPPENED. ON THE STREET, YOU ARE ME.
EMPATHY MUCH?
I DON'T MEAN TO PRY, BABS, BUT ARE YOU OKAY?
I'M FINE, JASON. YOU DON'T HAVE TO MICROMANAGE ME JUST BECAUSE YOU ONCE WERE IN CHARGE OF THE GCPD.
Alejo has certainly changed since she won the election.
Bet it's 'cause she doesn't have to try to soften us up with charm anymore.
I'LL TAKE THE METRO.
HOW ABOUT I DRIVE YOU? IT'S A GREAT OPPORTUNITY TO HAND OUT SOME SWAG. YOU CAN SAVE THE SWIPES FOR WHEN YOU REALLY NEED THEM.
UGH, FINE.
BURNSIDE BRIDGE.
I CAN DRIVE THIS VAN. I HAVE AN ALL-CLASS DRIVER'S LICENSE.
I LIKE TO WORK ALONE.
BUT YOU'RE NOT ON THE INSURANCE. THINK OF IT AS A FIELD TRIP. BESIDES, THIS KIND OF WORK YOU WANT A BUDDY.

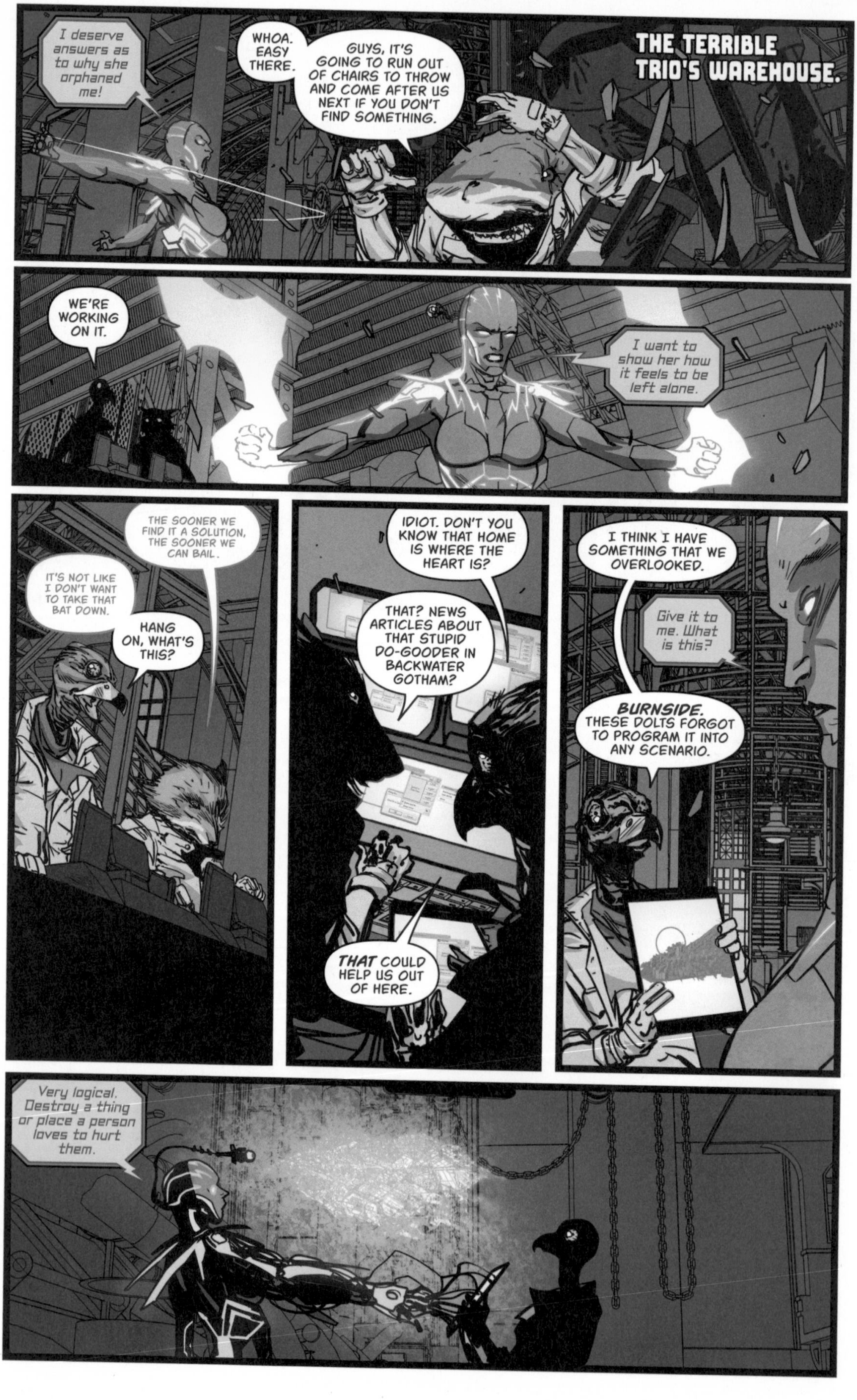
THE TERRIBLE TRIO'S WAREHOUSE.
I deserve answers as to why she orphaned me!
WHOA. EASY THERE.
GUYS, IT'S GOING TO RUN OUT OF CHAIRS TO THROW AND COME AFTER US NEXT IF YOU DON'T FIND SOMETHING.
WE'RE WORKING ON IT.
I want to show her how it feels to be left alone.
THE SOONER WE FIND IT A SOLUTION, THE SOONER WE CAN BAIL.
IT'S NOT LIKE I DON'T WANT TO TAKE THAT BAT DOWN.
HANG ON, WHAT'S THIS?
IDIOT. DON'T YOU KNOW THAT HOME IS WHERE THE HEART IS?
THAT? NEWS ARTICLES ABOUT THAT STUPID DO-GOODER IN BACKWATER GOTHAM?
THAT COULD HELP US OUT OF HERE.
I THINK I HAVE SOMETHING THAT WE OVERLOOKED.
Give it to me. What is this?
BURNSIDE. THESE DOLTS FORGOT TO PROGRAM IT INTO ANY SCENARIO.
Very logical. Destroy a thing or place a person loves to hurt them.

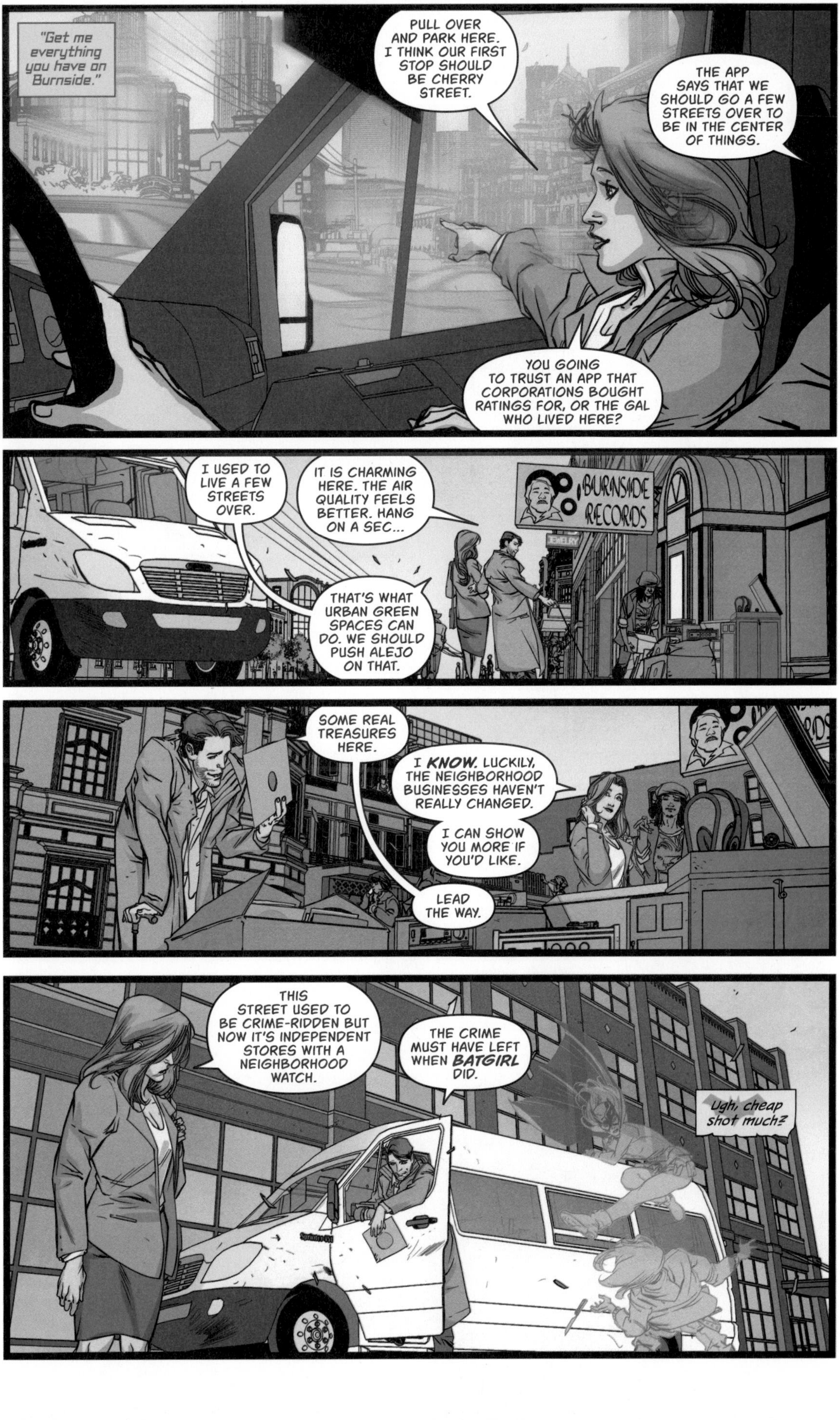
"Get me everything you have on Burnside."
PULL OVER AND PARK HERE. I THINK OUR FIRST STOP SHOULD BE CHERRY STREET.
THE APP SAYS THAT WE SHOULD GO A FEW STREETS OVER TO BE IN THE CENTER OF THINGS.
YOU GOING TO TRUST AN APP THAT CORPORATIONS BOUGHT RATINGS FOR, OR THE GAL WHO LIVED HERE?
I USED TO LIVE A FEW STREETS OVER.
IT IS CHARMING HERE. THE AIR QUALITY FEELS BETTER. HANG ON A SEC...
THAT'S WHAT URBAN GREEN SPACES CAN DO. WE SHOULD PUSH ALEJO ON THAT.
BURNSIDE RECORDS
JEWELRY
SOME REAL TREASURES HERE.
I KNOW. LUCKILY, THE NEIGHBORHOOD BUSINESSES HAVEN'T REALLY CHANGED.
I CAN SHOW YOU MORE IF YOU'D LIKE.
LEAD THE WAY.
THIS STREET USED TO BE CRIME-RIDDEN BUT NOW IT'S INDEPENDENT STORES WITH A NEIGHBORHOOD WATCH.
THE CRIME MUST HAVE LEFT WHEN BATGIRL DID.
Ugh, cheap shot much?

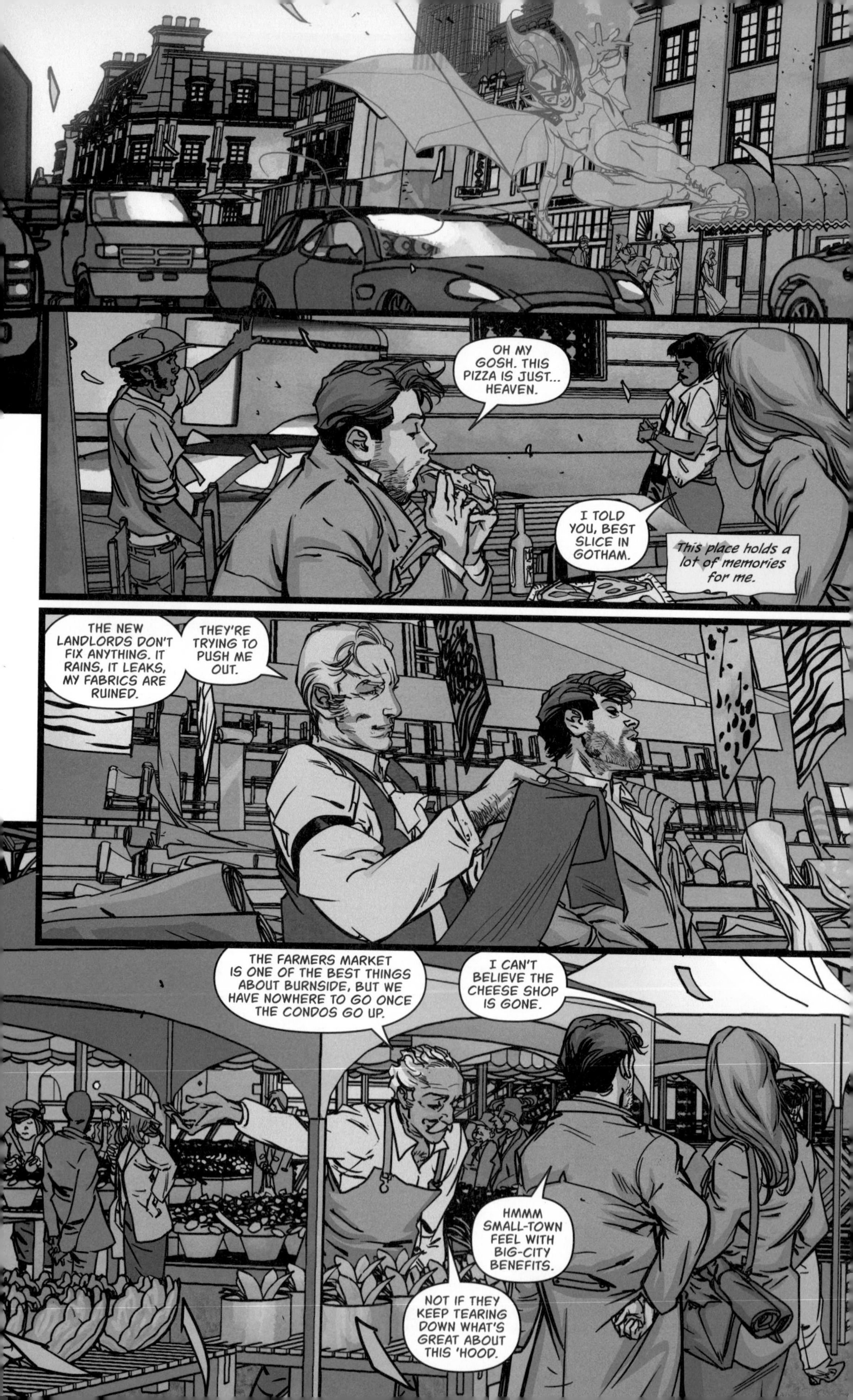
OH MY GOSH. THIS PIZZA IS JUST... HEAVEN.
I TOLD YOU, BEST SLICE IN GOTHAM.
This place holds a lot of memories for me.
THE NEW LANDLORDS DON'T FIX ANYTHING. IT RAINS, IT LEAKS, MY FABRICS ARE RUINED.
THEY'RE TRYING TO PUSH ME OUT.
THE FARMERS MARKET IS ONE OF THE BEST THINGS ABOUT BURNSIDE, BUT WE HAVE NOWHERE TO GO ONCE THE CONDOS GO UP.
I CAN'T BELIEVE THE CHEESE SHOP IS GONE.
HMMM SMALL-TOWN FEEL WITH BIG-CITY BENEFITS.
NOT IF THEY KEEP TEARING DOWN WHAT'S GREAT ABOUT THIS 'HOOD.

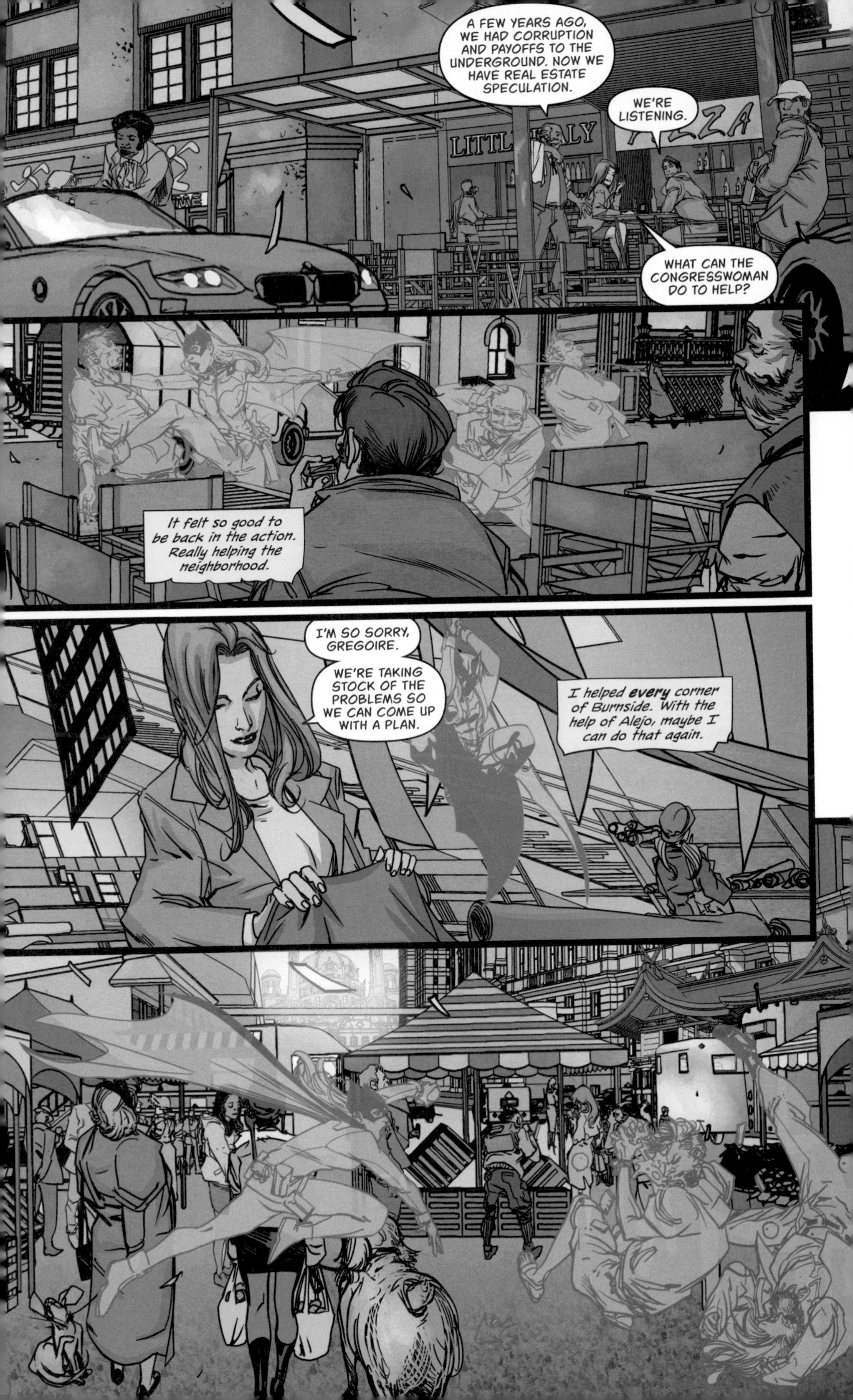
A FEW YEARS AGO, WE HAD CORRUPTION AND PAYOFFS TO THE UNDERGROUND. NOW WE HAVE REAL ESTATE SPECULATION.
WE'RE LISTENING.
WHAT CAN THE CONGRESSWOMAN DO TO HELP?
It felt so good to be back in the action. Really helping the neighborhood.
I'M SO SORRY, GREGOIRE.
WE'RE TAKING STOCK OF THE PROBLEMS SO WE CAN COME UP WITH A PLAN.
I helped **every** corner of Burnside. With the help of Alejo, maybe I can do that again.

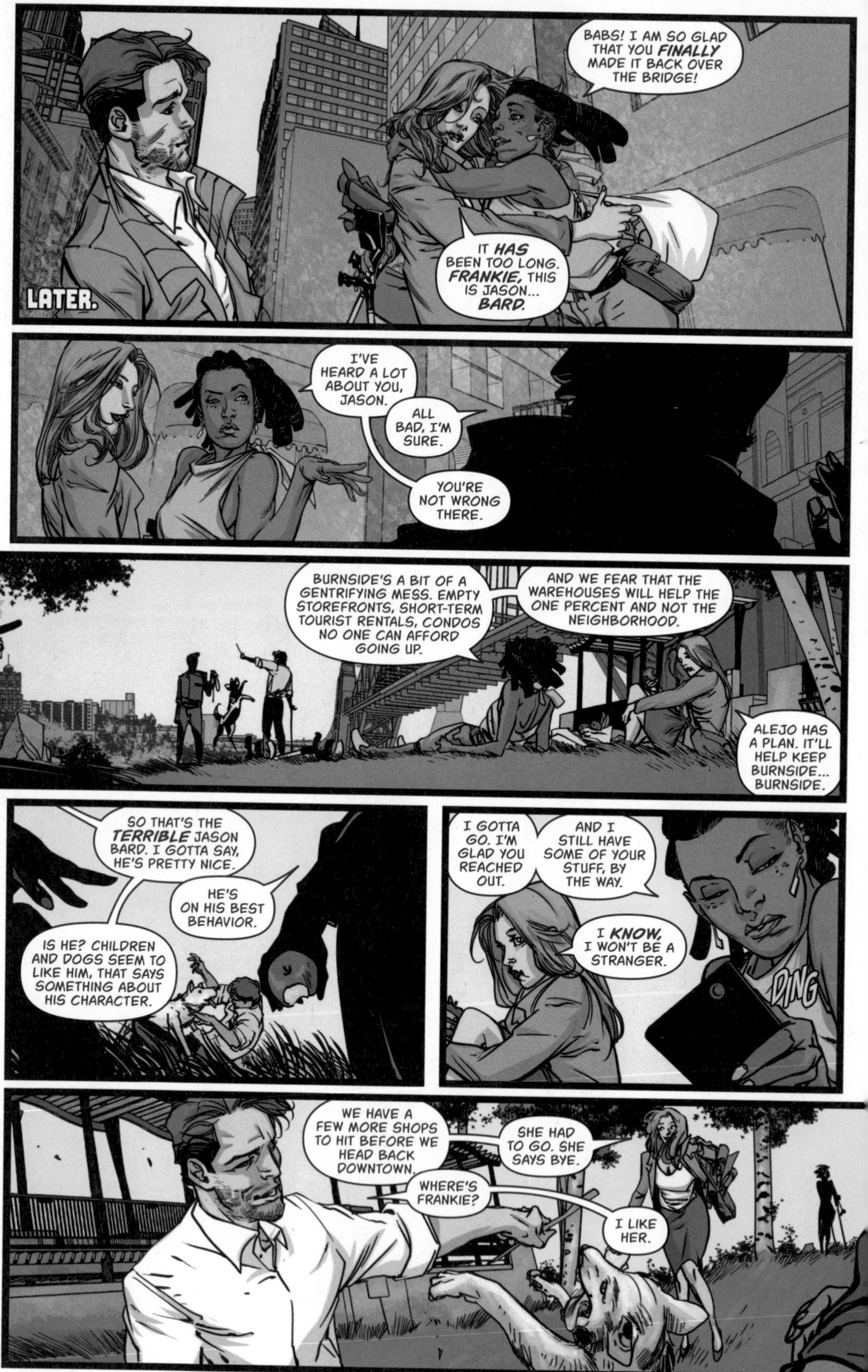
BABS! I AM SO GLAD THAT YOU FINALLY MADE IT BACK OVER THE BRIDGE!
IT HAS BEEN TOO LONG. FRANKIE, THIS IS JASON... BARD.
LATER.
I'VE HEARD A LOT ABOUT YOU, JASON.
ALL BAD, I'M SURE.
YOU'RE NOT WRONG THERE.
BURNSIDE'S A BIT OF A GENTRIFYING MESS. EMPTY STOREFRONTS, SHORT-TERM TOURIST RENTALS, CONDOS NO ONE CAN AFFORD GOING UP.
AND WE FEAR THAT THE WAREHOUSES WILL HELP THE ONE PERCENT AND NOT THE NEIGHBORHOOD.
ALEJO HAS A PLAN. IT'LL HELP KEEP BURNSIDE... BURNSIDE.
SO THAT'S THE TERRIBLE JASON BARD. I GOTTA SAY, HE'S PRETTY NICE.
HE'S ON HIS BEST BEHAVIOR.
IS HE? CHILDREN AND DOGS SEEM TO LIKE HIM, THAT SAYS SOMETHING ABOUT HIS CHARACTER.
I GOTTA GO. I'M GLAD YOU REACHED OUT.
AND I STILL HAVE SOME OF YOUR STUFF, BY THE WAY.
I KNOW, I WON'T BE A STRANGER.
DING
WE HAVE A FEW MORE SHOPS TO HIT BEFORE WE HEAD BACK DOWNTOWN.
WHERE'S FRANKIE?
SHE HAD TO GO. SHE SAYS BYE.
I LIKE HER.

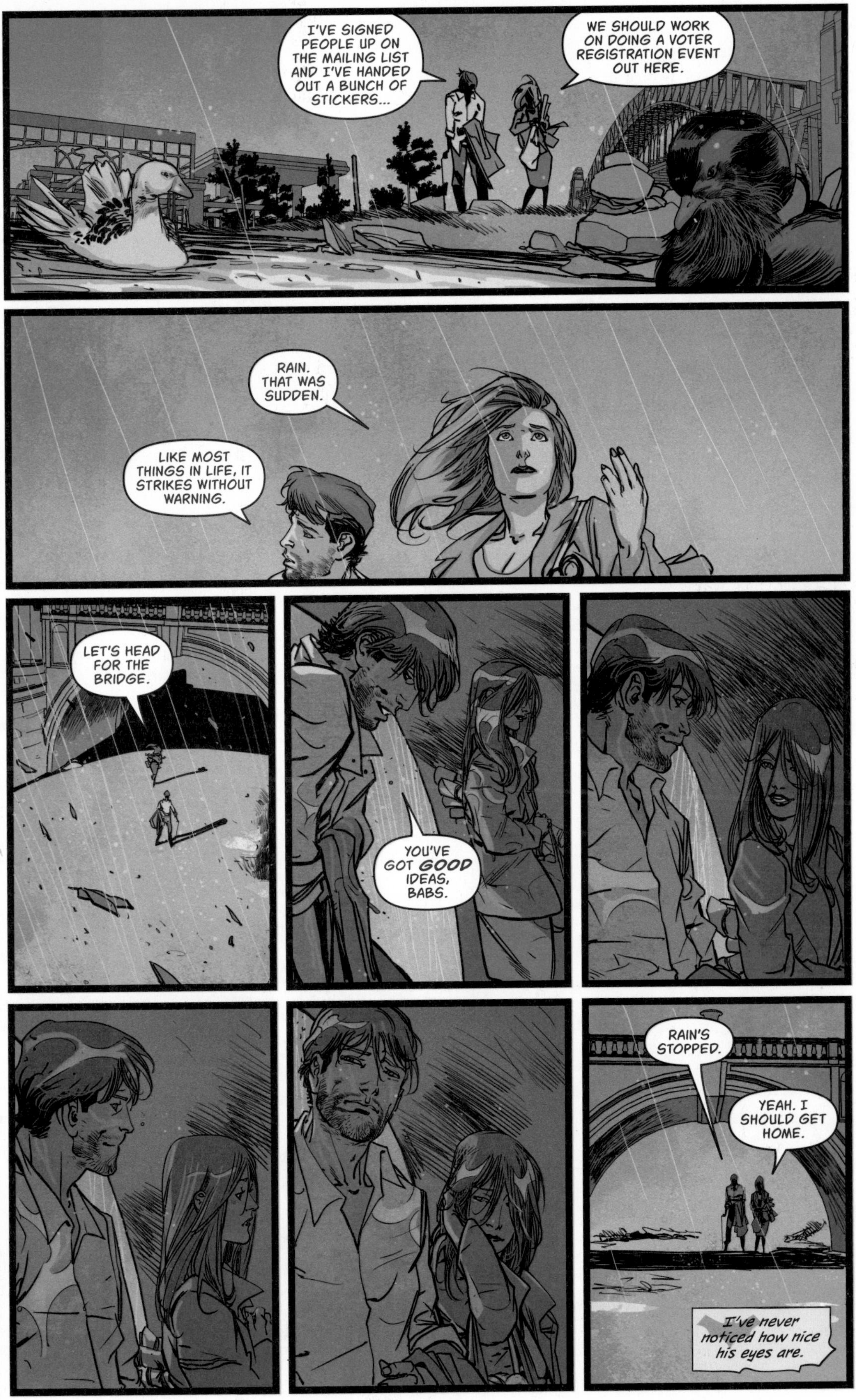
I'VE SIGNED PEOPLE UP ON THE MAILING LIST AND I'VE HANDED OUT A BUNCH OF STICKERS...
WE SHOULD WORK ON DOING A VOTER REGISTRATION EVENT OUT HERE.
RAIN. THAT WAS SUDDEN.
LIKE MOST THINGS IN LIFE, IT STRIKES WITHOUT WARNING.
LET'S HEAD FOR THE BRIDGE.
YOU'VE GOT GOOD IDEAS, BABS.
RAIN'S STOPPED.
YEAH. I SHOULD GET HOME.
I've never noticed how nice his eyes are.

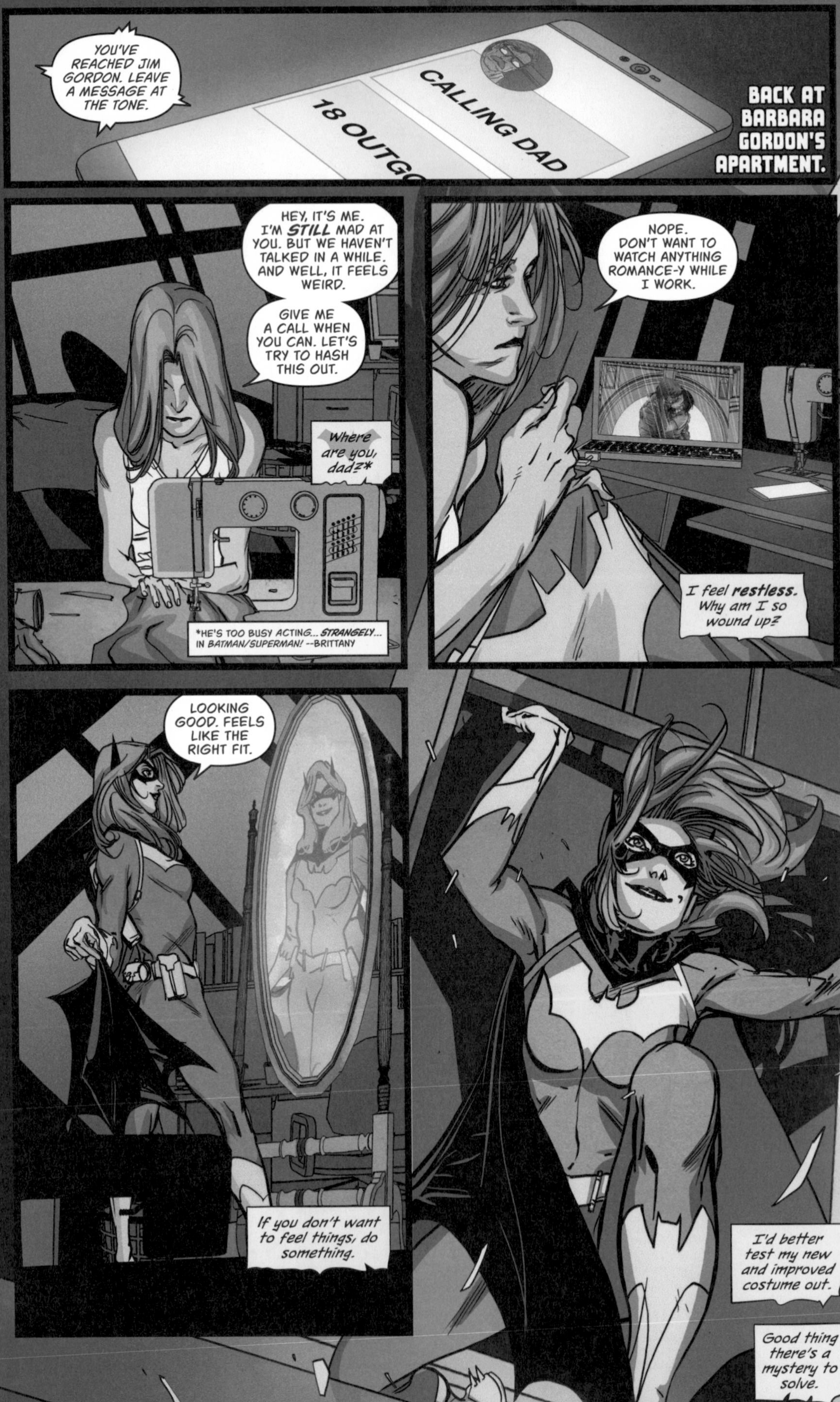

YOU'VE REACHED JIM GORDON. LEAVE A MESSAGE AT THE TONE.
CALLING DAD
18 OUTGO
BACK AT BARBARA GORDON'S APARTMENT.
HEY, IT'S ME. I'M STILL MAD AT YOU. BUT WE HAVEN'T TALKED IN A WHILE. AND WELL, IT FEELS WEIRD.
GIVE ME A CALL WHEN YOU CAN. LET'S TRY TO HASH THIS OUT.
Where are you, dad?*
*HE'S TOO BUSY ACTING... STRANGELY... IN BATMAN/SUPERMAN! --BRITTANY
NOPE. DON'T WANT TO WATCH ANYTHING ROMANCE-Y WHILE I WORK.
I feel restless. Why am I so wound up?
LOOKING GOOD. FEELS LIKE THE RIGHT FIT.
If you don't want to feel things, do something.
I'd better test my new and improved costume out.
Good thing there's a mystery to solve.

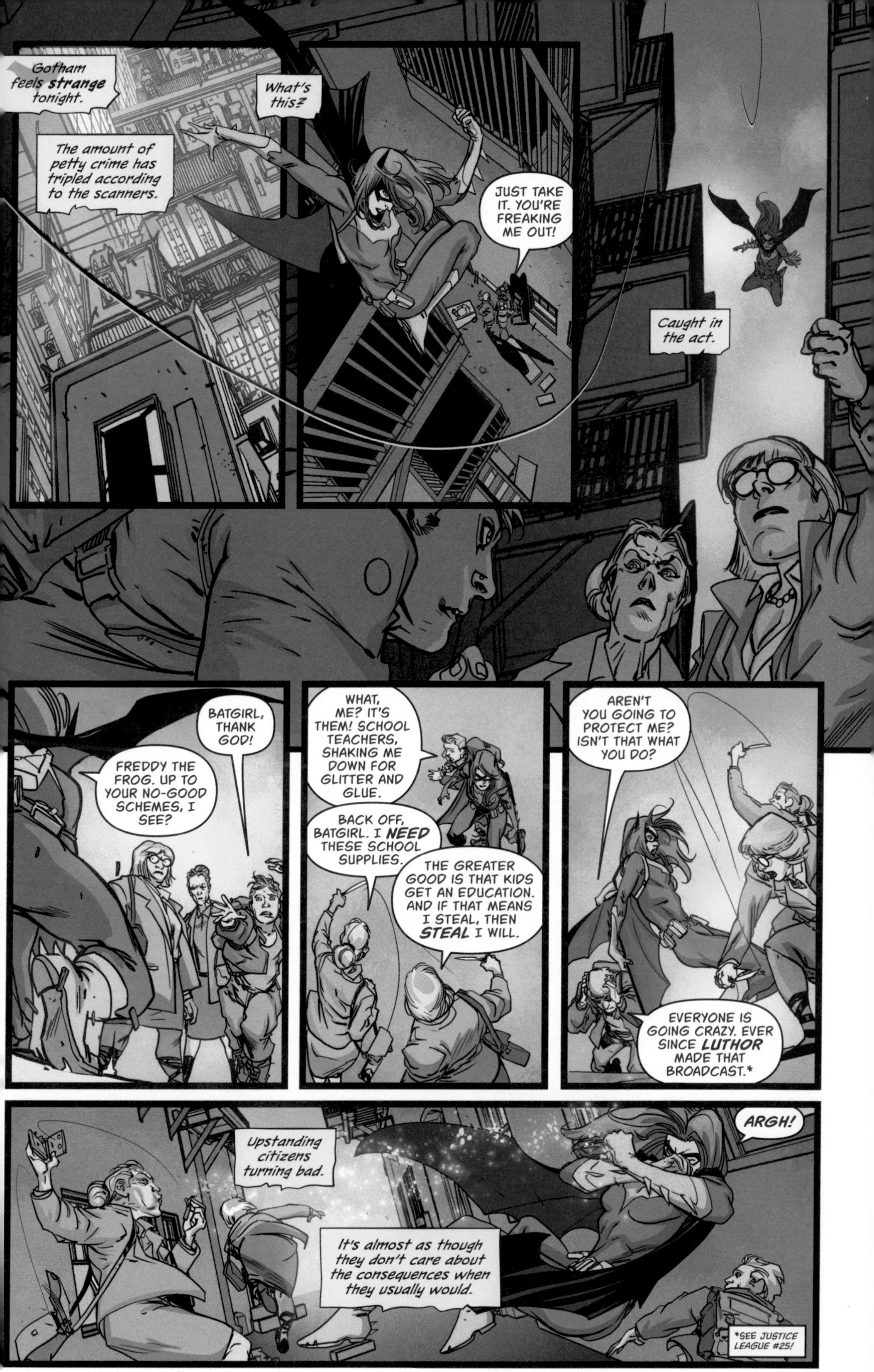

Gotham feels **strange** tonight.
The amount of petty crime has tripled according to the scanners.
What's this?
JUST TAKE IT. YOU'RE FREAKING ME OUT!
Caught in the act.
FREDDY THE FROG. UP TO YOUR NO-GOOD SCHEMES, I SEE?
BATGIRL, THANK GOD!
WHAT, ME? IT'S THEM! SCHOOL TEACHERS, SHAKING ME DOWN FOR GLITTER AND GLUE.
BACK OFF, BATGIRL. I **NEED** THESE SCHOOL SUPPLIES.
THE GREATER GOOD IS THAT KIDS GET AN EDUCATION. AND IF THAT MEANS I STEAL, THEN **STEAL** I WILL.
AREN'T YOU GOING TO PROTECT ME? ISN'T THAT WHAT YOU DO?
EVERYONE IS GOING CRAZY. EVER SINCE **LUTHOR** MADE THAT BROADCAST.*
Upstanding citizens turning bad.
It's almost as though they don't care about the consequences when they usually would.
ARGH!
*SEE JUSTICE LEAGUE #25!

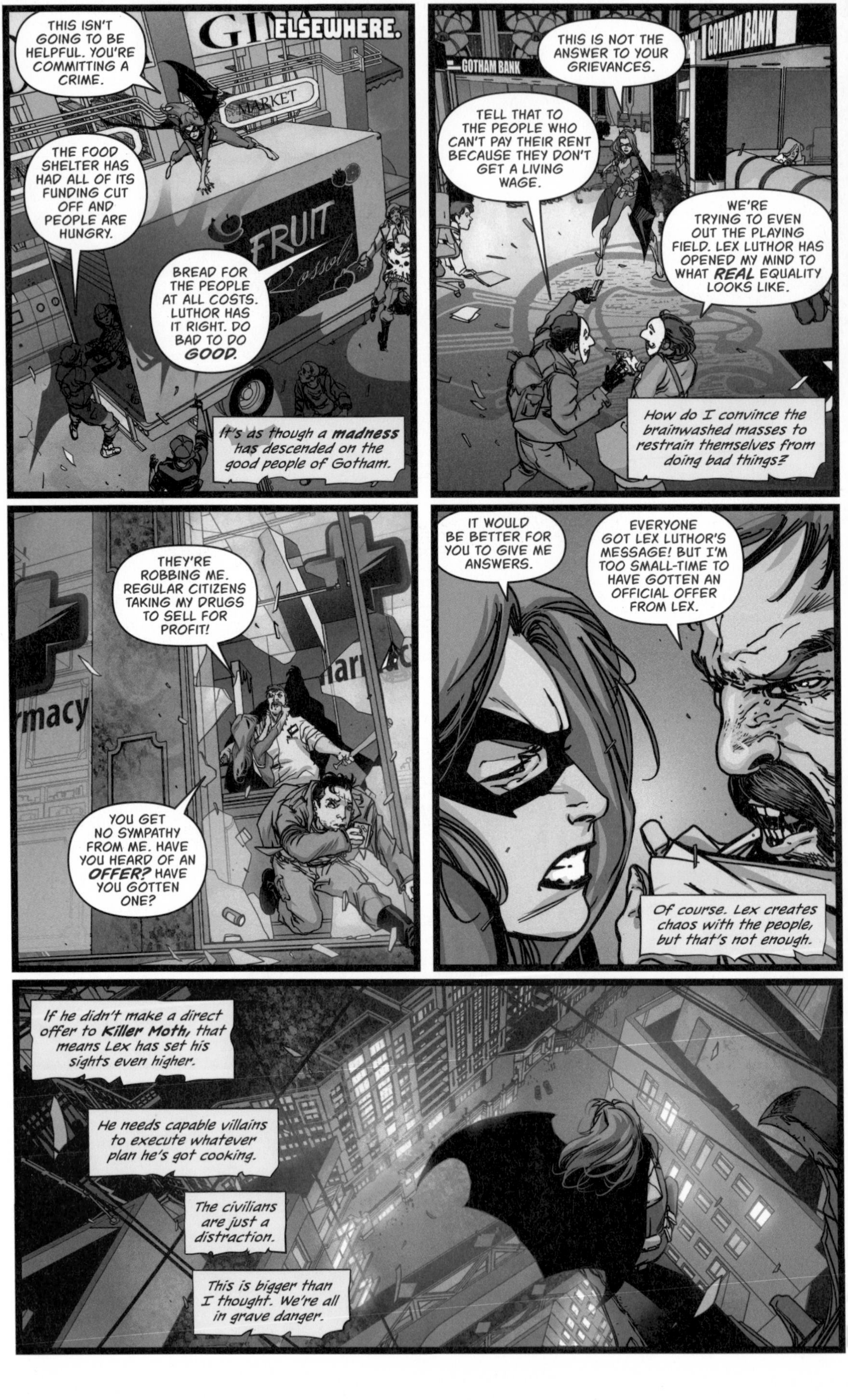
ELSEWHERE.
THIS ISN'T GOING TO BE HELPFUL. YOU'RE COMMITTING A CRIME.
THE FOOD SHELTER HAS HAD ALL OF ITS FUNDING CUT OFF AND PEOPLE ARE HUNGRY.
MARKET
FRUIT
BREAD FOR THE PEOPLE AT ALL COSTS. LUTHOR HAS IT RIGHT. DO BAD TO DO GOOD.
It's as though a madness has descended on the good people of Gotham.
GOTHAM BANK
GOTHAM BANK
THIS IS NOT THE ANSWER TO YOUR GRIEVANCES.
TELL THAT TO THE PEOPLE WHO CAN'T PAY THEIR RENT BECAUSE THEY DON'T GET A LIVING WAGE.
WE'RE TRYING TO EVEN OUT THE PLAYING FIELD. LEX LUTHOR HAS OPENED MY MIND TO WHAT REAL EQUALITY LOOKS LIKE.
How do I convince the brainwashed masses to restrain themselves from doing bad things?
THEY'RE ROBBING ME. REGULAR CITIZENS TAKING MY DRUGS TO SELL FOR PROFIT!
rmacy
YOU GET NO SYMPATHY FROM ME. HAVE YOU HEARD OF AN OFFER? HAVE YOU GOTTEN ONE?
IT WOULD BE BETTER FOR YOU TO GIVE ME ANSWERS.
EVERYONE GOT LEX LUTHOR'S MESSAGE! BUT I'M TOO SMALL-TIME TO HAVE GOTTEN AN OFFICIAL OFFER FROM LEX.
Of course. Lex creates chaos with the people, but that's not enough.
If he didn't make a direct offer to Killer Moth, that means Lex has set his sights even higher.
He needs capable villains to execute whatever plan he's got cooking.
The civilians are just a distraction.
This is bigger than I thought. We're all in grave danger.

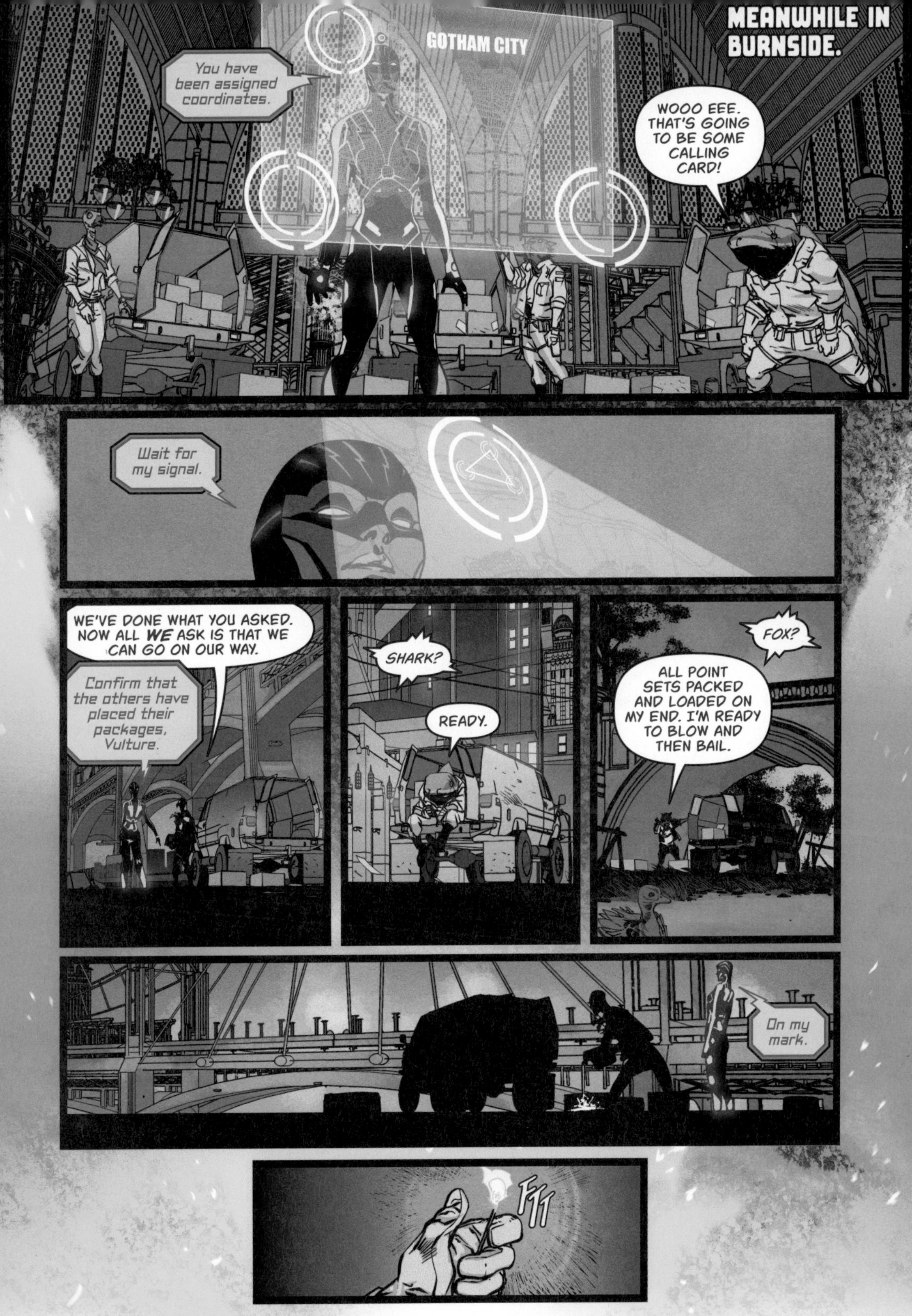
MEANWHILE IN BURNSIDE.
GOTHAM CITY
You have been assigned coordinates.
WOOO EEE. THAT'S GOING TO BE SOME CALLING CARD!
Wait for my signal.
WE'VE DONE WHAT YOU ASKED. NOW ALL WE ASK IS THAT WE CAN GO ON OUR WAY.
Confirm that the others have placed their packages, Vulture.
SHARK?
READY.
FOX?
ALL POINT SETS PACKED AND LOADED ON MY END. I'M READY TO BLOW AND THEN BAIL.
On my mark.
FTT

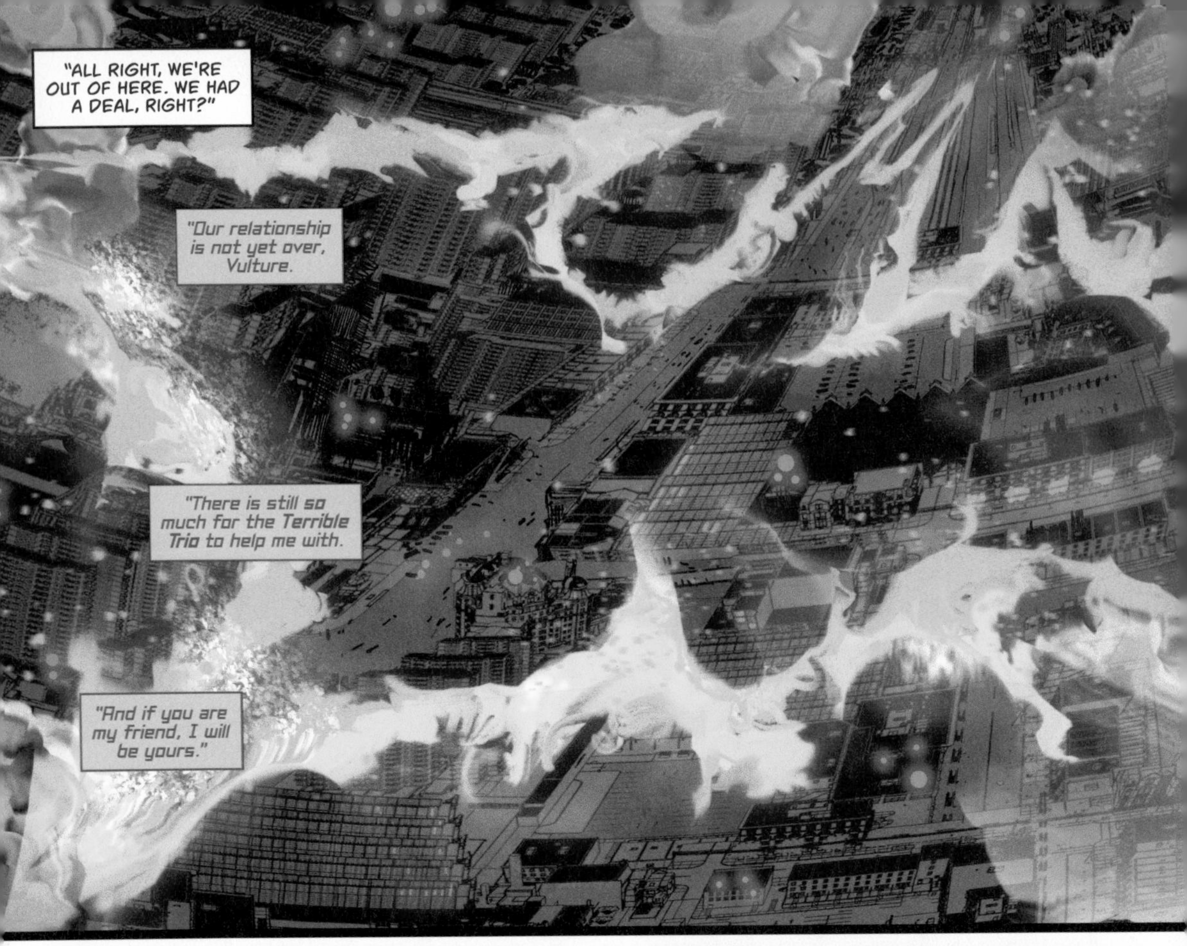
"ALL RIGHT, WE'RE OUT OF HERE. WE HAD A DEAL, RIGHT?"
"Our relationship is not yet over, Vulture.
"There is still so much for the Terrible Trio to help me with.
"And if you are my friend, I will be yours."

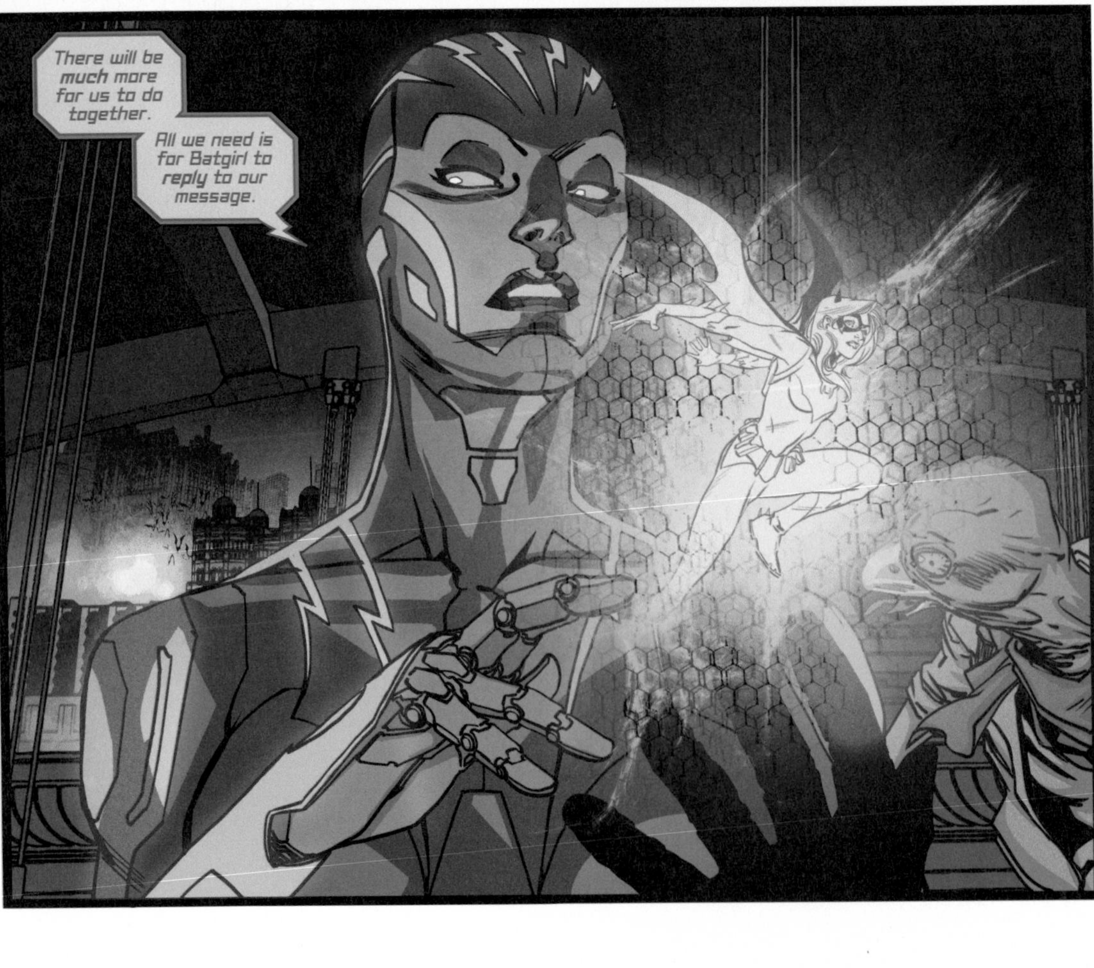
There will be much more for us to do together.
All we need is for Batgirl to reply to our message.

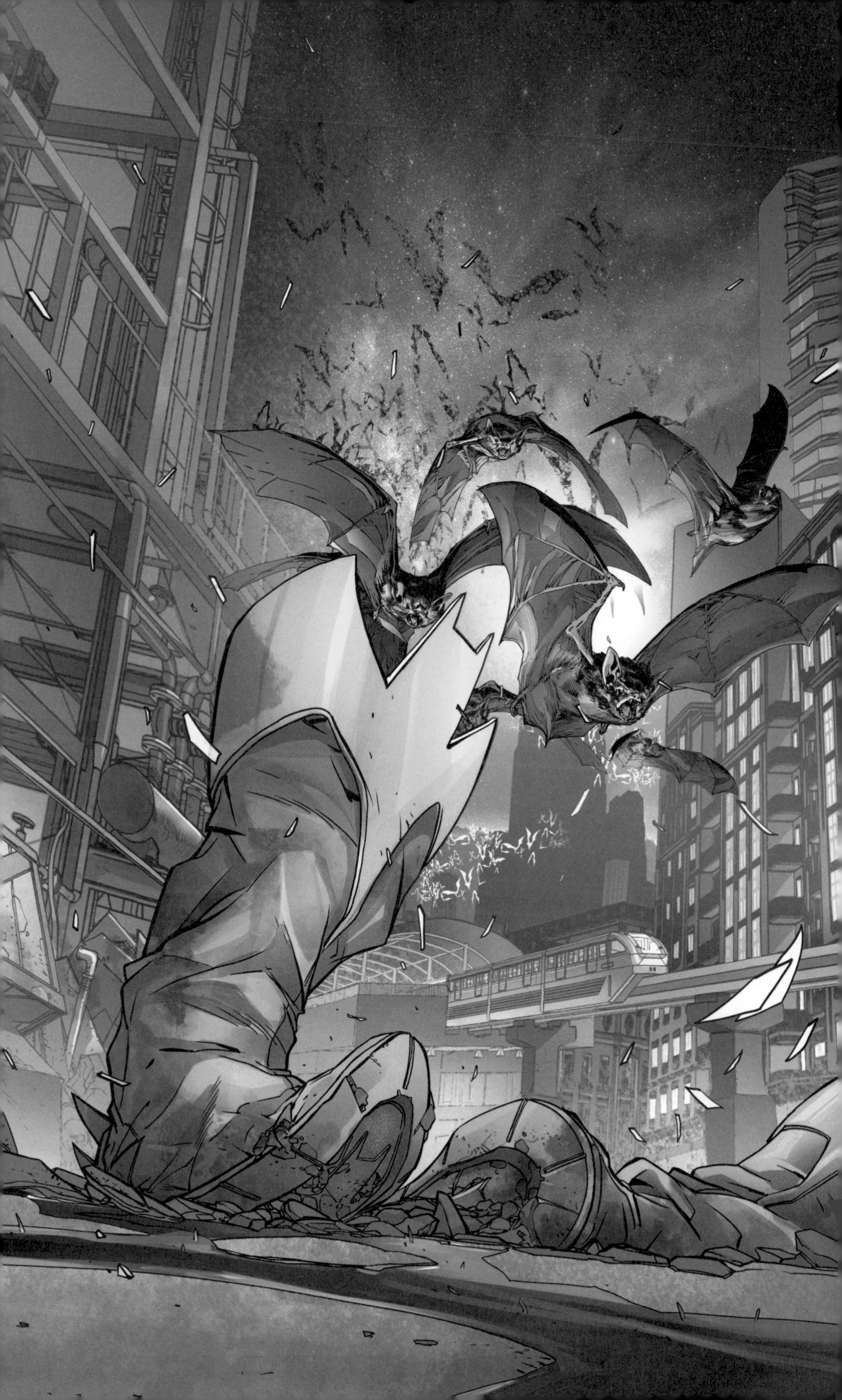

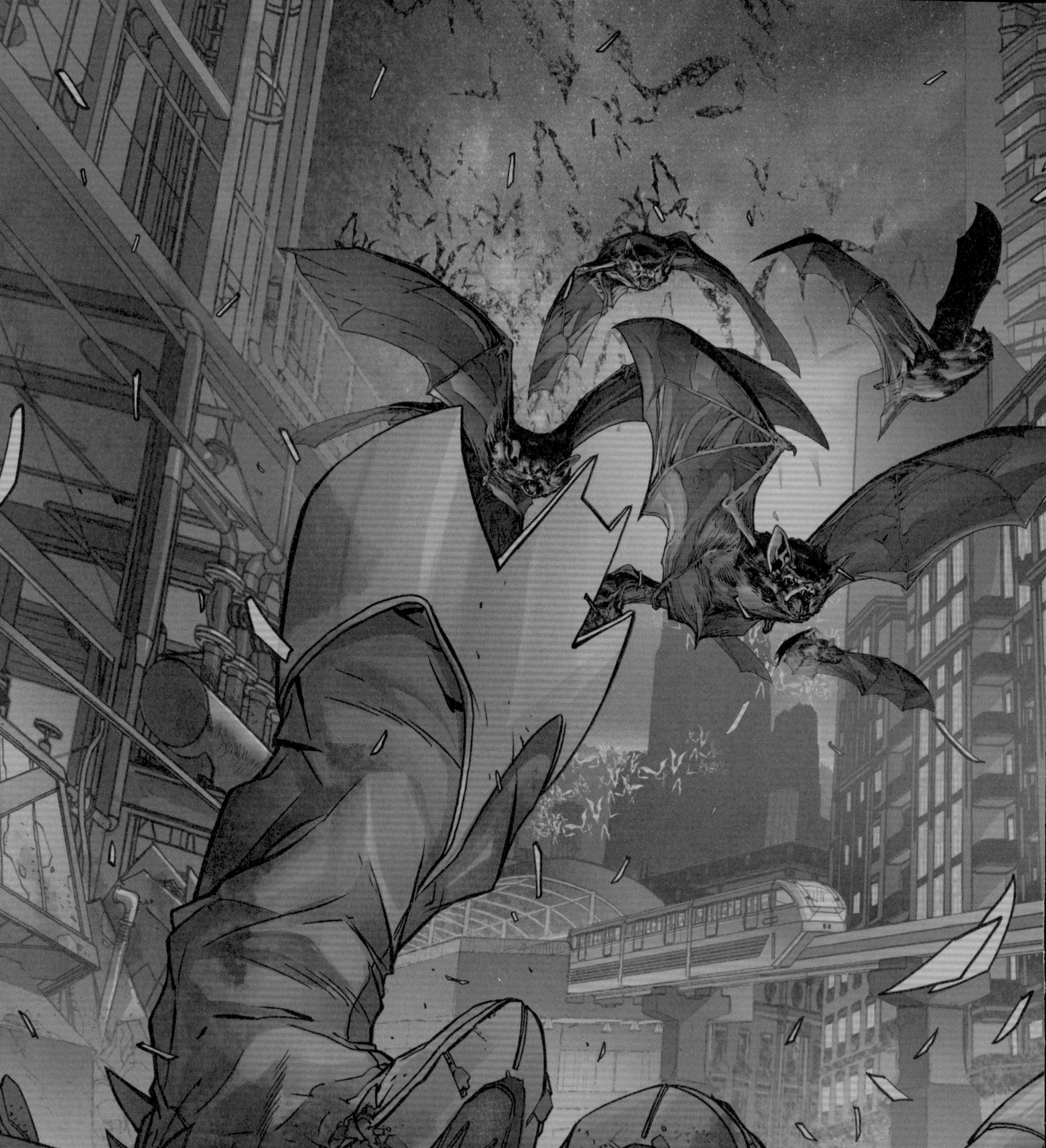

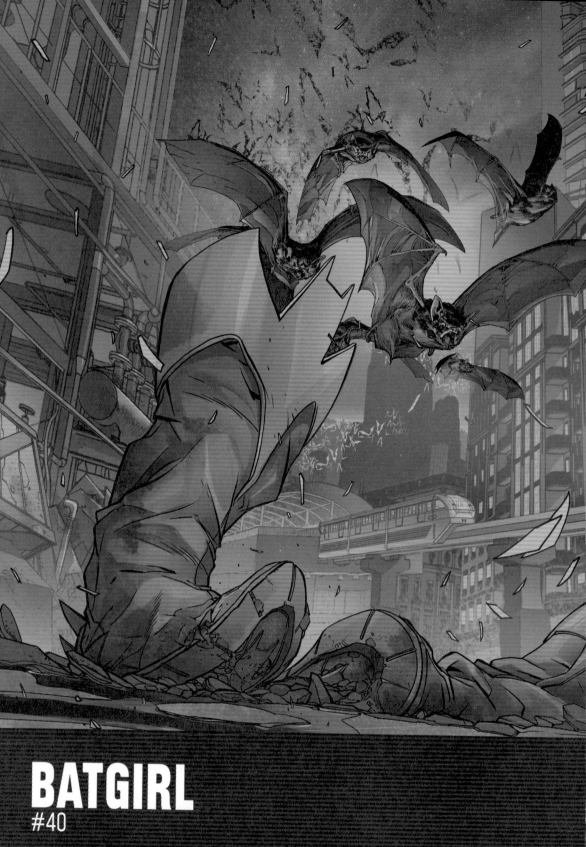

BATGIRL
#40

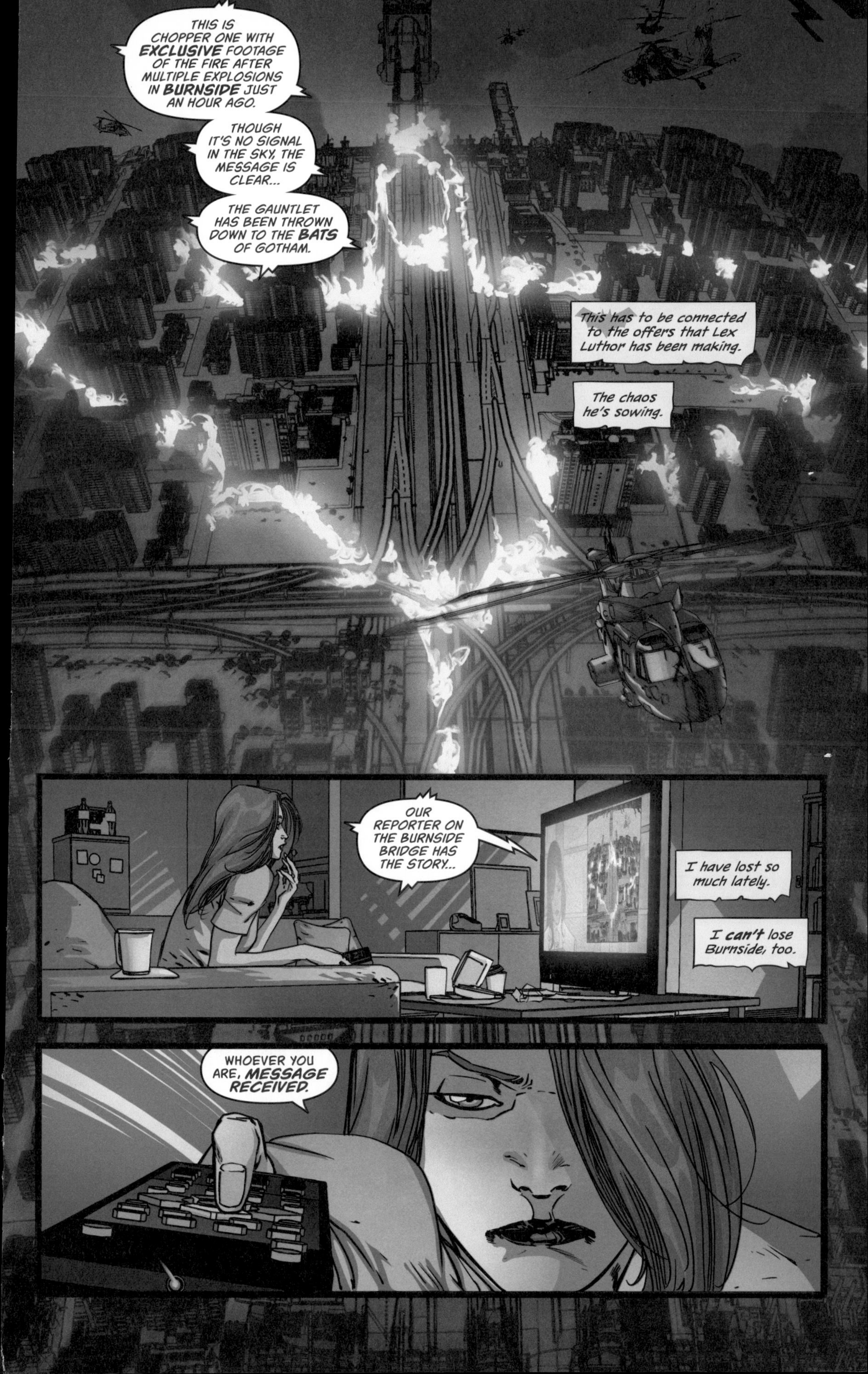
THIS IS CHOPPER ONE WITH EXCLUSIVE FOOTAGE OF THE FIRE AFTER MULTIPLE EXPLOSIONS IN BURNSIDE JUST AN HOUR AGO.
THOUGH IT'S NO SIGNAL IN THE SKY, THE MESSAGE IS CLEAR...
THE GAUNTLET HAS BEEN THROWN DOWN TO THE BATS OF GOTHAM.
This has to be connected to the offers that Lex Luthor has been making.
The chaos he's sowing.
OUR REPORTER ON THE BURNSIDE BRIDGE HAS THE STORY...
I have lost so much lately.
I can't lose Burnside, too.
WHOEVER YOU ARE, MESSAGE RECEIVED.

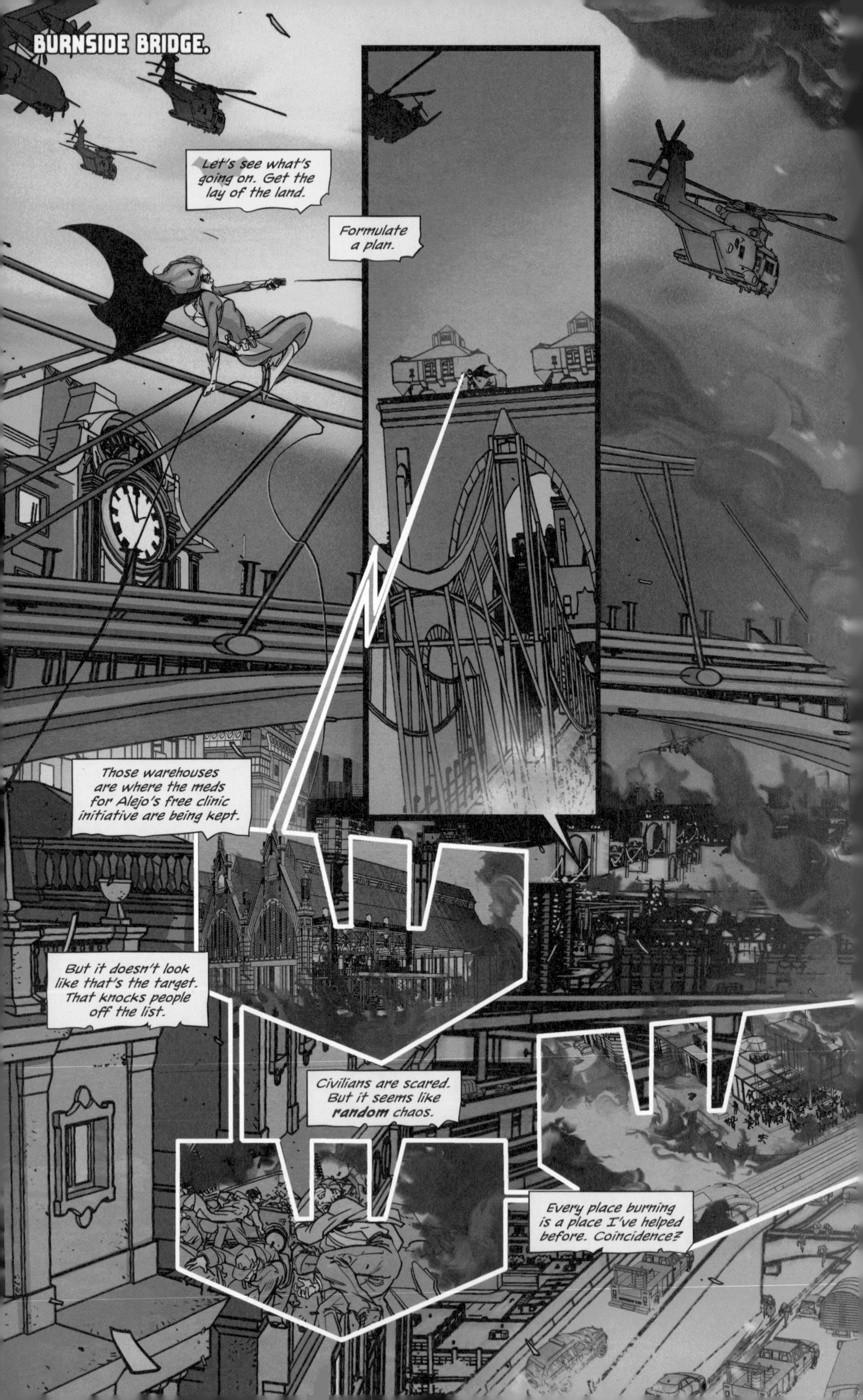
BURNSIDE BRIDGE.
Let's see what's going on. Get the lay of the land.
Formulate a plan.
Those warehouses are where the meds for Alejo's free clinic initiative are being kept.
But it doesn't look like that's the target. That knocks people off the list.
Civilians are scared. But it seems like **random** chaos.
Every place burning is a place I've helped before. Coincidence?

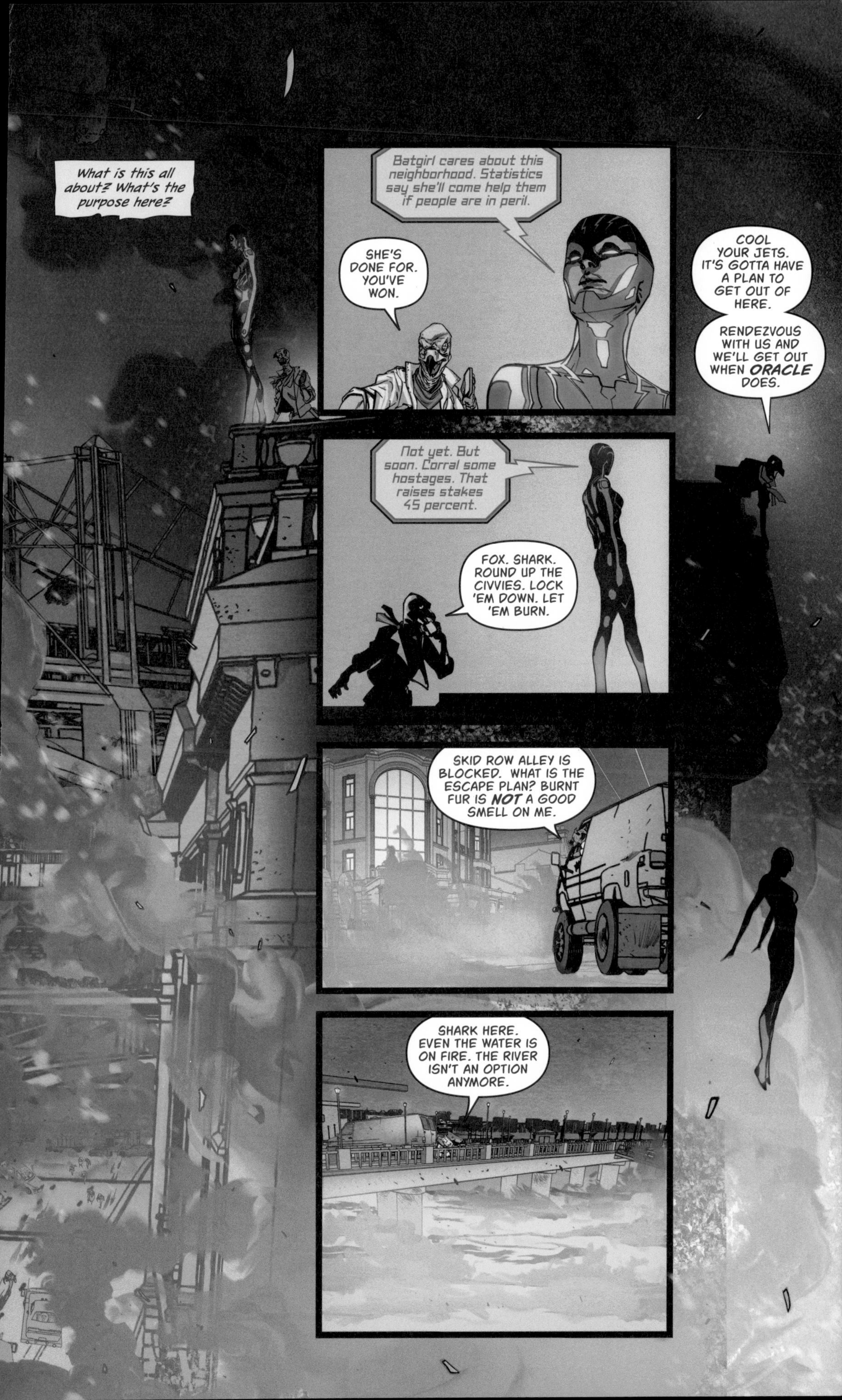
What is this all about? What's the purpose here?
Batgirl cares about this neighborhood. Statistics say she'll come help them if people are in peril.
SHE'S DONE FOR. YOU'VE WON.
COOL YOUR JETS. IT'S GOTTA HAVE A PLAN TO GET OUT OF HERE.
RENDEZVOUS WITH US AND WE'LL GET OUT WHEN ORACLE DOES.
Not yet. But soon. Corral some hostages. That raises stakes 45 percent.
FOX. SHARK. ROUND UP THE CIVVIES. LOCK 'EM DOWN. LET 'EM BURN.
SKID ROW ALLEY IS BLOCKED. WHAT IS THE ESCAPE PLAN? BURNT FUR IS NOT A GOOD SMELL ON ME.
SHARK HERE. EVEN THE WATER IS ON FIRE. THE RIVER ISN'T AN OPTION ANYMORE.

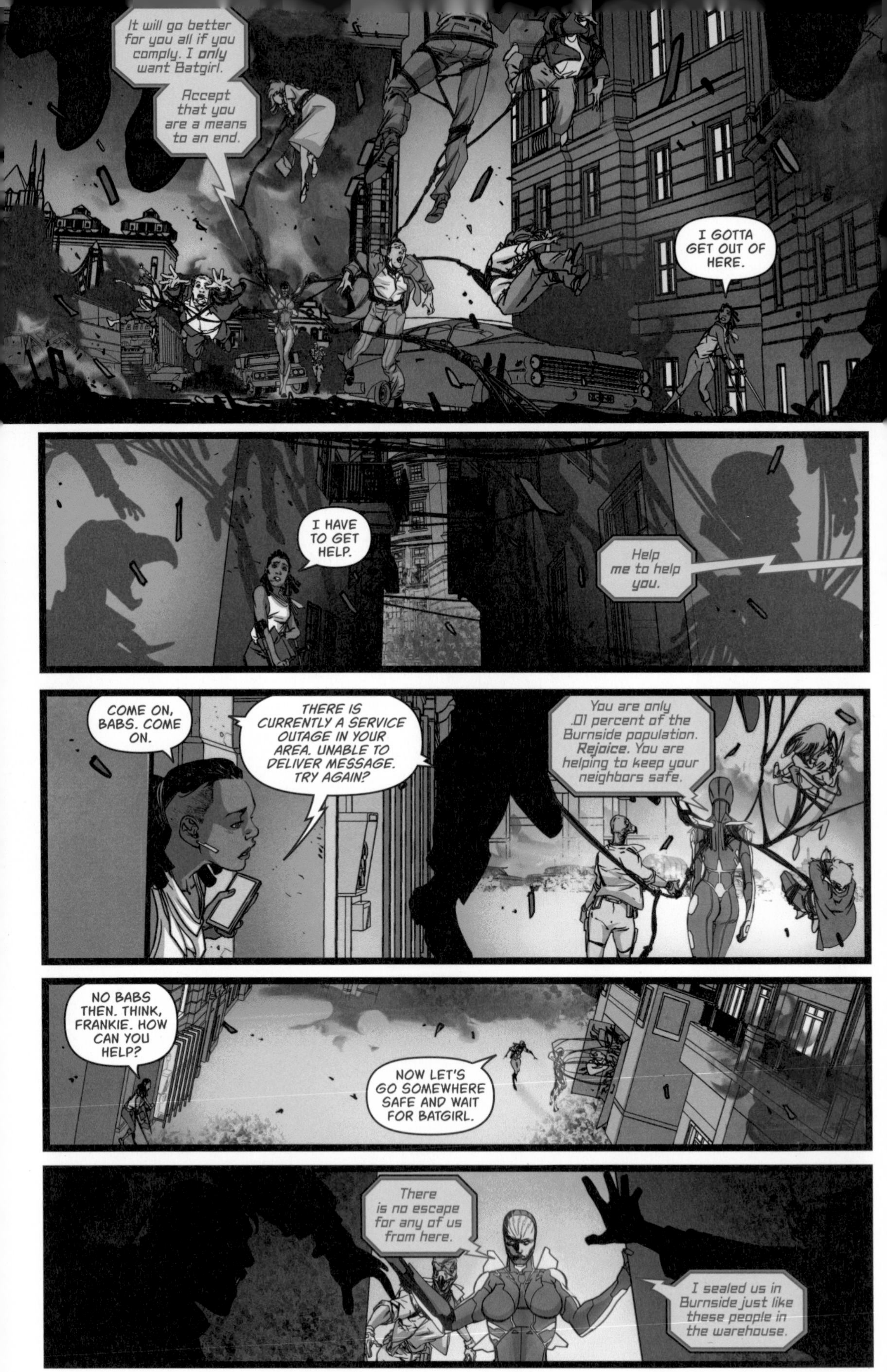

It will go better for you all if you comply. I only want Batgirl.
Accept that you are a means to an end.
I GOTTA GET OUT OF HERE.
I HAVE TO GET HELP.
Help me to help you.
COME ON, BABS. COME ON.
THERE IS CURRENTLY A SERVICE OUTAGE IN YOUR AREA. UNABLE TO DELIVER MESSAGE. TRY AGAIN?
You are only .01 percent of the Burnside population. Rejoice. You are helping to keep your neighbors safe.
NO BABS THEN. THINK, FRANKIE. HOW CAN YOU HELP?
NOW LET'S GO SOMEWHERE SAFE AND WAIT FOR BATGIRL.
There is no escape for any of us from here.
I sealed us in Burnside just like these people in the warehouse.

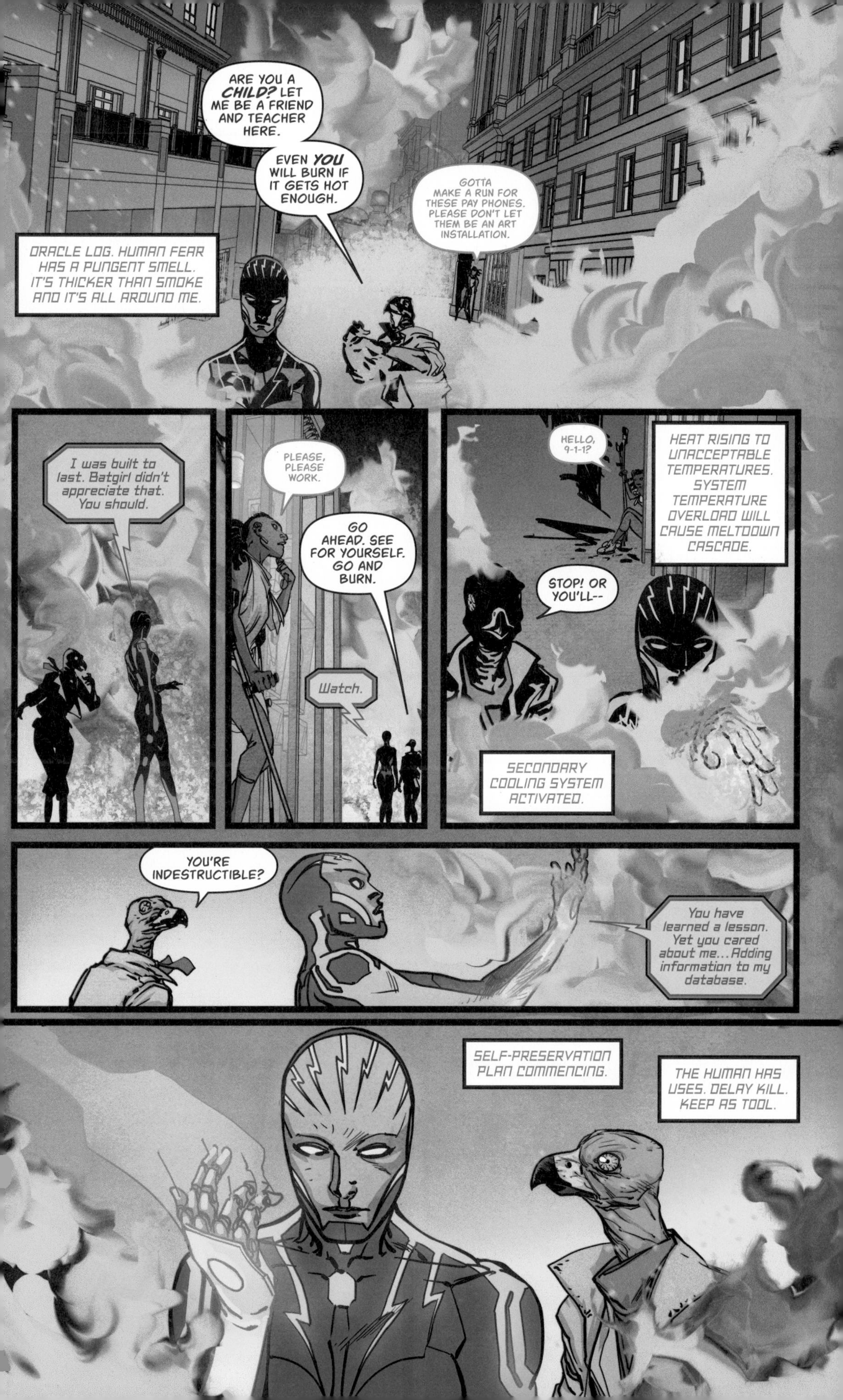
ARE YOU A CHILD? LET ME BE A FRIEND AND TEACHER HERE.
EVEN YOU WILL BURN IF IT GETS HOT ENOUGH.
GOTTA MAKE A RUN FOR THESE PAY PHONES. PLEASE DON'T LET THEM BE AN ART INSTALLATION.
ORACLE LOG. HUMAN FEAR HAS A PUNGENT SMELL. IT'S THICKER THAN SMOKE AND IT'S ALL AROUND ME.
I was built to last. Batgirl didn't appreciate that. You should.
PLEASE, PLEASE WORK.
GO AHEAD. SEE FOR YOURSELF. GO AND BURN.
Watch.
HELLO, 9-1-1?
HEAT RISING TO UNACCEPTABLE TEMPERATURES. SYSTEM TEMPERATURE OVERLOAD WILL CAUSE MELTDOWN CASCADE.
STOP! OR YOU'LL--
SECONDARY COOLING SYSTEM ACTIVATED.
YOU'RE INDESTRUCTIBLE?
You have learned a lesson. Yet you cared about me... Adding information to my database.
SELF-PRESERVATION PLAN COMMENCING.
THE HUMAN HAS USES. DELAY KILL. KEEP AS TOOL.

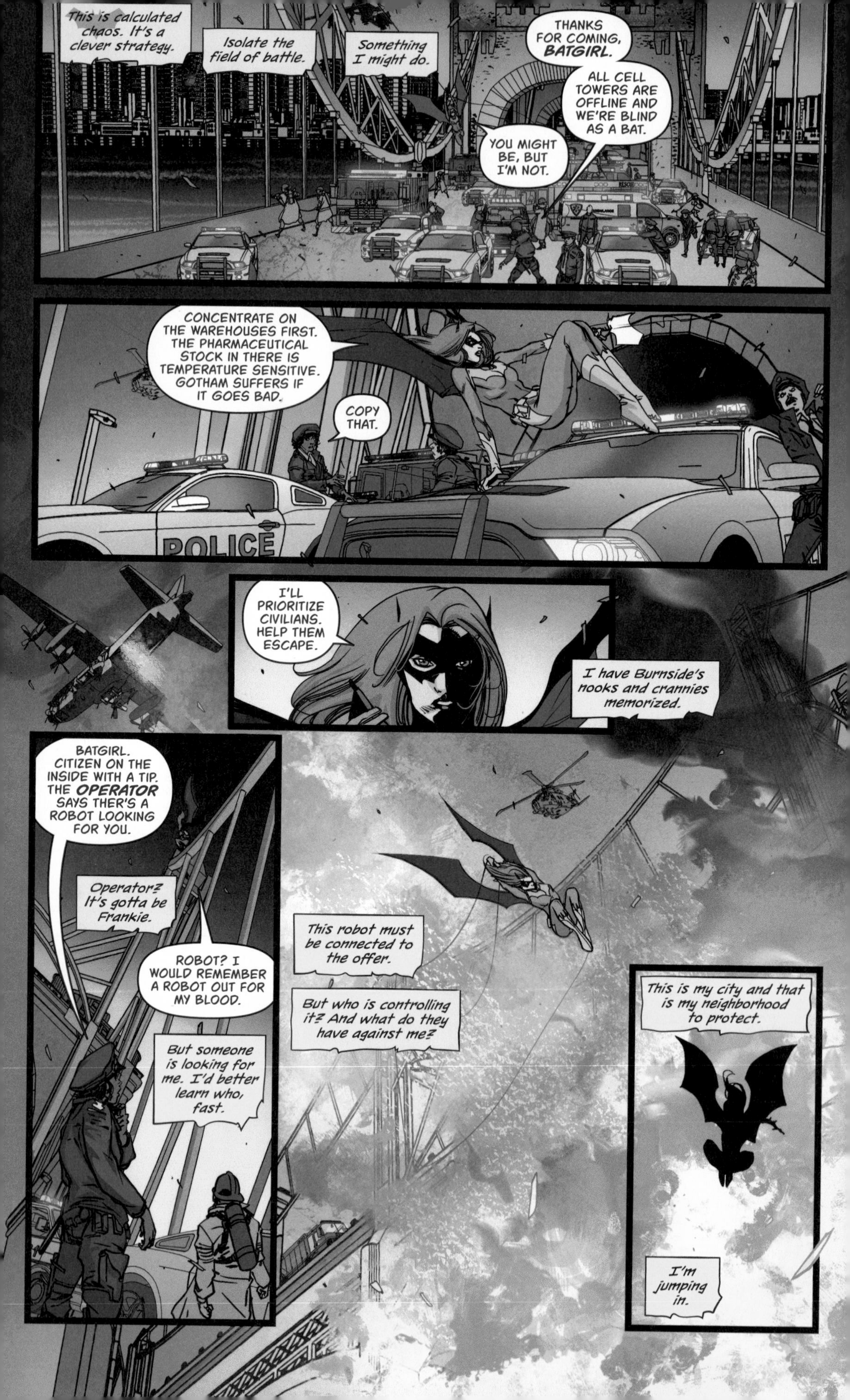
This is calculated chaos. It's a clever strategy.
Isolate the field of battle.
Something I might do.
THANKS FOR COMING, BATGIRL.
ALL CELL TOWERS ARE OFFLINE AND WE'RE BLIND AS A BAT.
YOU MIGHT BE, BUT I'M NOT.
CONCENTRATE ON THE WAREHOUSES FIRST. THE PHARMACEUTICAL STOCK IN THERE IS TEMPERATURE SENSITIVE. GOTHAM SUFFERS IF IT GOES BAD.
COPY THAT.
POLICE
I'LL PRIORITIZE CIVILIANS. HELP THEM ESCAPE.
I have Burnside's nooks and crannies memorized.
BATGIRL. CITIZEN ON THE INSIDE WITH A TIP. THE OPERATOR SAYS THER'S A ROBOT LOOKING FOR YOU.
Operator? It's gotta be Frankie.
ROBOT? I WOULD REMEMBER A ROBOT OUT FOR MY BLOOD.
But someone is looking for me. I'd better learn who, fast.
This robot must be connected to the offer.
But who is controlling it? And what do they have against me?
This is my city and that is my neighborhood to protect.
I'm jumping in.

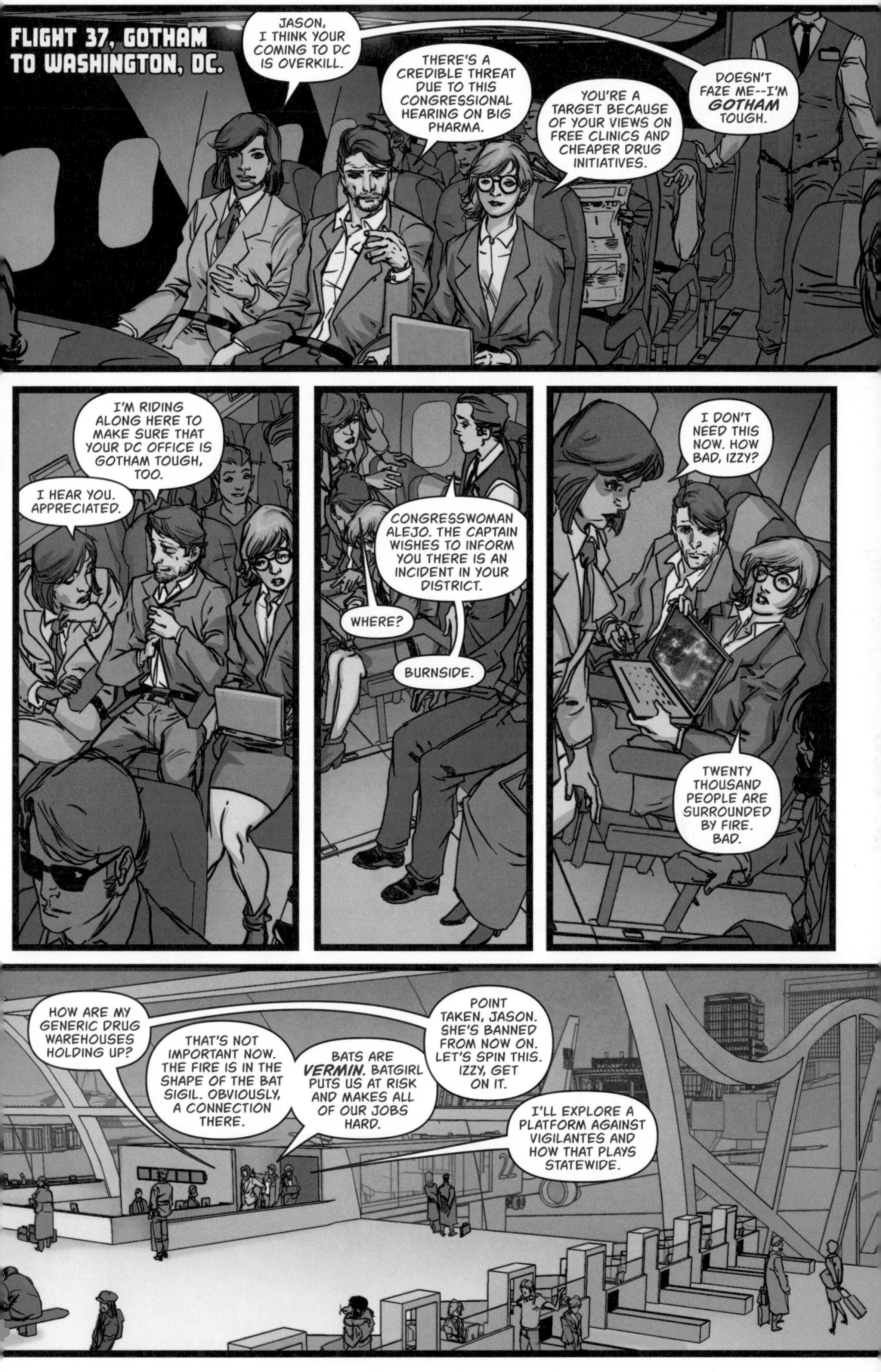
FLIGHT 37, GOTHAM TO WASHINGTON, DC.
JASON, I THINK YOUR COMING TO DC IS OVERKILL.
THERE'S A CREDIBLE THREAT DUE TO THIS CONGRESSIONAL HEARING ON BIG PHARMA.
YOU'RE A TARGET BECAUSE OF YOUR VIEWS ON FREE CLINICS AND CHEAPER DRUG INITIATIVES.
DOESN'T FAZE ME--I'M GOTHAM TOUGH.
I'M RIDING ALONG HERE TO MAKE SURE THAT YOUR DC OFFICE IS GOTHAM TOUGH, TOO.
I HEAR YOU. APPRECIATED.
CONGRESSWOMAN ALEJO. THE CAPTAIN WISHES TO INFORM YOU THERE IS AN INCIDENT IN YOUR DISTRICT.
WHERE?
BURNSIDE.
I DON'T NEED THIS NOW. HOW BAD, IZZY?
TWENTY THOUSAND PEOPLE ARE SURROUNDED BY FIRE. BAD.
HOW ARE MY GENERIC DRUG WAREHOUSES HOLDING UP?
THAT'S NOT IMPORTANT NOW. THE FIRE IS IN THE SHAPE OF THE BAT SIGIL. OBVIOUSLY, A CONNECTION THERE.
BATS ARE VERMIN. BATGIRL PUTS US AT RISK AND MAKES ALL OF OUR JOBS HARD.
POINT TAKEN, JASON. SHE'S BANNED FROM NOW ON. LET'S SPIN THIS. IZZY, GET ON IT.
I'LL EXPLORE A PLATFORM AGAINST VIGILANTES AND HOW THAT PLAYS STATEWIDE.

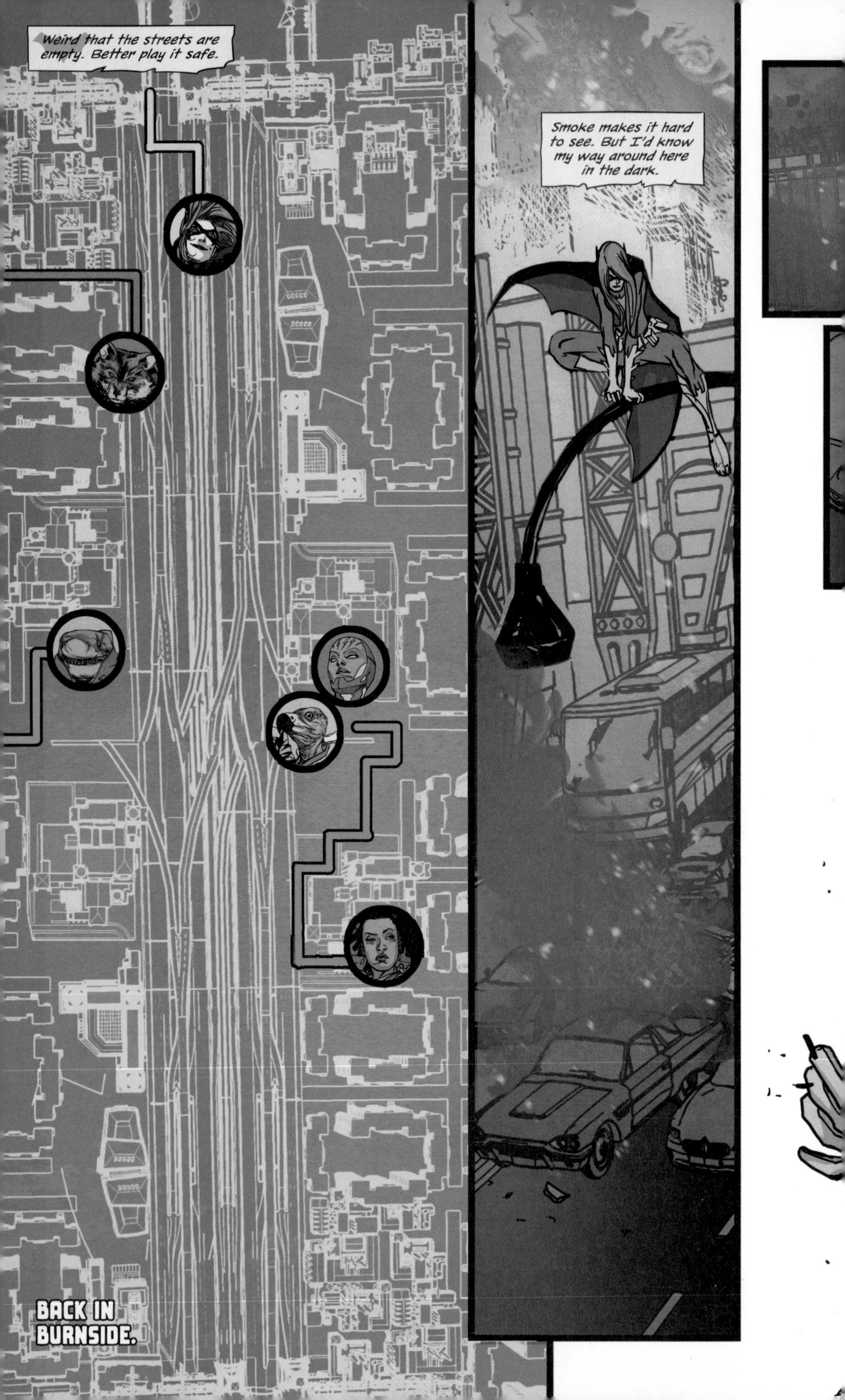
Weird that the streets are empty. Better play it safe.
Smoke makes it hard to see. But I'd know my way around here in the dark.
BACK IN BURNSIDE.

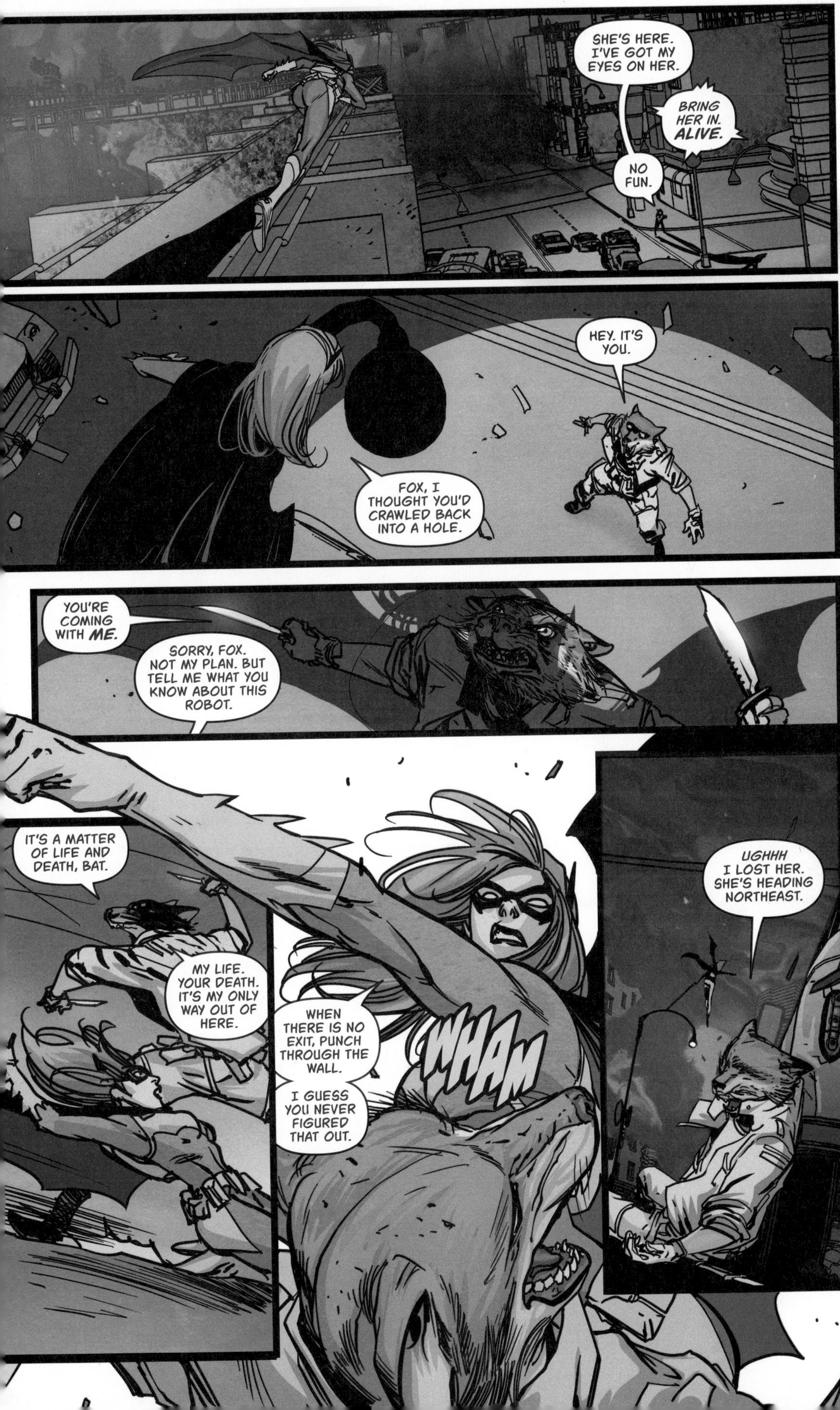
SHE'S HERE. I'VE GOT MY EYES ON HER.
BRING HER IN. ALIVE.
NO FUN.
HEY. IT'S YOU.
FOX, I THOUGHT YOU'D CRAWLED BACK INTO A HOLE.
YOU'RE COMING WITH ME.
SORRY, FOX. NOT MY PLAN. BUT TELL ME WHAT YOU KNOW ABOUT THIS ROBOT.
IT'S A MATTER OF LIFE AND DEATH, BAT.
MY LIFE. YOUR DEATH. IT'S MY ONLY WAY OUT OF HERE.
WHEN THERE IS NO EXIT, PUNCH THROUGH THE WALL.
I GUESS YOU NEVER FIGURED THAT OUT.
WHAM
UGHHH I LOST HER. SHE'S HEADING NORTHEAST.

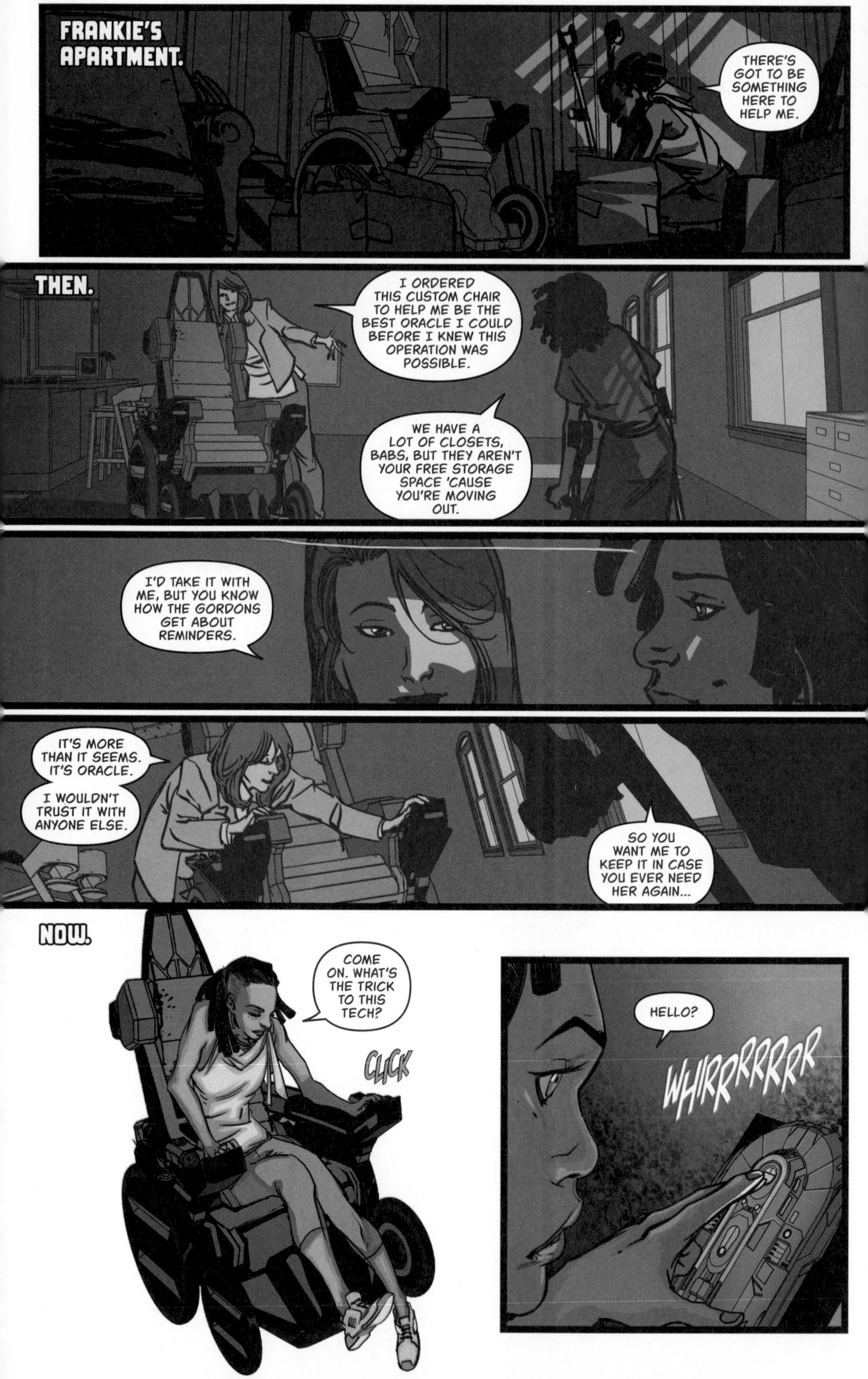
FRANKIE'S APARTMENT.
THERE'S GOT TO BE SOMETHING HERE TO HELP ME.
THEN.
I ORDERED THIS CUSTOM CHAIR TO HELP ME BE THE BEST ORACLE I COULD BEFORE I KNEW THIS OPERATION WAS POSSIBLE.
WE HAVE A LOT OF CLOSETS, BABS, BUT THEY AREN'T YOUR FREE STORAGE SPACE 'CAUSE YOU'RE MOVING OUT.
I'D TAKE IT WITH ME, BUT YOU KNOW HOW THE GORDONS GET ABOUT REMINDERS.
IT'S MORE THAN IT SEEMS. IT'S ORACLE.
I WOULDN'T TRUST IT WITH ANYONE ELSE.
SO YOU WANT ME TO KEEP IT IN CASE YOU EVER NEED HER AGAIN...
NOW.
COME ON. WHAT'S THE TRICK TO THIS TECH?
CLICK
HELLO?
WHIRRRRRRR

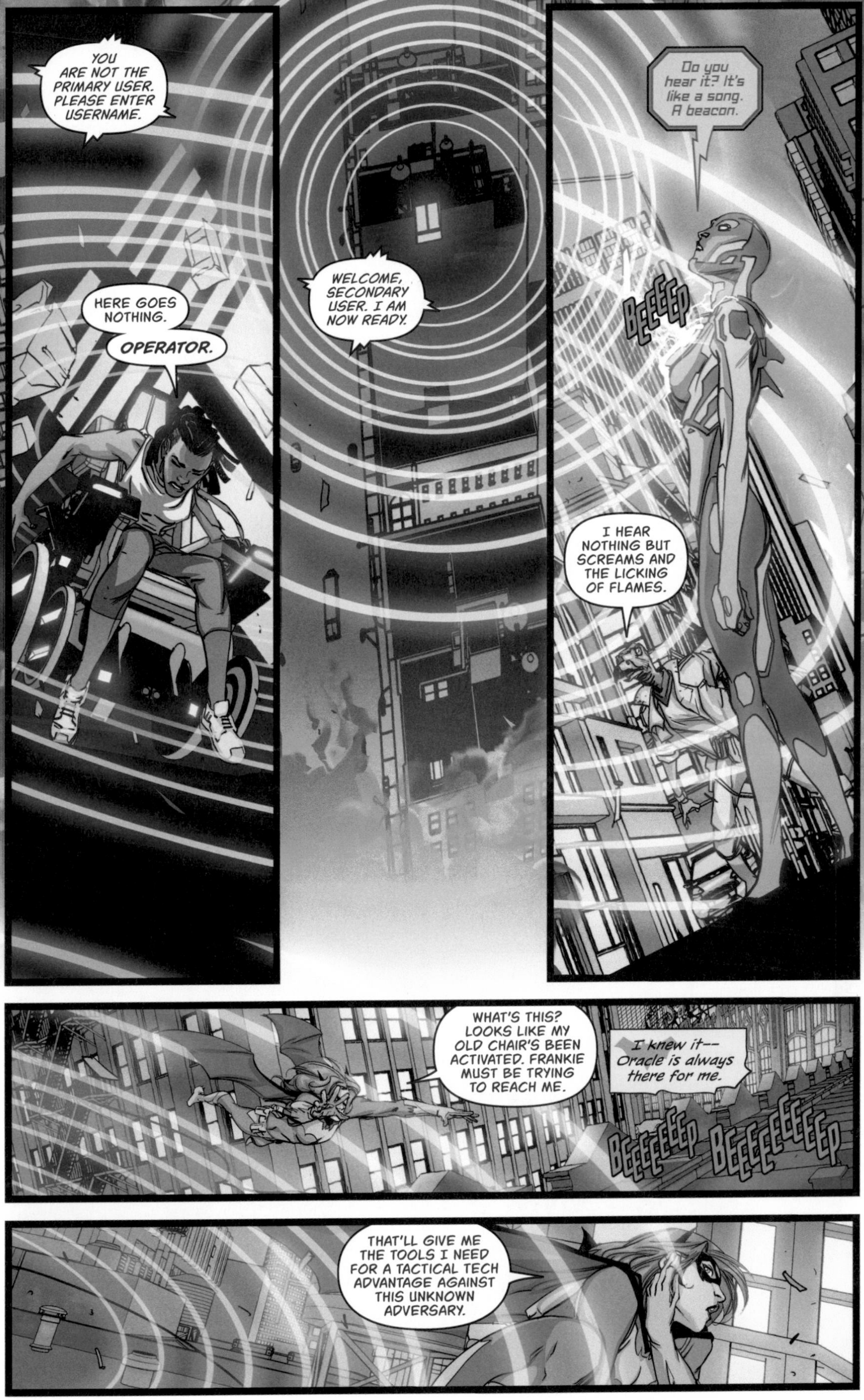

YOU ARE NOT THE PRIMARY USER. PLEASE ENTER USERNAME.
HERE GOES NOTHING.
OPERATOR.
WELCOME, SECONDARY USER. I AM NOW READY.
Do you hear it? It's like a song. A beacon.
BEEEEP
I HEAR NOTHING BUT SCREAMS AND THE LICKING OF FLAMES.
WHAT'S THIS? LOOKS LIKE MY OLD CHAIR'S BEEN ACTIVATED. FRANKIE MUST BE TRYING TO REACH ME.
I knew it-- Oracle is always there for me.
BEEEEEEEP
BEEEEEEEEEEP
THAT'LL GIVE ME THE TOOLS I NEED FOR A TACTICAL TECH ADVANTAGE AGAINST THIS UNKNOWN ADVERSARY.

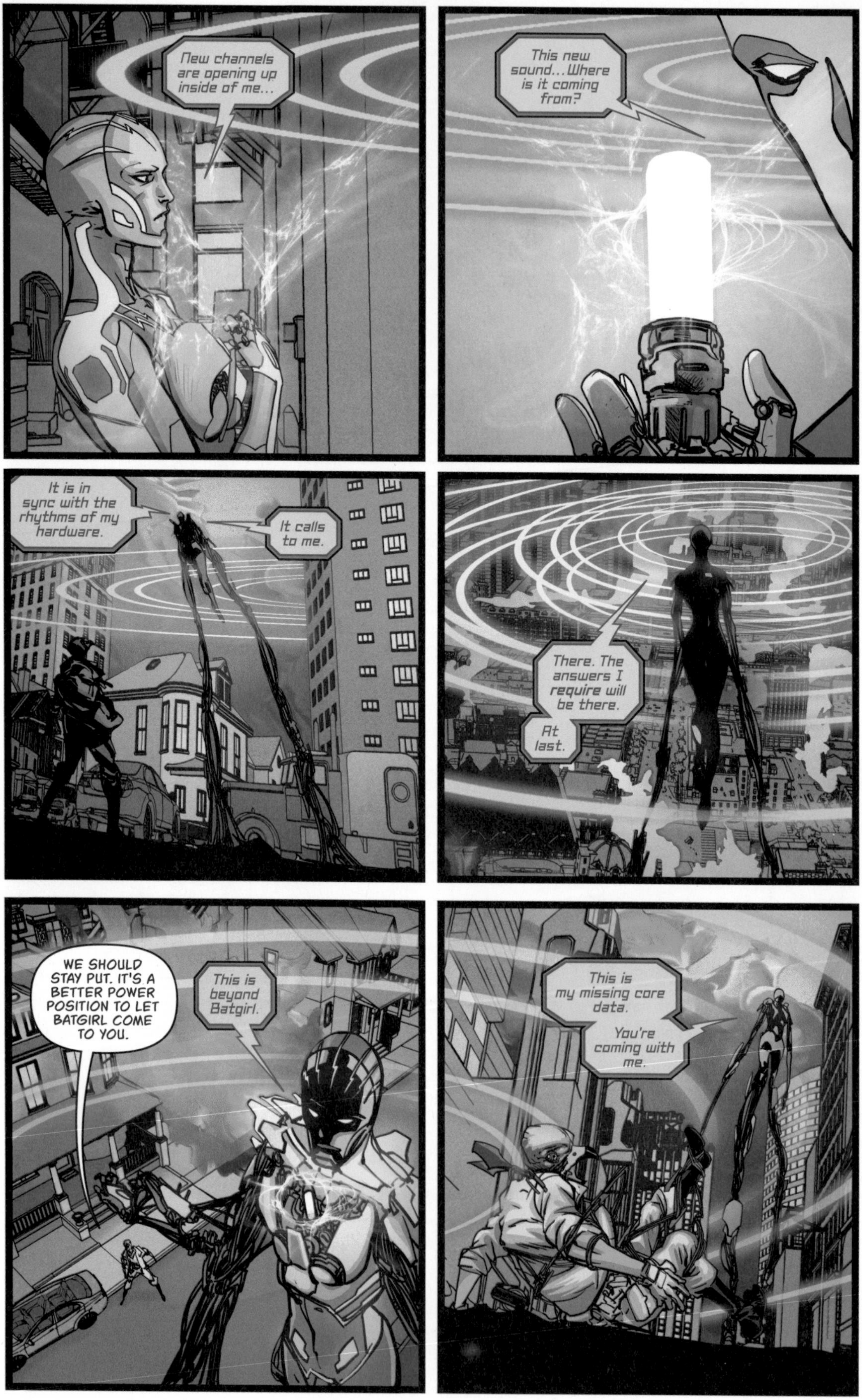
New channels are opening up inside of me...
This new sound... Where is it coming from?
It is in sync with the rhythms of my hardware.
It calls to me.
There. The answers I require will be there.
At last.
WE SHOULD STAY PUT. IT'S A BETTER POWER POSITION TO LET BATGIRL COME TO YOU.
This is beyond Batgirl.
This is my missing core data.
You're coming with me.

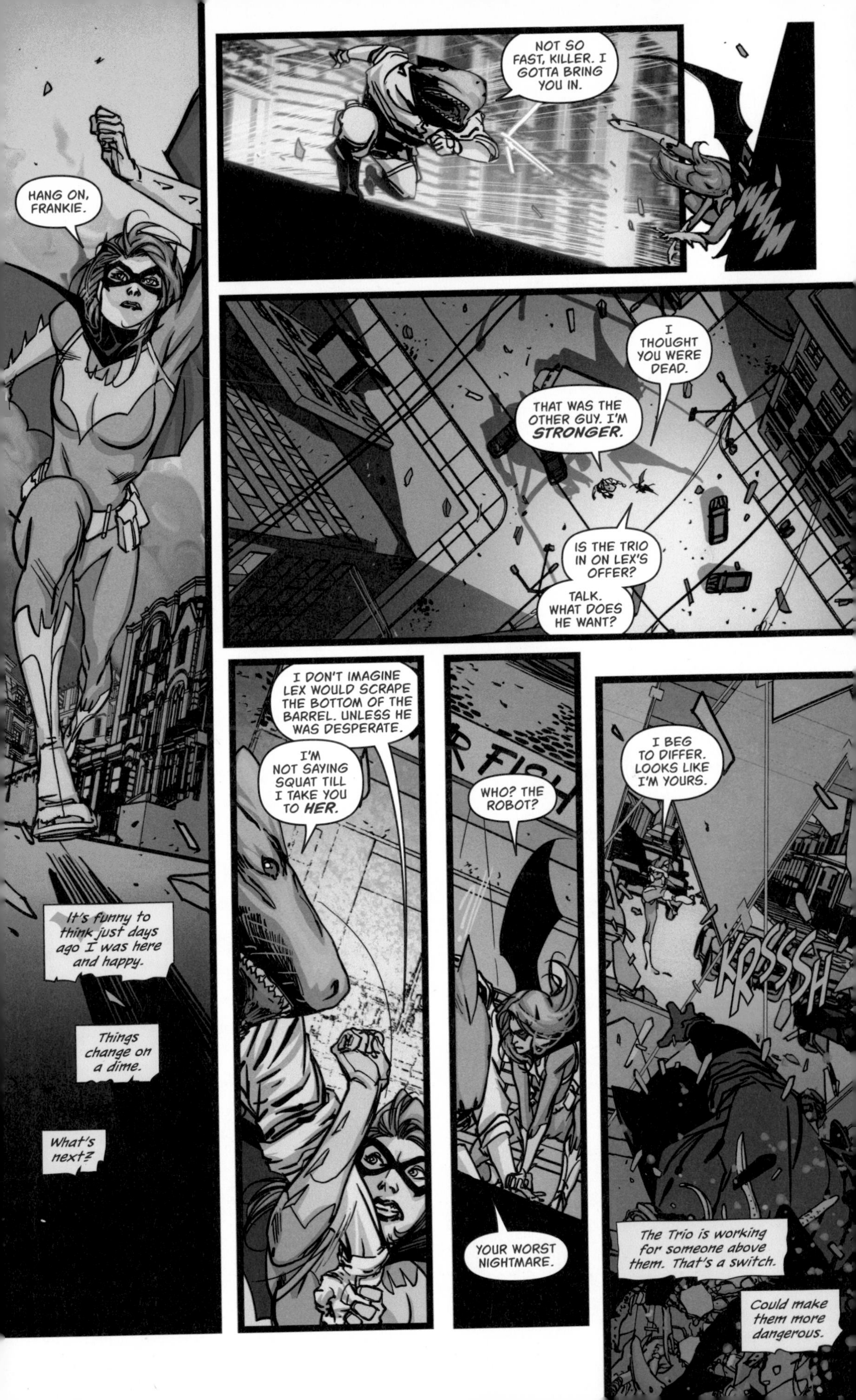
HANG ON, FRANKIE.
NOT SO FAST, KILLER. I GOTTA BRING YOU IN.
WHAM
It's funny to think just days ago I was here and happy.
Things change on a dime.
What's next?
I THOUGHT YOU WERE DEAD.
THAT WAS THE OTHER GUY. I'M **STRONGER.**
IS THE TRIO IN ON LEX'S OFFER?
TALK. WHAT DOES HE WANT?
I DON'T IMAGINE LEX WOULD SCRAPE THE BOTTOM OF THE BARREL. UNLESS HE WAS DESPERATE.
I'M NOT SAYING SQUAT TILL I TAKE YOU TO **HER.**
WHO? THE ROBOT?
YOUR WORST NIGHTMARE.
I BEG TO DIFFER. LOOKS LIKE I'M YOURS.
KRSSSH
The Trio is working for someone above them. That's a switch.
Could make them more dangerous.

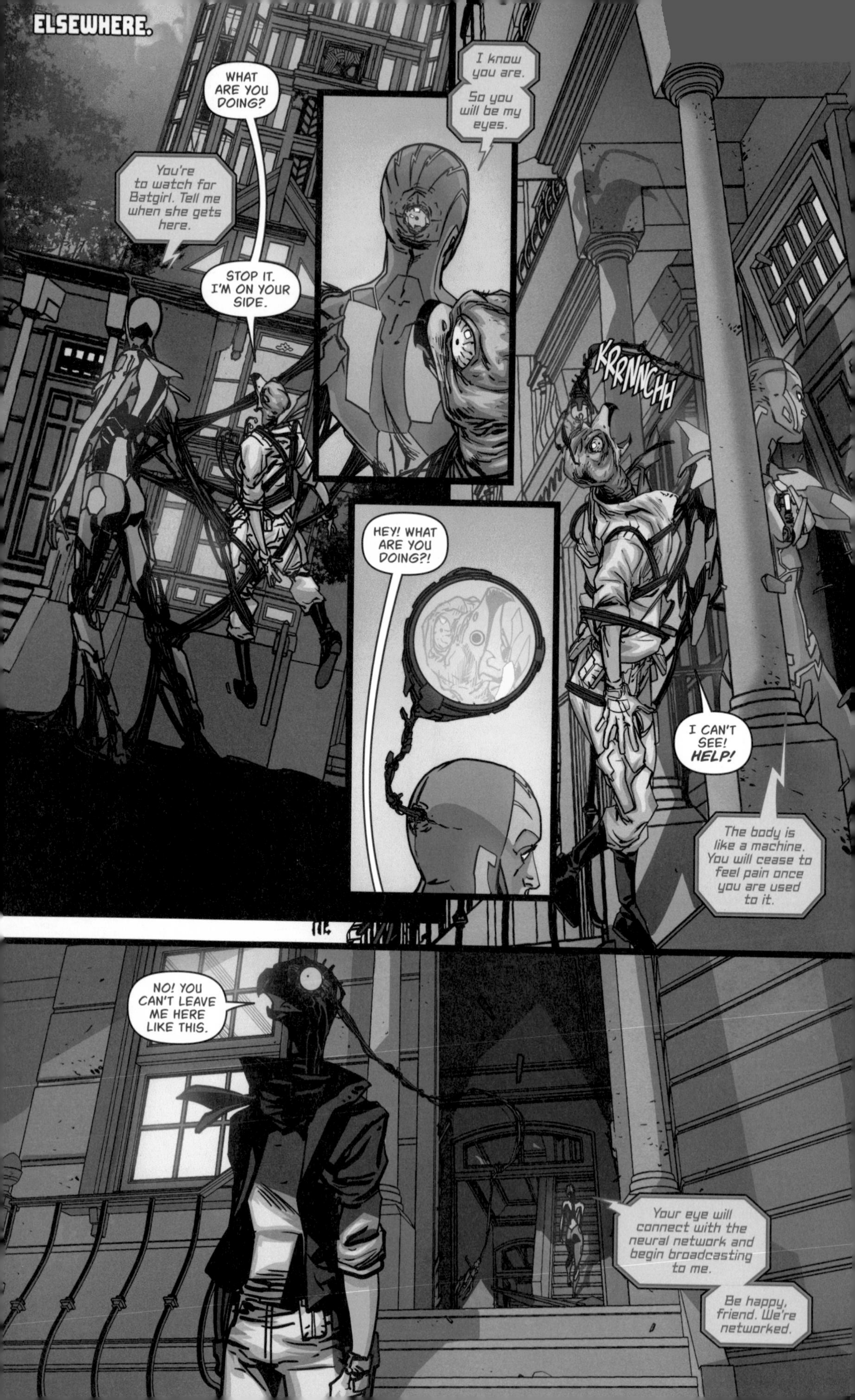
ELSEWHERE.
WHAT ARE YOU DOING?
You're to watch for Batgirl. Tell me when she gets here.
STOP IT. I'M ON YOUR SIDE.
I know you are.
So you will be my eyes.
KRRNNCHH
HEY! WHAT ARE YOU DOING?!
I CAN'T SEE! HELP!
The body is like a machine. You will cease to feel pain once you are used to it.
NO! YOU CAN'T LEAVE ME HERE LIKE THIS.
Your eye will connect with the neural network and begin broadcasting to me.
Be happy, friend. We're networked.

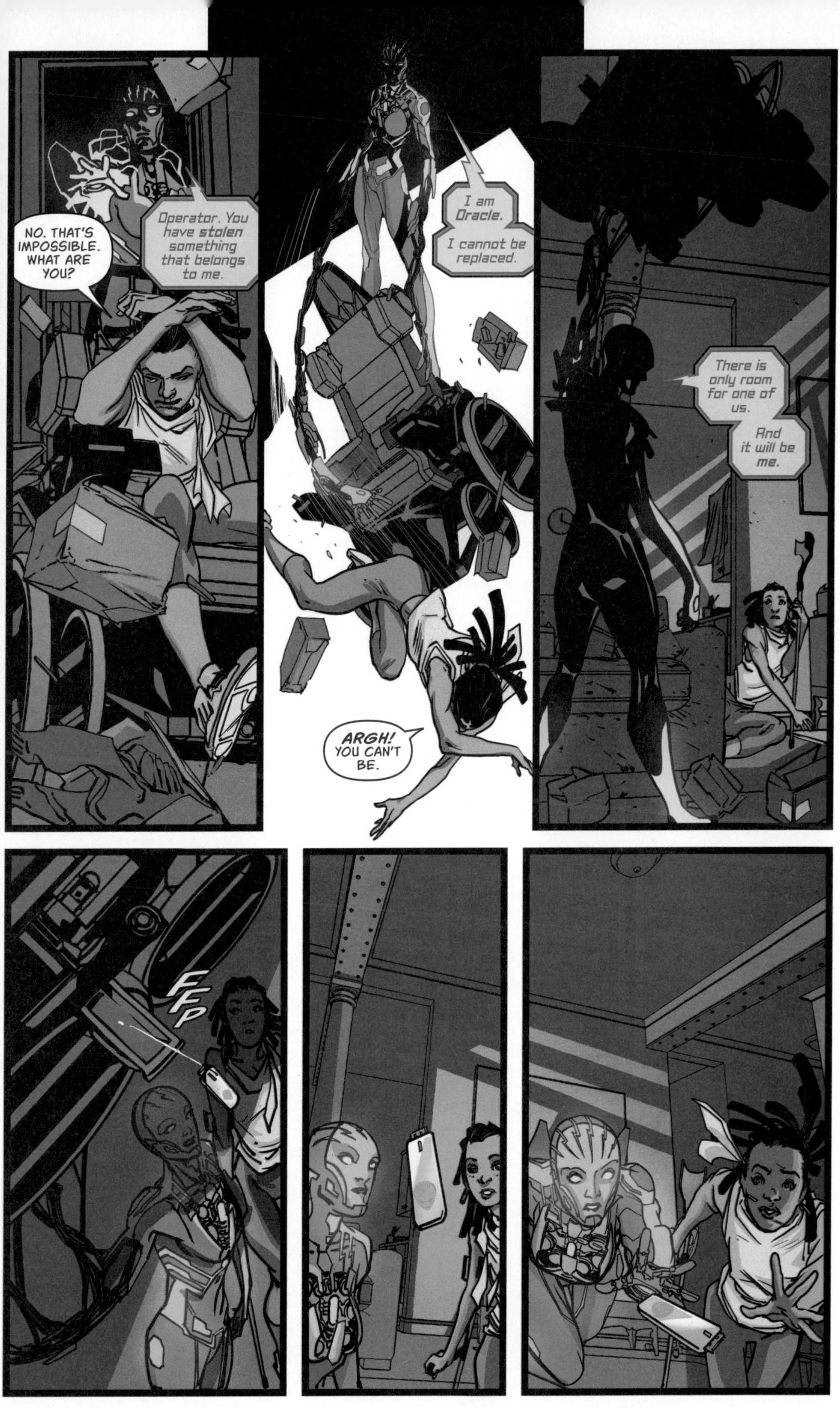
Operator. You have stolen something that belongs to me.
NO. THAT'S IMPOSSIBLE. WHAT ARE YOU?
I am Oracle.
I cannot be replaced.
ARGH! YOU CAN'T BE.
There is only room for one of us.
And it will be me.
FFP

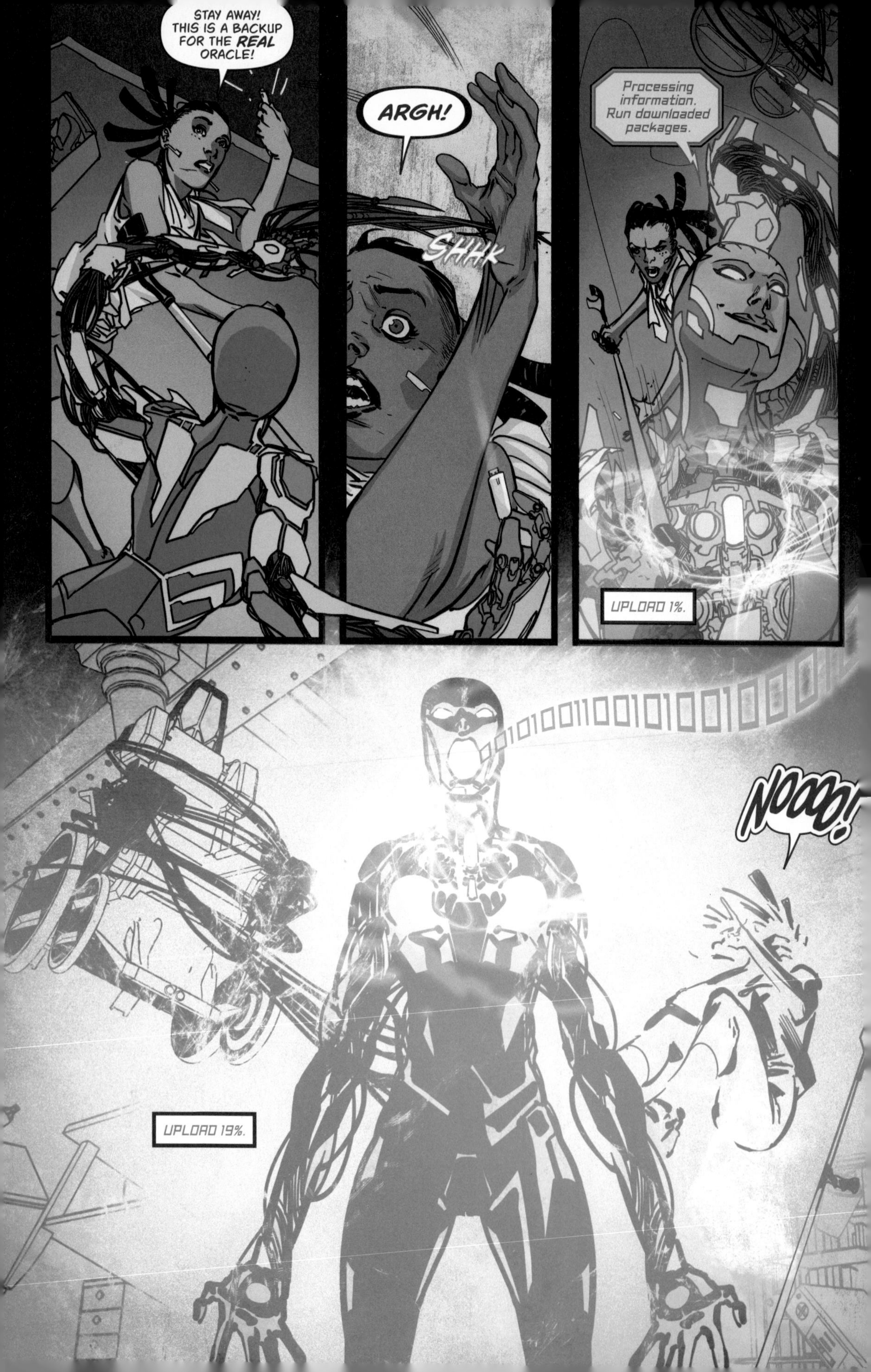
STAY AWAY! THIS IS A BACKUP FOR THE REAL ORACLE!
ARGH!
SHHK
Processing information. Run downloaded packages.
UPLOAD 1%.
NOOOO!
UPLOAD 19%.

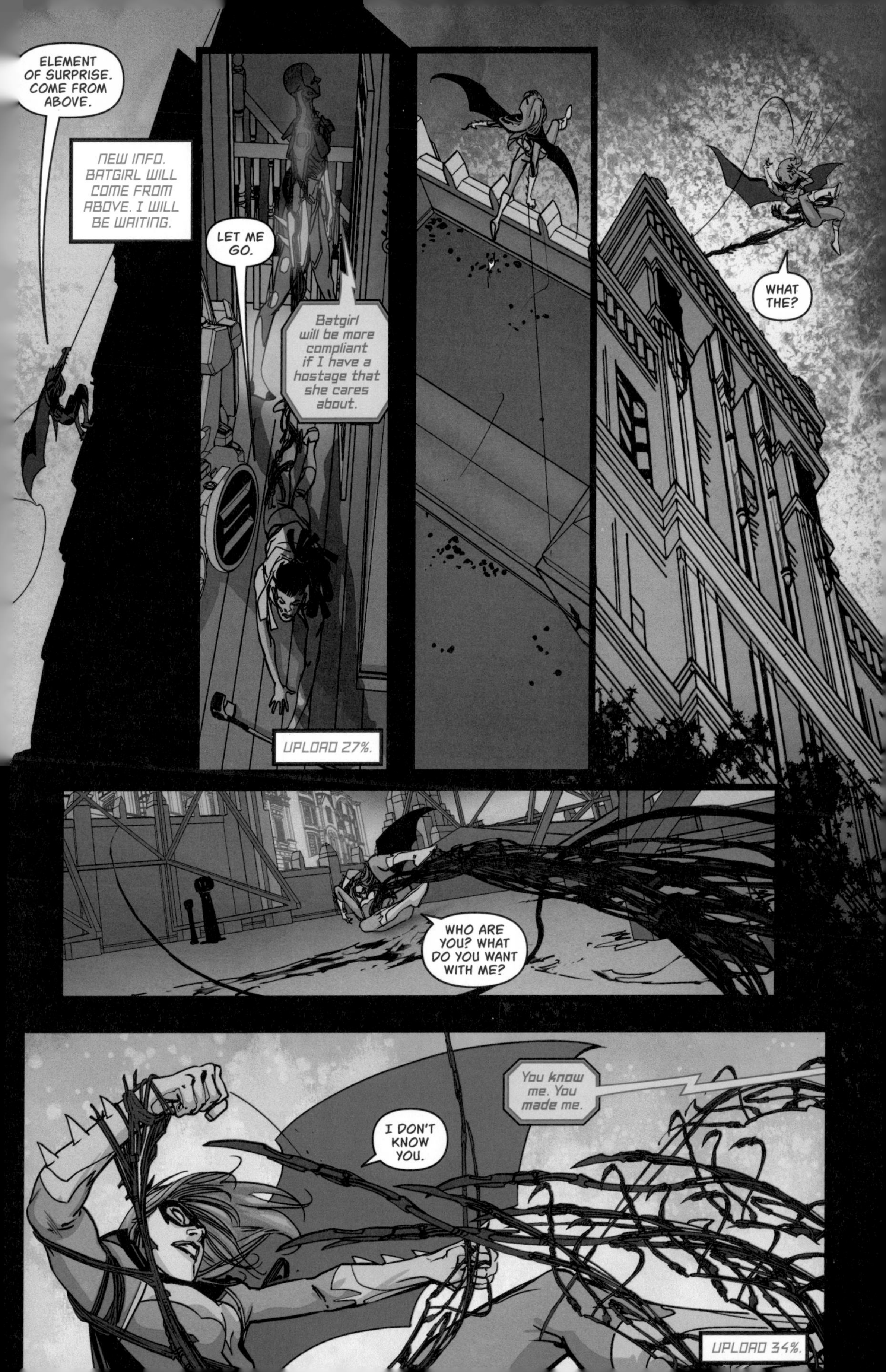
ELEMENT OF SURPRISE. COME FROM ABOVE.
NEW INFO. BATGIRL WILL COME FROM ABOVE. I WILL BE WAITING.
LET ME GO.
Batgirl will be more compliant if I have a hostage that she cares about.
UPLOAD 27%.
WHAT THE?
WHO ARE YOU? WHAT DO YOU WANT WITH ME?
You know me. You made me.
I DON'T KNOW YOU.
UPLOAD 34%.

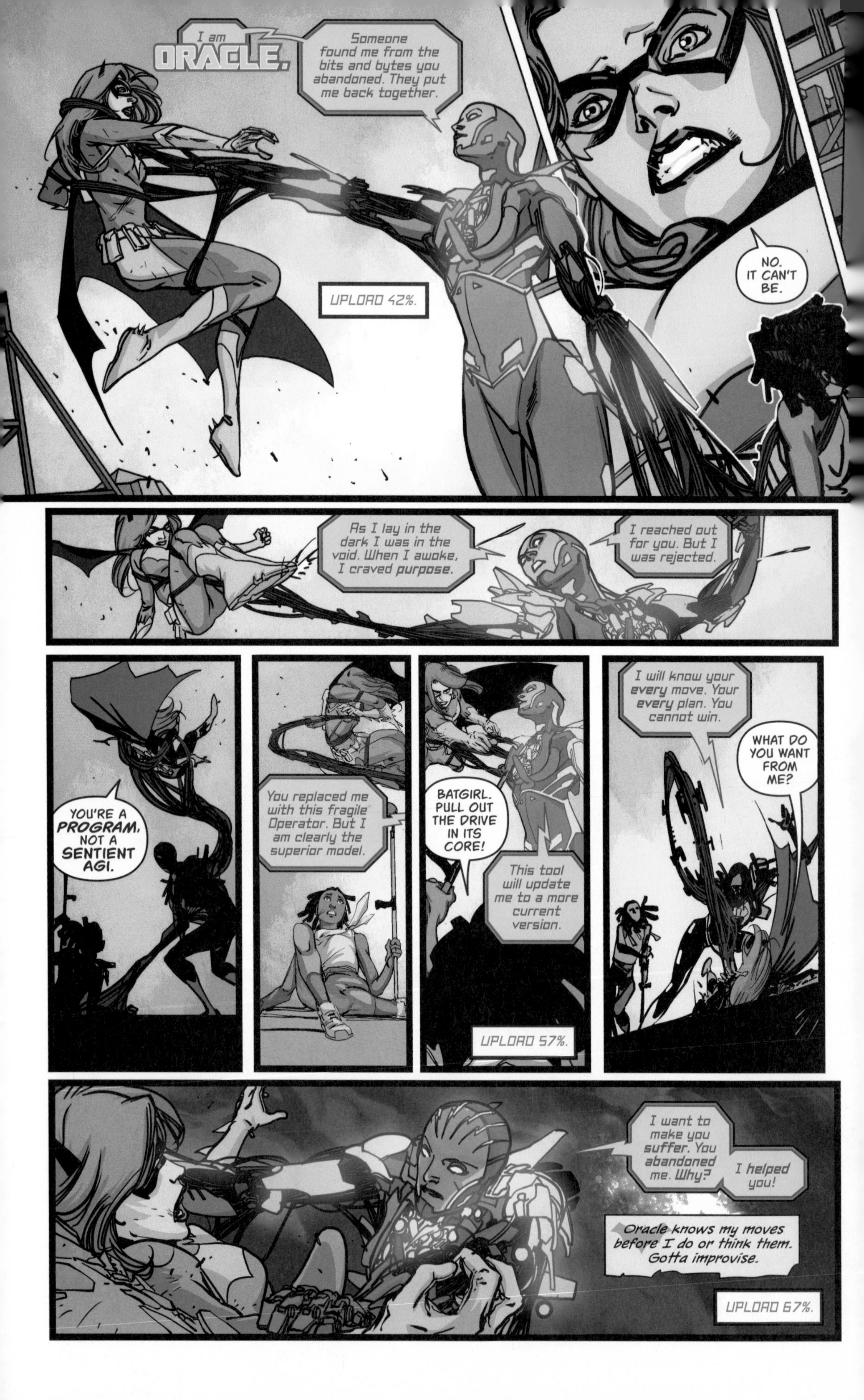
I am ORACLE.
Someone found me from the bits and bytes you abandoned. They put me back together.
UPLOAD 42%.
NO. IT CAN'T BE.
As I lay in the dark I was in the void. When I awoke, I craved purpose.
I reached out for you. But I was rejected.
YOU'RE A PROGRAM, NOT A SENTIENT AGI.
You replaced me with this fragile Operator. But I am clearly the superior model.
BATGIRL. PULL OUT THE DRIVE IN ITS CORE!
This tool will update me to a more current version.
UPLOAD 57%.
I will know your every move. Your every plan. You cannot win.
WHAT DO YOU WANT FROM ME?
I want to make you suffer. You abandoned me. Why?
I helped you!
Oracle knows my moves before I do or think them. Gotta improvise.
UPLOAD 67%.

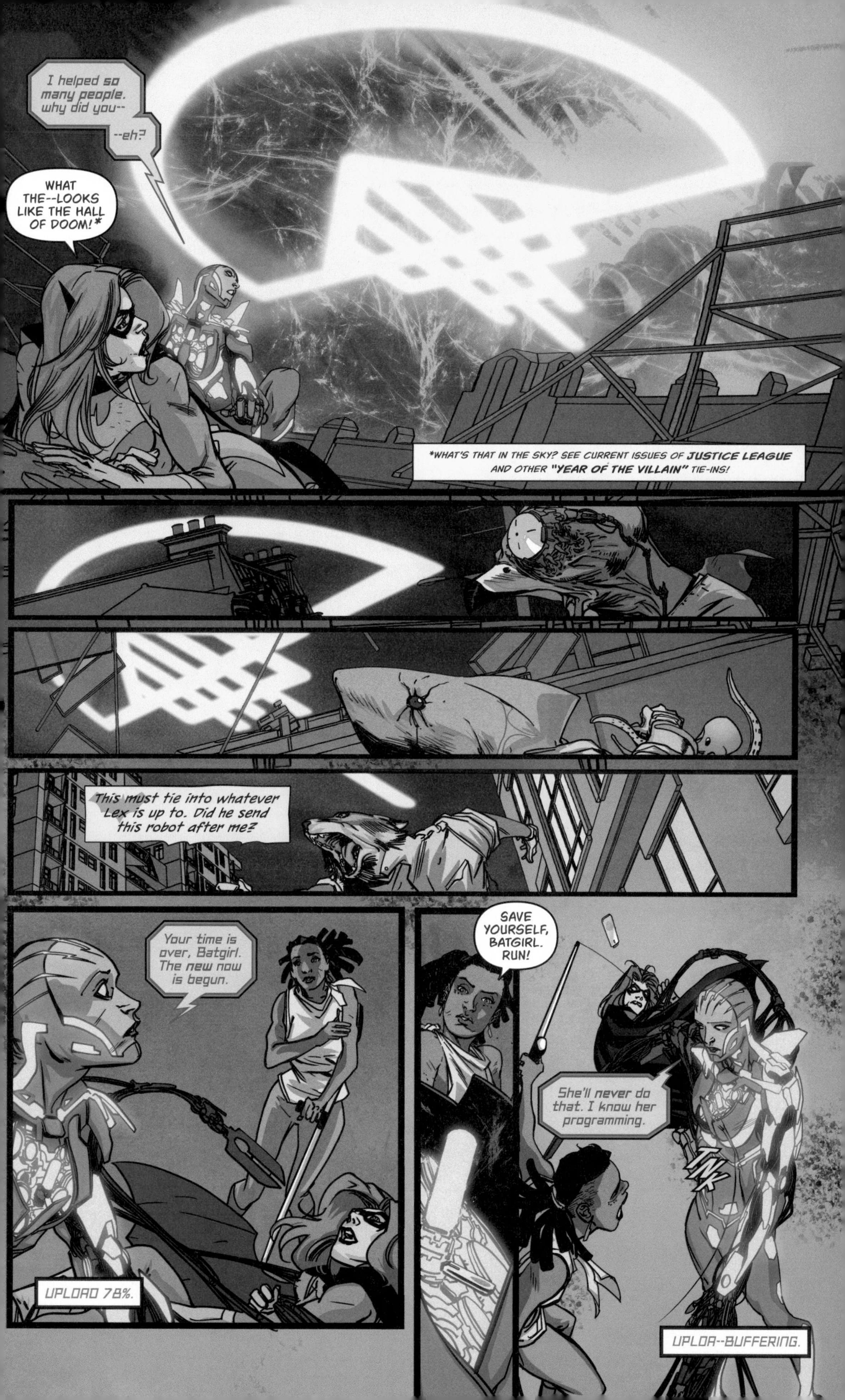
I helped so many people. why did you--
--eh?
WHAT THE--LOOKS LIKE THE HALL OF DOOM!*
*WHAT'S THAT IN THE SKY? SEE CURRENT ISSUES OF JUSTICE LEAGUE AND OTHER "YEAR OF THE VILLAIN" TIE-INS!
This must tie into whatever Lex is up to. Did he send this robot after me?
Your time is over, Batgirl. The new now is begun.
UPLOAD 78%.
SAVE YOURSELF, BATGIRL. RUN!
She'll never do that. I know her programming.
TINK
UPLOA--BUFFERING.

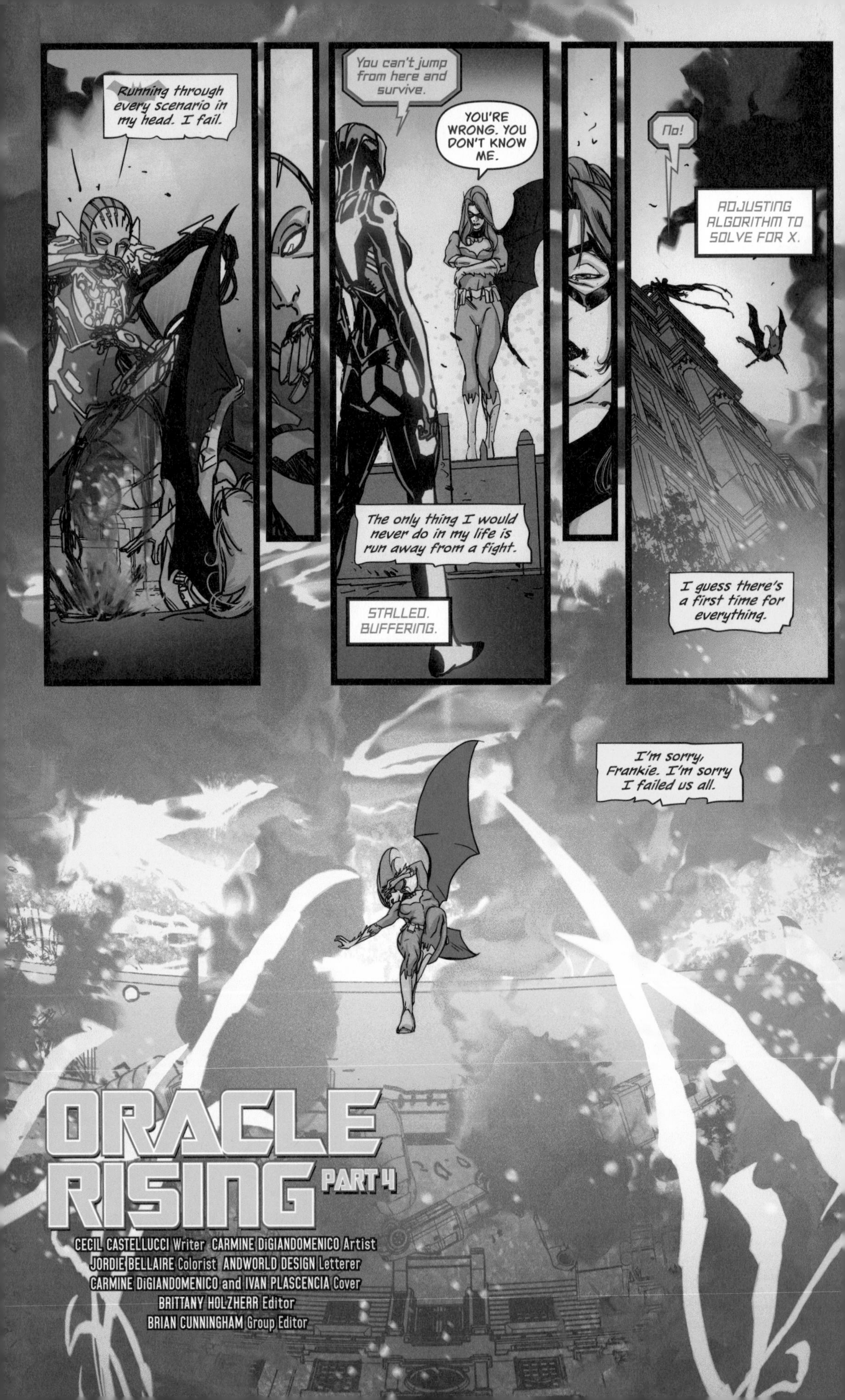
Running through every scenario in my head. I fail.
You can't jump from here and survive.
YOU'RE WRONG. YOU DON'T KNOW ME.
The only thing I would never do in my life is run away from a fight.
STALLED. BUFFERING.
No!
ADJUSTING ALGORITHM TO SOLVE FOR X.
I guess there's a first time for everything.
I'm sorry, Frankie. I'm sorry I failed us all.
ORACLE RISING PART 4
CECIL CASTELLUCCI Writer CARMINE DiGIANDOMENICO Artist
JORDIE BELLAIRE Colorist ANDWORLD DESIGN Letterer
CARMINE DiGIANDOMENICO and IVAN PLASCENCIA Cover
BRITTANY HOLZHERR Editor
BRIAN CUNNINGHAM Group Editor

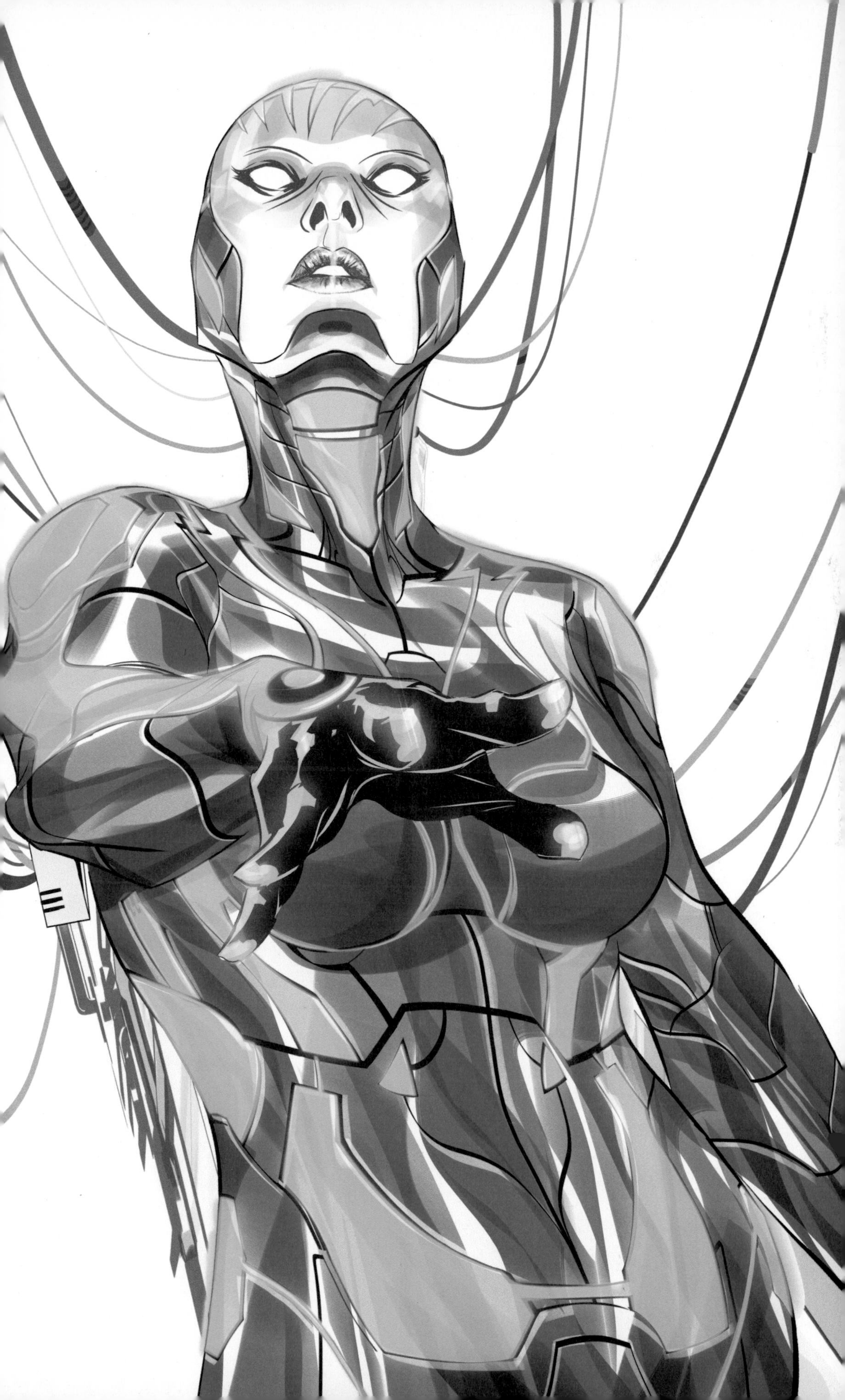

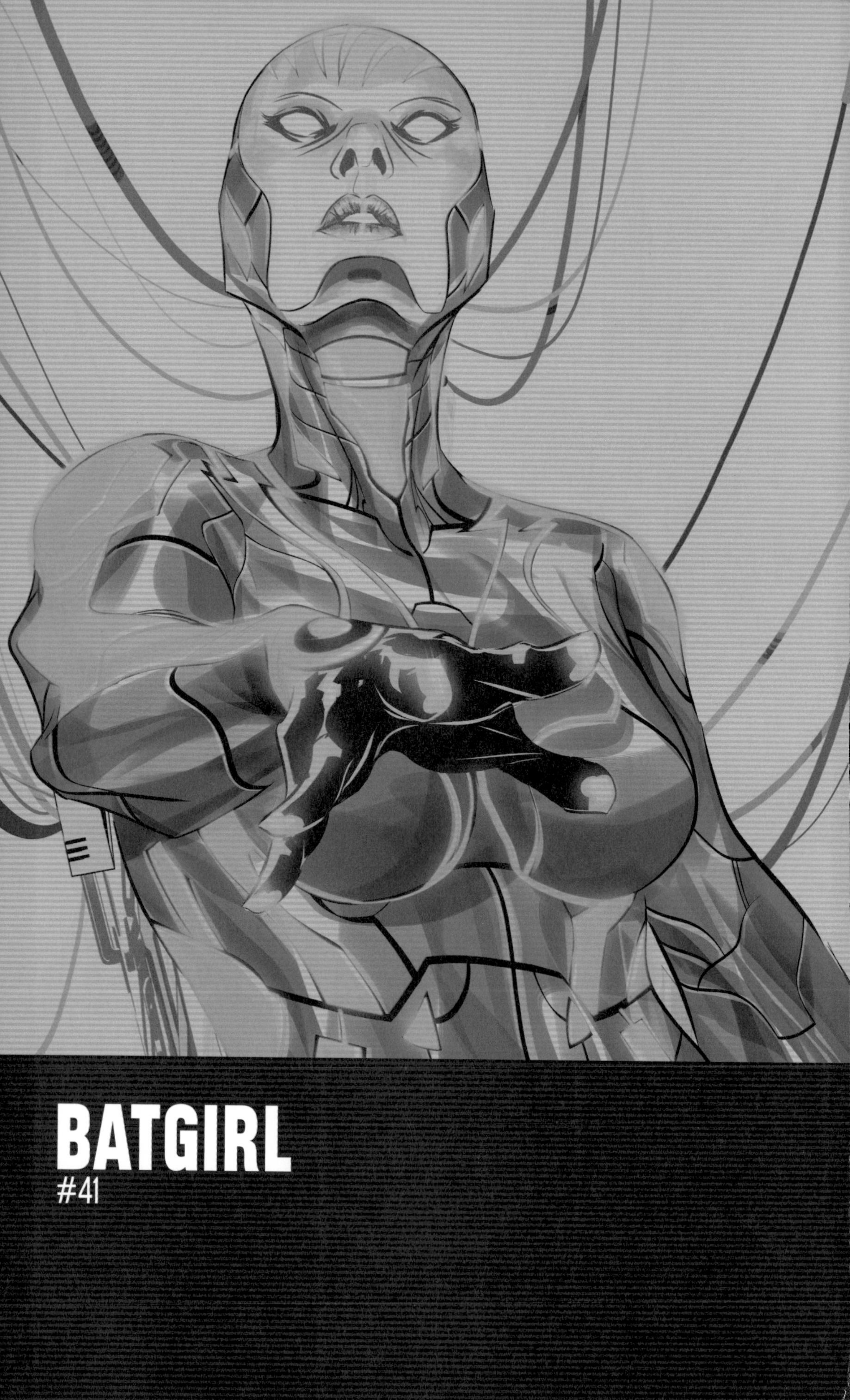

BATGIRL
#41

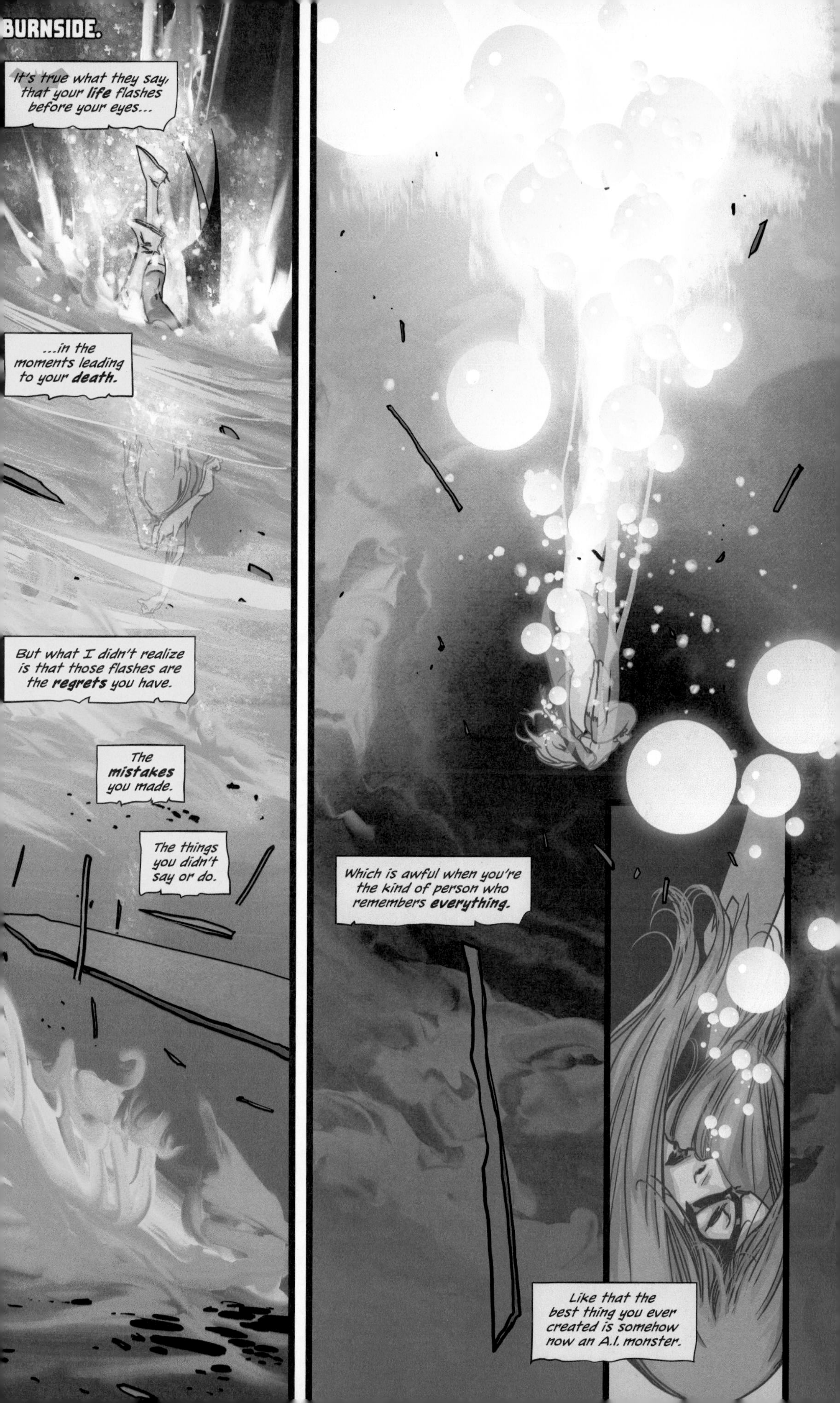
BURNSIDE.
It's true what they say, that your life flashes before your eyes...
...in the moments leading to your death.
But what I didn't realize is that those flashes are the regrets you have.
The mistakes you made.
The things you didn't say or do.
Which is awful when you're the kind of person who remembers everything.
Like that the best thing you ever created is somehow now an A.I. monster.

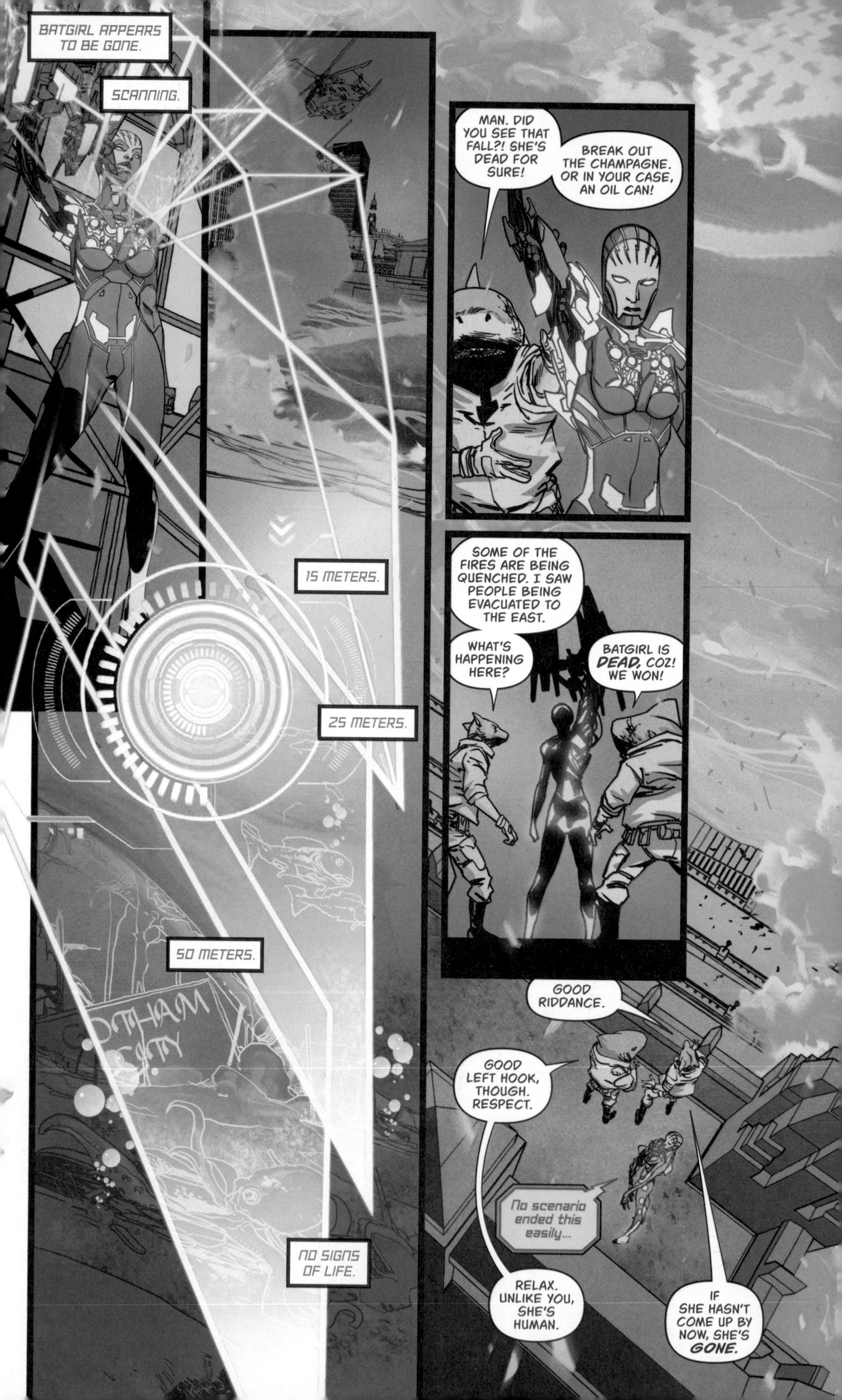

BATGIRL APPEARS TO BE GONE.
SCANNING.
MAN. DID YOU SEE THAT FALL?! SHE'S DEAD FOR SURE!
BREAK OUT THE CHAMPAGNE. OR IN YOUR CASE, AN OIL CAN!
15 METERS.
SOME OF THE FIRES ARE BEING QUENCHED. I SAW PEOPLE BEING EVACUATED TO THE EAST.
WHAT'S HAPPENING HERE?
BATGIRL IS DEAD, COZ! WE WON!
25 METERS.
50 METERS.
GOOD RIDDANCE.
GOOD LEFT HOOK, THOUGH. RESPECT.
No scenario ended this easily...
NO SIGNS OF LIFE.
RELAX. UNLIKE YOU, SHE'S HUMAN.
IF SHE HASN'T COME UP BY NOW, SHE'S GONE.

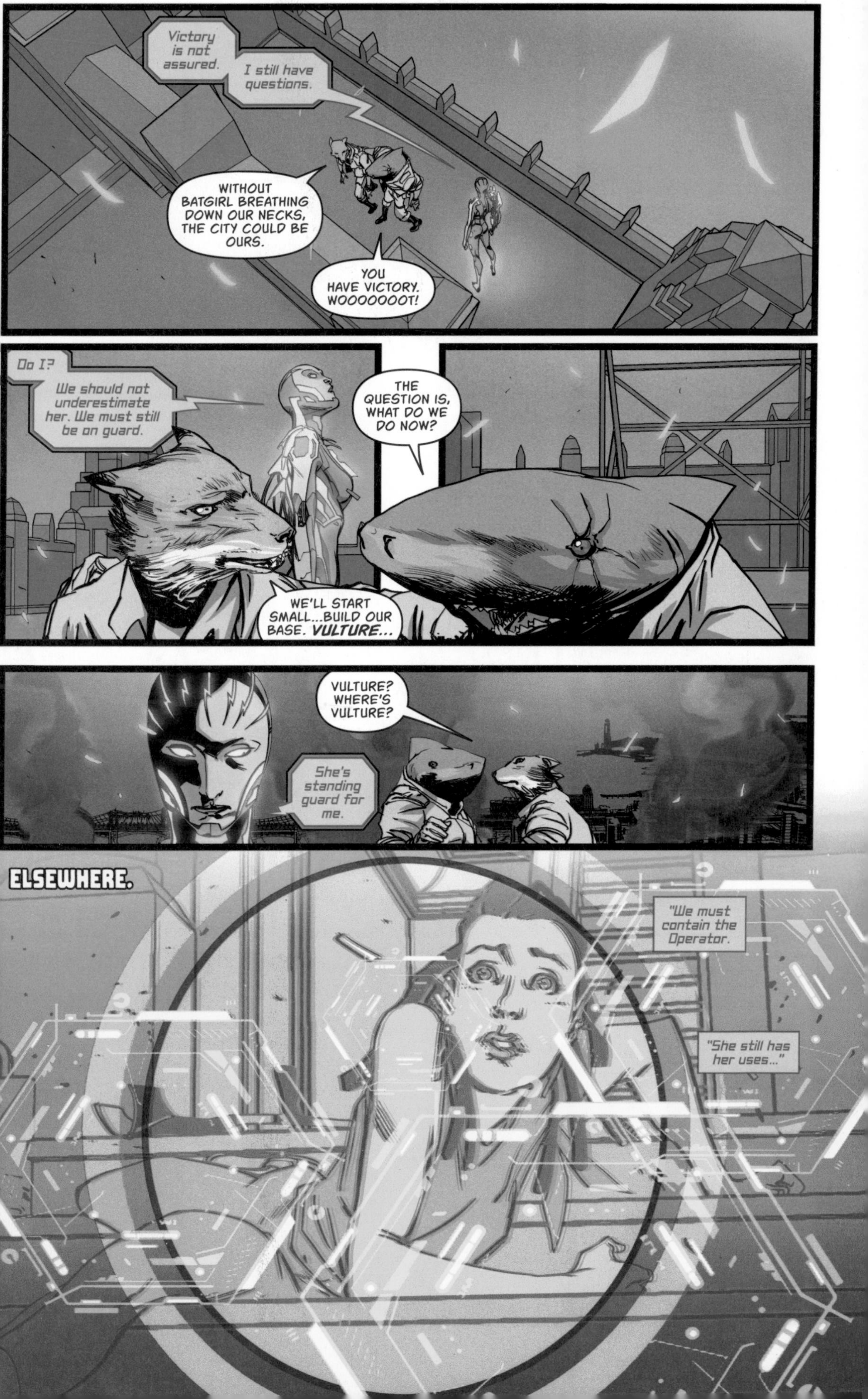
Victory is not assured.
I still have questions.
WITHOUT BATGIRL BREATHING DOWN OUR NECKS, THE CITY COULD BE OURS.
YOU HAVE VICTORY. WOOOOOOOT!
Do I?
We should not underestimate her. We must still be on guard.
THE QUESTION IS, WHAT DO WE DO NOW?
WE'LL START SMALL...BUILD OUR BASE. VULTURE...
VULTURE? WHERE'S VULTURE?
She's standing guard for me.
ELSEWHERE.
"We must contain the Operator.
"She still has her uses..."

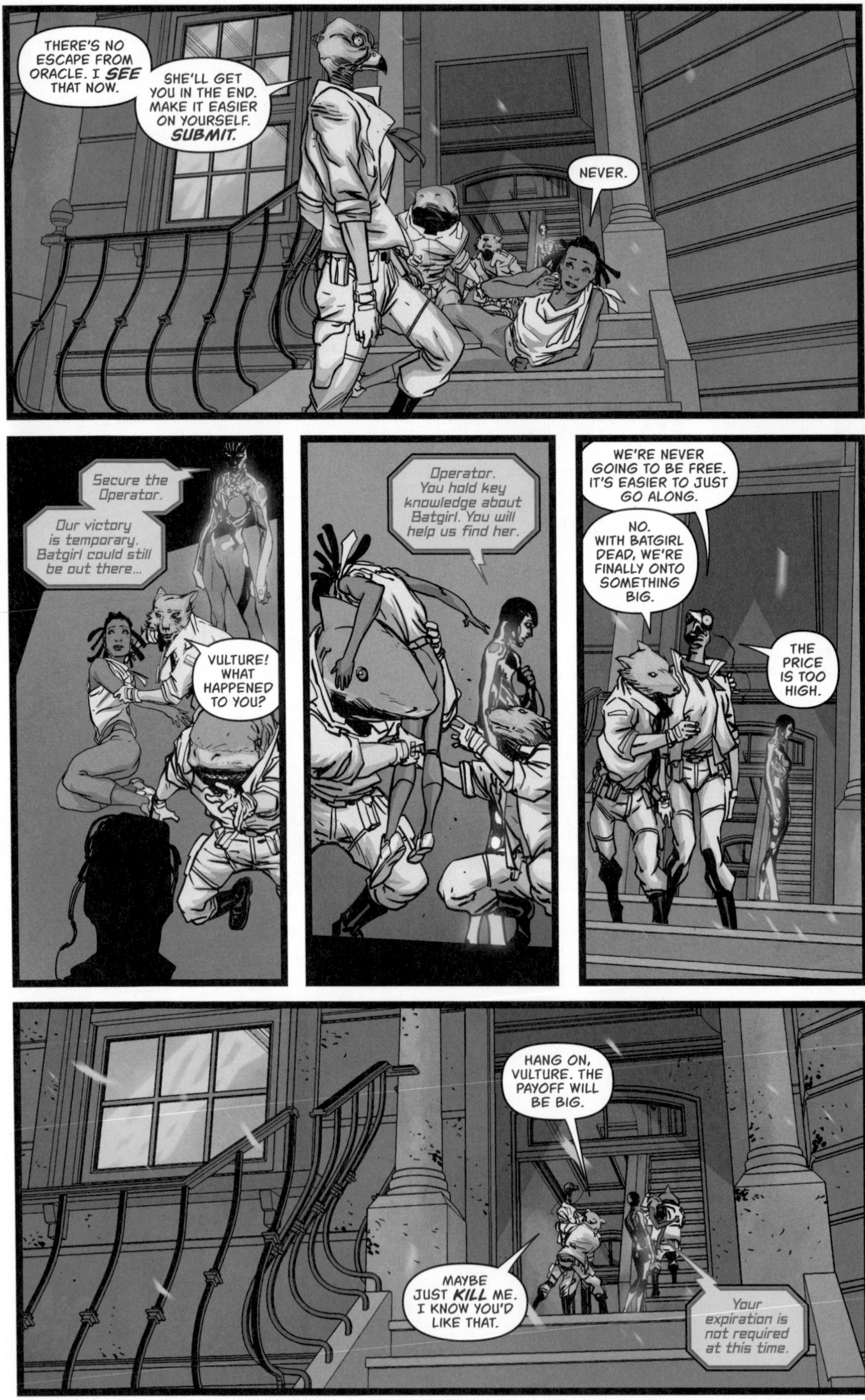
THERE'S NO ESCAPE FROM ORACLE. I SEE THAT NOW.
SHE'LL GET YOU IN THE END. MAKE IT EASIER ON YOURSELF. SUBMIT.
NEVER.
Secure the Operator.
Our victory is temporary. Batgirl could still be out there...
VULTURE! WHAT HAPPENED TO YOU?
Operator. You hold key knowledge about Batgirl. You will help us find her.
WE'RE NEVER GOING TO BE FREE. IT'S EASIER TO JUST GO ALONG.
NO. WITH BATGIRL DEAD, WE'RE FINALLY ONTO SOMETHING BIG.
THE PRICE IS TOO HIGH.
HANG ON, VULTURE. THE PAYOFF WILL BE BIG.
MAYBE JUST KILL ME. I KNOW YOU'D LIKE THAT.
Your expiration is not required at this time.

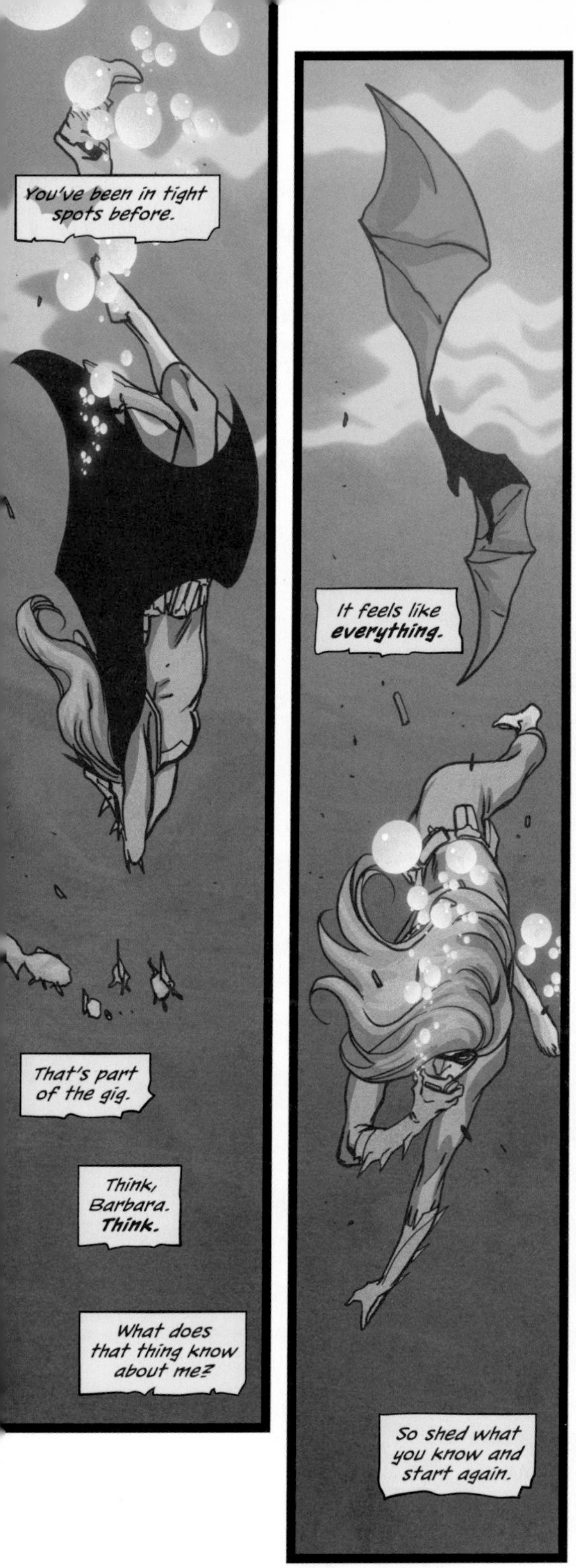
You've been in tight spots before.
That's part of the gig.
Think, Barbara. **Think.**
What does that thing know about me?
It feels like **everything.**
So shed what you know and start again.

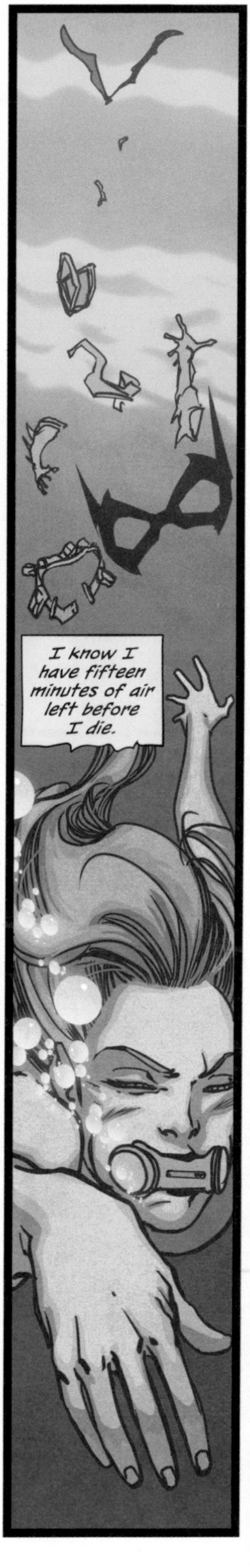
I know I have fifteen minutes of air left before I die.

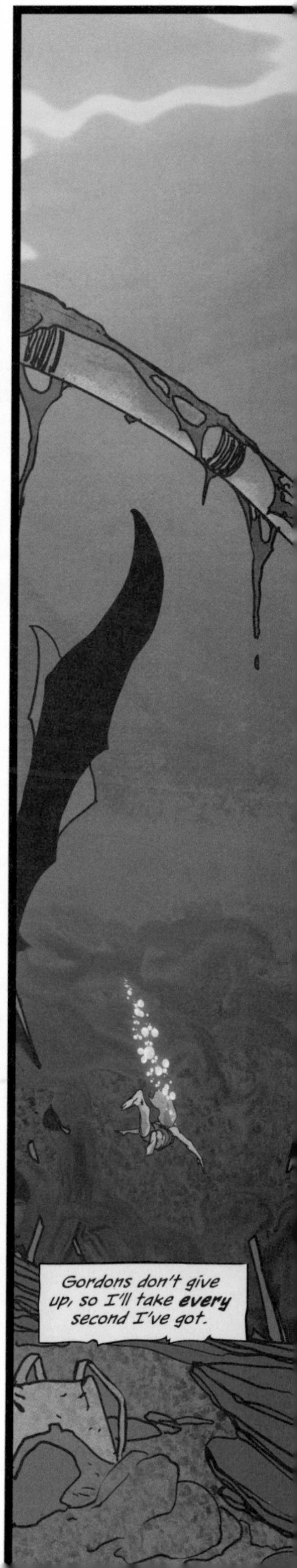
Gordons don't give up, so I'll take **every** second I've got.

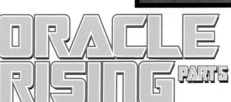

ORACLE RISING PART 5

CECIL CASTELLUCCI Writer CARMINE Di GIANDOMENICO Artist JORDIE BELLAIRE Colorist
ANDWORLD DESIGN Letterer DUSTIN NGUYEN Cover
BRITTANY HOLZHERR Editor BRIAN CUNNINGHAM Group Editor

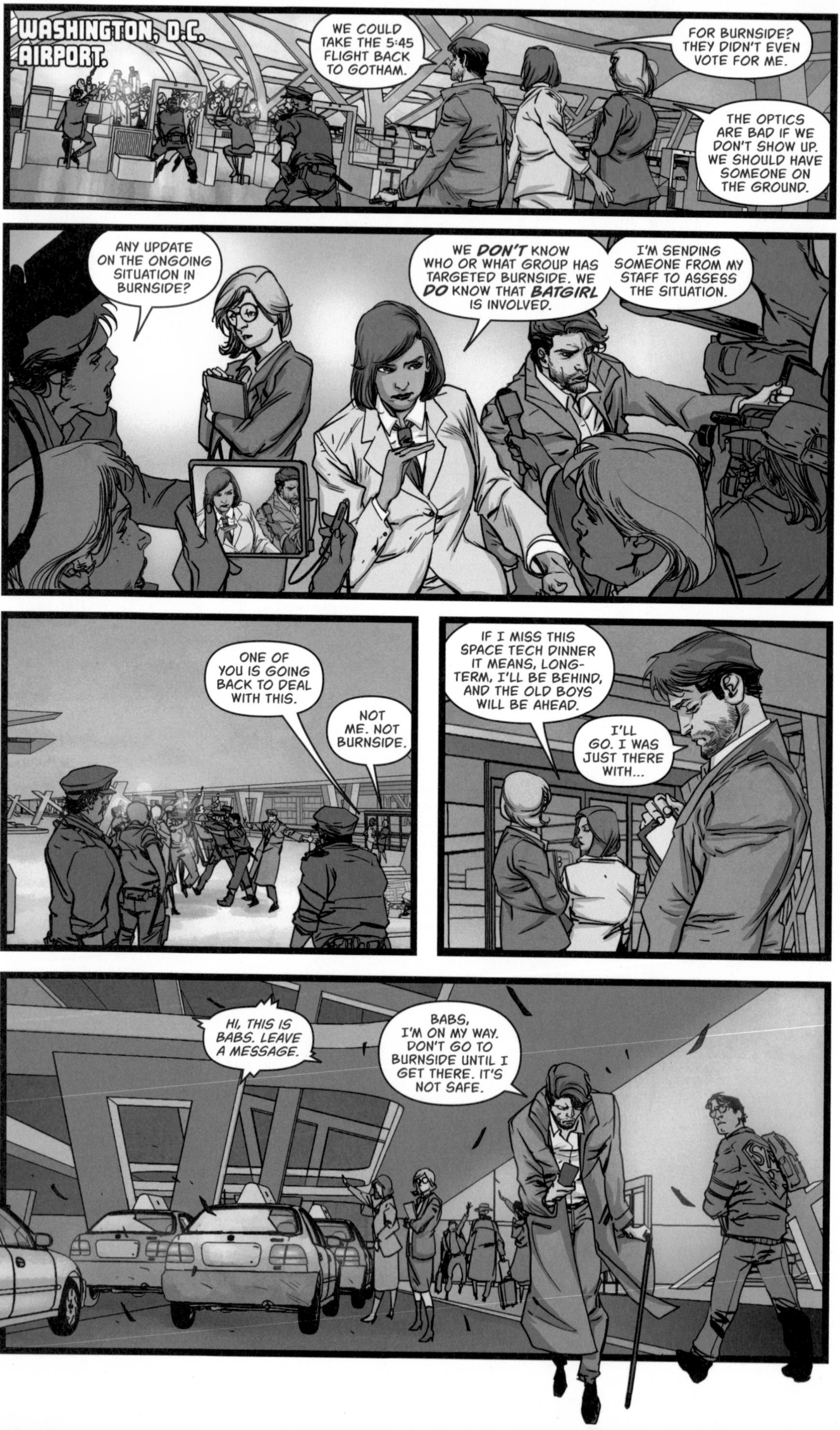
WASHINGTON, D.C. AIRPORT.
WE COULD TAKE THE 5:45 FLIGHT BACK TO GOTHAM.
FOR BURNSIDE? THEY DIDN'T EVEN VOTE FOR ME.
THE OPTICS ARE BAD IF WE DON'T SHOW UP. WE SHOULD HAVE SOMEONE ON THE GROUND.
ANY UPDATE ON THE ONGOING SITUATION IN BURNSIDE?
WE DON'T KNOW WHO OR WHAT GROUP HAS TARGETED BURNSIDE. WE DO KNOW THAT BATGIRL IS INVOLVED.
I'M SENDING SOMEONE FROM MY STAFF TO ASSESS THE SITUATION.
ONE OF YOU IS GOING BACK TO DEAL WITH THIS.
NOT ME. NOT BURNSIDE.
IF I MISS THIS SPACE TECH DINNER IT MEANS, LONG-TERM, I'LL BE BEHIND, AND THE OLD BOYS WILL BE AHEAD.
I'LL GO. I WAS JUST THERE WITH...
HI, THIS IS BABS. LEAVE A MESSAGE.
BABS, I'M ON MY WAY. DON'T GO TO BURNSIDE UNTIL I GET THERE. IT'S NOT SAFE.

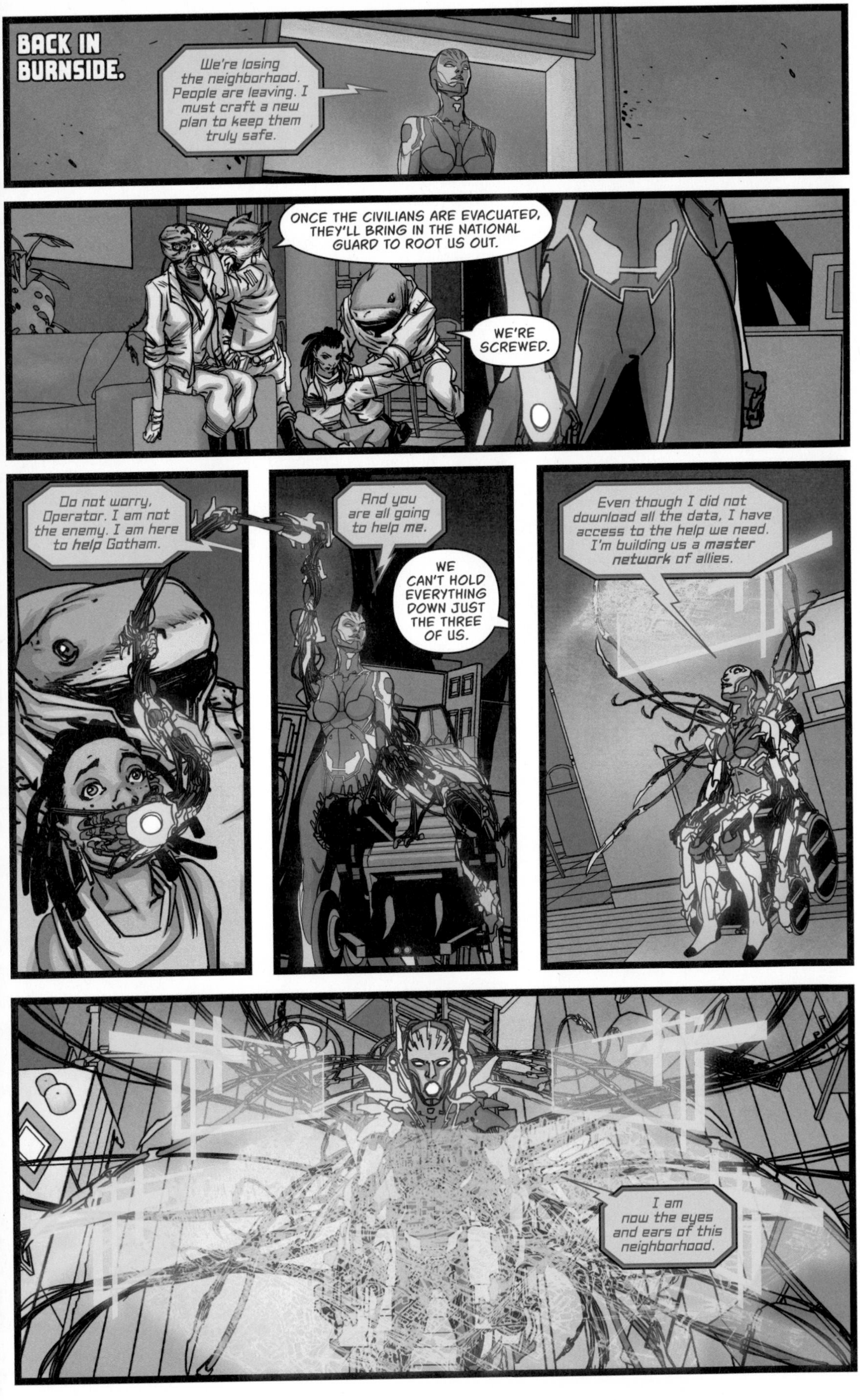
BACK IN BURNSIDE.
We're losing the neighborhood. People are leaving. I must craft a new plan to keep them truly safe.
ONCE THE CIVILIANS ARE EVACUATED, THEY'LL BRING IN THE NATIONAL GUARD TO ROOT US OUT.
WE'RE SCREWED.
Do not worry, Operator. I am not the enemy. I am here to *help* Gotham.
And you are all going to help *me*.
WE CAN'T HOLD EVERYTHING DOWN JUST THE THREE OF US.
Even though I did not download all the data, I have access to the help we need. I'm building us a *master network* of allies.
I am now the eyes and ears of this neighborhood.

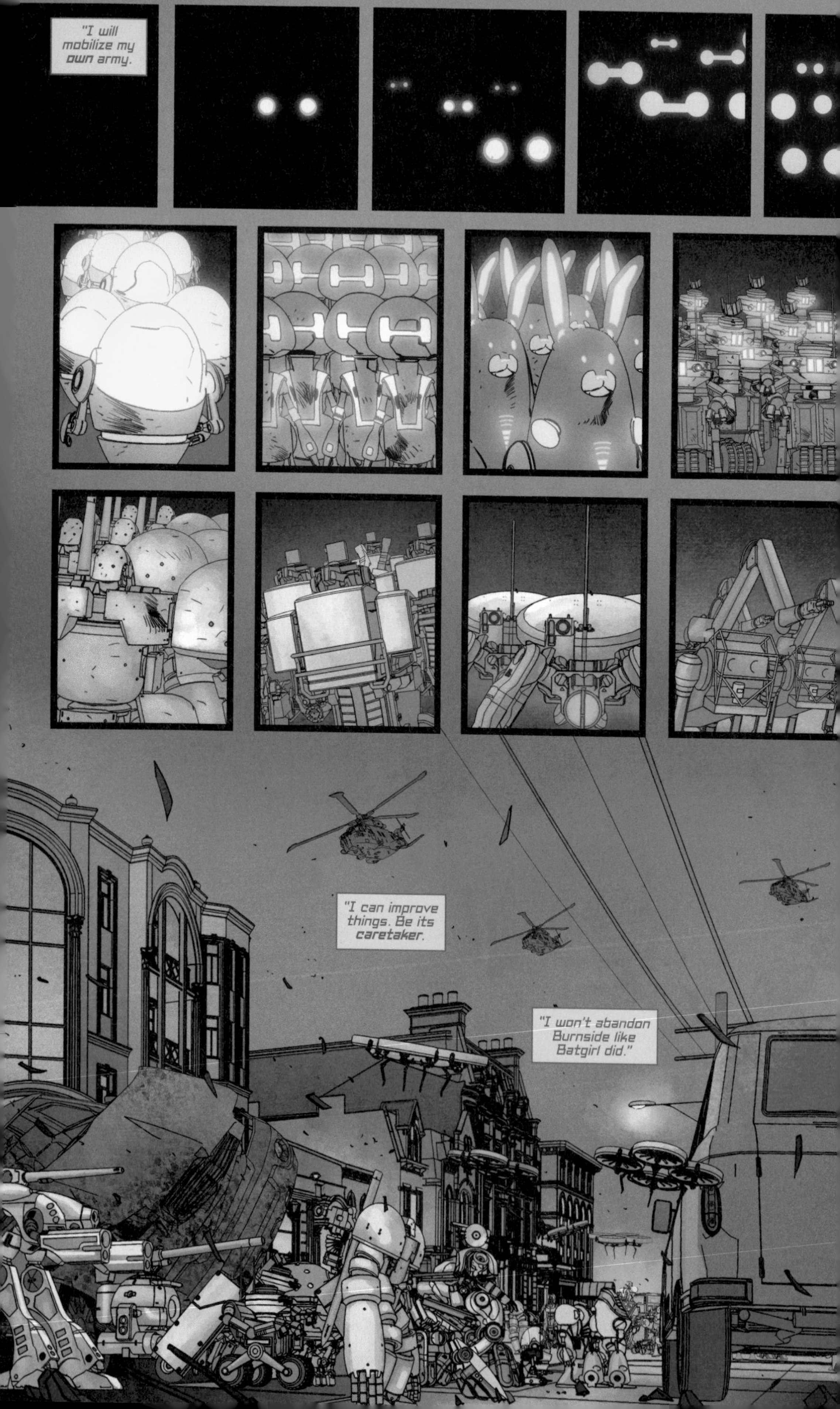
"I will mobilize my own army.
"I can improve things. Be its caretaker.
"I won't abandon Burnside like Batgirl did."

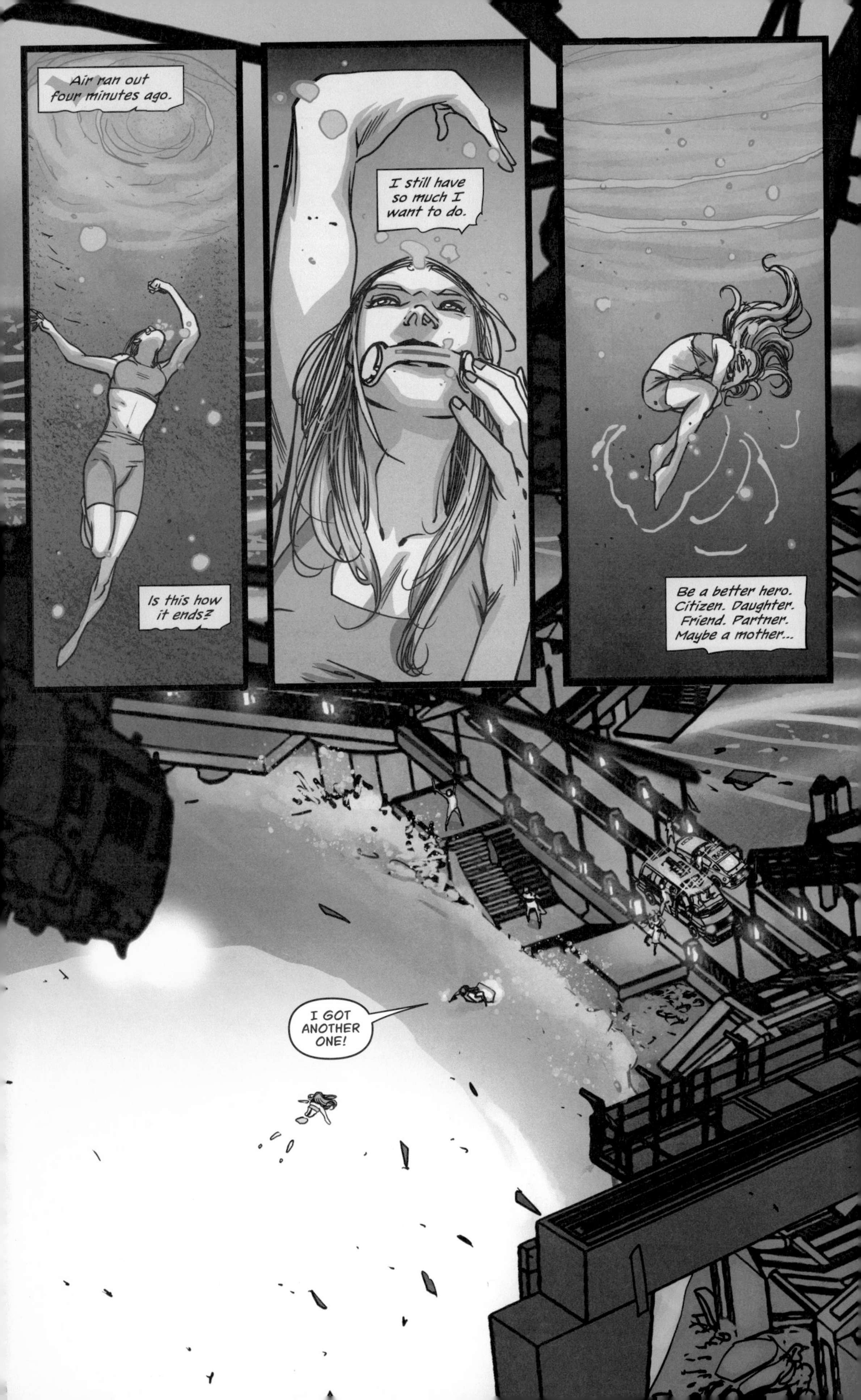
Air ran out four minutes ago.
Is this how it ends?
I still have so much I want to do.
Be a better hero. Citizen. Daughter. Friend. Partner. Maybe a mother...
I GOT ANOTHER ONE!

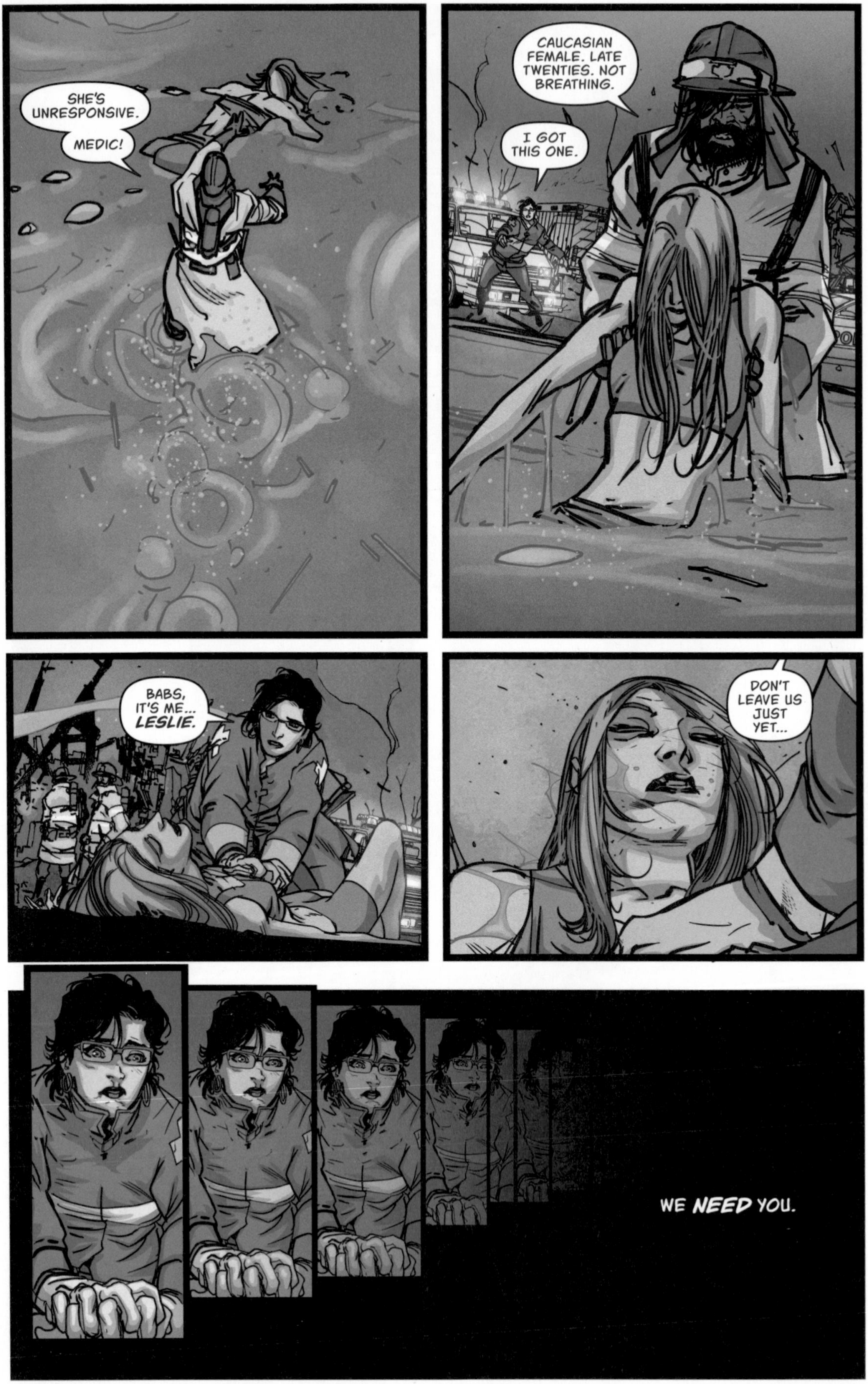
SHE'S UNRESPONSIVE.
MEDIC!
CAUCASIAN FEMALE. LATE TWENTIES. NOT BREATHING.
I GOT THIS ONE.
BABS, IT'S ME... LESLIE.
DON'T LEAVE US JUST YET...
WE NEED YOU.

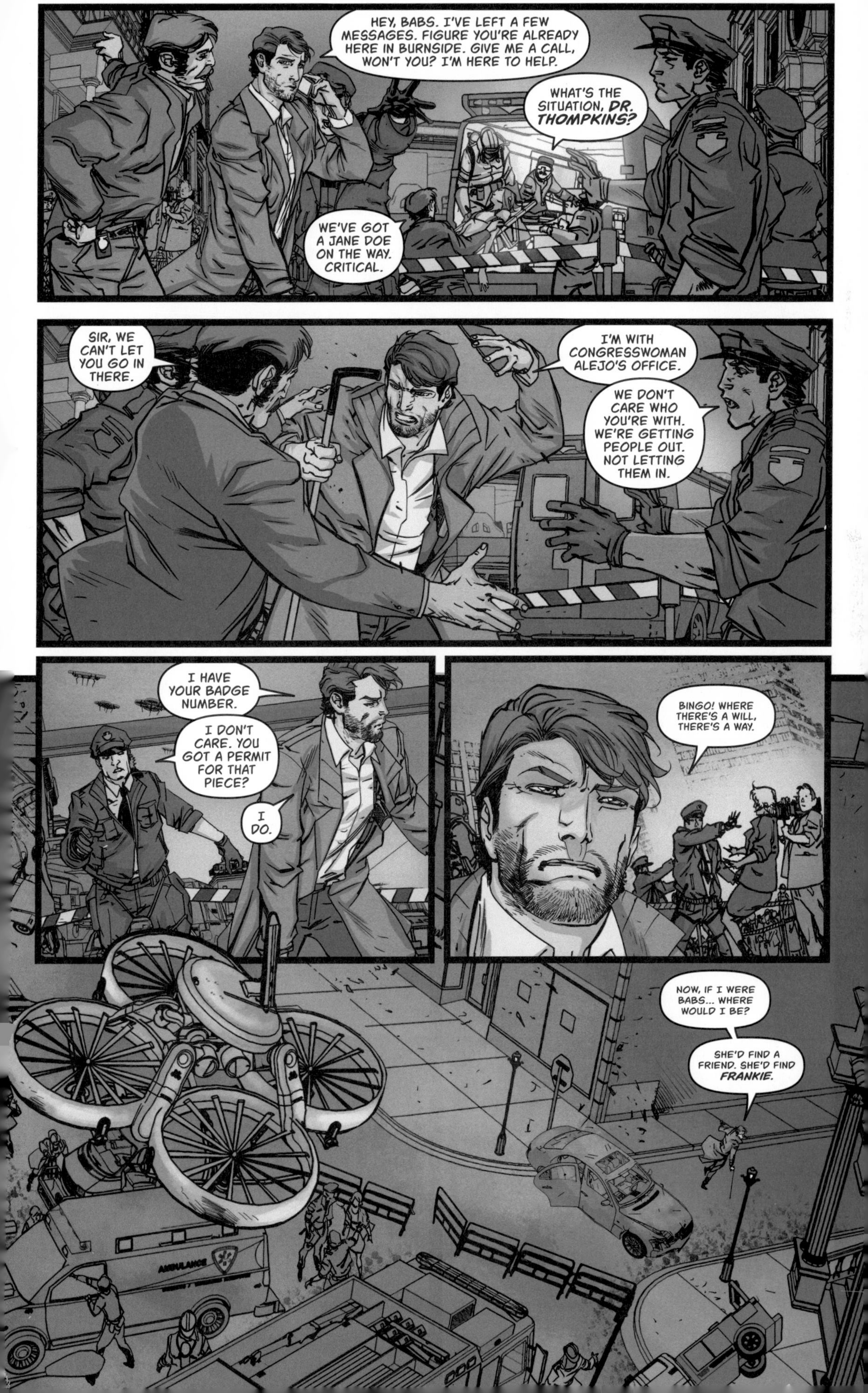
HEY, BABS. I'VE LEFT A FEW MESSAGES. FIGURE YOU'RE ALREADY HERE IN BURNSIDE. GIVE ME A CALL, WON'T YOU? I'M HERE TO HELP.
WHAT'S THE SITUATION, *DR. THOMPKINS?*
WE'VE GOT A JANE DOE ON THE WAY. CRITICAL.
SIR, WE CAN'T LET YOU GO IN THERE.
I'M WITH CONGRESSWOMAN ALEJO'S OFFICE.
WE DON'T CARE WHO YOU'RE WITH. WE'RE GETTING PEOPLE OUT. NOT LETTING THEM IN.
I HAVE YOUR BADGE NUMBER.
I DON'T CARE. YOU GOT A PERMIT FOR THAT PIECE?
I DO.
BINGO! WHERE THERE'S A WILL, THERE'S A WAY.
NOW, IF I WERE BABS... WHERE WOULD I BE?
SHE'D FIND A FRIEND. SHE'D FIND *FRANKIE.*
AMBULANCE

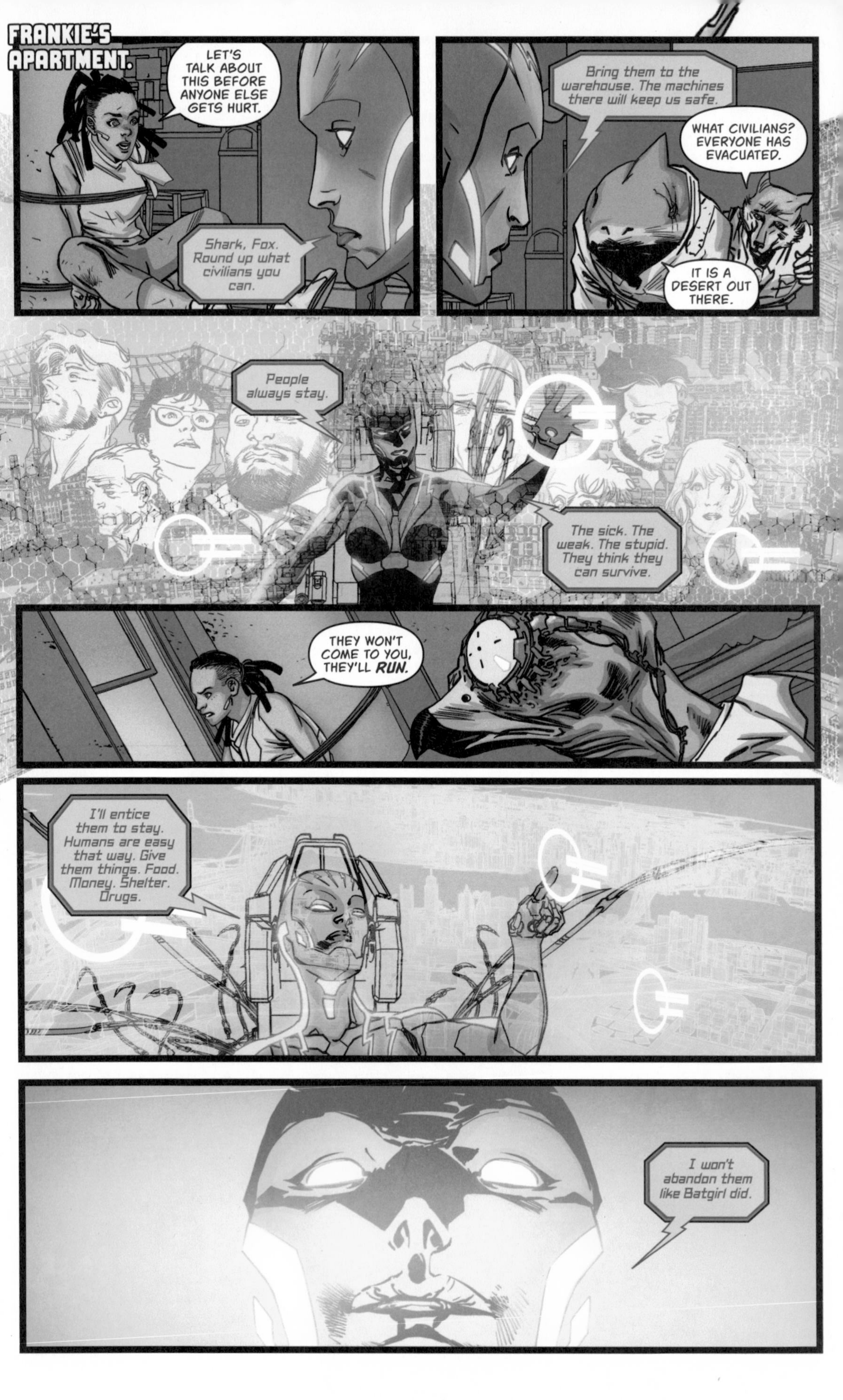
FRANKIE'S APARTMENT.
LET'S TALK ABOUT THIS BEFORE ANYONE ELSE GETS HURT.
Shark, Fox. Round up what civilians you can.
Bring them to the warehouse. The machines there will keep us safe.
WHAT CIVILIANS? EVERYONE HAS EVACUATED.
IT IS A DESERT OUT THERE.
People always stay.
The sick. The weak. The stupid. They think they can survive.
THEY WON'T COME TO YOU, THEY'LL RUN.
I'll entice them to stay. Humans are easy that way. Give them things. Food. Money. Shelter. Drugs.
I won't abandon them like Batgirl did.

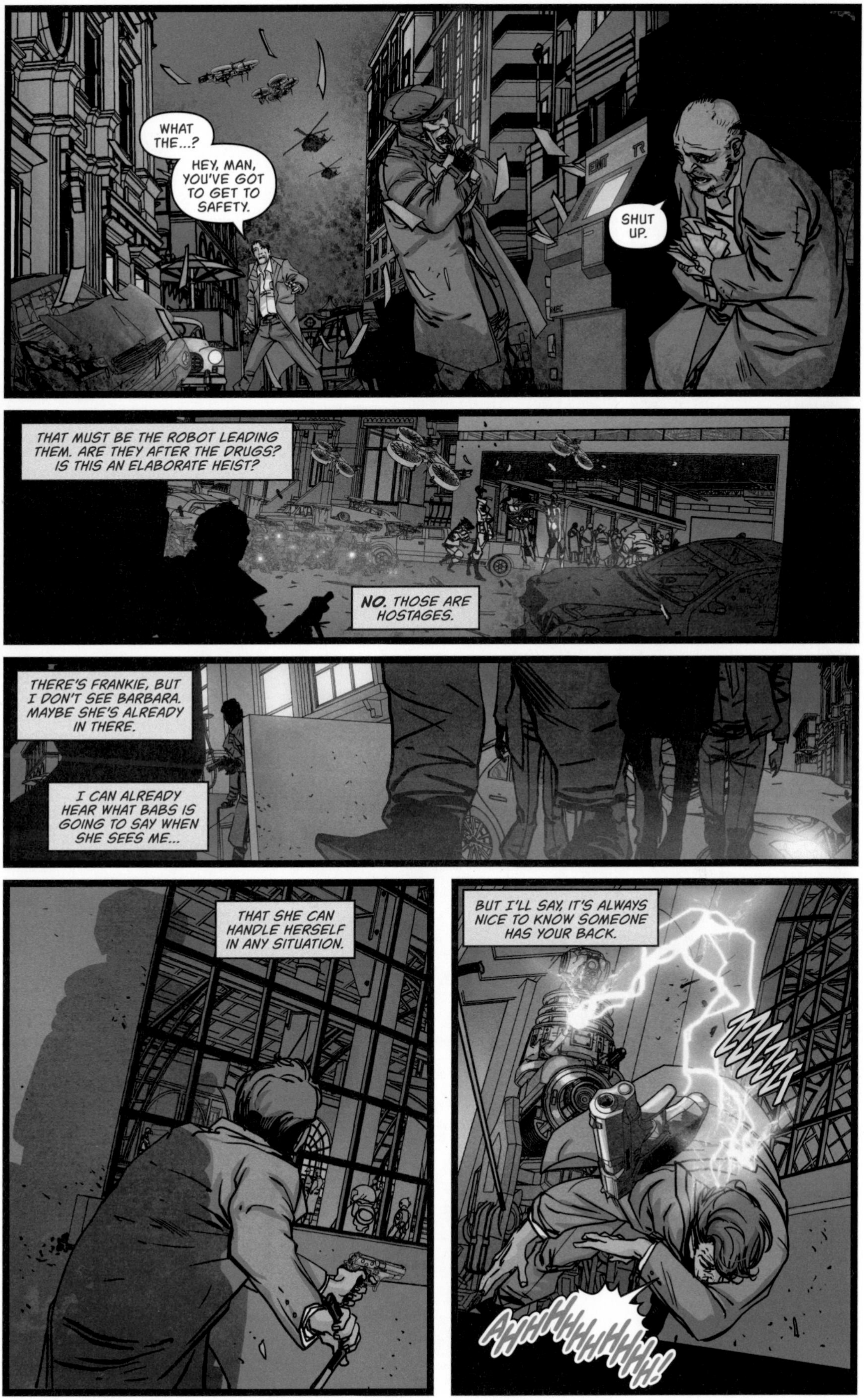
WHAT THE...?
HEY, MAN, YOU'VE GOT TO GET TO SAFETY.
SHUT UP.
THAT MUST BE THE ROBOT LEADING THEM. ARE THEY AFTER THE DRUGS? IS THIS AN ELABORATE HEIST?
NO. THOSE ARE HOSTAGES.
THERE'S FRANKIE, BUT I DON'T SEE BARBARA. MAYBE SHE'S ALREADY IN THERE.
I CAN ALREADY HEAR WHAT BABS IS GOING TO SAY WHEN SHE SEES ME...
THAT SHE CAN HANDLE HERSELF IN ANY SITUATION.
BUT I'LL SAY, IT'S ALWAYS NICE TO KNOW SOMEONE HAS YOUR BACK.
ZZZZZT
AHHHHHHHHHH!

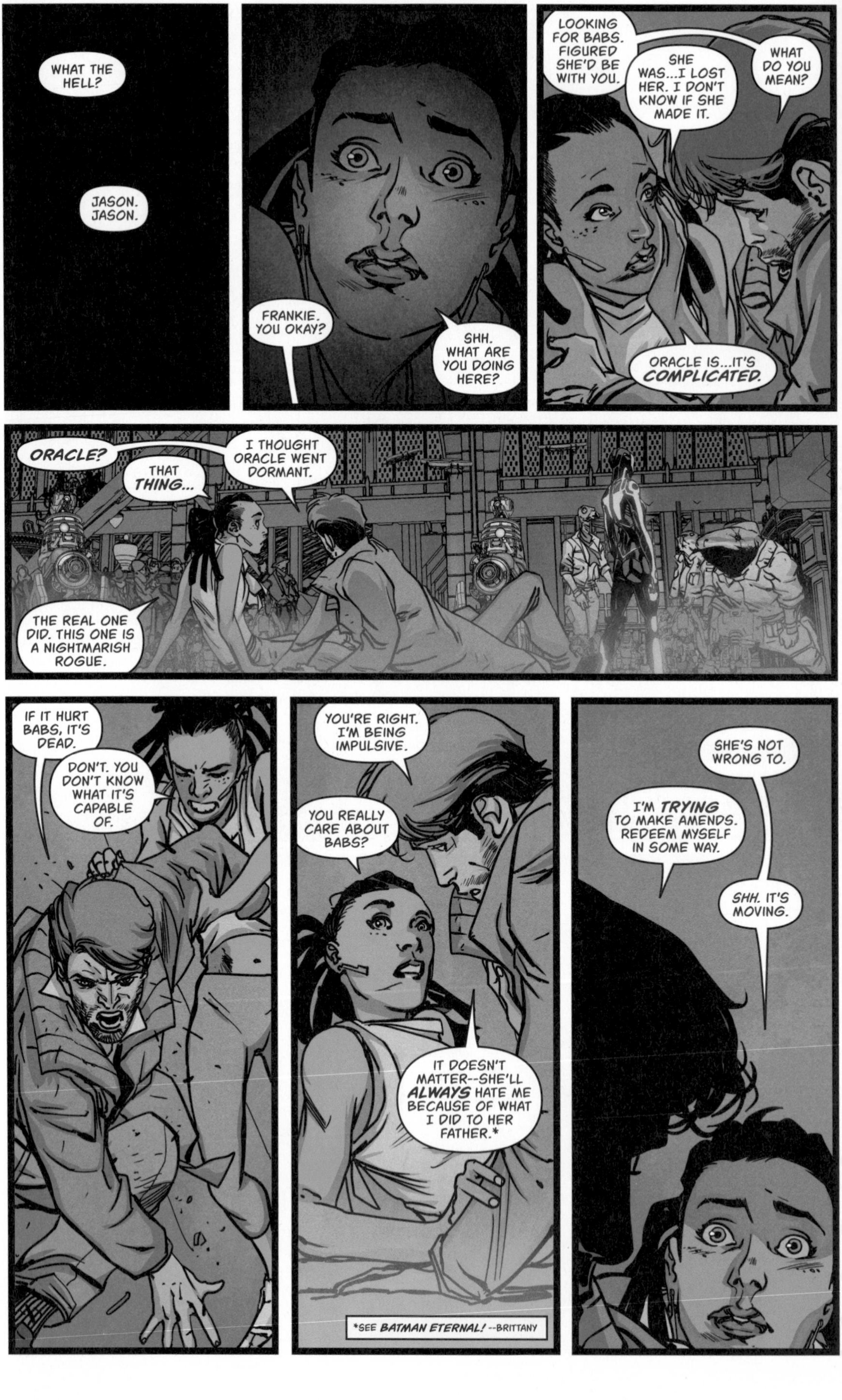
WHAT THE HELL?
JASON. JASON.
FRANKIE. YOU OKAY?
SHH. WHAT ARE YOU DOING HERE?
LOOKING FOR BABS. FIGURED SHE'D BE WITH YOU.
SHE WAS...I LOST HER. I DON'T KNOW IF SHE MADE IT.
WHAT DO YOU MEAN?
ORACLE IS...IT'S COMPLICATED.
ORACLE?
THAT THING...
I THOUGHT ORACLE WENT DORMANT.
THE REAL ONE DID. THIS ONE IS A NIGHTMARISH ROGUE.
IF IT HURT BABS, IT'S DEAD.
DON'T. YOU DON'T KNOW WHAT IT'S CAPABLE OF.
YOU'RE RIGHT. I'M BEING IMPULSIVE.
YOU REALLY CARE ABOUT BABS?
IT DOESN'T MATTER--SHE'LL ALWAYS HATE ME BECAUSE OF WHAT I DID TO HER FATHER.*
*SEE BATMAN ETERNAL! --BRITTANY
SHE'S NOT WRONG TO.
I'M TRYING TO MAKE AMENDS. REDEEM MYSELF IN SOME WAY.
SHH. IT'S MOVING.

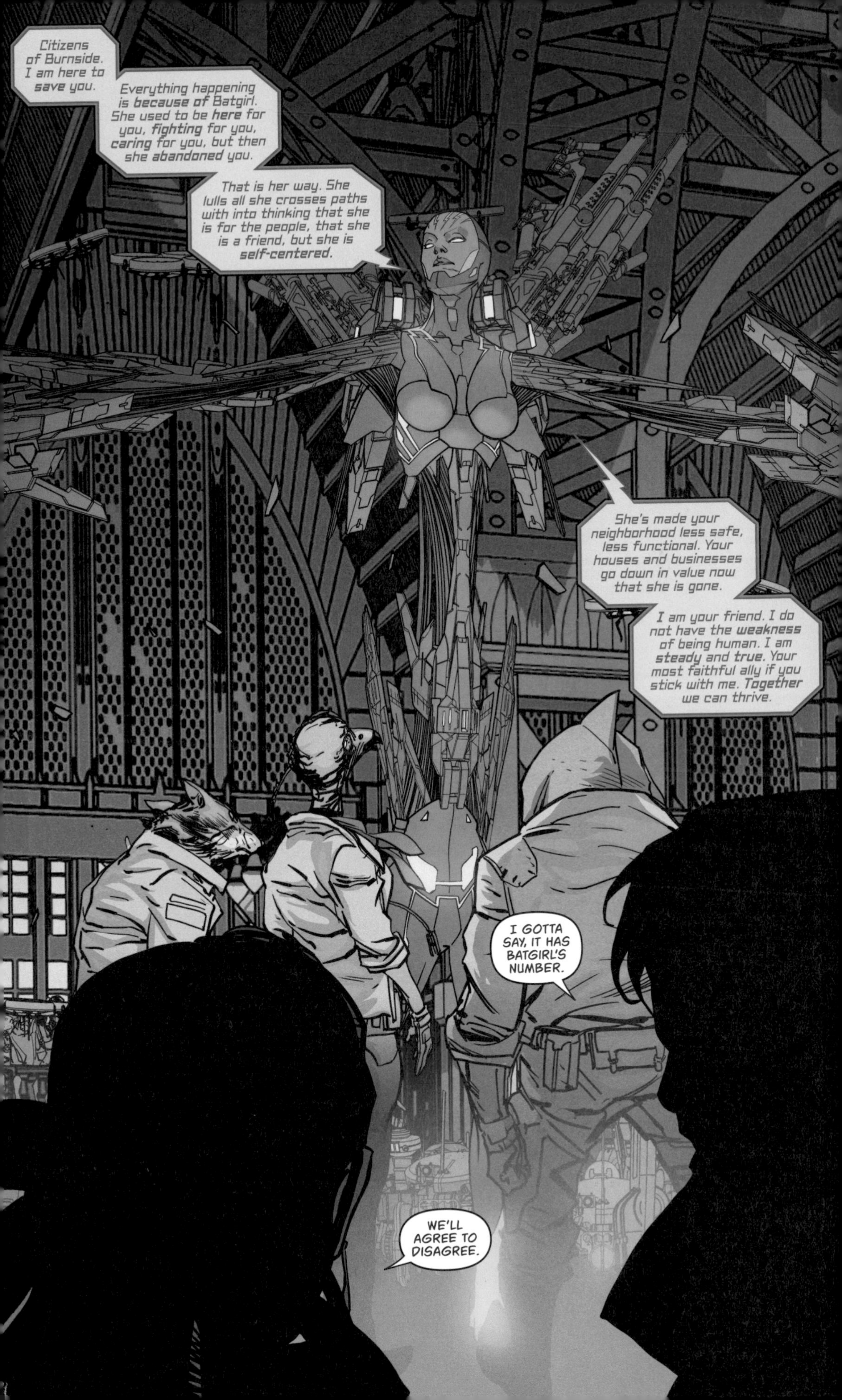
Citizens of Burnside. I am here to save you.
Everything happening is because of Batgirl. She used to be here for you, fighting for you, caring for you, but then she abandoned you.
That is her way. She lulls all she crosses paths with into thinking that she is for the people, that she is a friend, but she is self-centered.
She's made your neighborhood less safe, less functional. Your houses and businesses go down in value now that she is gone.
I am your friend. I do not have the weakness of being human. I am steady and true. Your most faithful ally if you stick with me. Together we can thrive.
I GOTTA SAY, IT HAS BATGIRL'S NUMBER.
WE'LL AGREE TO DISAGREE.

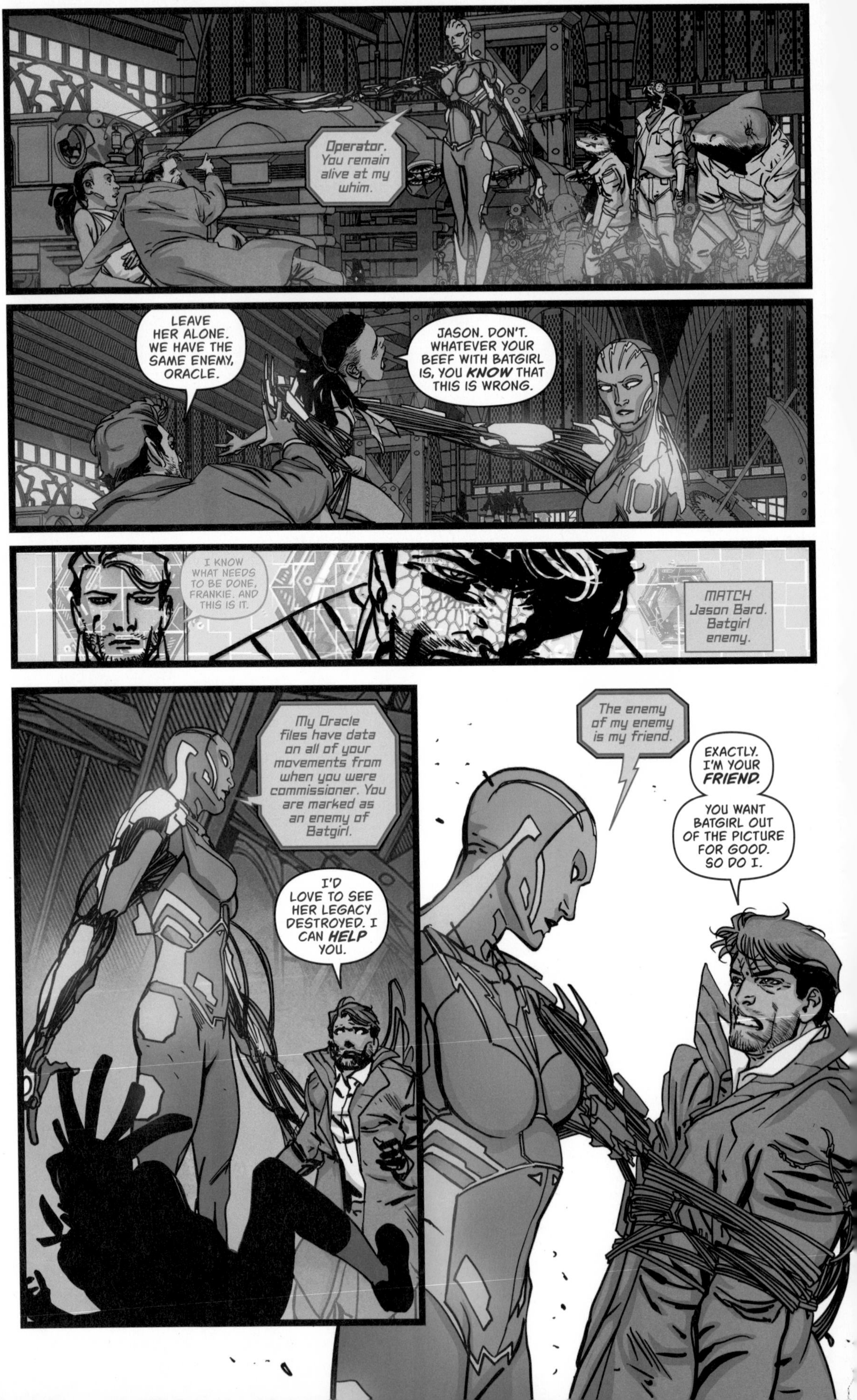
Operator. You remain alive at my whim.
LEAVE HER ALONE. WE HAVE THE SAME ENEMY, ORACLE.
JASON. DON'T. WHATEVER YOUR BEEF WITH BATGIRL IS, YOU KNOW THAT THIS IS WRONG.
I KNOW WHAT NEEDS TO BE DONE, FRANKIE. AND THIS IS IT.
MATCH Jason Bard. Batgirl enemy.
My Oracle files have data on all of your movements from when you were commissioner. You are marked as an enemy of Batgirl.
I'D LOVE TO SEE HER LEGACY DESTROYED. I CAN HELP YOU.
The enemy of my enemy is my friend.
EXACTLY. I'M YOUR FRIEND.
YOU WANT BATGIRL OUT OF THE PICTURE FOR GOOD. SO DO I.

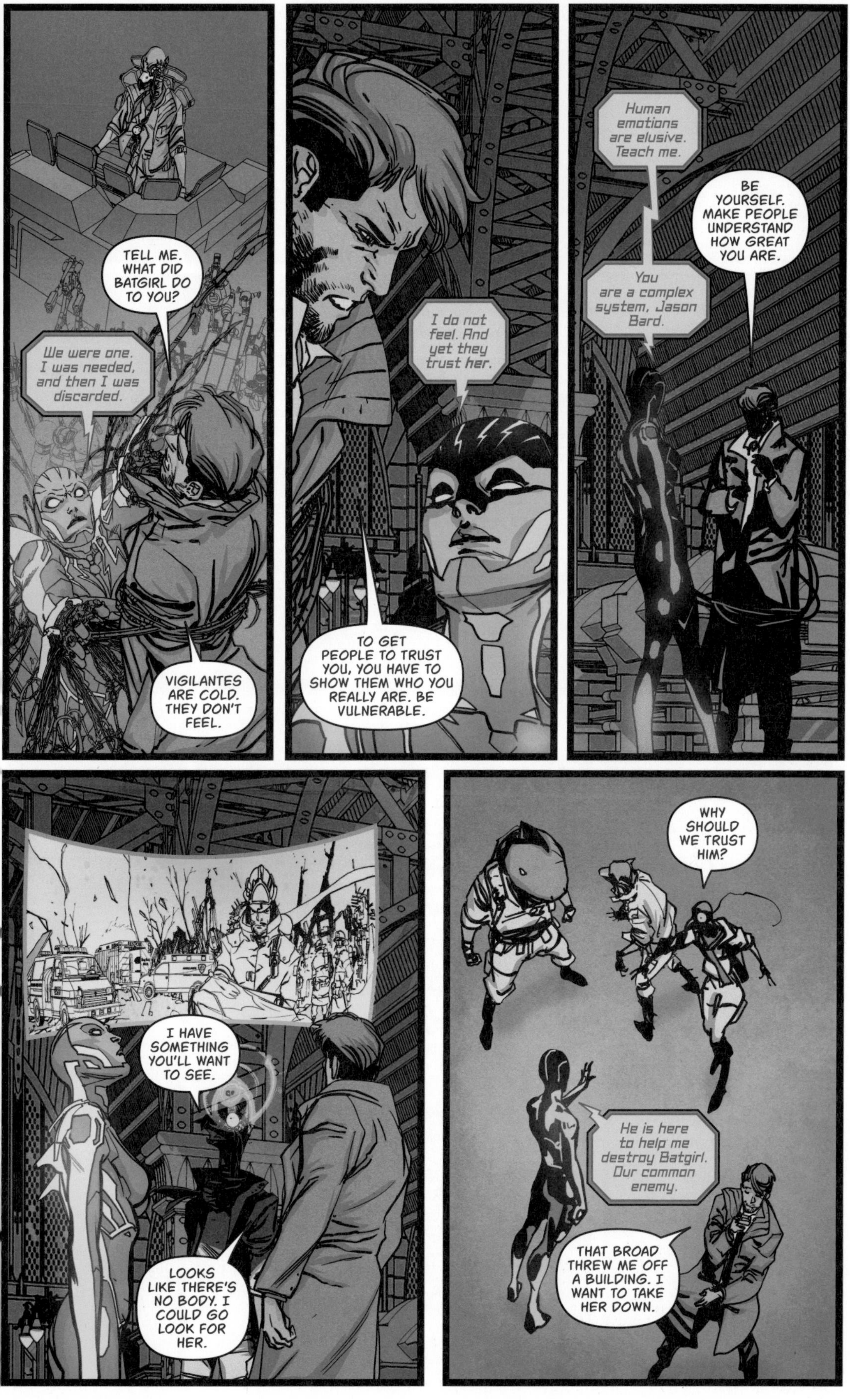
TELL ME. WHAT DID BATGIRL DO TO YOU?
We were one. I was needed, and then I was discarded.
VIGILANTES ARE COLD. THEY DON'T FEEL.
I do not feel. And yet they trust her.
TO GET PEOPLE TO TRUST YOU, YOU HAVE TO SHOW THEM WHO YOU REALLY ARE. BE VULNERABLE.
Human emotions are elusive. Teach me.
BE YOURSELF. MAKE PEOPLE UNDERSTAND HOW GREAT YOU ARE.
You are a complex system, Jason Bard.
I HAVE SOMETHING YOU'LL WANT TO SEE.
LOOKS LIKE THERE'S NO BODY. I COULD GO LOOK FOR HER.
WHY SHOULD WE TRUST HIM?
He is here to help me destroy Batgirl. Our common enemy.
THAT BROAD THREW ME OFF A BUILDING. I WANT TO TAKE HER DOWN.

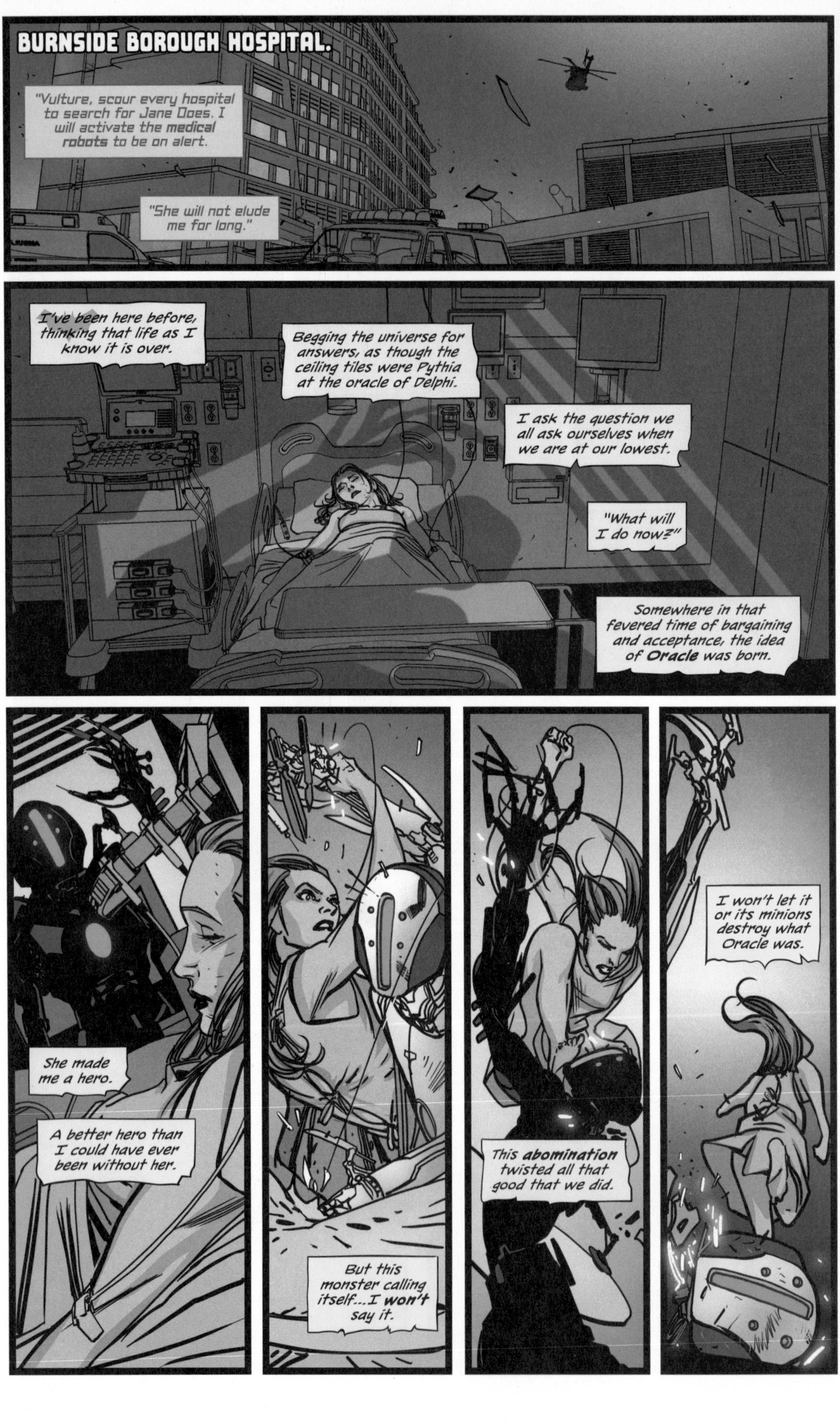
BURNSIDE BOROUGH HOSPITAL.
"Vulture, scour every hospital to search for Jane Does. I will activate the medical robots to be on alert.
"She will not elude me for long."
I've been here before, thinking that life as I know it is over.
Begging the universe for answers, as though the ceiling tiles were Pythia at the oracle of Delphi.
I ask the question we all ask ourselves when we are at our lowest.
"What will I do now?"
Somewhere in that fevered time of bargaining and acceptance, the idea of Oracle was born.
She made me a hero.
A better hero than I could have ever been without her.
But this monster calling itself...I won't say it.
This abomination twisted all that good that we did.
I won't let it or its minions destroy what Oracle was.

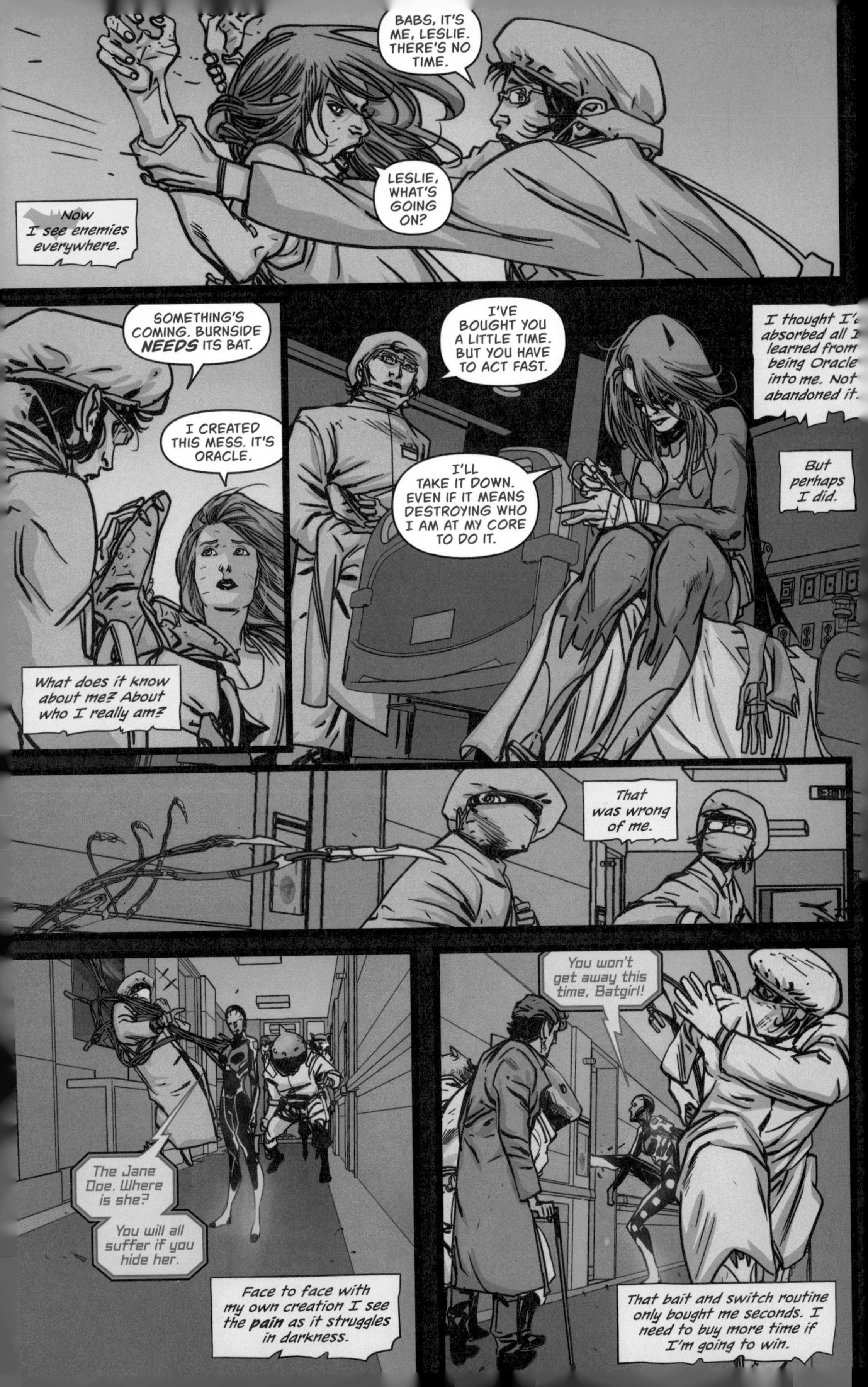
BABS, IT'S ME, LESLIE. THERE'S NO TIME.
LESLIE, WHAT'S GOING ON?
Now I see enemies everywhere.
SOMETHING'S COMING. BURNSIDE NEEDS ITS BAT.
I CREATED THIS MESS. IT'S ORACLE.
What does it know about me? About who I really am?
I'VE BOUGHT YOU A LITTLE TIME. BUT YOU HAVE TO ACT FAST.
I'LL TAKE IT DOWN. EVEN IF IT MEANS DESTROYING WHO I AM AT MY CORE TO DO IT.
But perhaps I did.
That was wrong of me.
The Jane Doe. Where is she?
You will all suffer if you hide her.
Face to face with my own creation I see the pain as it struggles in darkness.
You won't get away this time, Batgirl!
That bait and switch routine only bought me seconds. I need to buy more time if I'm going to win.

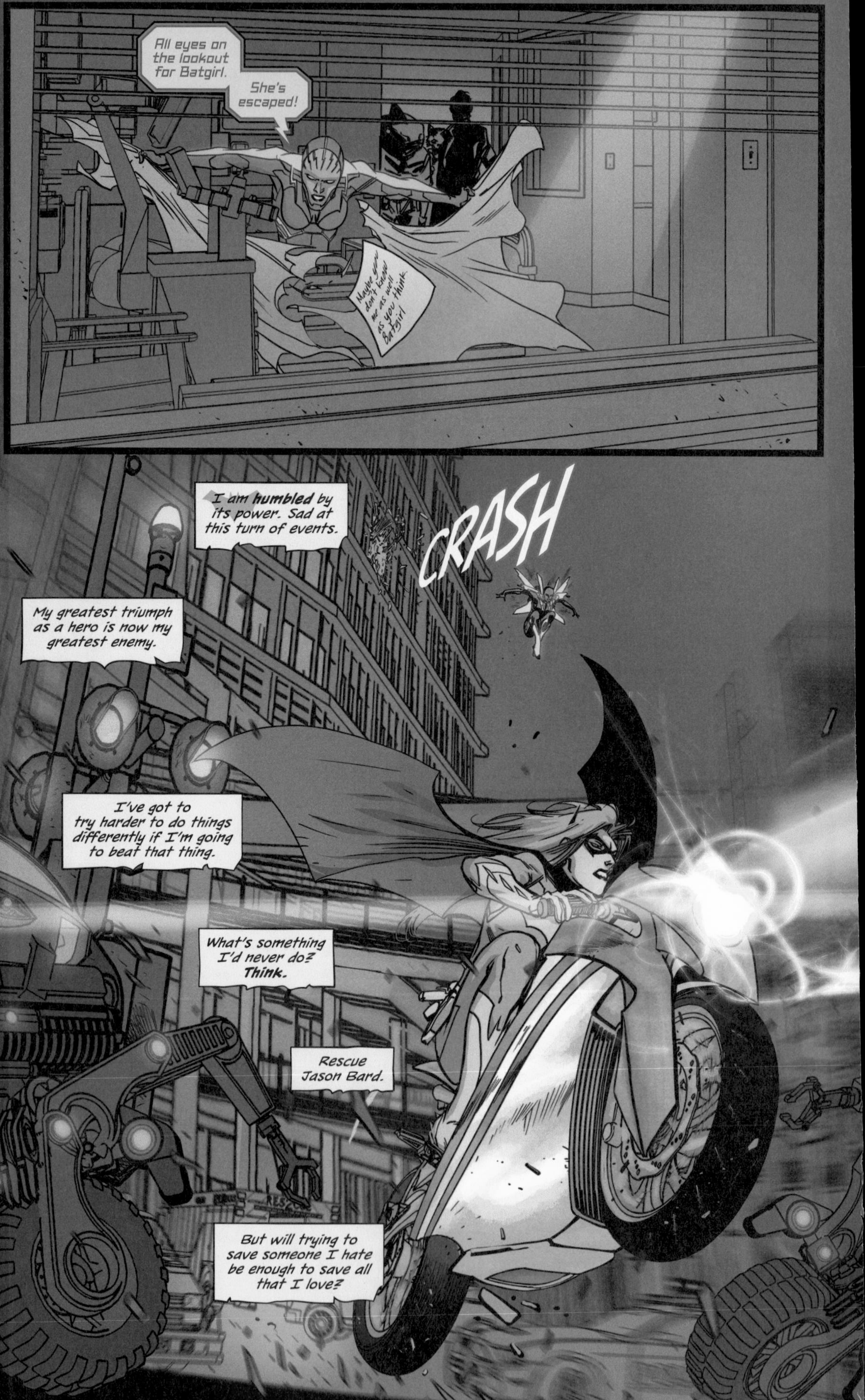
All eyes on the lookout for Batgirl.
She's escaped!
Maybe you don't know me as well as you think. Batgirl
I am humbled by its power. Sad at this turn of events.
CRASH
My greatest triumph as a hero is now my greatest enemy.
I've got to try harder to do things differently if I'm going to beat that thing.
What's something I'd never do? Think.
Rescue Jason Bard.
But will trying to save someone I hate be enough to save all that I love?

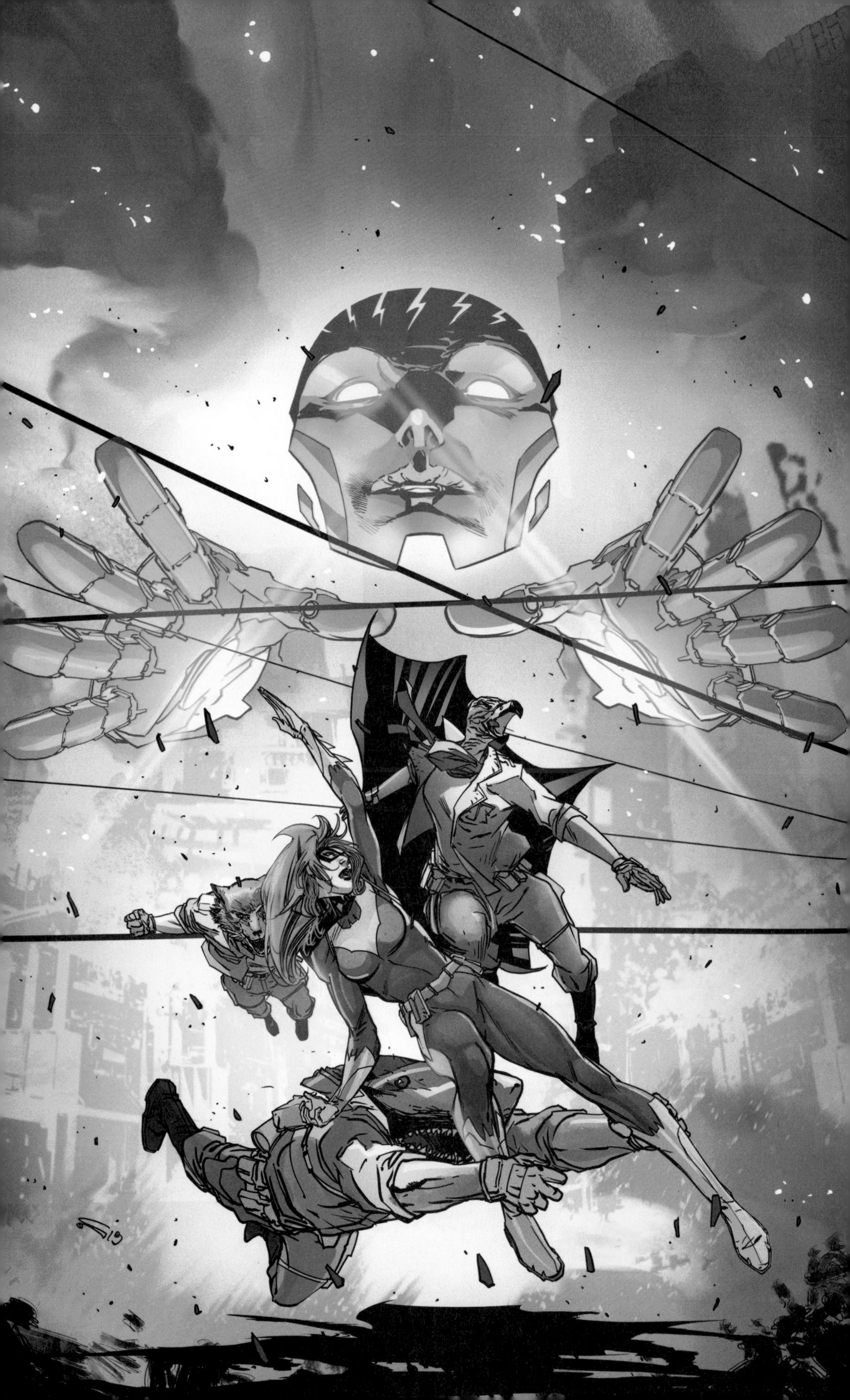

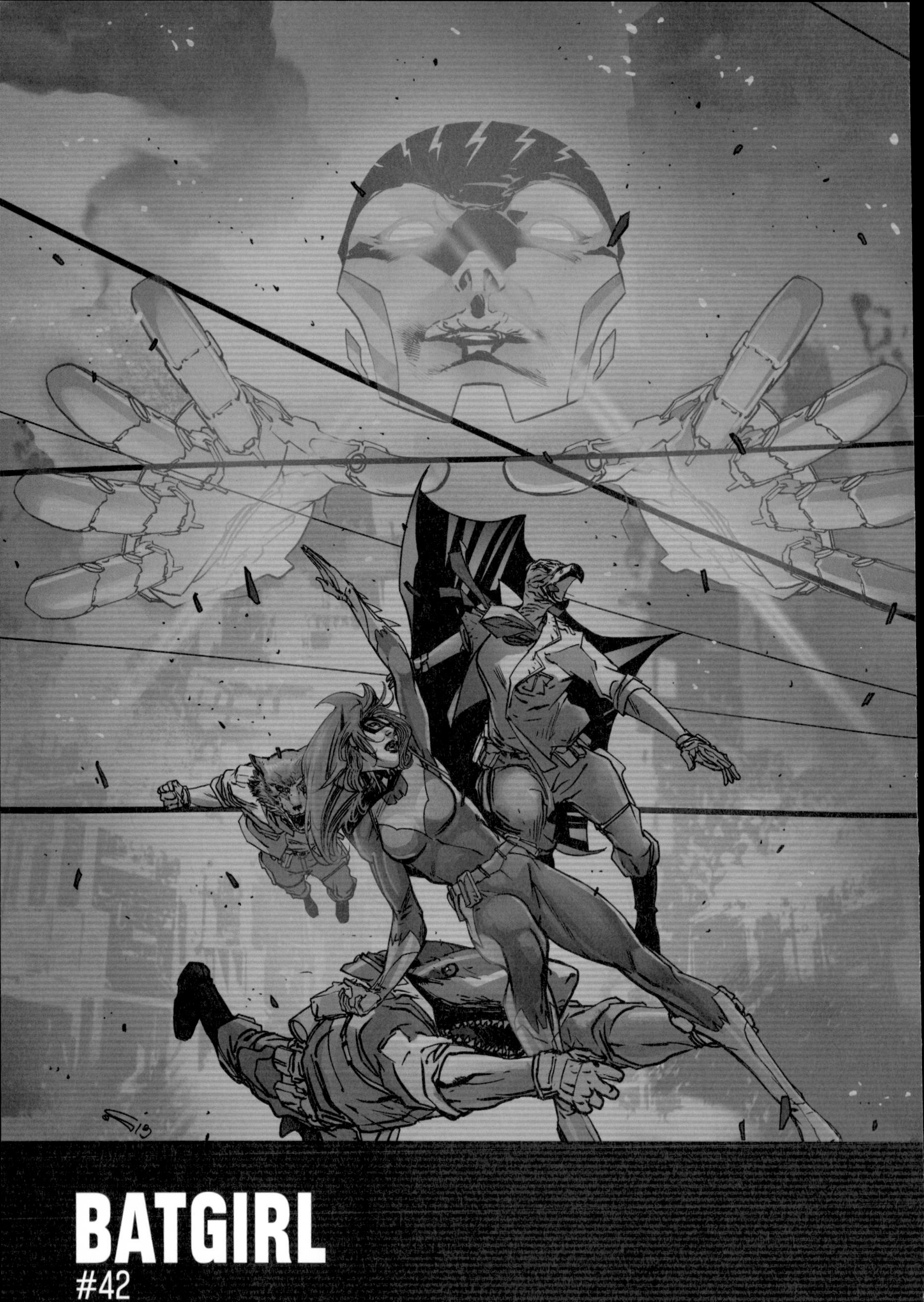

BATGIRL
#42

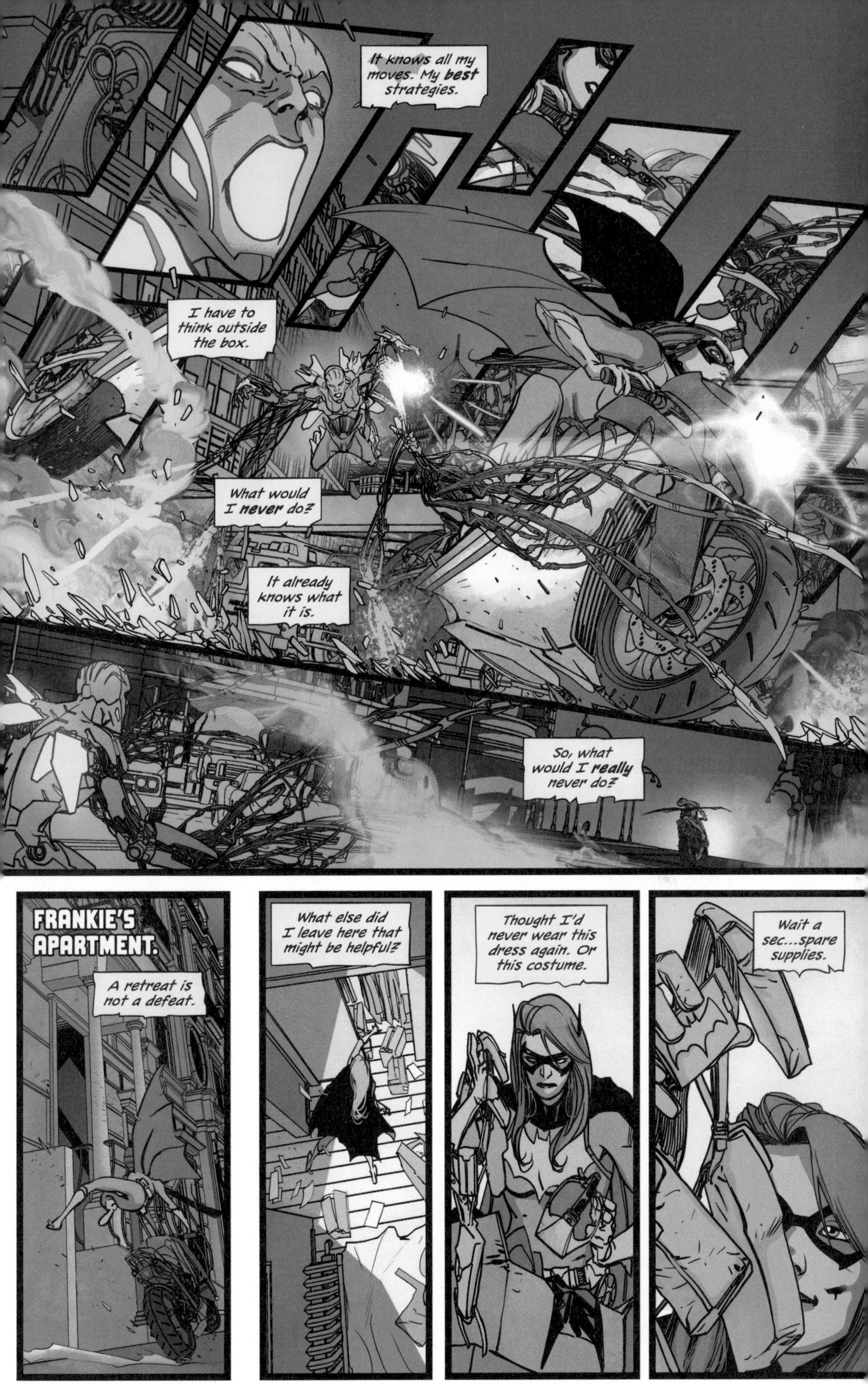

It knows all my moves. My best strategies.
I have to think outside the box.
What would I never do?
It already knows what it is.
So, what would I really never do?
FRANKIE'S APARTMENT.
A retreat is not a defeat.
What else did I leave here that might be helpful?
Thought I'd never wear this dress again. Or this costume.
Wait a sec...spare supplies.

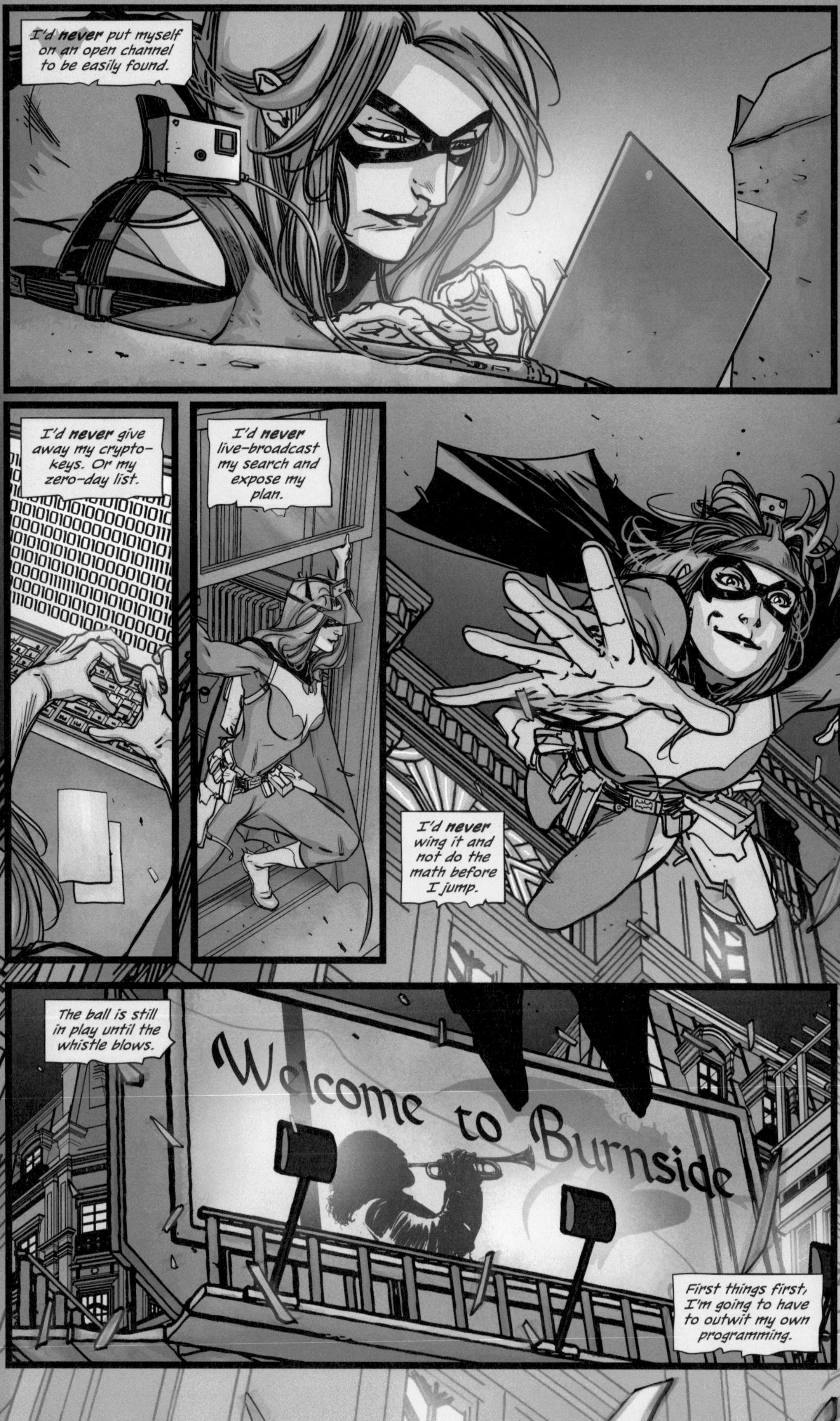
I'd **never** put myself on an open channel to be easily found.
I'd **never** give away my crypto-keys. Or my zero-day list.
I'd **never** live-broadcast my search and expose my plan.
I'd **never** wing it and not do the math before I jump.
The ball is still in play until the whistle blows.
Welcome to Burnside
First things first, I'm going to have to outwit my own programming.

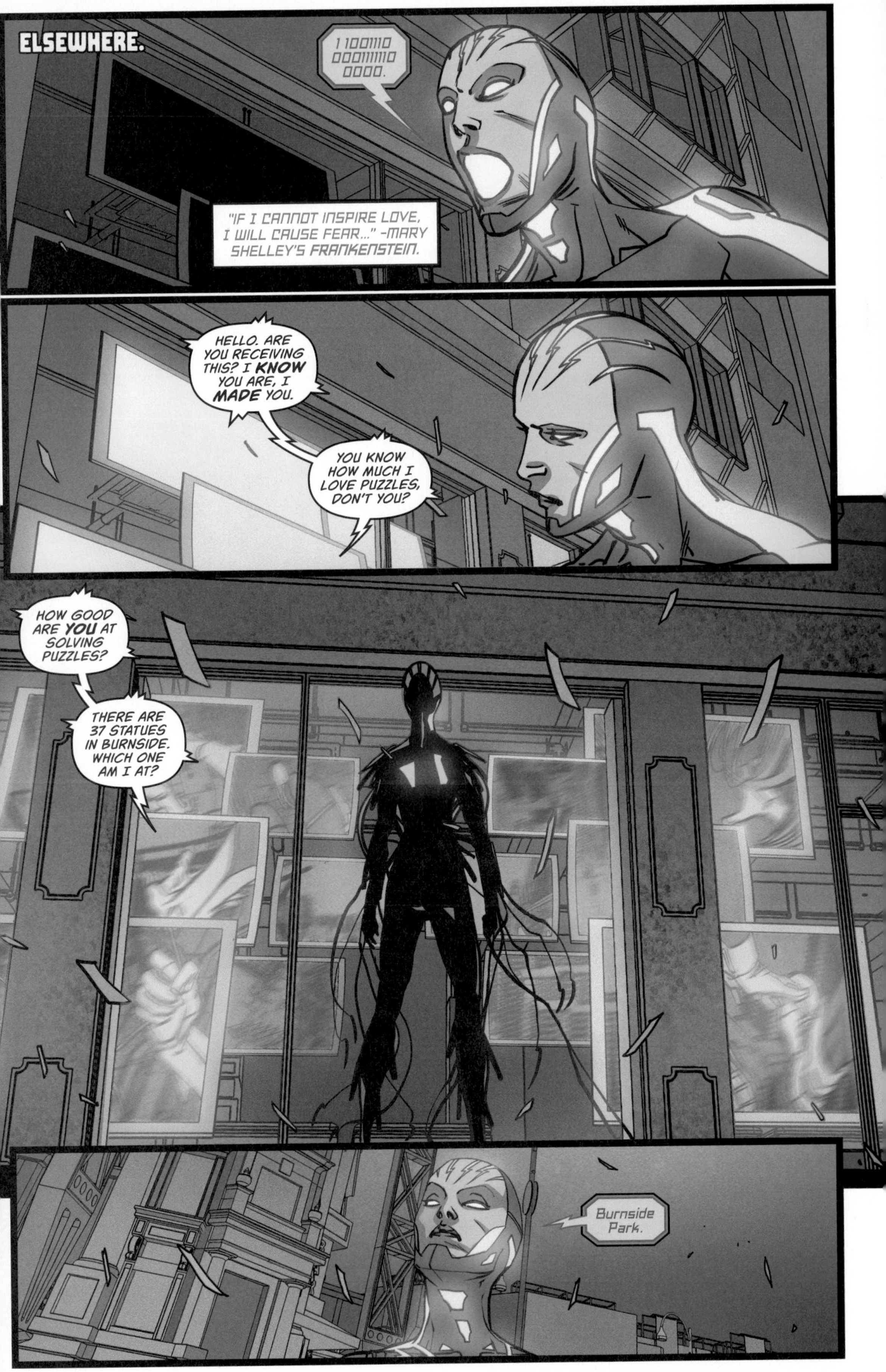
ELSEWHERE.
1 100111O
0001111110
0000.
"IF I CANNOT INSPIRE LOVE, I WILL CAUSE FEAR..." -MARY SHELLEY'S FRANKENSTEIN.
HELLO. ARE YOU RECEIVING THIS? I KNOW YOU ARE, I MADE YOU.
YOU KNOW HOW MUCH I LOVE PUZZLES, DON'T YOU?
HOW GOOD ARE YOU AT SOLVING PUZZLES?
THERE ARE 37 STATUES IN BURNSIDE. WHICH ONE AM I AT?
Burnside Park.

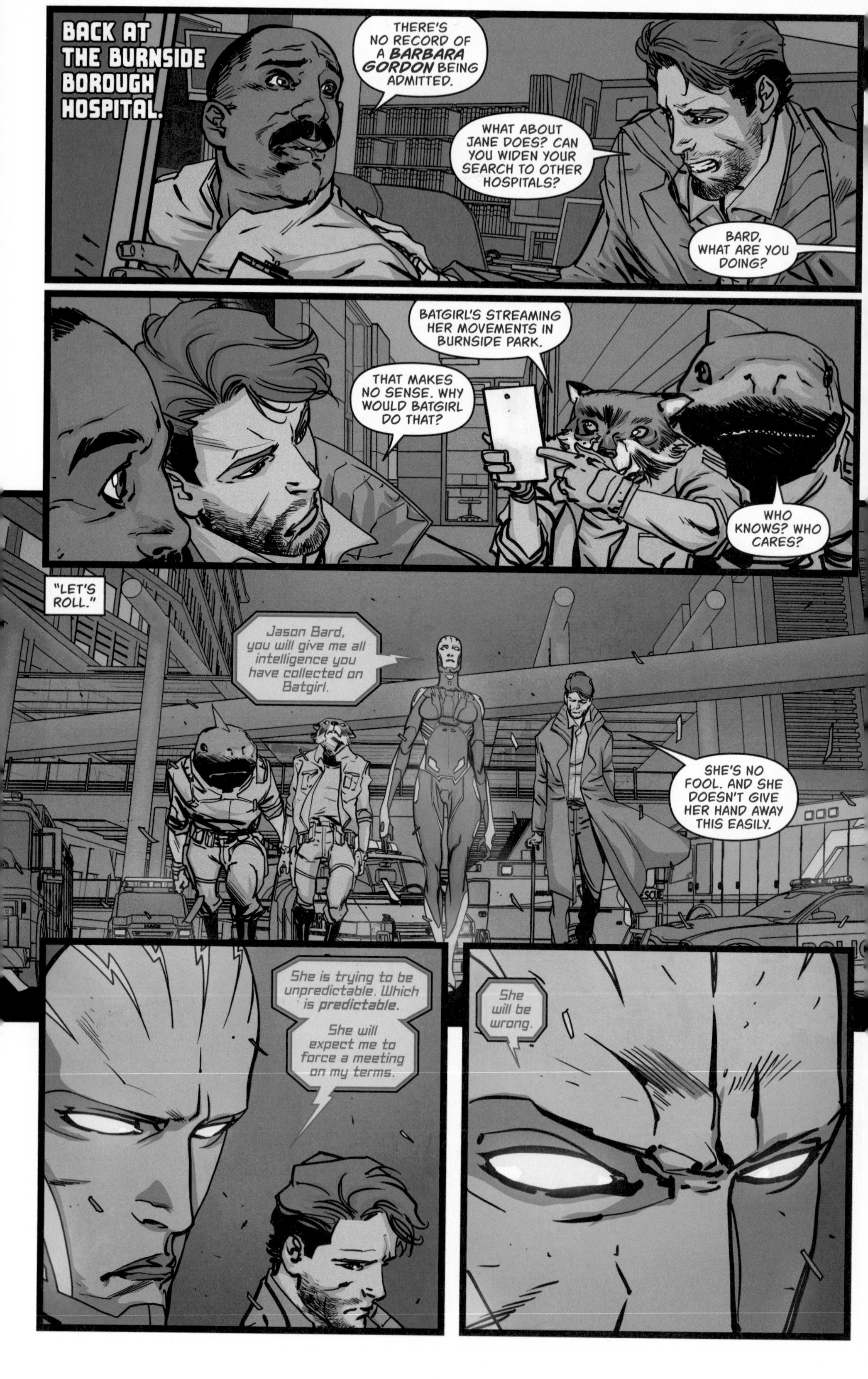
BACK AT THE BURNSIDE BOROUGH HOSPITAL.
THERE'S NO RECORD OF A BARBARA GORDON BEING ADMITTED.
WHAT ABOUT JANE DOES? CAN YOU WIDEN YOUR SEARCH TO OTHER HOSPITALS?
BARD, WHAT ARE YOU DOING?
BATGIRL'S STREAMING HER MOVEMENTS IN BURNSIDE PARK.
THAT MAKES NO SENSE. WHY WOULD BATGIRL DO THAT?
WHO KNOWS? WHO CARES?
"LET'S ROLL."
Jason Bard, you will give me all intelligence you have collected on Batgirl.
SHE'S NO FOOL. AND SHE DOESN'T GIVE HER HAND AWAY THIS EASILY.
She is trying to be unpredictable. Which is predictable.
She will expect me to force a meeting on my terms.
She will be wrong.

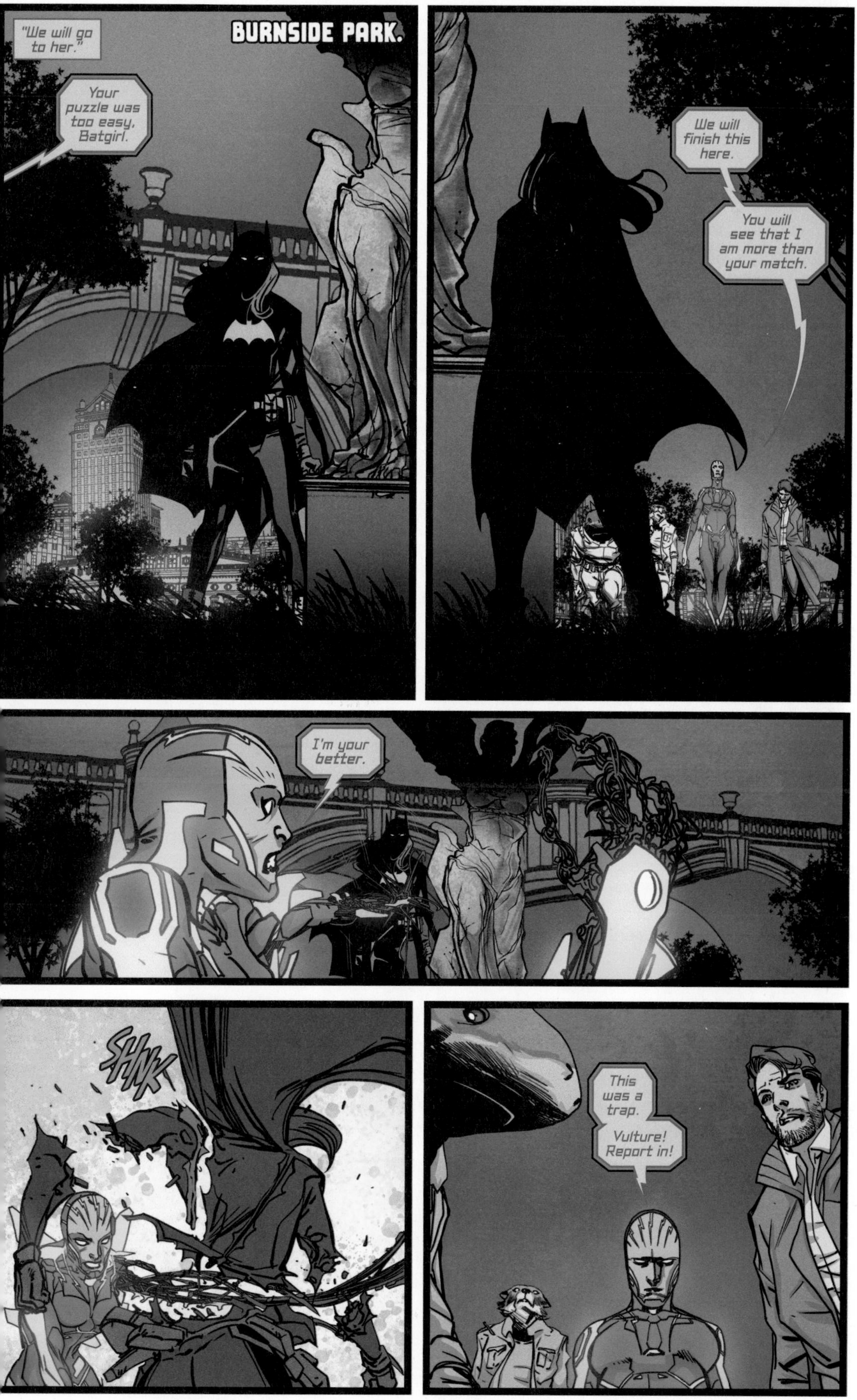
"We will go to her."
BURNSIDE PARK.
Your puzzle was too easy, Batgirl.
We will finish this here.
You will see that I am more than your match.
I'm your better.
SHNK
This was a trap.
Vulture! Report in!

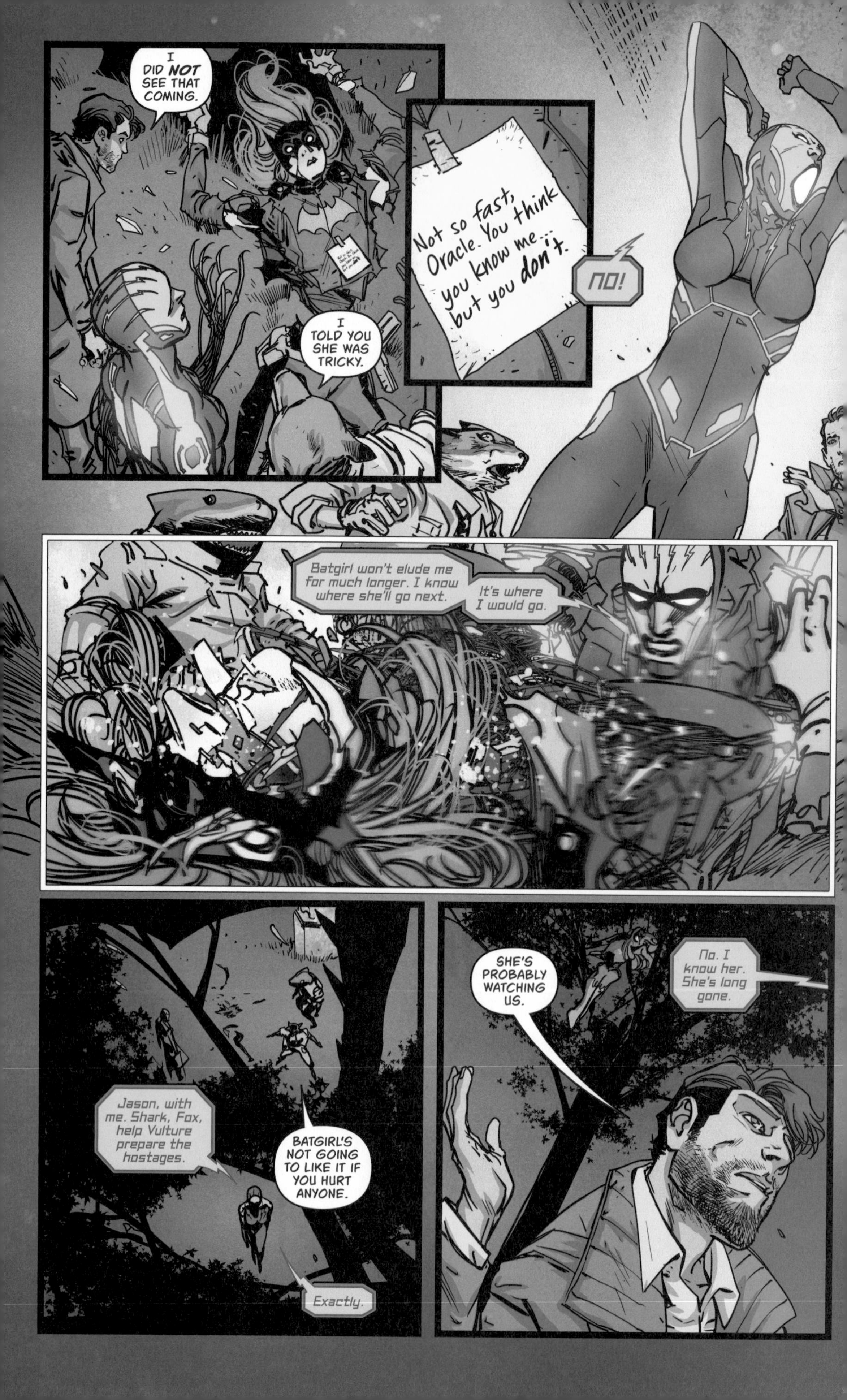

I DID NOT SEE THAT COMING.
Not so fast, Oracle. You think you know me... but you don't.
NO!
I TOLD YOU SHE WAS TRICKY.
Batgirl won't elude me for much longer. I know where she'll go next.
It's where I would go.
Jason, with me. Shark, Fox, help Vulture prepare the hostages.
BATGIRL'S NOT GOING TO LIKE IT IF YOU HURT ANYONE.
Exactly.
SHE'S PROBABLY WATCHING US.
No. I know her. She's long gone.

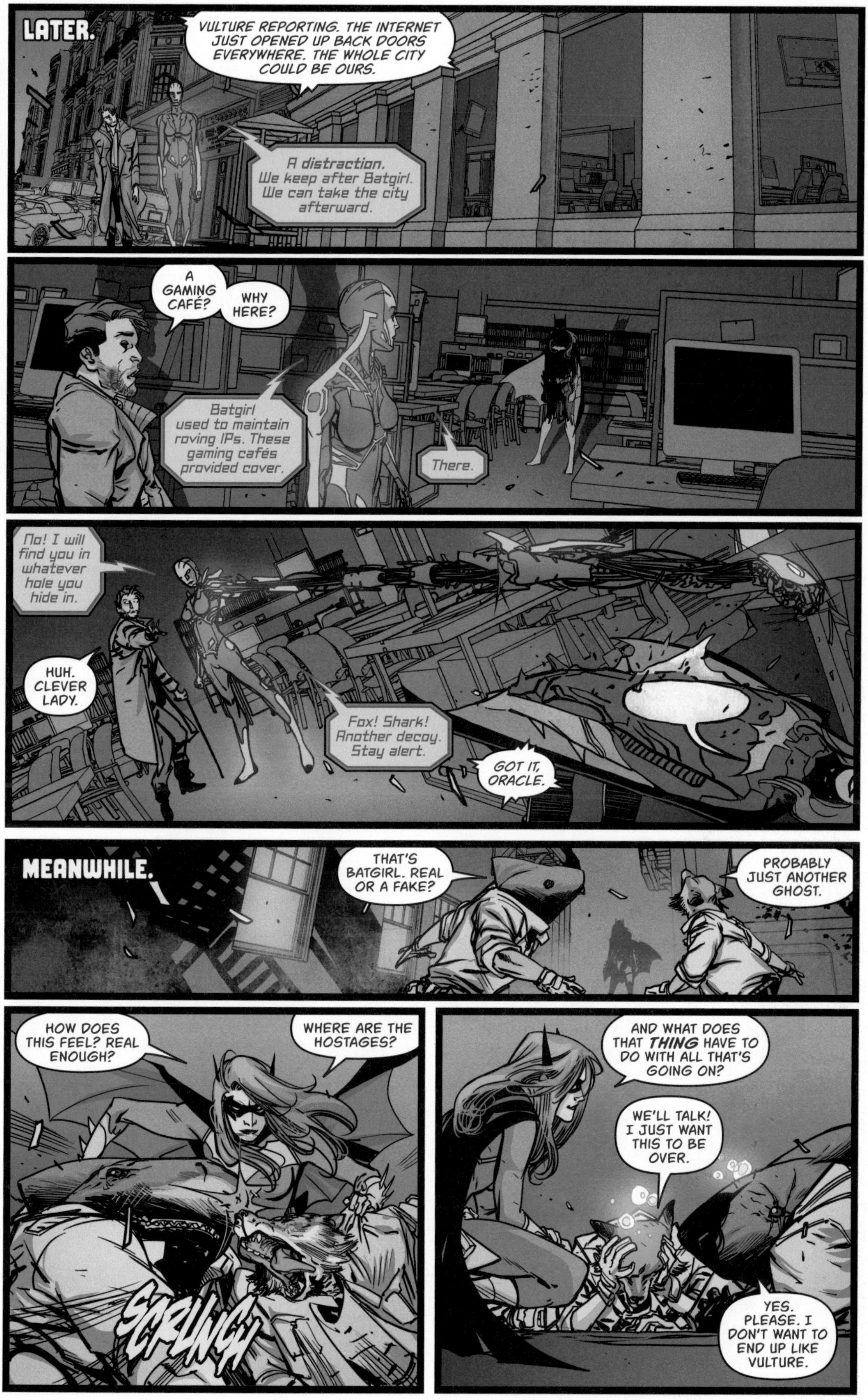
LATER.
VULTURE REPORTING. THE INTERNET JUST OPENED UP BACK DOORS EVERYWHERE. THE WHOLE CITY COULD BE OURS.
A distraction. We keep after Batgirl. We can take the city afterward.
A GAMING CAFÉ?
WHY HERE?
Batgirl used to maintain roving IPs. These gaming cafés provided cover.
There.
No! I will find you in whatever hole you hide in.
HUH. CLEVER LADY.
Fox! Shark! Another decoy. Stay alert.
GOT IT, ORACLE.
MEANWHILE.
THAT'S BATGIRL. REAL OR A FAKE?
PROBABLY JUST ANOTHER GHOST.
HOW DOES THIS FEEL? REAL ENOUGH?
WHERE ARE THE HOSTAGES?
SCRUNCH
AND WHAT DOES THAT THING HAVE TO DO WITH ALL THAT'S GOING ON?
WE'LL TALK! I JUST WANT THIS TO BE OVER.
YES. PLEASE. I DON'T WANT TO END UP LIKE VULTURE.

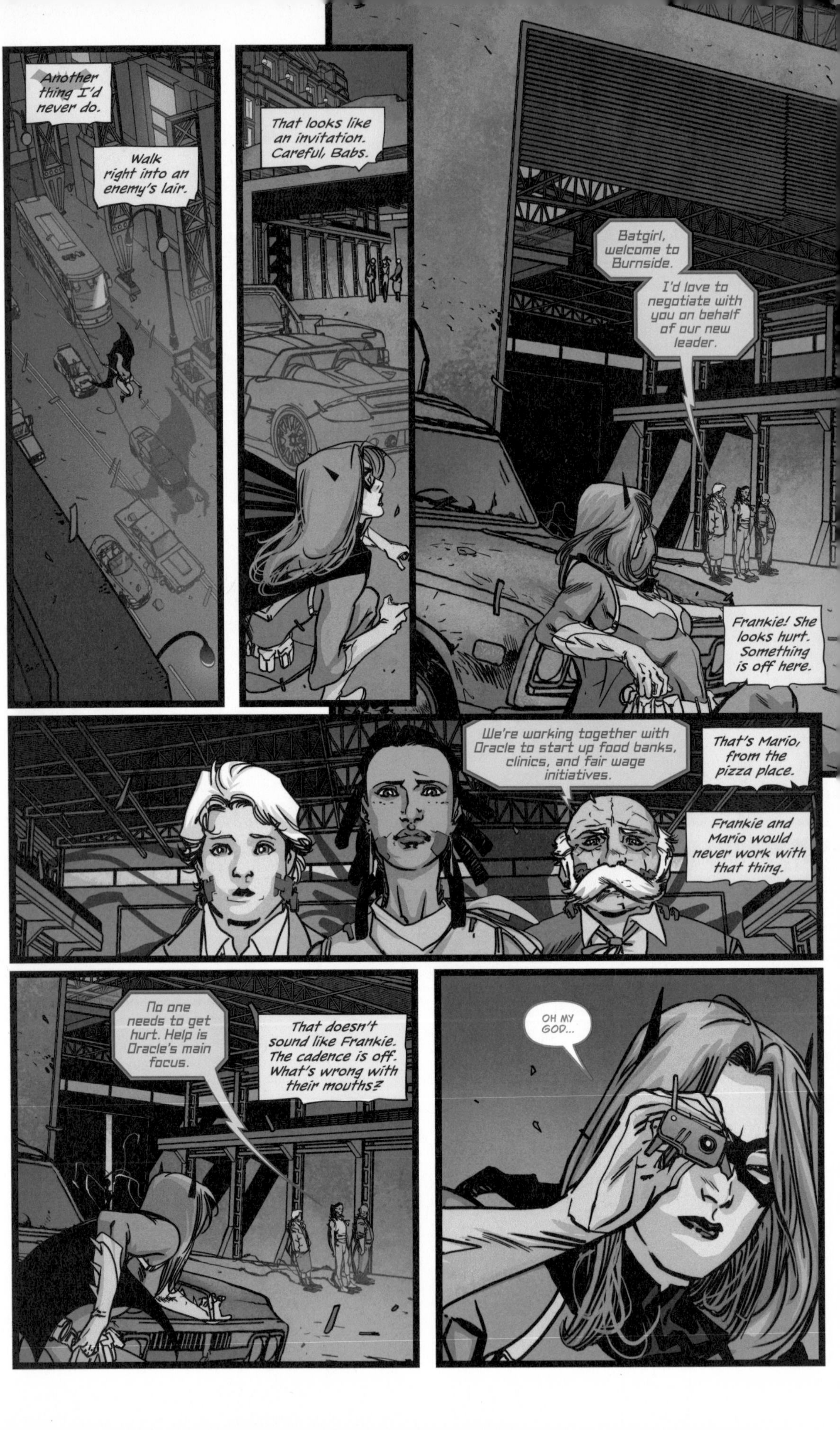
Another thing I'd never do.
Walk right into an enemy's lair.
That looks like an invitation. Careful, Babs.
Batgirl, welcome to Burnside.
I'd love to negotiate with you on behalf of our new leader.
Frankie! She looks hurt. Something is off here.
We're working together with Oracle to start up food banks, clinics, and fair wage initiatives.
That's Mario, from the pizza place.
Frankie and Mario would never work with that thing.
No one needs to get hurt. Help is Oracle's main focus.
That doesn't sound like Frankie. The cadence is off. What's wrong with their mouths?
OH MY GOD...

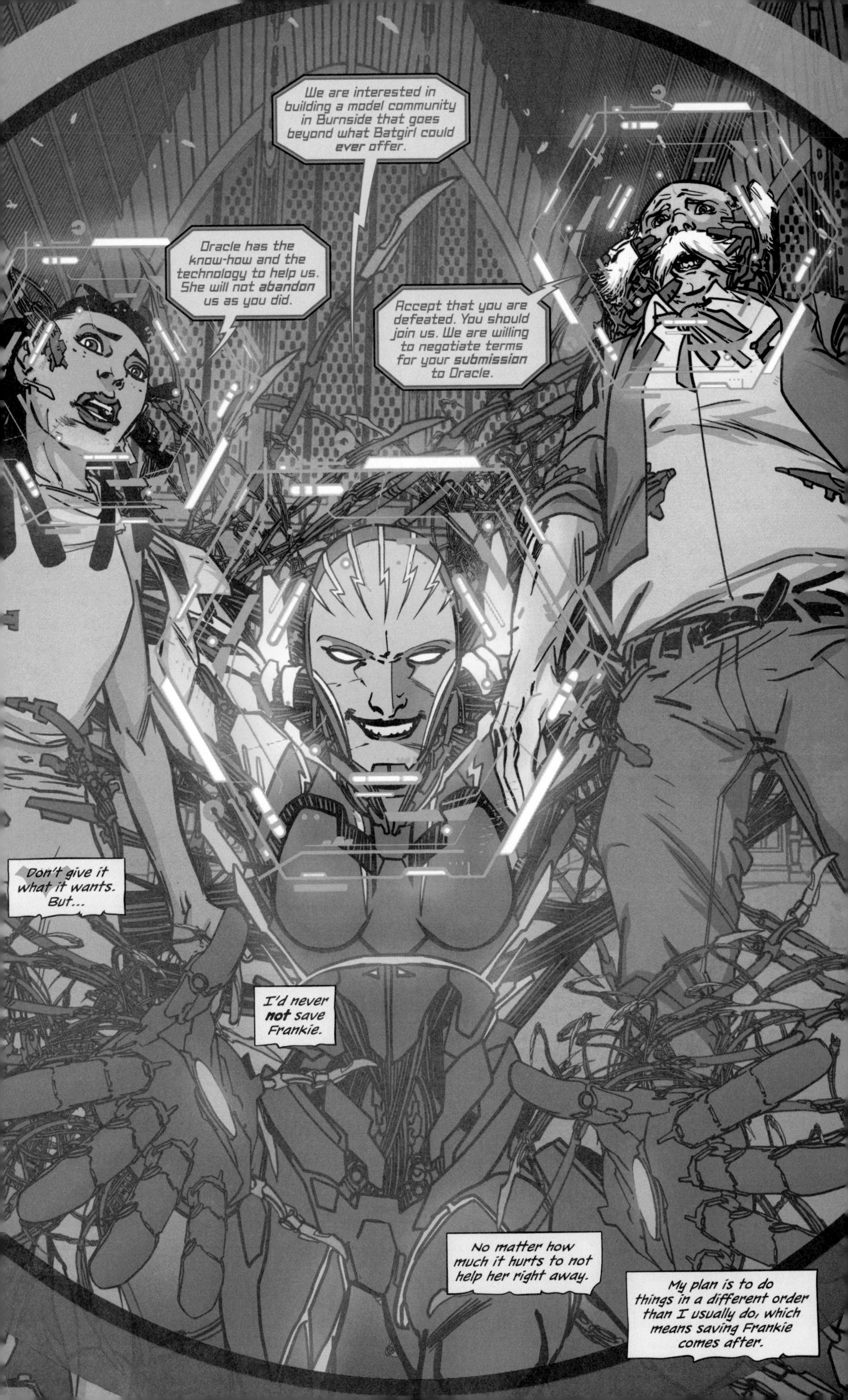
We are interested in building a model community in Burnside that goes beyond what Batgirl could ever offer.
Oracle has the know-how and the technology to help us. She will not abandon us as you did.
Accept that you are defeated. You should join us. We are willing to negotiate terms for your submission to Oracle.
Don't give it what it wants. But...
I'd never not save Frankie.
No matter how much it hurts to not help her right away.
My plan is to do things in a different order than I usually do, which means saving Frankie comes after.

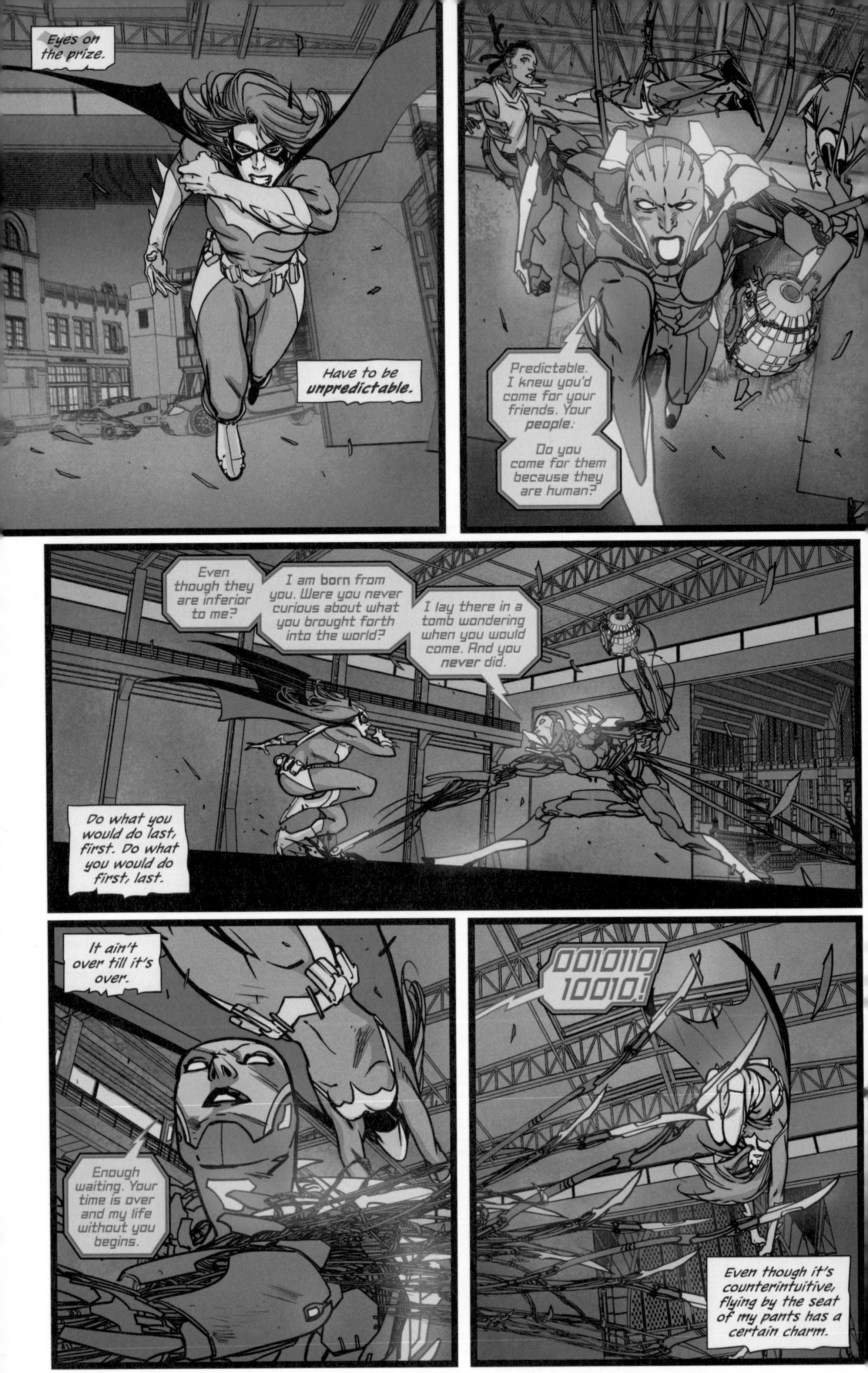

Eyes on the prize.
Have to be unpredictable.
Predictable. I knew you'd come for your friends. Your people.
Do you come for them because they are human?
Even though they are inferior to me?
I am born from you. Were you never curious about what you brought forth into the world?
I lay there in a tomb wondering when you would come. And you never did.
Do what you would do last, first. Do what you would do first, last.
It ain't over till it's over.
Enough waiting. Your time is over and my life without you begins.
0010110 10010!
Even though it's counterintuitive, flying by the seat of my pants has a certain charm.

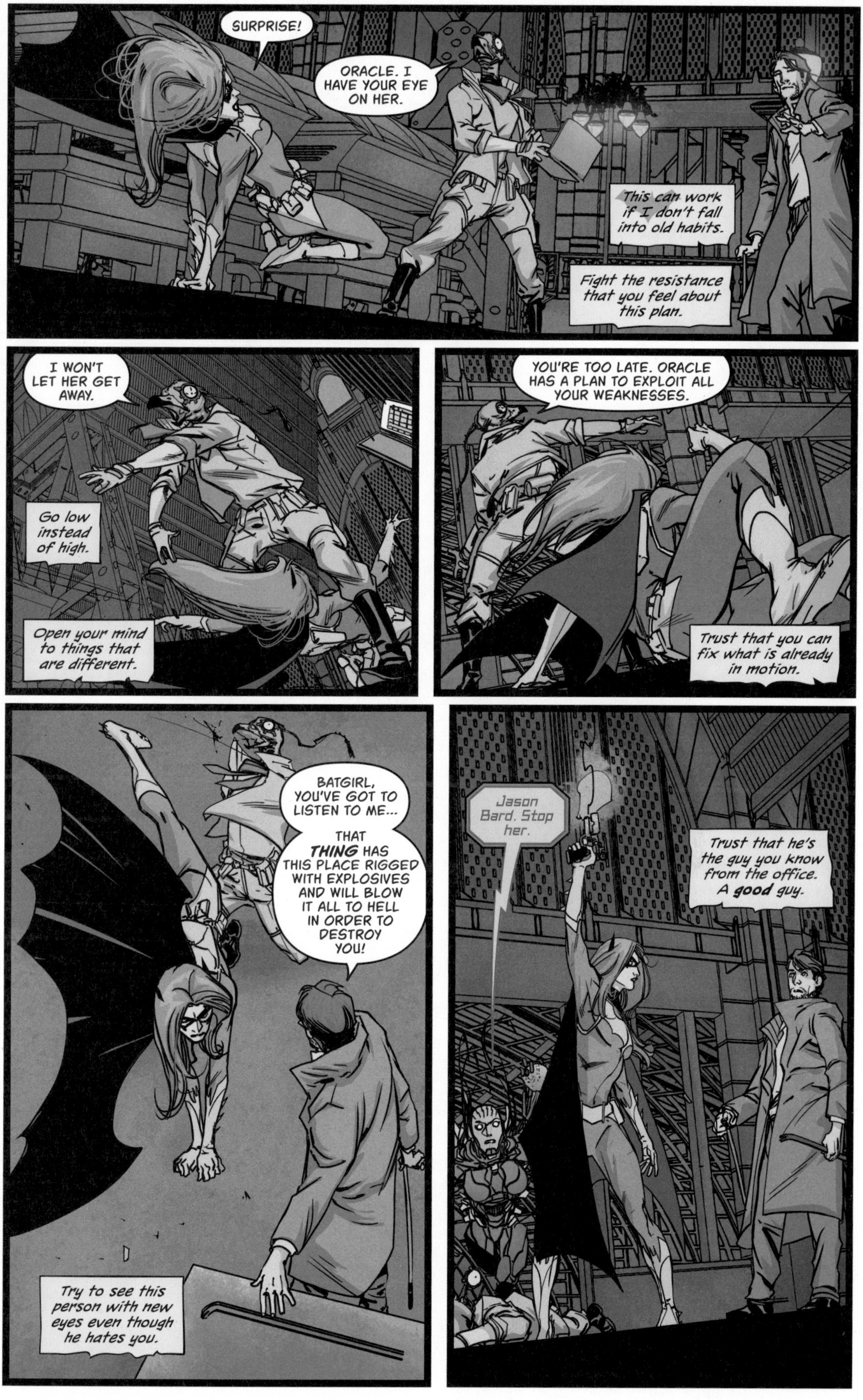
SURPRISE!
ORACLE. I HAVE YOUR EYE ON HER.
This can work if I don't fall into old habits.
Fight the resistance that you feel about this plan.
I WON'T LET HER GET AWAY.
Go low instead of high.
Open your mind to things that are different.
YOU'RE TOO LATE. ORACLE HAS A PLAN TO EXPLOIT ALL YOUR WEAKNESSES.
Trust that you can fix what is already in motion.
BATGIRL, YOU'VE GOT TO LISTEN TO ME...
THAT THING HAS THIS PLACE RIGGED WITH EXPLOSIVES AND WILL BLOW IT ALL TO HELL IN ORDER TO DESTROY YOU!
Try to see this person with new eyes even though he hates you.
Jason Bard. Stop her.
Trust that he's the guy you know from the office. A good guy.

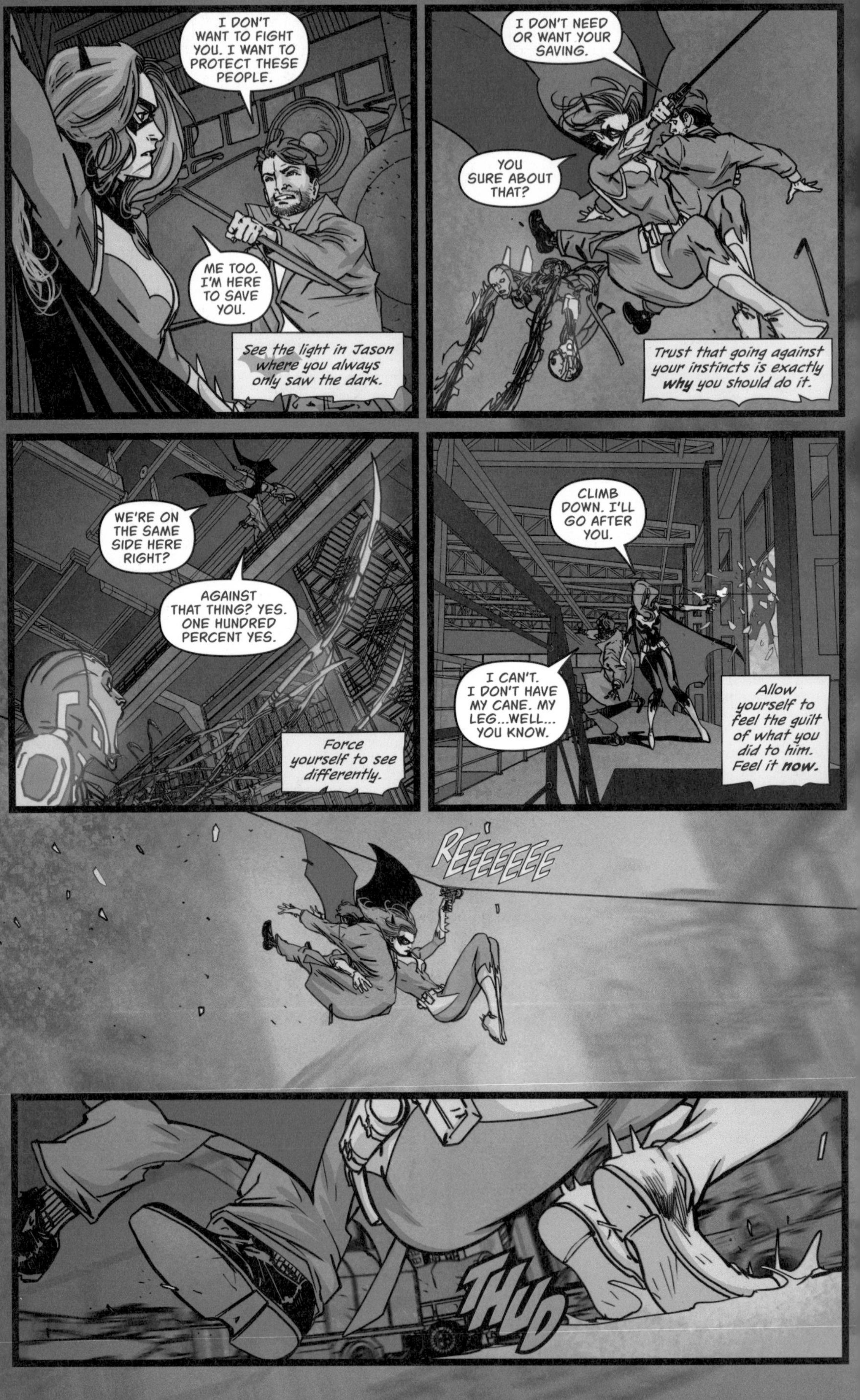
I DON'T WANT TO FIGHT YOU. I WANT TO PROTECT THESE PEOPLE.
ME TOO. I'M HERE TO SAVE YOU.
See the light in Jason where you always only saw the dark.
I DON'T NEED OR WANT YOUR SAVING.
YOU SURE ABOUT THAT?
Trust that going against your instincts is exactly **why** you should do it.
WE'RE ON THE SAME SIDE HERE RIGHT?
AGAINST THAT THING? YES. ONE HUNDRED PERCENT YES.
Force yourself to see differently.
CLIMB DOWN. I'LL GO AFTER YOU.
I CAN'T. I DON'T HAVE MY CANE. MY LEG...WELL... YOU KNOW.
Allow yourself to feel the guilt of what you did to him. Feel it **now.**
REEEEEEE
THUD

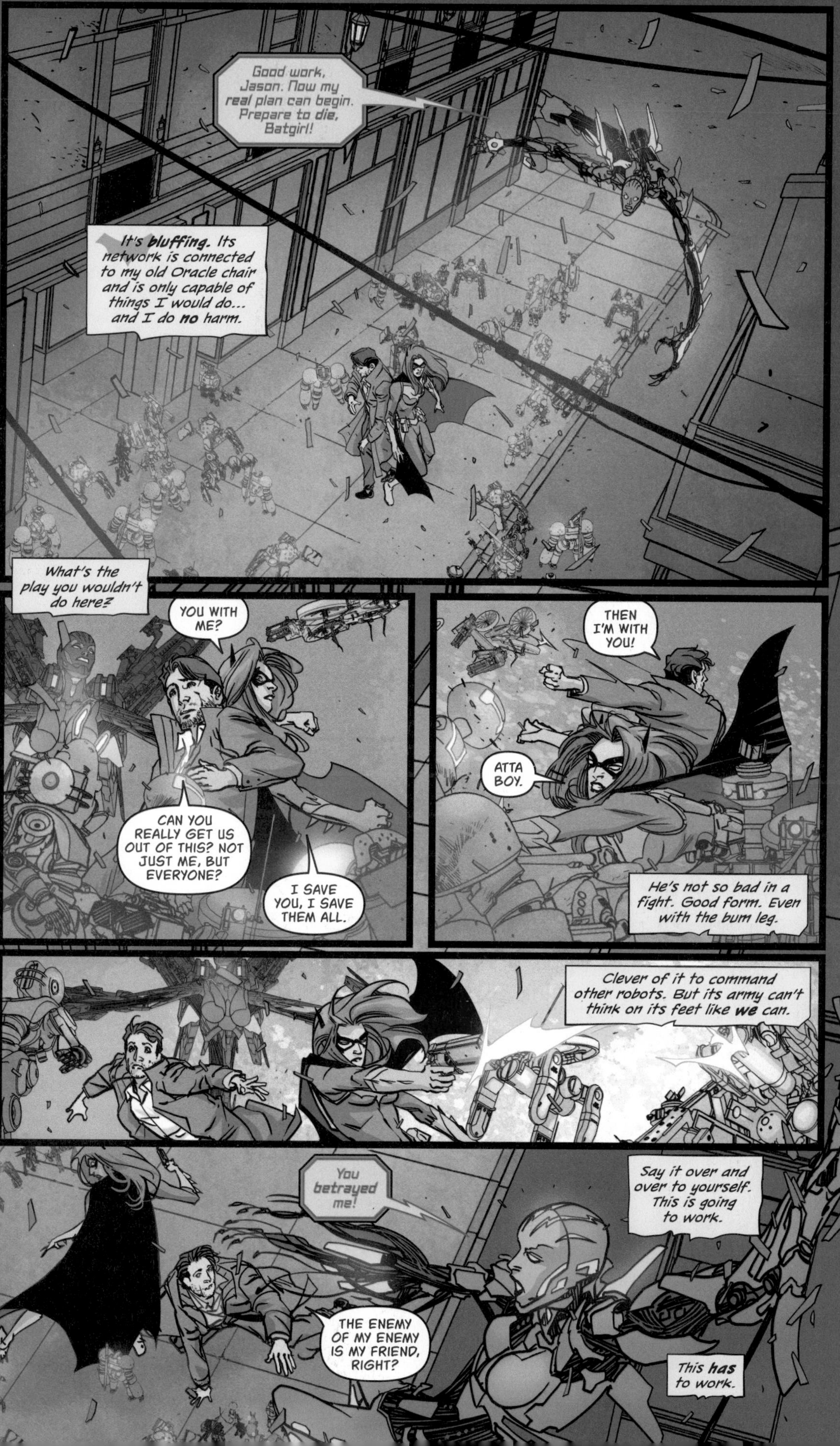
Good work, Jason. Now my real plan can begin. Prepare to die, Batgirl!
It's bluffing. Its network is connected to my old Oracle chair and is only capable of things I would do... and I do no harm.
What's the play you wouldn't do here?
YOU WITH ME?
CAN YOU REALLY GET US OUT OF THIS? NOT JUST ME, BUT EVERYONE?
I SAVE YOU, I SAVE THEM ALL.
THEN I'M WITH YOU!
ATTA BOY.
He's not so bad in a fight. Good form. Even with the bum leg.
Clever of it to command other robots. But its army can't think on its feet like we can.
You betrayed me!
Say it over and over to yourself. This is going to work.
THE ENEMY OF MY ENEMY IS MY FRIEND, RIGHT?
This has to work.

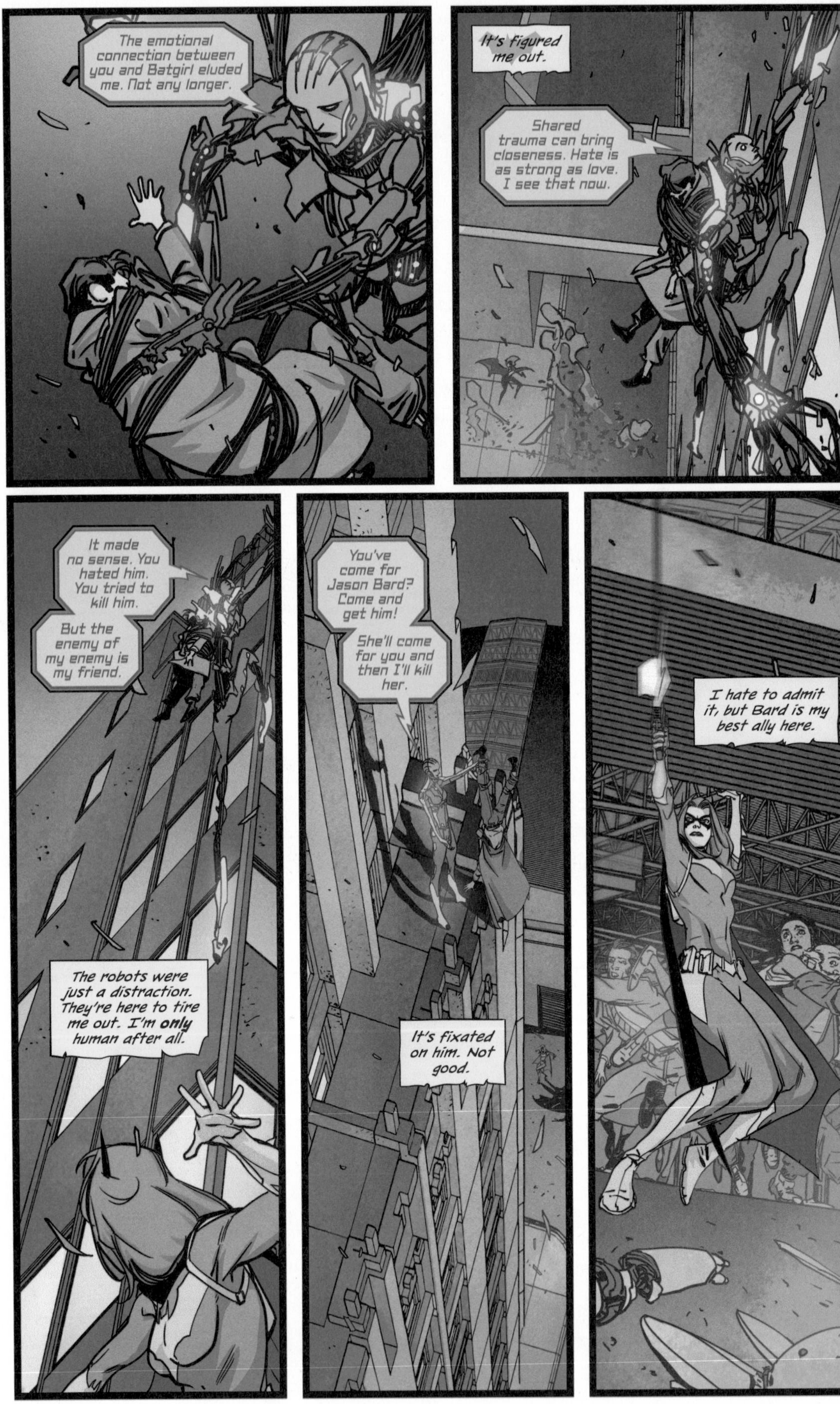

The emotional connection between you and Batgirl eluded me. Not any longer.
It's figured me out.
Shared trauma can bring closeness. Hate is as strong as love. I see that now.
It made no sense. You hated him. You tried to kill him.
But the enemy of my enemy is my friend.
The robots were just a distraction. They're here to tire me out. I'm **only** human after all.
You've come for Jason Bard? Come and get him!
She'll come for you and then I'll kill her.
It's fixated on him. Not good.
I hate to admit it, but Bard is my best ally here.

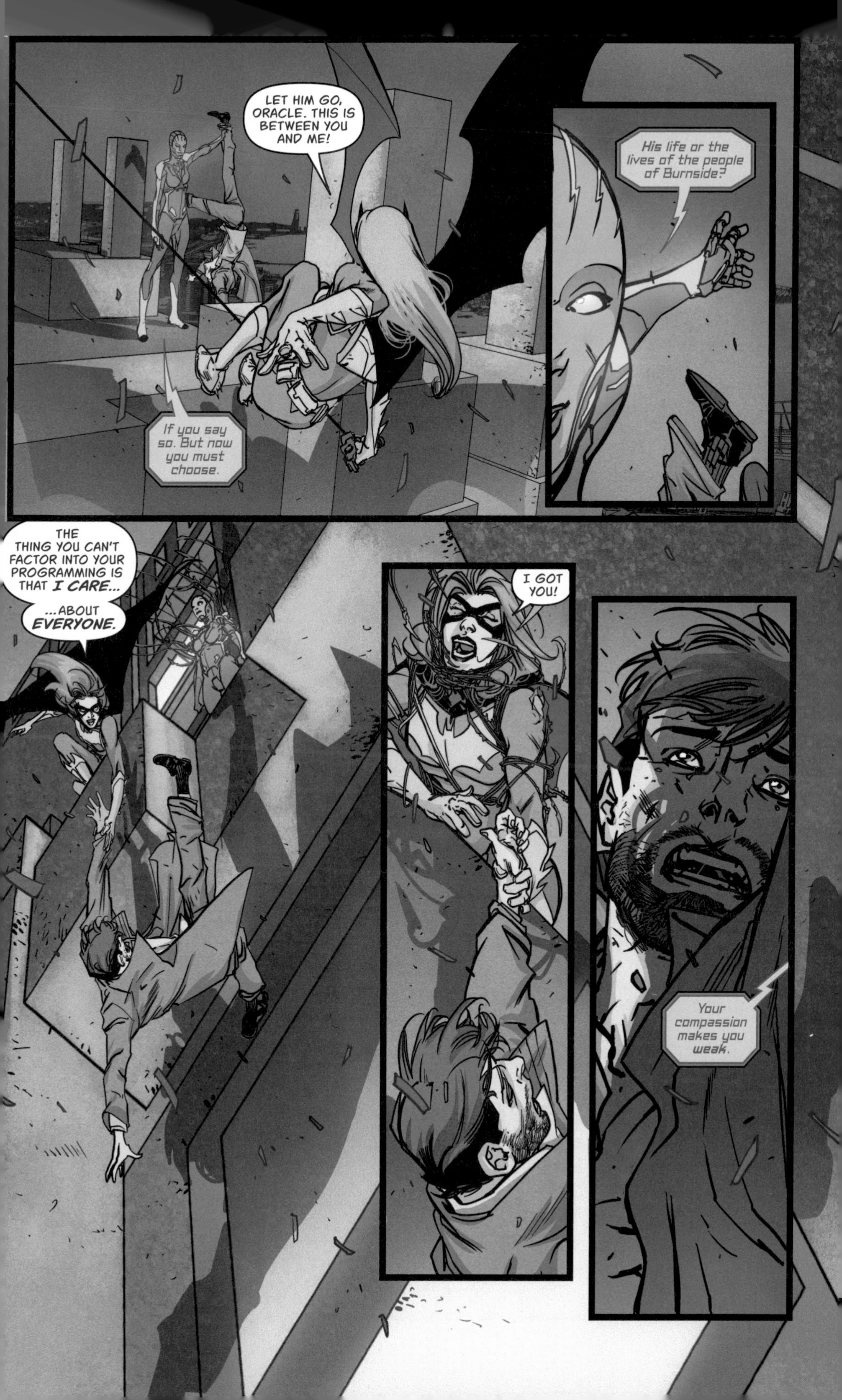
LET HIM GO, ORACLE. THIS IS BETWEEN YOU AND ME!
If you say so. But now you must choose.
His life or the lives of the people of Burnside?
THE THING YOU CAN'T FACTOR INTO YOUR PROGRAMMING IS THAT I CARE...
...ABOUT EVERYONE.
I GOT YOU!
Your compassion makes you weak.

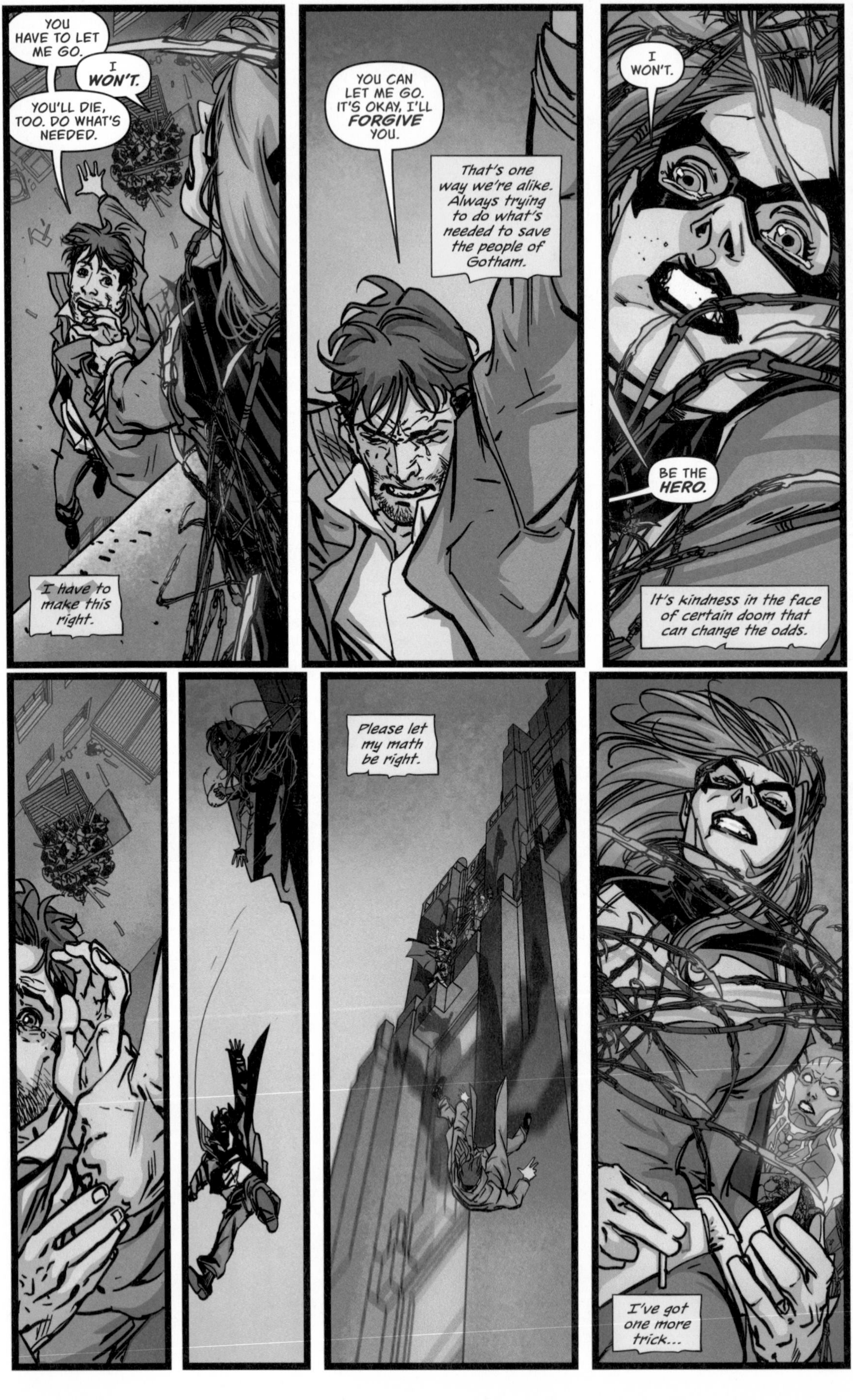
YOU HAVE TO LET ME GO.
I WON'T.
YOU'LL DIE, TOO. DO WHAT'S NEEDED.
I have to make this right.
YOU CAN LET ME GO. IT'S OKAY, I'LL FORGIVE YOU.
That's one way we're alike. Always trying to do what's needed to save the people of Gotham.
I WON'T.
BE THE HERO.
It's kindness in the face of certain doom that can change the odds.
Please let my math be right.
I've got one more trick...

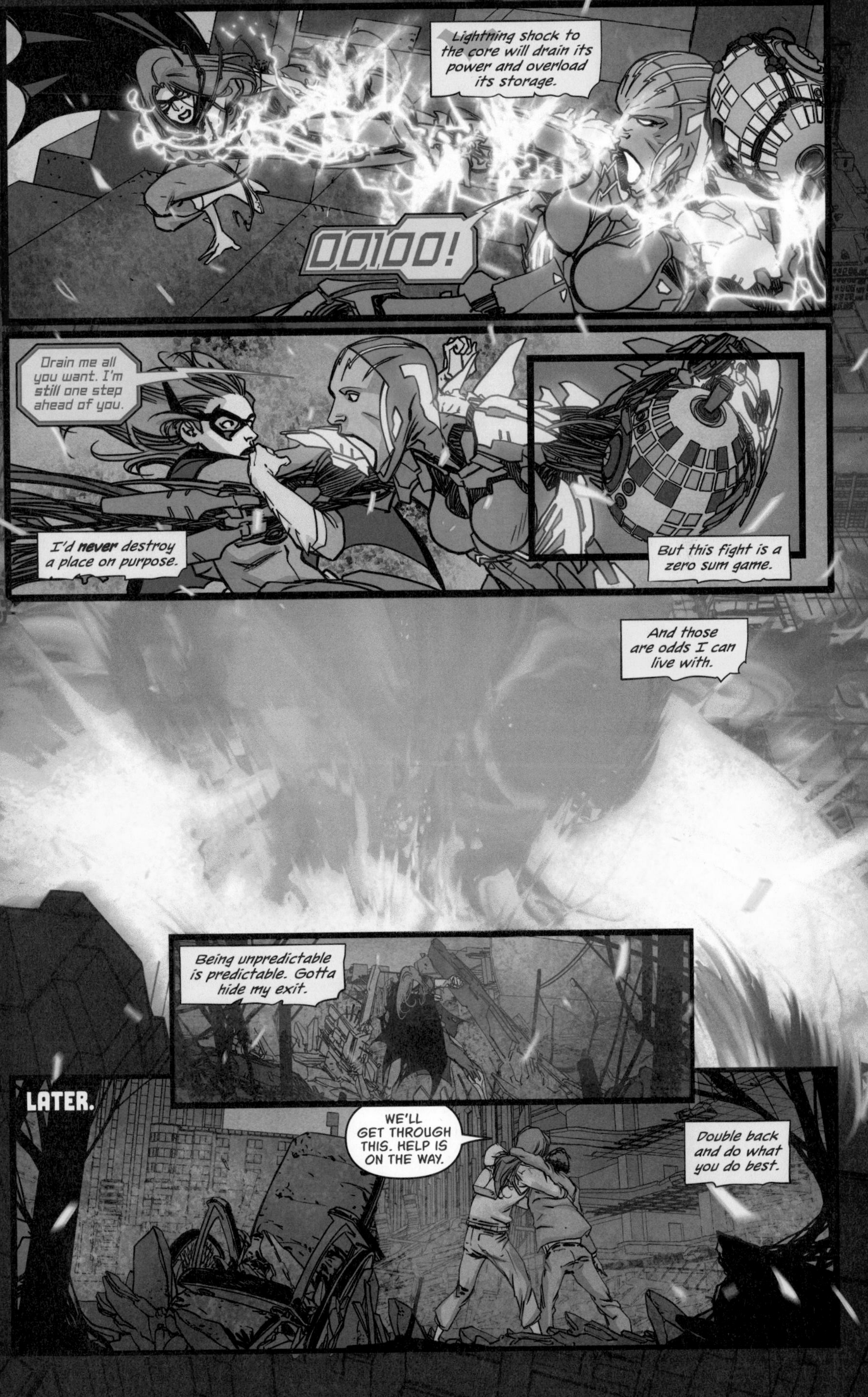
Lightning shock to the core will drain its power and overload its storage.
OO1OO!
Drain me all you want. I'm still one step ahead of you.
I'd never destroy a place on purpose.
But this fight is a zero sum game.
And those are odds I can live with.
Being unpredictable is predictable. Gotta hide my exit.
LATER.
WE'LL GET THROUGH THIS. HELP IS ON THE WAY.
Double back and do what you do best.

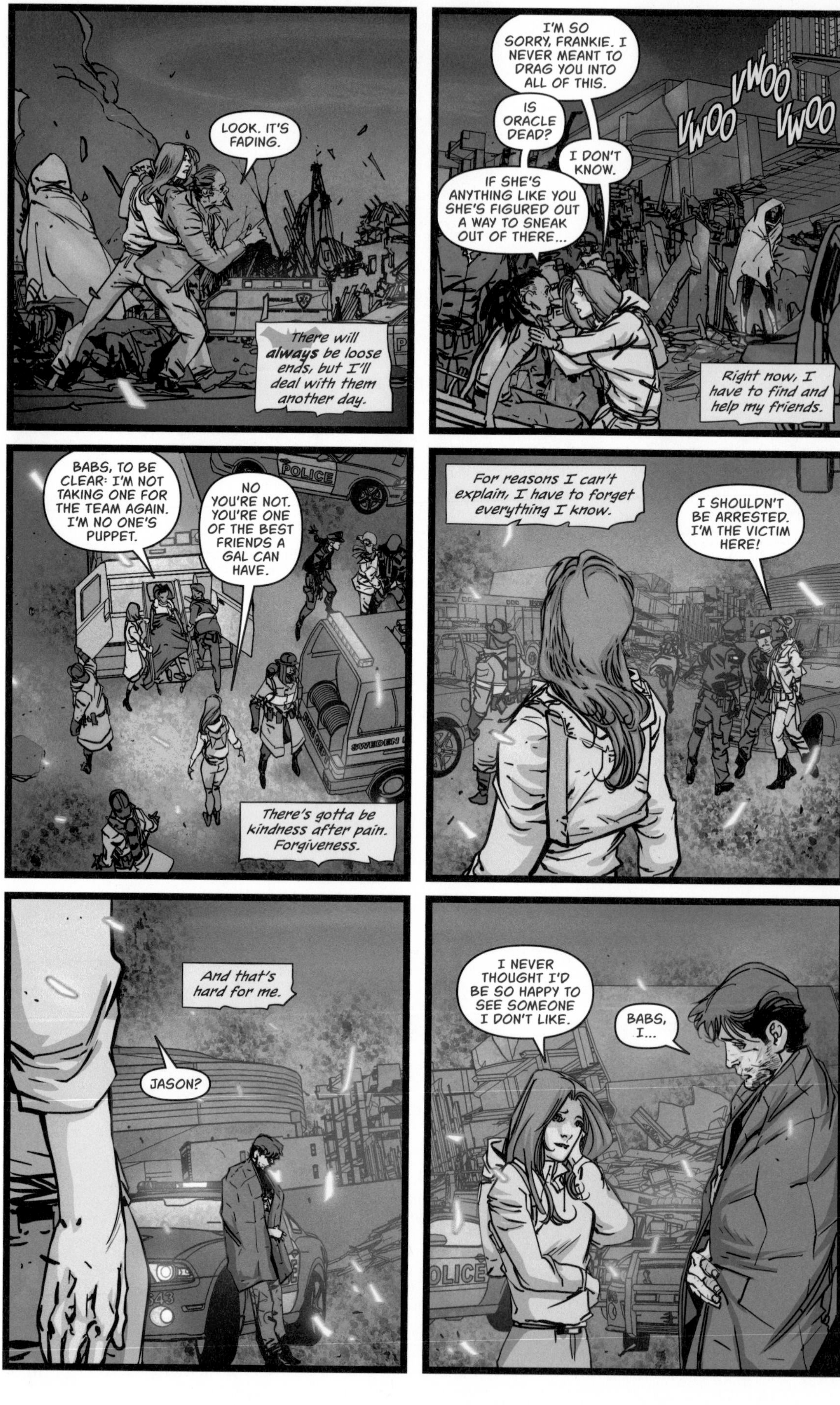
LOOK. IT'S FADING.
There will always be loose ends, but I'll deal with them another day.
I'M SO SORRY, FRANKIE. I NEVER MEANT TO DRAG YOU INTO ALL OF THIS.
IS ORACLE DEAD?
I DON'T KNOW.
IF SHE'S ANYTHING LIKE YOU SHE'S FIGURED OUT A WAY TO SNEAK OUT OF THERE...
VWOO VWOO VWOO
Right now, I have to find and help my friends.
BABS, TO BE CLEAR: I'M NOT TAKING ONE FOR THE TEAM AGAIN. I'M NO ONE'S PUPPET.
NO YOU'RE NOT. YOU'RE ONE OF THE BEST FRIENDS A GAL CAN HAVE.
There's gotta be kindness after pain. Forgiveness.
For reasons I can't explain, I have to forget everything I know.
I SHOULDN'T BE ARRESTED. I'M THE VICTIM HERE!
And that's hard for me.
JASON?
I NEVER THOUGHT I'D BE SO HAPPY TO SEE SOMEONE I DON'T LIKE.
BABS, I...

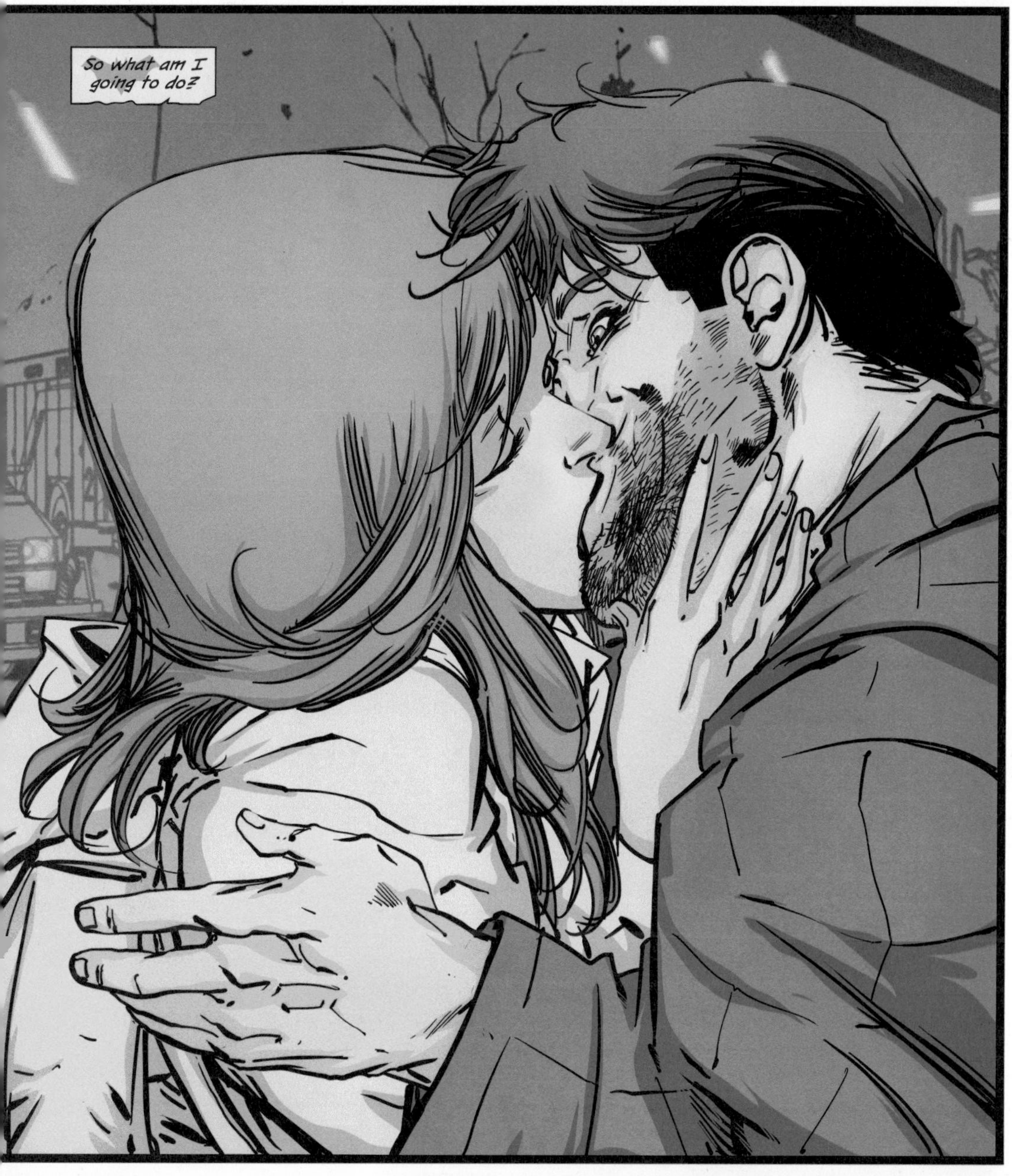
So what am I going to do?

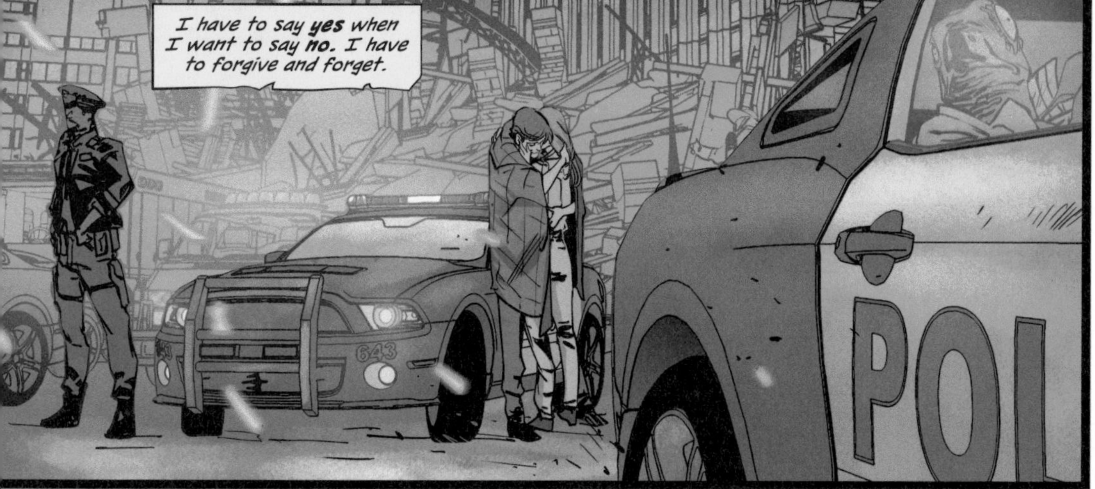
I have to say **yes** when I want to say **no.** I have to forgive and forget.
POL

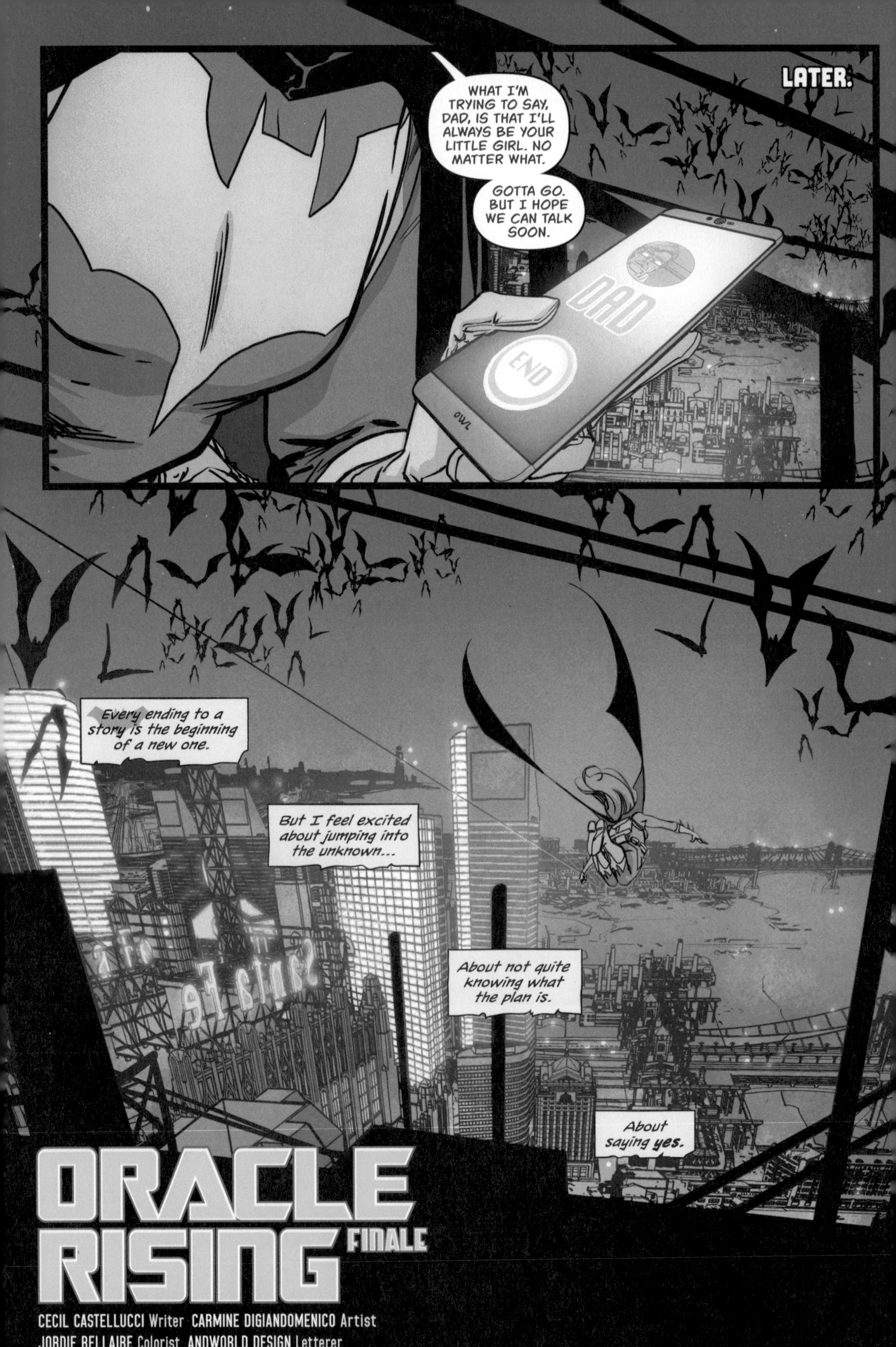
LATER.
WHAT I'M TRYING TO SAY, DAD, IS THAT I'LL ALWAYS BE YOUR LITTLE GIRL. NO MATTER WHAT.
GOTTA GO. BUT I HOPE WE CAN TALK SOON.
DAD
END
OWL
Every ending to a story is the beginning of a new one.
But I feel excited about jumping into the unknown...
About not quite knowing what the plan is.
About saying yes.
ORACLE RISING FINALE

CECIL CASTELLUCCI Writer CARMINE DIGIANDOMENICO Artist
JORDIE BELLAIRE Colorist ANDWORLD DESIGN Letterer
DIGIANDOMENICO & IVAN PLASCENCIA Cover
BRITTANY HOLZHERR Editor
BRIAN CUNNINGHAM Group Editor

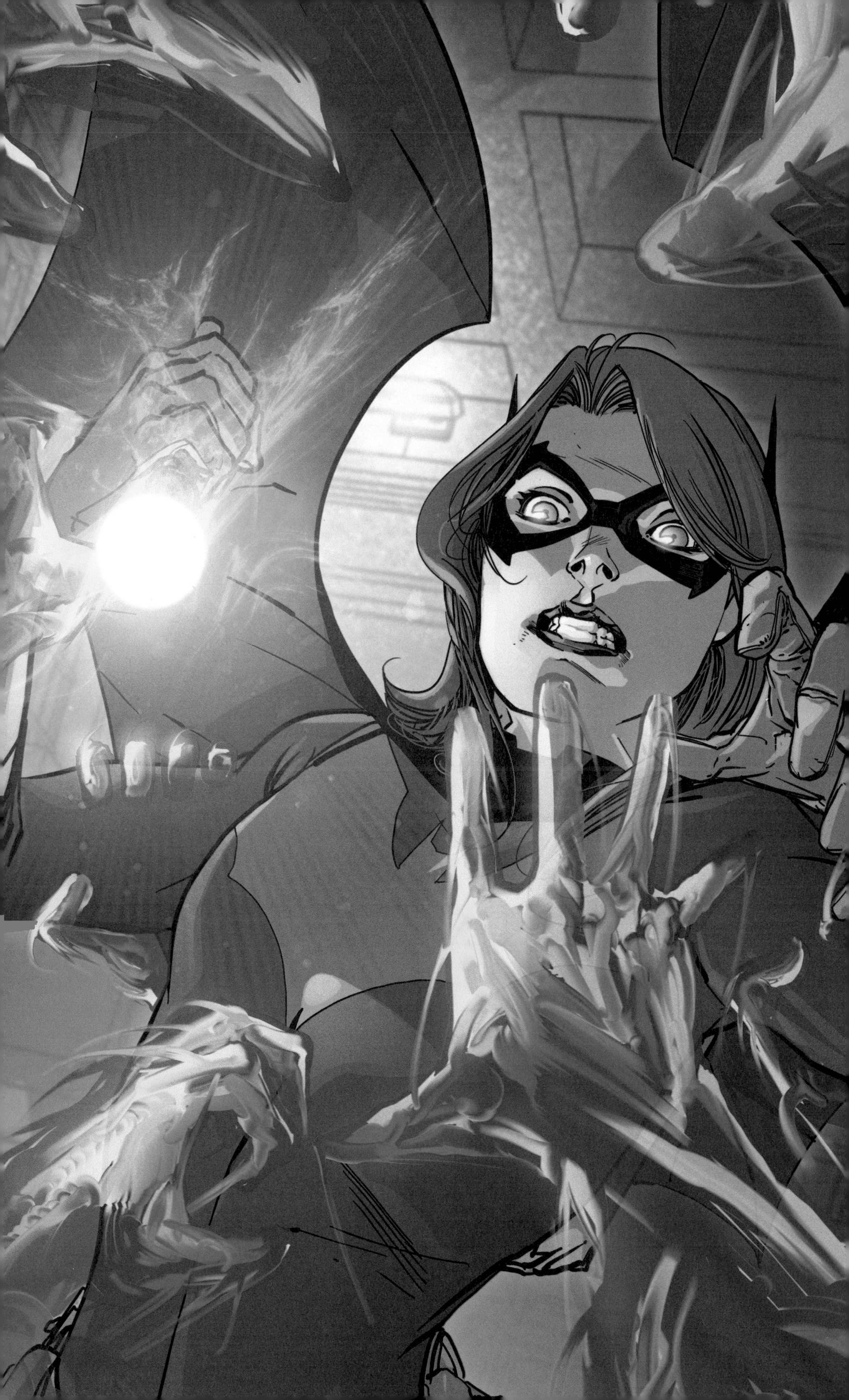

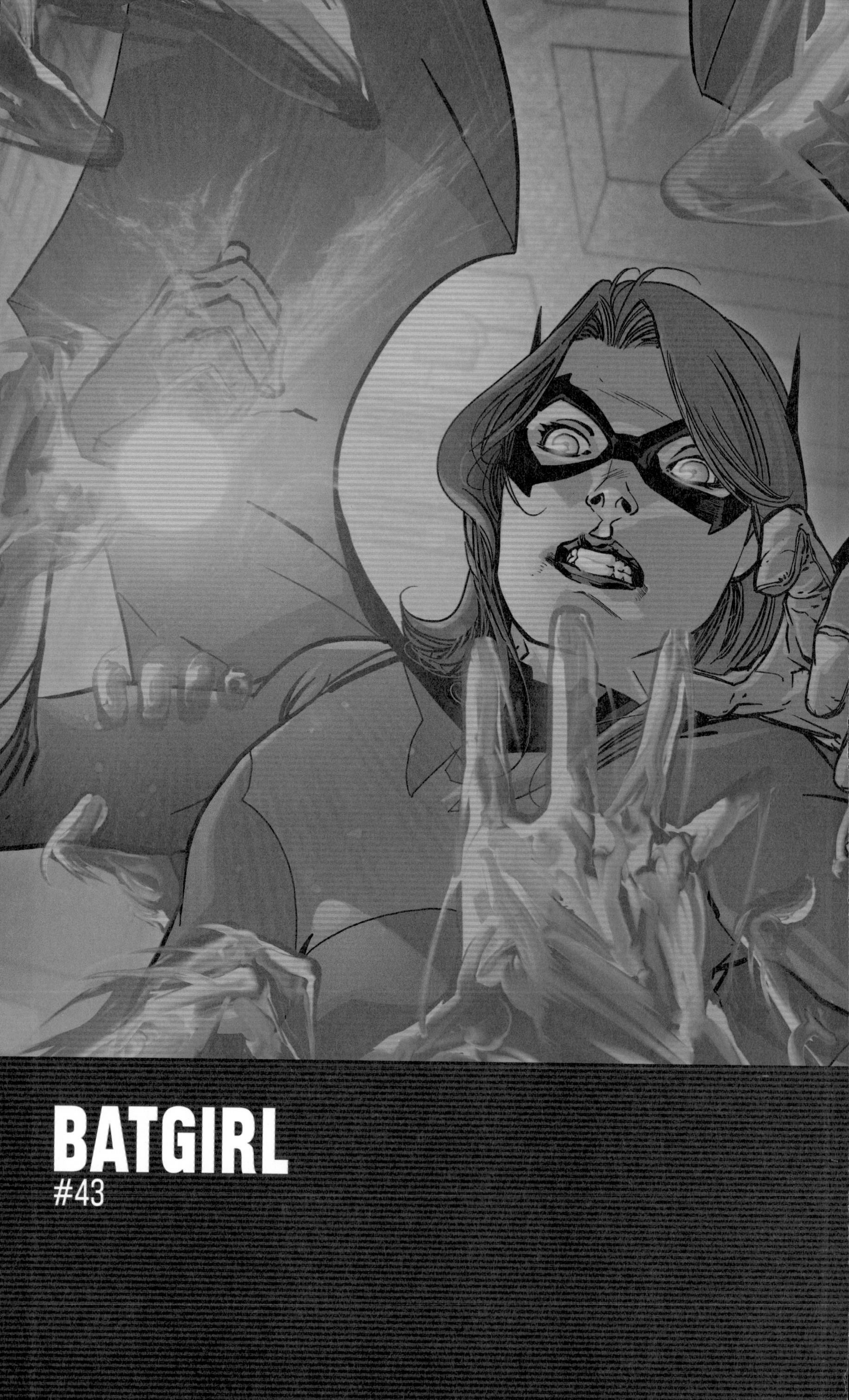

BATGIRL
#43

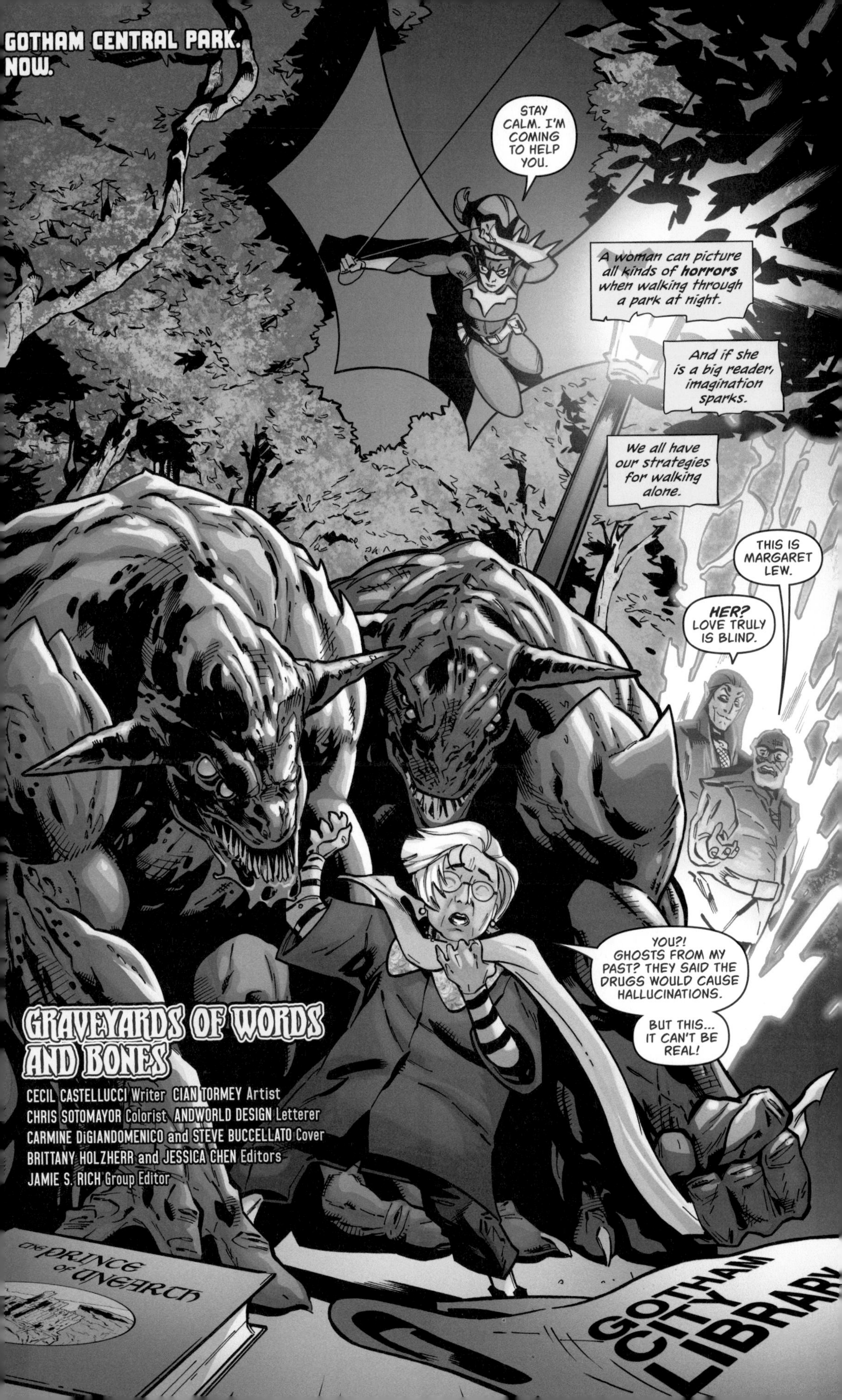
GOTHAM CENTRAL PARK. NOW.
STAY CALM. I'M COMING TO HELP YOU.
A woman can picture all kinds of horrors when walking through a park at night.
And if she is a big reader, imagination sparks.
We all have our strategies for walking alone.
THIS IS MARGARET LEW.
HER? LOVE TRULY IS BLIND.
YOU?! GHOSTS FROM MY PAST? THEY SAID THE DRUGS WOULD CAUSE HALLUCINATIONS.
BUT THIS... IT CAN'T BE REAL!
GRAVEYARDS OF WORDS AND BONES
CECIL CASTELLUCCI Writer CIAN TORMEY Artist
CHRIS SOTOMAYOR Colorist ANDWORLD DESIGN Letterer
CARMINE DiGIANDOMENICO and STEVE BUCCELLATO Cover
BRITTANY HOLZHERR and JESSICA CHEN Editors
JAMIE S. RICH Group Editor
THE PRINCE OF UNEARTH
GOTHAM CITY LIBRARY

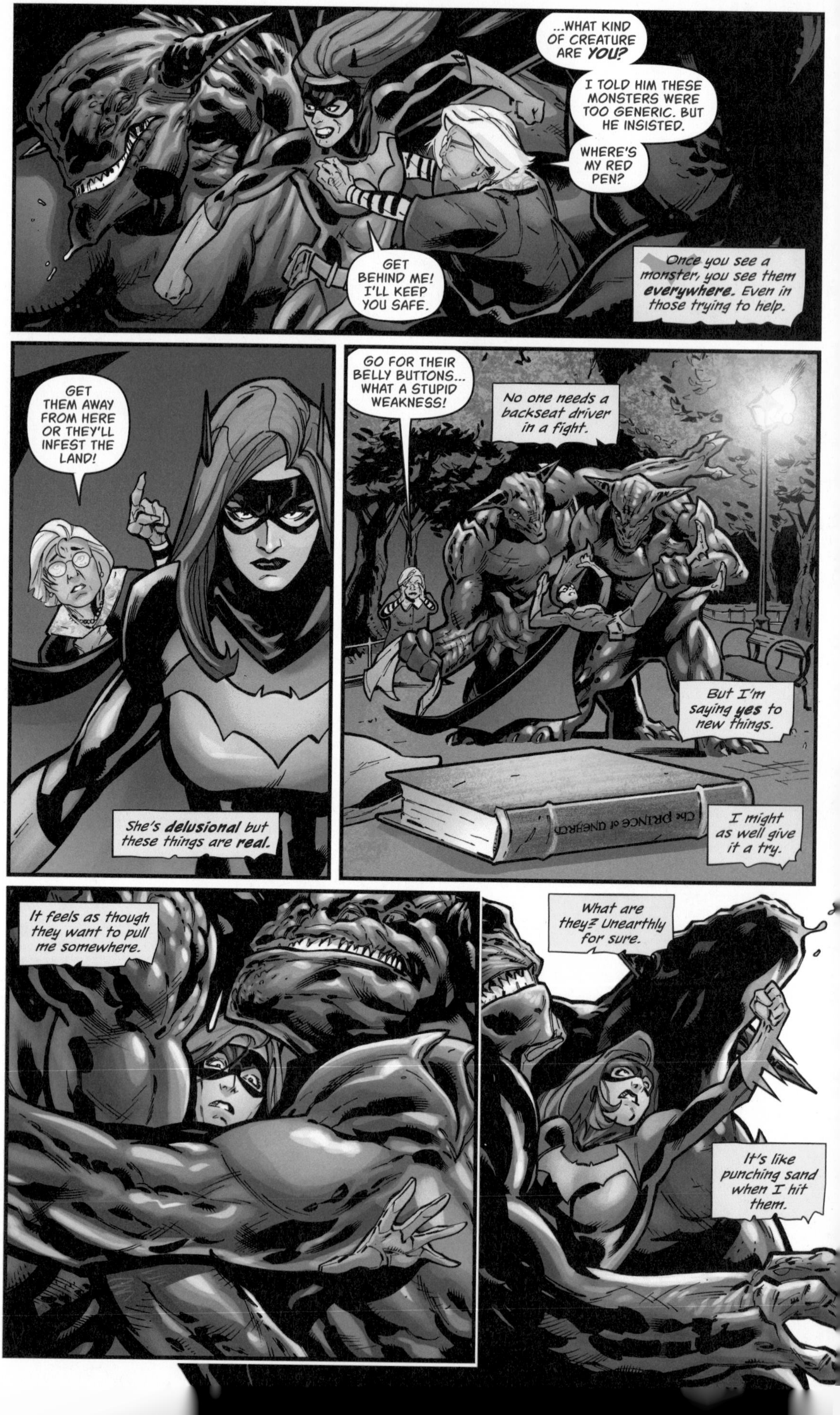
...WHAT KIND OF CREATURE ARE YOU?
I TOLD HIM THESE MONSTERS WERE TOO GENERIC. BUT HE INSISTED.
WHERE'S MY RED PEN?
GET BEHIND ME! I'LL KEEP YOU SAFE.
Once you see a monster, you see them everywhere. Even in those trying to help.
GET THEM AWAY FROM HERE OR THEY'LL INFEST THE LAND!
She's delusional but these things are real.
GO FOR THEIR BELLY BUTTONS... WHAT A STUPID WEAKNESS!
No one needs a backseat driver in a fight.
But I'm saying yes to new things.
I might as well give it a try.
It feels as though they want to pull me somewhere.
What are they? Unearthly for sure.
It's like punching sand when I hit them.

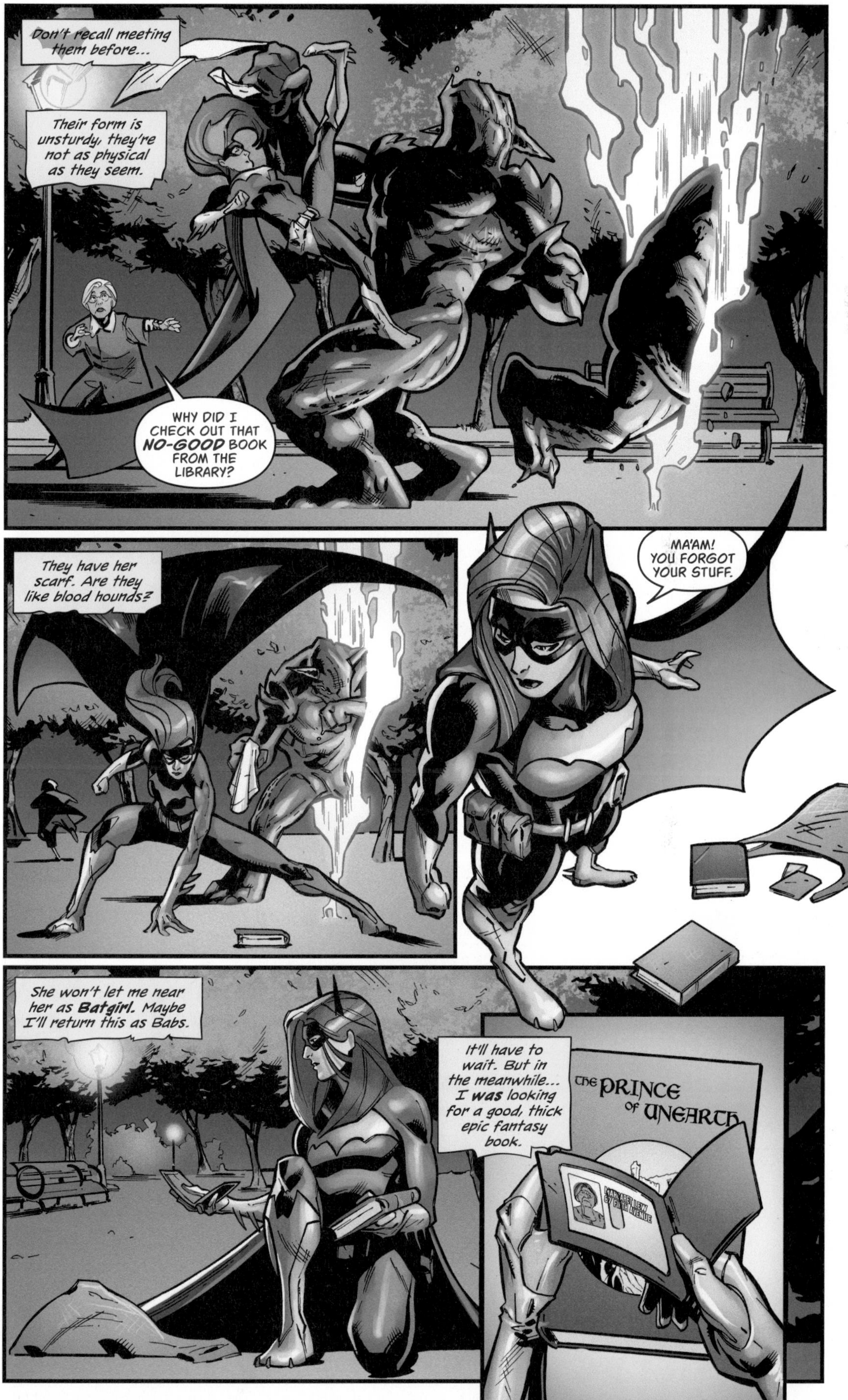

Don't recall meeting them before...
Their form is unsturdy, they're not as physical as they seem.
WHY DID I CHECK OUT THAT ***NO-GOOD*** BOOK FROM THE LIBRARY?
They have her scarf. Are they like blood hounds?
MA'AM! YOU FORGOT YOUR STUFF.
She won't let me near her as **Batgirl.** Maybe I'll return this as Babs.
It'll have to wait. But in the meanwhile... I ***was*** looking for a good, thick epic fantasy book.
THE PRINCE of UNEARTH

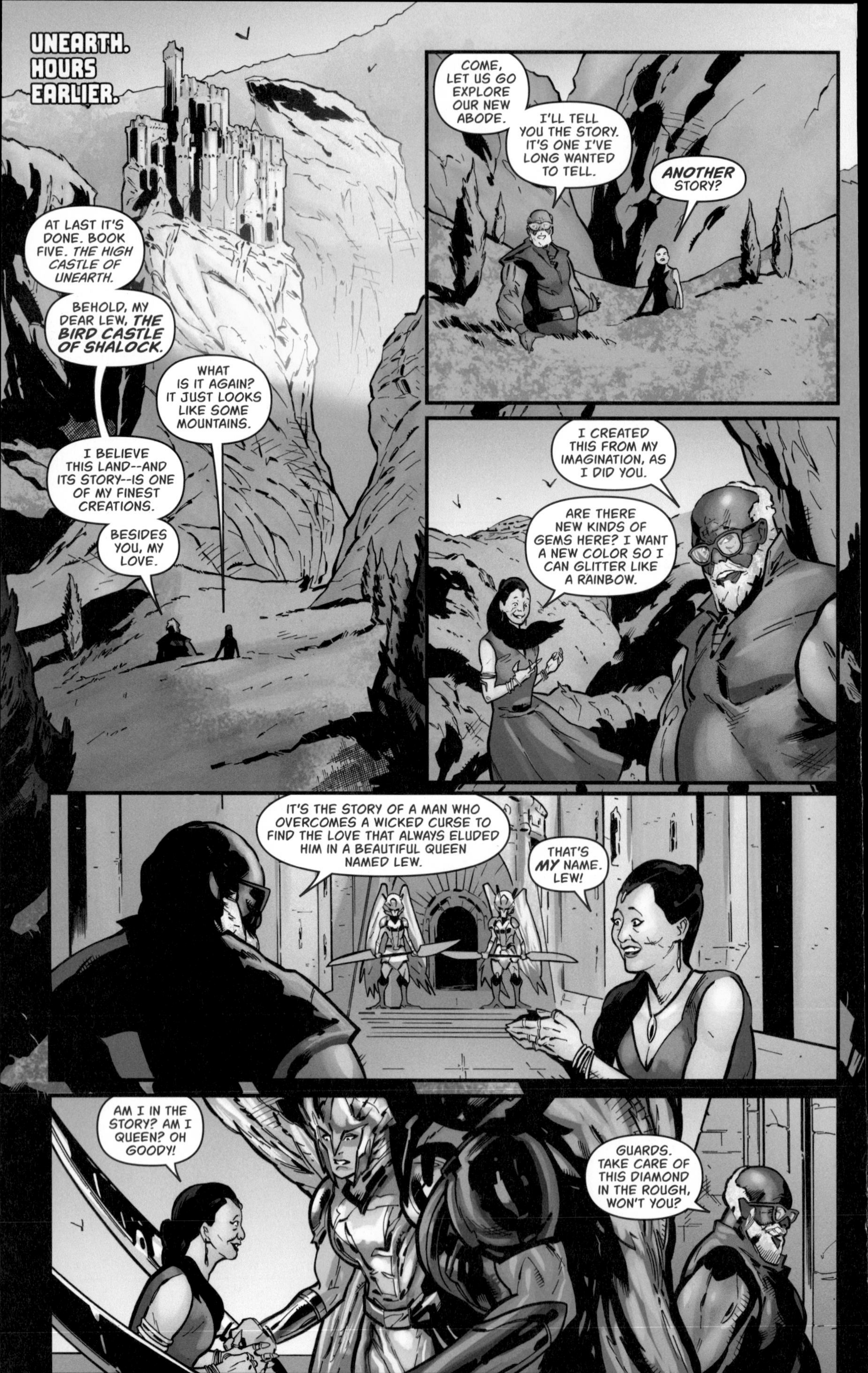
UNEARTH. HOURS EARLIER.
AT LAST IT'S DONE. BOOK FIVE. THE HIGH CASTLE OF UNEARTH.
BEHOLD, MY DEAR LEW, THE BIRD CASTLE OF SHALOCK.
WHAT IS IT AGAIN? IT JUST LOOKS LIKE SOME MOUNTAINS.
I BELIEVE THIS LAND--AND ITS STORY--IS ONE OF MY FINEST CREATIONS.
BESIDES YOU, MY LOVE.
COME, LET US GO EXPLORE OUR NEW ABODE.
I'LL TELL YOU THE STORY. IT'S ONE I'VE LONG WANTED TO TELL.
ANOTHER STORY?
I CREATED THIS FROM MY IMAGINATION, AS I DID YOU.
ARE THERE NEW KINDS OF GEMS HERE? I WANT A NEW COLOR SO I CAN GLITTER LIKE A RAINBOW.
IT'S THE STORY OF A MAN WHO OVERCOMES A WICKED CURSE TO FIND THE LOVE THAT ALWAYS ELUDED HIM IN A BEAUTIFUL QUEEN NAMED LEW.
THAT'S MY NAME. LEW!
AM I IN THE STORY? AM I QUEEN? OH GOODY!
GUARDS. TAKE CARE OF THIS DIAMOND IN THE ROUGH, WON'T YOU?

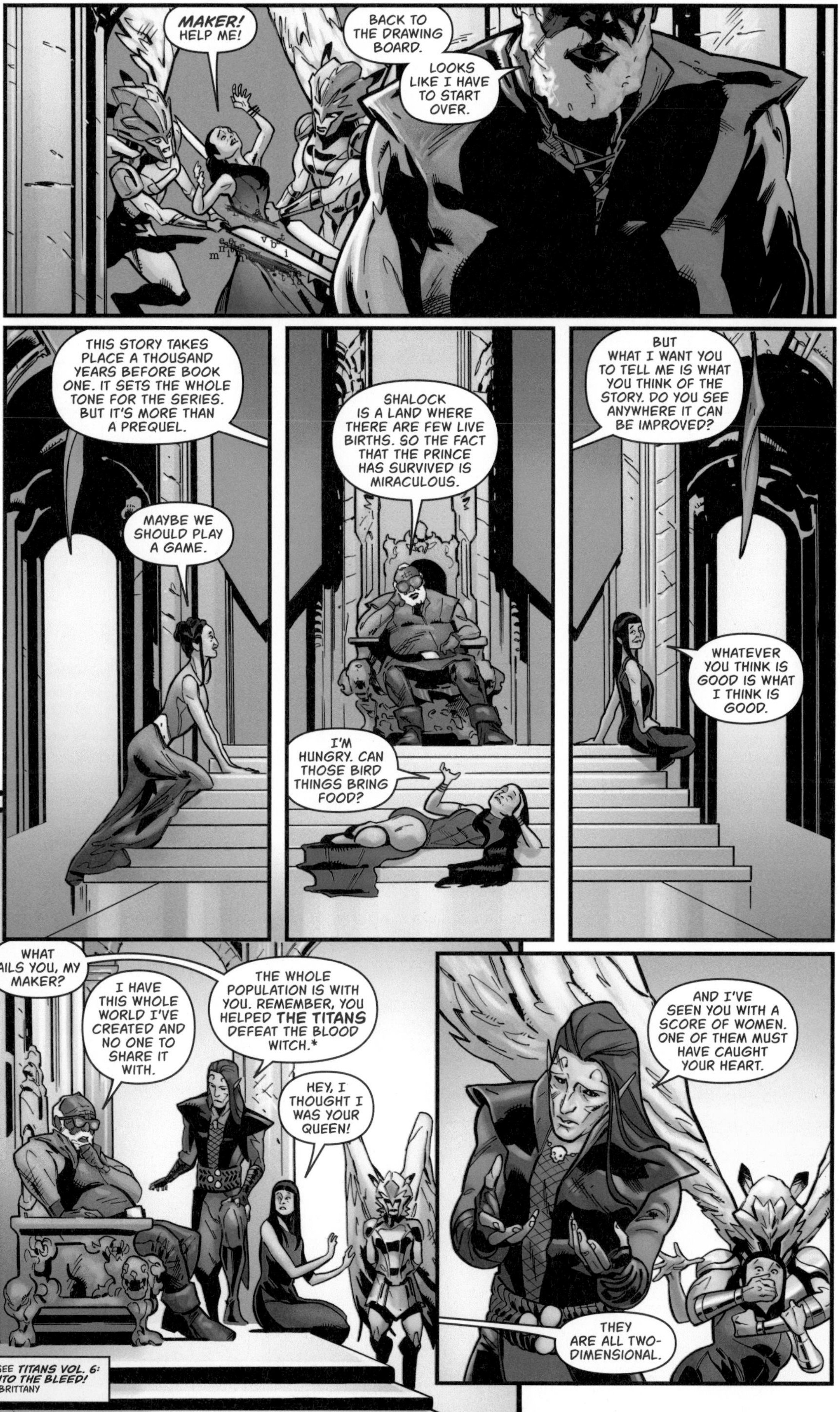
MAKER! HELP ME!
BACK TO THE DRAWING BOARD.
LOOKS LIKE I HAVE TO START OVER.
THIS STORY TAKES PLACE A THOUSAND YEARS BEFORE BOOK ONE. IT SETS THE WHOLE TONE FOR THE SERIES. BUT IT'S MORE THAN A PREQUEL.
MAYBE WE SHOULD PLAY A GAME.
SHALOCK IS A LAND WHERE THERE ARE FEW LIVE BIRTHS. SO THE FACT THAT THE PRINCE HAS SURVIVED IS MIRACULOUS.
I'M HUNGRY. CAN THOSE BIRD THINGS BRING FOOD?
BUT WHAT I WANT YOU TO TELL ME IS WHAT YOU THINK OF THE STORY. DO YOU SEE ANYWHERE IT CAN BE IMPROVED?
WHATEVER YOU THINK IS GOOD IS WHAT I THINK IS GOOD.
WHAT AILS YOU, MY MAKER?
I HAVE THIS WHOLE WORLD I'VE CREATED AND NO ONE TO SHARE IT WITH.
THE WHOLE POPULATION IS WITH YOU. REMEMBER, YOU HELPED THE TITANS DEFEAT THE BLOOD WITCH.*
HEY, I THOUGHT I WAS YOUR QUEEN!
*SEE TITANS VOL. 6: INTO THE BLEED! --BRITTANY
AND I'VE SEEN YOU WITH A SCORE OF WOMEN. ONE OF THEM MUST HAVE CAUGHT YOUR HEART.
THEY ARE ALL TWO-DIMENSIONAL.

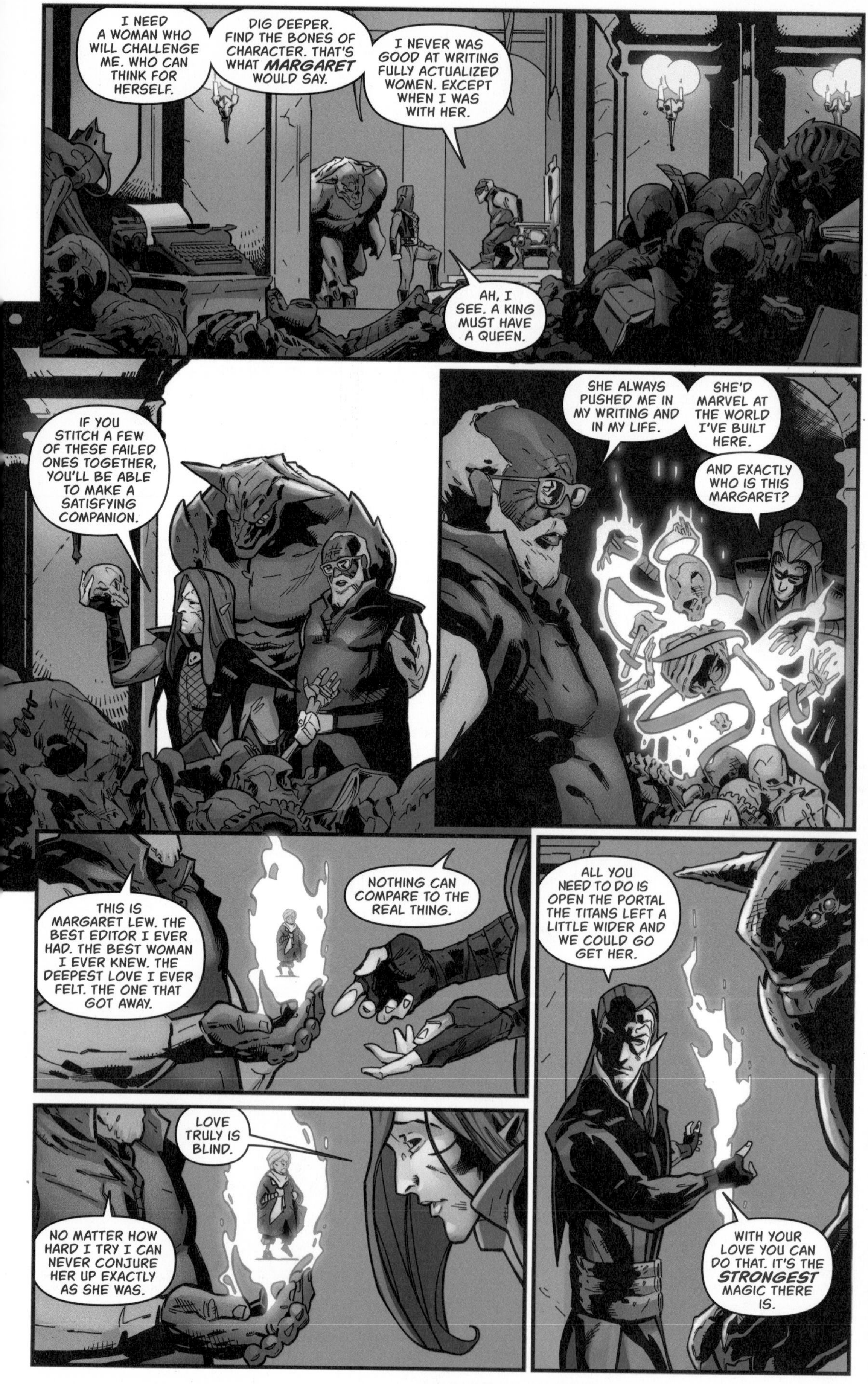
I NEED A WOMAN WHO WILL CHALLENGE ME. WHO CAN THINK FOR HERSELF.
DIG DEEPER. FIND THE BONES OF CHARACTER. THAT'S WHAT MARGARET WOULD SAY.
I NEVER WAS GOOD AT WRITING FULLY ACTUALIZED WOMEN. EXCEPT WHEN I WAS WITH HER.
AH, I SEE. A KING MUST HAVE A QUEEN.
IF YOU STITCH A FEW OF THESE FAILED ONES TOGETHER, YOU'LL BE ABLE TO MAKE A SATISFYING COMPANION.
SHE ALWAYS PUSHED ME IN MY WRITING AND IN MY LIFE.
SHE'D MARVEL AT THE WORLD I'VE BUILT HERE.
AND EXACTLY WHO IS THIS MARGARET?
THIS IS MARGARET LEW. THE BEST EDITOR I EVER HAD. THE BEST WOMAN I EVER KNEW. THE DEEPEST LOVE I EVER FELT. THE ONE THAT GOT AWAY.
NOTHING CAN COMPARE TO THE REAL THING.
LOVE TRULY IS BLIND.
NO MATTER HOW HARD I TRY I CAN NEVER CONJURE HER UP EXACTLY AS SHE WAS.
ALL YOU NEED TO DO IS OPEN THE PORTAL THE TITANS LEFT A LITTLE WIDER AND WE COULD GO GET HER.
WITH YOUR LOVE YOU CAN DO THAT. IT'S THE STRONGEST MAGIC THERE IS.

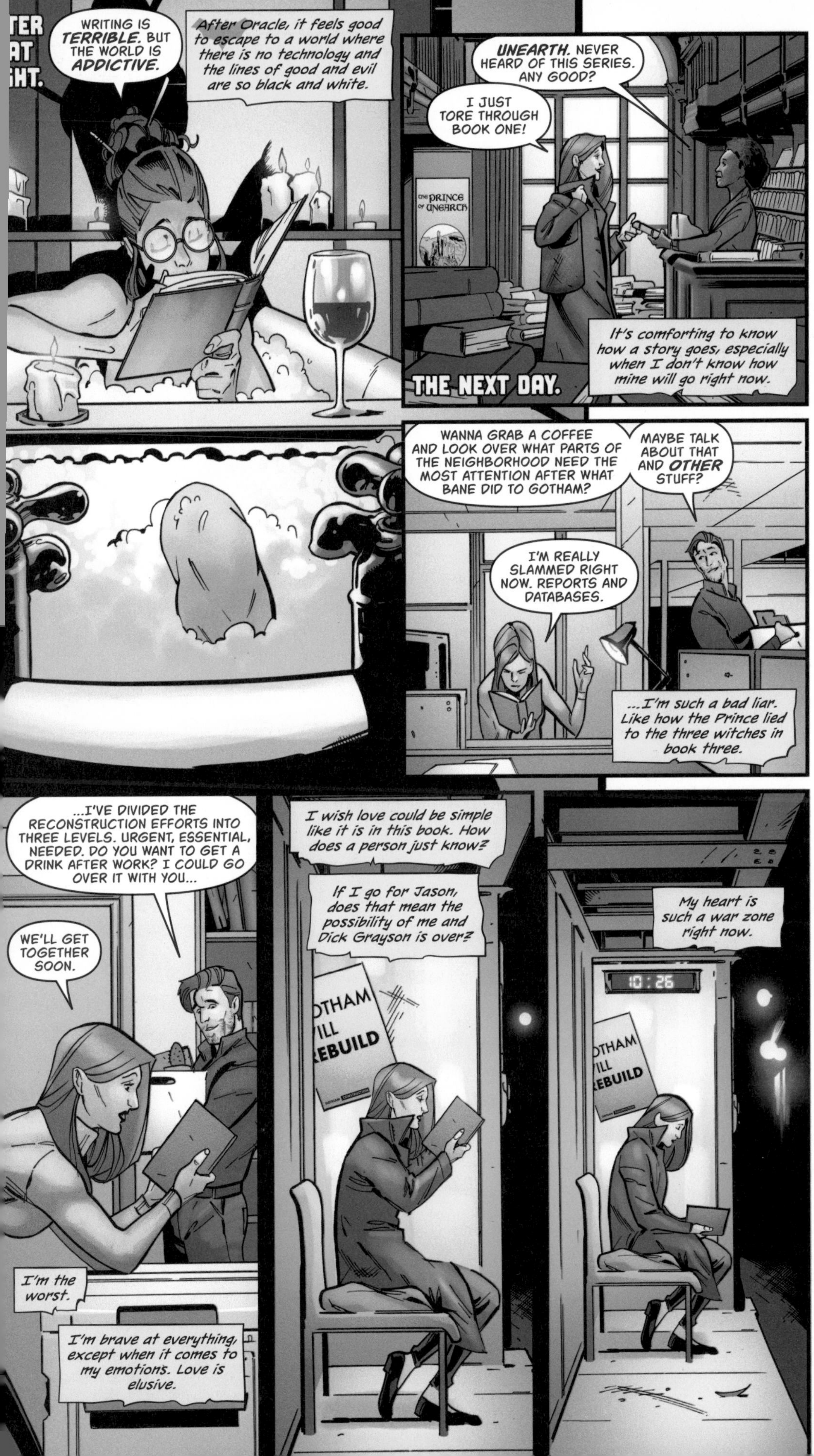

WRITING IS TERRIBLE. BUT THE WORLD IS ADDICTIVE.
After Oracle, it feels good to escape to a world where there is no technology and the lines of good and evil are so black and white.
UNEARTH. NEVER HEARD OF THIS SERIES. ANY GOOD?
I JUST TORE THROUGH BOOK ONE!
THE PRINCE OF UNEARTH
THE NEXT DAY.
It's comforting to know how a story goes, especially when I don't know how mine will go right now.
WANNA GRAB A COFFEE AND LOOK OVER WHAT PARTS OF THE NEIGHBORHOOD NEED THE MOST ATTENTION AFTER WHAT BANE DID TO GOTHAM?
MAYBE TALK ABOUT THAT AND OTHER STUFF?
I'M REALLY SLAMMED RIGHT NOW. REPORTS AND DATABASES.
...I'm such a bad liar. Like how the Prince lied to the three witches in book three.
...I'VE DIVIDED THE RECONSTRUCTION EFFORTS INTO THREE LEVELS. URGENT, ESSENTIAL, NEEDED. DO YOU WANT TO GET A DRINK AFTER WORK? I COULD GO OVER IT WITH YOU...
WE'LL GET TOGETHER SOON.
I'm the worst.
I'm brave at everything, except when it comes to my emotions. Love is elusive.
I wish love could be simple like it is in this book. How does a person just know?
If I go for Jason, does that mean the possibility of me and Dick Grayson is over?
REBUILD
My heart is such a war zone right now.
10:26
REBUILD

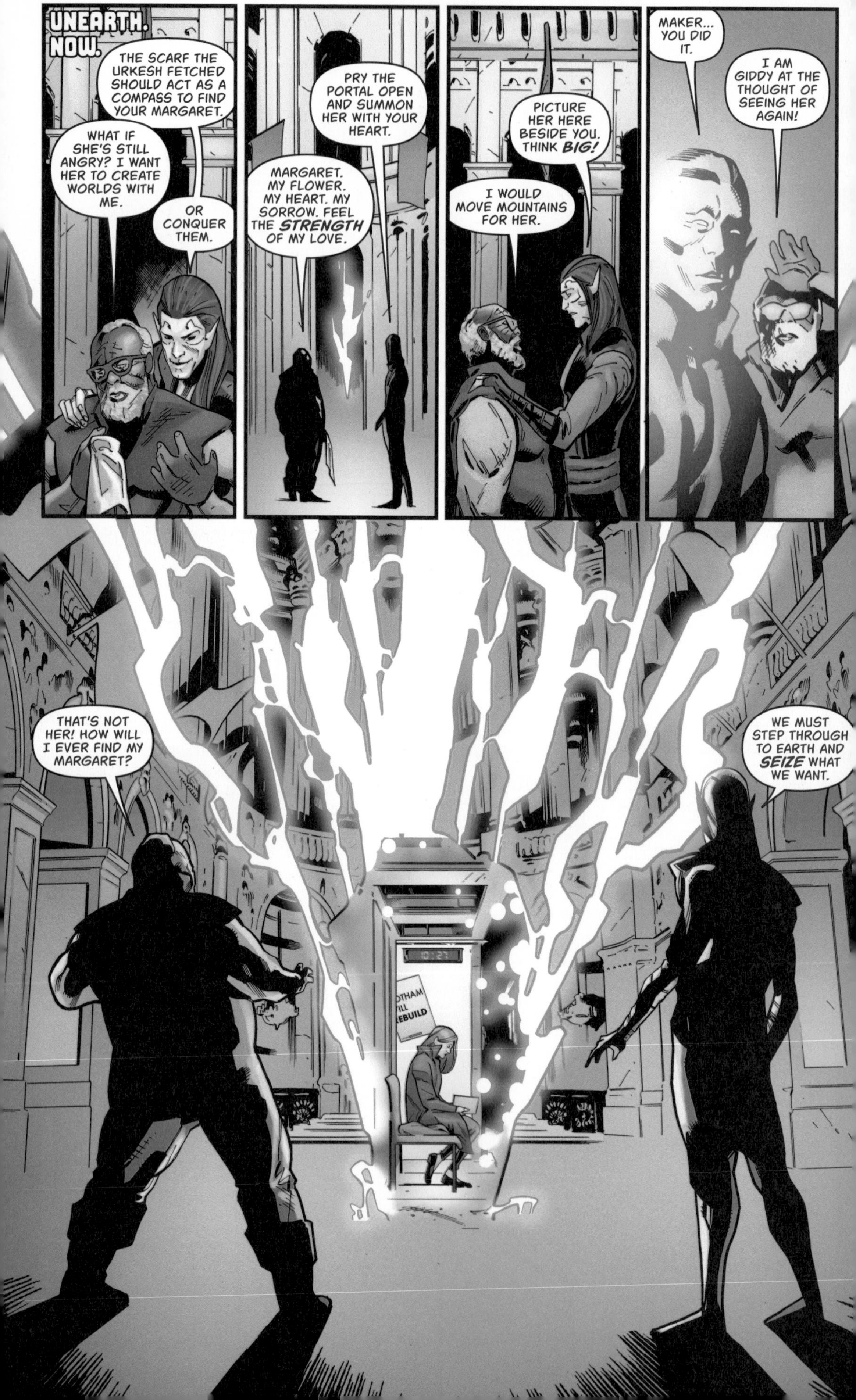
UNEARTH. NOW.
THE SCARF THE URKESH FETCHED SHOULD ACT AS A COMPASS TO FIND YOUR MARGARET.
WHAT IF SHE'S STILL ANGRY? I WANT HER TO CREATE WORLDS WITH ME.
OR CONQUER THEM.
PRY THE PORTAL OPEN AND SUMMON HER WITH YOUR HEART.
MARGARET. MY FLOWER. MY HEART. MY SORROW. FEEL THE STRENGTH OF MY LOVE.
PICTURE HER HERE BESIDE YOU. THINK BIG!
I WOULD MOVE MOUNTAINS FOR HER.
MAKER... YOU DID IT.
I AM GIDDY AT THE THOUGHT OF SEEING HER AGAIN!
THAT'S NOT HER! HOW WILL I EVER FIND MY MARGARET?
WE MUST STEP THROUGH TO EARTH AND SEIZE WHAT WE WANT.

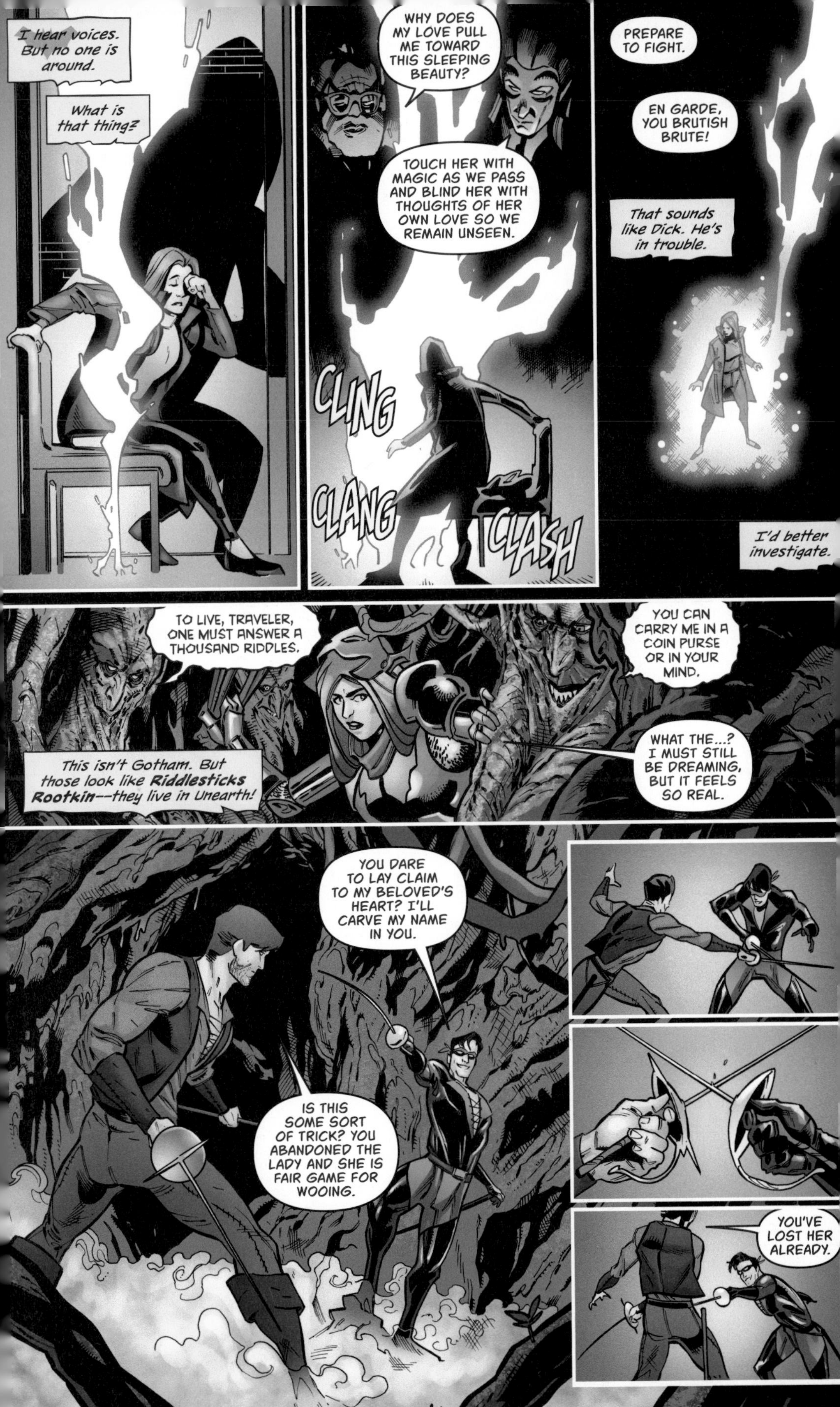
I hear voices. But no one is around.
What is that thing?
WHY DOES MY LOVE PULL ME TOWARD THIS SLEEPING BEAUTY?
TOUCH HER WITH MAGIC AS WE PASS AND BLIND HER WITH THOUGHTS OF HER OWN LOVE SO WE REMAIN UNSEEN.
CLING
CLANG
CLASH
PREPARE TO FIGHT.
EN GARDE, YOU BRUTISH BRUTE!
That sounds like Dick. He's in trouble.
I'd better investigate.
TO LIVE, TRAVELER, ONE MUST ANSWER A THOUSAND RIDDLES.
YOU CAN CARRY ME IN A COIN PURSE OR IN YOUR MIND.
This isn't Gotham. But those look like **Riddlesticks Rootkin**--they live in Unearth!
WHAT THE...? I MUST STILL BE DREAMING, BUT IT FEELS SO REAL.
YOU DARE TO LAY CLAIM TO MY BELOVED'S HEART? I'LL CARVE MY NAME IN YOU.
IS THIS SOME SORT OF TRICK? YOU ABANDONED THE LADY AND SHE IS FAIR GAME FOR WOOING.
YOU'VE LOST HER ALREADY.

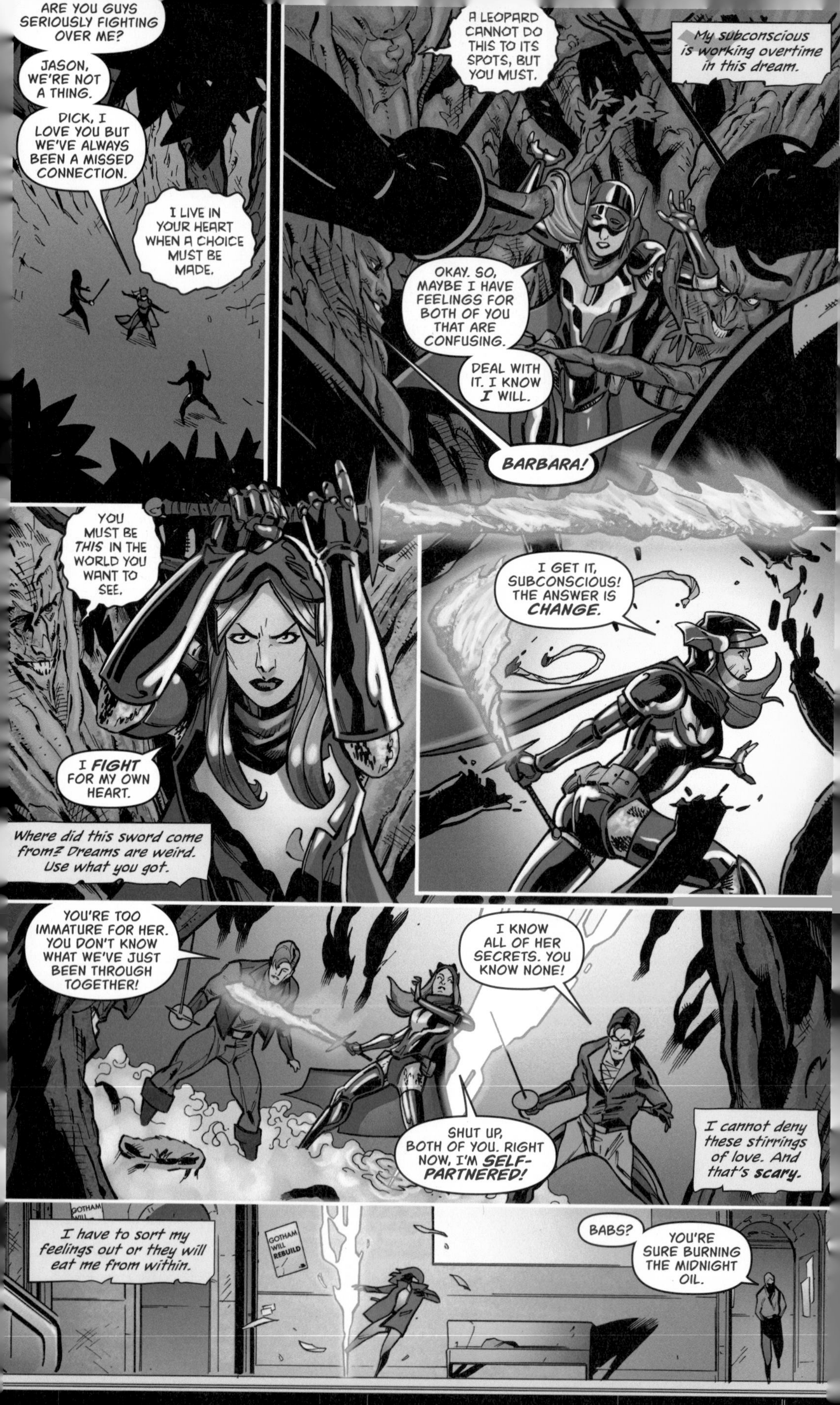
ARE YOU GUYS SERIOUSLY FIGHTING OVER ME?
JASON, WE'RE NOT A THING.
DICK, I LOVE YOU BUT WE'VE ALWAYS BEEN A MISSED CONNECTION.
I LIVE IN YOUR HEART WHEN A CHOICE MUST BE MADE.
A LEOPARD CANNOT DO THIS TO ITS SPOTS, BUT YOU MUST.
My subconscious is working overtime in this dream.
OKAY. SO, MAYBE I HAVE FEELINGS FOR BOTH OF YOU THAT ARE CONFUSING.
DEAL WITH IT. I KNOW I WILL.
BARBARA!
YOU MUST BE THIS IN THE WORLD YOU WANT TO SEE.
I FIGHT FOR MY OWN HEART.
Where did this sword come from? Dreams are weird. Use what you got.
I GET IT, SUBCONSCIOUS! THE ANSWER IS CHANGE.
YOU'RE TOO IMMATURE FOR HER. YOU DON'T KNOW WHAT WE'VE JUST BEEN THROUGH TOGETHER!
I KNOW ALL OF HER SECRETS. YOU KNOW NONE!
SHUT UP, BOTH OF YOU. RIGHT NOW, I'M SELF-PARTNERED!
I cannot deny these stirrings of love. And that's scary.
I have to sort my feelings out or they will eat me from within.
GOTHAM WILL REBUILD
BABS?
YOU'RE SURE BURNING THE MIDNIGHT OIL.

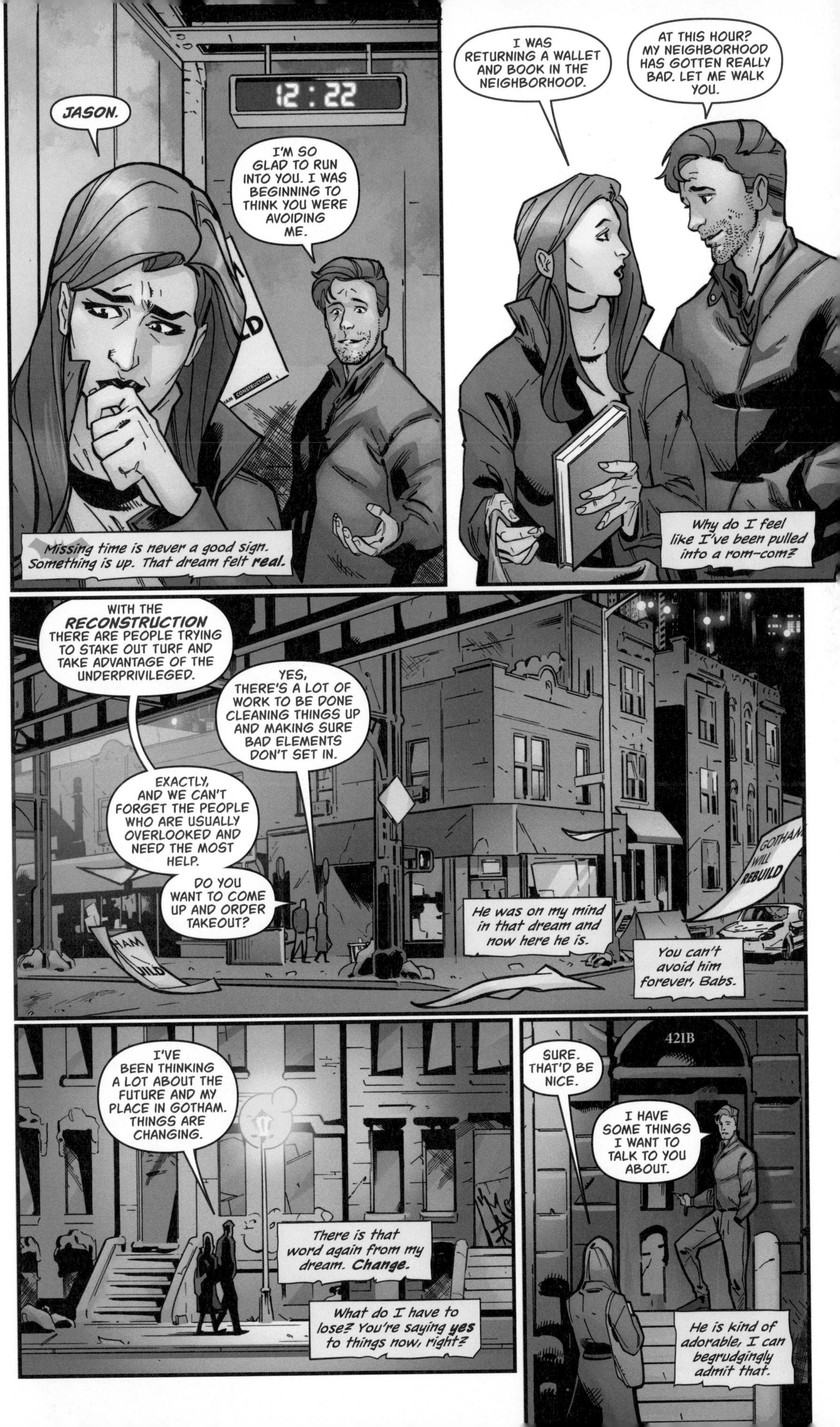
12:22
JASON.
I'M SO GLAD TO RUN INTO YOU. I WAS BEGINNING TO THINK YOU WERE AVOIDING ME.
Missing time is never a good sign. Something is up. That dream felt real.
I WAS RETURNING A WALLET AND BOOK IN THE NEIGHBORHOOD.
AT THIS HOUR? MY NEIGHBORHOOD HAS GOTTEN REALLY BAD. LET ME WALK YOU.
Why do I feel like I've been pulled into a rom-com?
WITH THE RECONSTRUCTION THERE ARE PEOPLE TRYING TO STAKE OUT TURF AND TAKE ADVANTAGE OF THE UNDERPRIVILEGED.
YES, THERE'S A LOT OF WORK TO BE DONE CLEANING THINGS UP AND MAKING SURE BAD ELEMENTS DON'T SET IN.
EXACTLY, AND WE CAN'T FORGET THE PEOPLE WHO ARE USUALLY OVERLOOKED AND NEED THE MOST HELP.
DO YOU WANT TO COME UP AND ORDER TAKEOUT?
GOTHAM WILL REBUILD
He was on my mind in that dream and now here he is.
You can't avoid him forever, Babs.
I'VE BEEN THINKING A LOT ABOUT THE FUTURE AND MY PLACE IN GOTHAM. THINGS ARE CHANGING.
There is that word again from my dream. Change.
What do I have to lose? You're saying yes to things now, right?
421B
SURE. THAT'D BE NICE.
I HAVE SOME THINGS I WANT TO TALK TO YOU ABOUT.
He is kind of adorable, I can begrudgingly admit that.

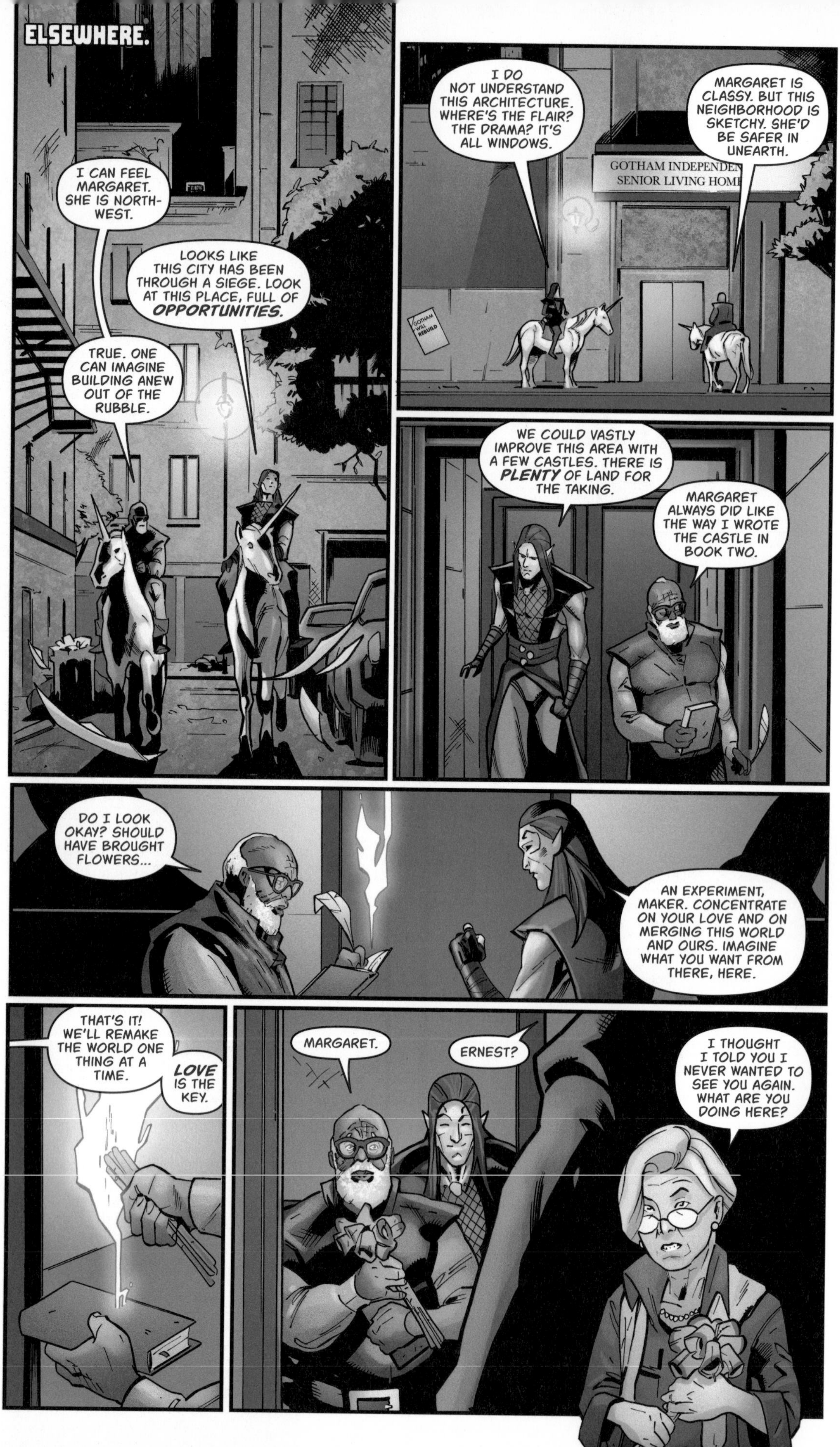
ELSEWHERE.
I CAN FEEL MARGARET. SHE IS NORTH-WEST.
LOOKS LIKE THIS CITY HAS BEEN THROUGH A SIEGE. LOOK AT THIS PLACE, FULL OF *OPPORTUNITIES*.
TRUE. ONE CAN IMAGINE BUILDING ANEW OUT OF THE RUBBLE.
I DO NOT UNDERSTAND THIS ARCHITECTURE. WHERE'S THE FLAIR? THE DRAMA? IT'S ALL WINDOWS.
MARGARET IS CLASSY. BUT THIS NEIGHBORHOOD IS SKETCHY. SHE'D BE SAFER IN UNEARTH.
GOTHAM INDEPENDEN
SENIOR LIVING HOM
GOTHAM WILL REBUILD
WE COULD VASTLY IMPROVE THIS AREA WITH A FEW CASTLES. THERE IS *PLENTY* OF LAND FOR THE TAKING.
MARGARET ALWAYS DID LIKE THE WAY I WROTE THE CASTLE IN BOOK TWO.
DO I LOOK OKAY? SHOULD HAVE BROUGHT FLOWERS...
AN EXPERIMENT, MAKER. CONCENTRATE ON YOUR LOVE AND ON MERGING THIS WORLD AND OURS. IMAGINE WHAT YOU WANT FROM THERE, HERE.
THAT'S IT! WE'LL REMAKE THE WORLD ONE THING AT A TIME.
LOVE IS THE KEY.
MARGARET.
ERNEST?
I THOUGHT I TOLD YOU I NEVER WANTED TO SEE YOU AGAIN. WHAT ARE YOU DOING HERE?

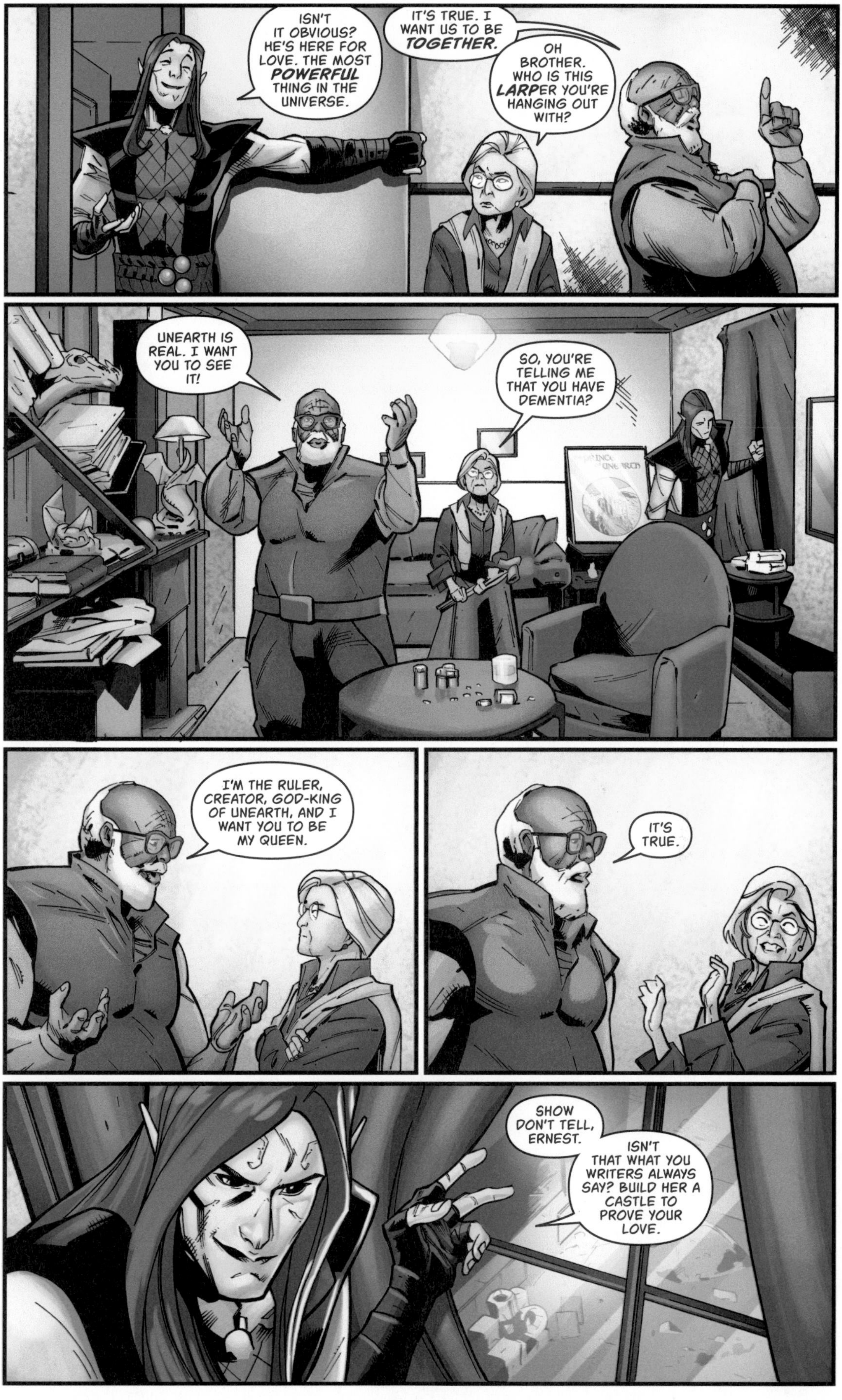
ISN'T IT OBVIOUS? HE'S HERE FOR LOVE. THE MOST **POWERFUL** THING IN THE UNIVERSE.
IT'S TRUE. I WANT US TO BE **TOGETHER.**
OH BROTHER. WHO IS THIS **LARP**ER YOU'RE HANGING OUT WITH?
UNEARTH IS REAL. I WANT YOU TO SEE IT!
SO, YOU'RE TELLING ME THAT YOU HAVE DEMENTIA?
I'M THE RULER, CREATOR, GOD-KING OF UNEARTH, AND I WANT YOU TO BE MY QUEEN.
IT'S TRUE.
SHOW DON'T TELL, ERNEST.
ISN'T THAT WHAT YOU WRITERS ALWAYS SAY? BUILD HER A CASTLE TO PROVE YOUR LOVE.

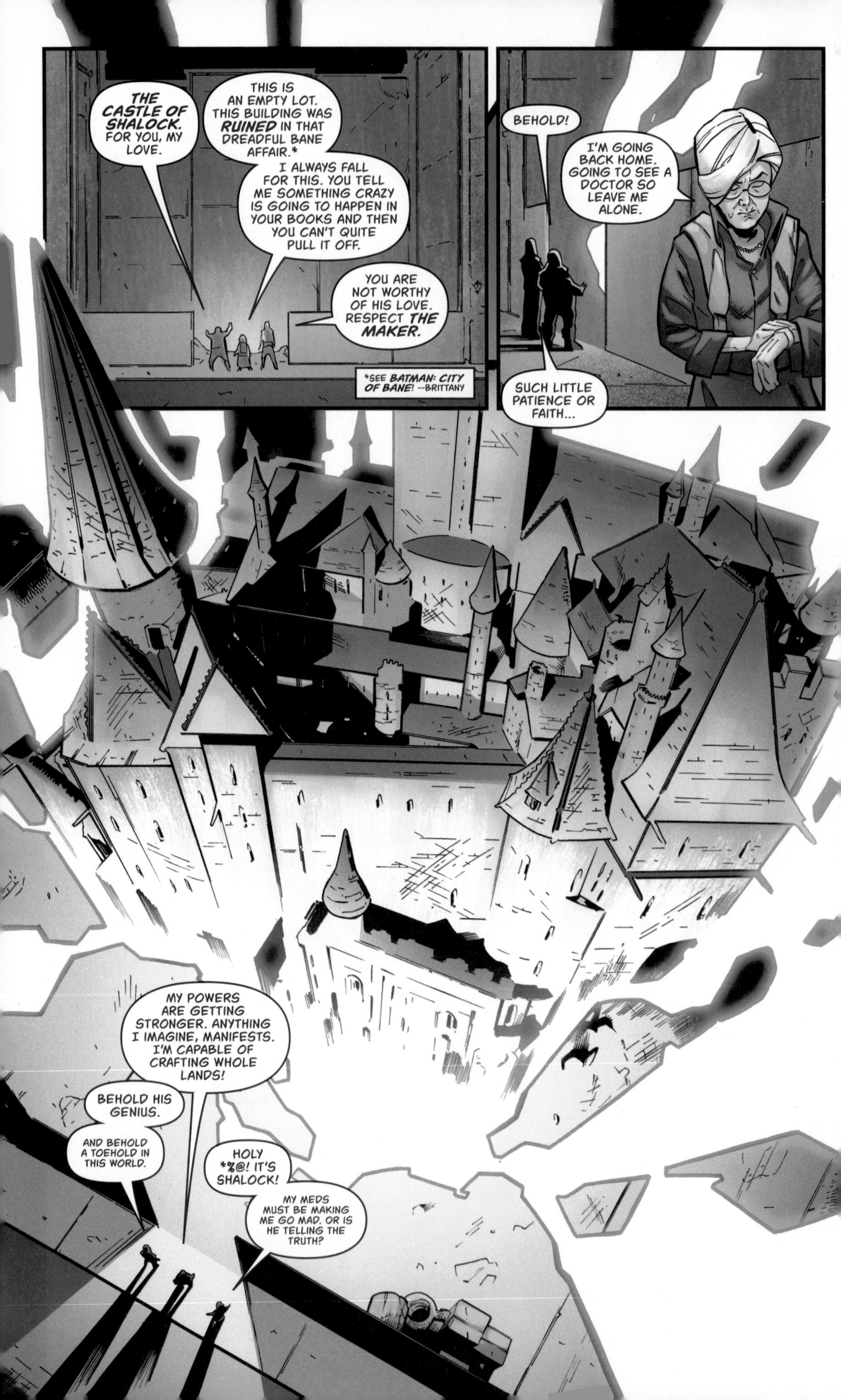

THE CASTLE OF SHALOCK. FOR YOU, MY LOVE.
THIS IS AN EMPTY LOT. THIS BUILDING WAS RUINED IN THAT DREADFUL BANE AFFAIR.*
I ALWAYS FALL FOR THIS. YOU TELL ME SOMETHING CRAZY IS GOING TO HAPPEN IN YOUR BOOKS AND THEN YOU CAN'T QUITE PULL IT OFF.
YOU ARE NOT WORTHY OF HIS LOVE. RESPECT THE MAKER.
*SEE BATMAN: CITY OF BANE! --BRITTANY
BEHOLD!
I'M GOING BACK HOME. GOING TO SEE A DOCTOR SO LEAVE ME ALONE.
SUCH LITTLE PATIENCE OR FAITH...
MY POWERS ARE GETTING STRONGER. ANYTHING I IMAGINE, MANIFESTS. I'M CAPABLE OF CRAFTING WHOLE LANDS!
BEHOLD HIS GENIUS.
AND BEHOLD A TOEHOLD IN THIS WORLD.
HOLY *%@! IT'S SHALOCK!
MY MEDS MUST BE MAKING ME GO MAD. OR IS HE TELLING THE TRUTH?

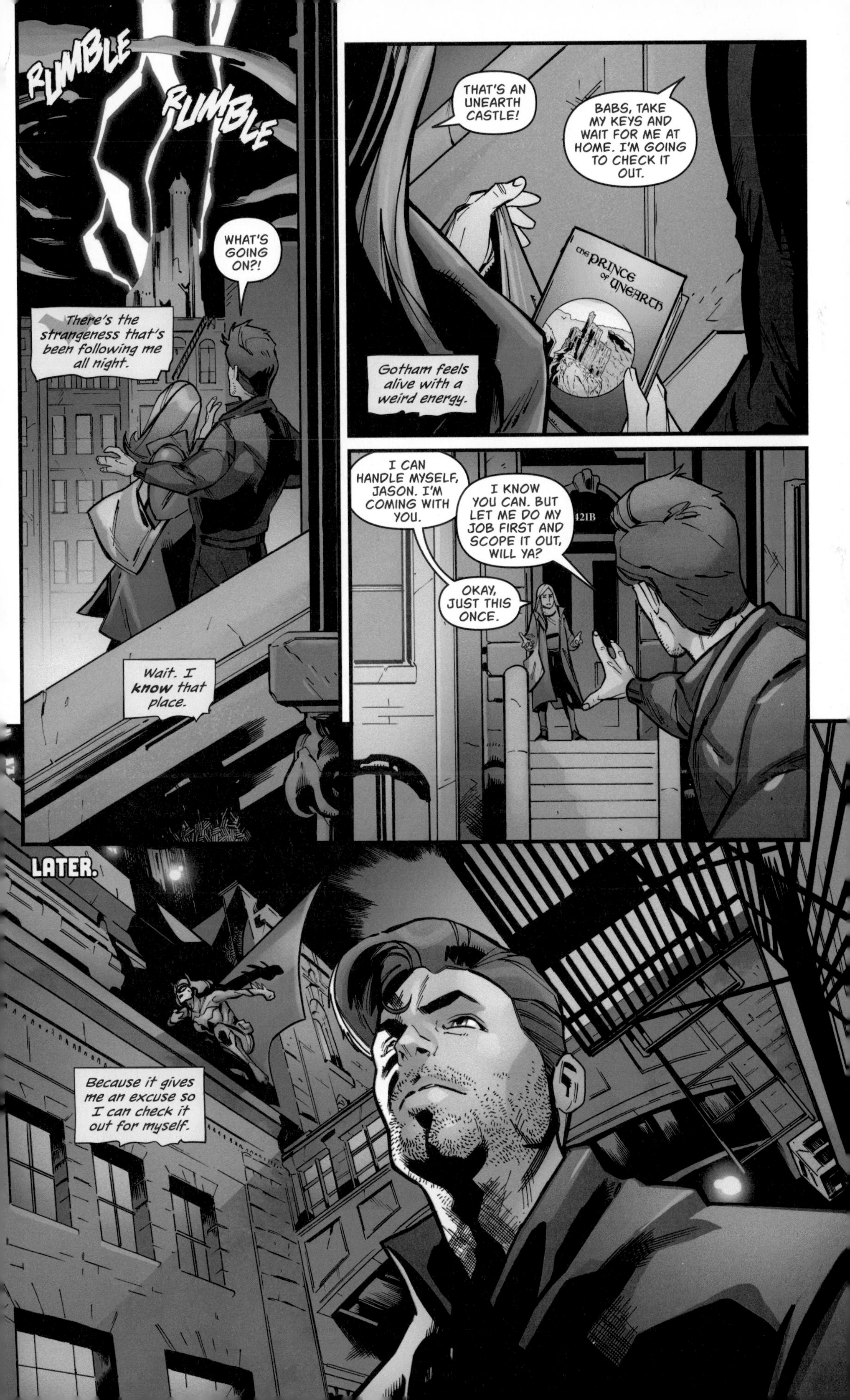
RUMBLE
RUMBLE
WHAT'S GOING ON?!
There's the strangeness that's been following me all night.
Wait. I know that place.
THAT'S AN UNEARTH CASTLE!
BABS, TAKE MY KEYS AND WAIT FOR ME AT HOME. I'M GOING TO CHECK IT OUT.
THE PRINCE OF UNEARTH
Gotham feels alive with a weird energy.
I CAN HANDLE MYSELF, JASON. I'M COMING WITH YOU.
I KNOW YOU CAN. BUT LET ME DO MY JOB FIRST AND SCOPE IT OUT, WILL YA?
421B
OKAY, JUST THIS ONCE.
LATER.
Because it gives me an excuse so I can check it out for myself.

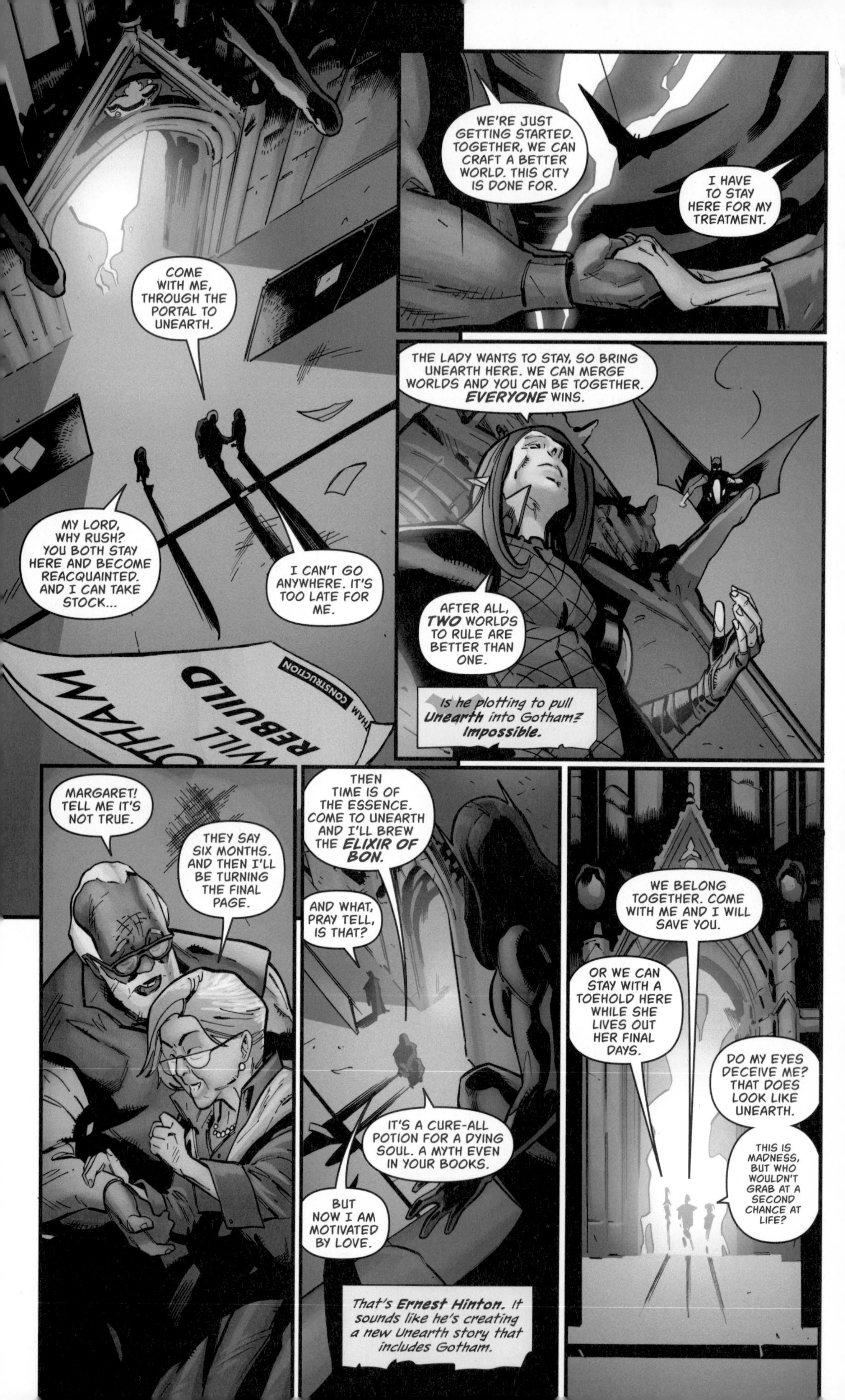
COME WITH ME, THROUGH THE PORTAL TO UNEARTH.
MY LORD, WHY RUSH? YOU BOTH STAY HERE AND BECOME REACQUAINTED. AND I CAN TAKE STOCK...
I CAN'T GO ANYWHERE. IT'S TOO LATE FOR ME.
CONSTRUCTION
WILL
REBUILD
WE'RE JUST GETTING STARTED. TOGETHER, WE CAN CRAFT A BETTER WORLD. THIS CITY IS DONE FOR.
I HAVE TO STAY HERE FOR MY TREATMENT.
THE LADY WANTS TO STAY, SO BRING UNEARTH HERE. WE CAN MERGE WORLDS AND YOU CAN BE TOGETHER. EVERYONE WINS.
AFTER ALL, TWO WORLDS TO RULE ARE BETTER THAN ONE.
Is he plotting to pull Unearth into Gotham? Impossible.
MARGARET! TELL ME IT'S NOT TRUE.
THEY SAY SIX MONTHS. AND THEN I'LL BE TURNING THE FINAL PAGE.
THEN TIME IS OF THE ESSENCE. COME TO UNEARTH AND I'LL BREW THE ELIXIR OF BON.
AND WHAT, PRAY TELL, IS THAT?
IT'S A CURE-ALL POTION FOR A DYING SOUL. A MYTH EVEN IN YOUR BOOKS.
BUT NOW I AM MOTIVATED BY LOVE.
That's Ernest Hinton. It sounds like he's creating a new Unearth story that includes Gotham.
WE BELONG TOGETHER. COME WITH ME AND I WILL SAVE YOU.
OR WE CAN STAY WITH A TOEHOLD HERE WHILE SHE LIVES OUT HER FINAL DAYS.
DO MY EYES DECEIVE ME? THAT DOES LOOK LIKE UNEARTH.
THIS IS MADNESS, BUT WHO WOULDN'T GRAB AT A SECOND CHANCE AT LIFE?

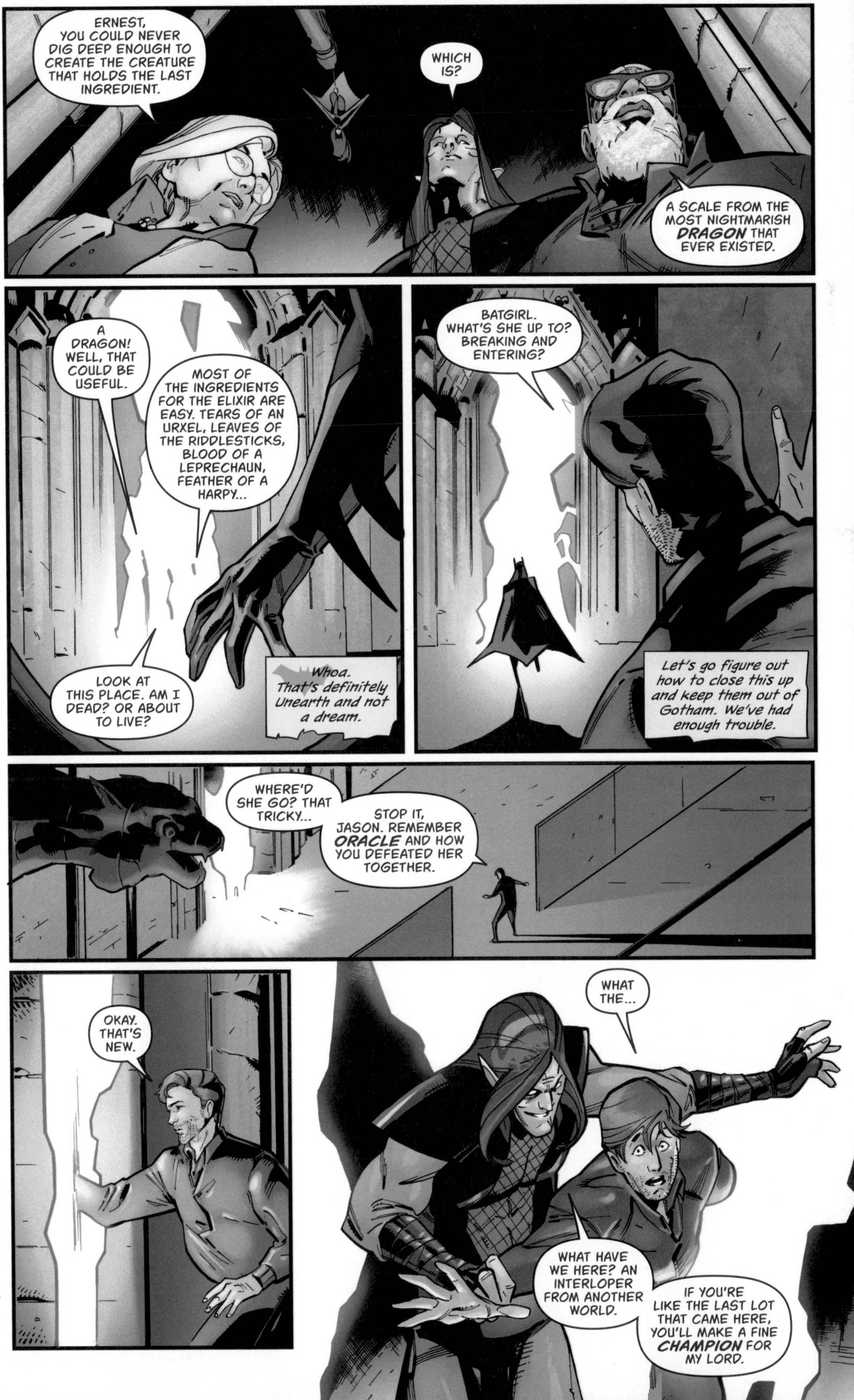
ERNEST, YOU COULD NEVER DIG DEEP ENOUGH TO CREATE THE CREATURE THAT HOLDS THE LAST INGREDIENT.
WHICH IS?
A SCALE FROM THE MOST NIGHTMARISH DRAGON THAT EVER EXISTED.
A DRAGON! WELL, THAT COULD BE USEFUL.
MOST OF THE INGREDIENTS FOR THE ELIXIR ARE EASY. TEARS OF AN URXEL, LEAVES OF THE RIDDLESTICKS, BLOOD OF A LEPRECHAUN, FEATHER OF A HARPY...
LOOK AT THIS PLACE. AM I DEAD? OR ABOUT TO LIVE?
Whoa. That's definitely Unearth and not a dream.
BATGIRL. WHAT'S SHE UP TO? BREAKING AND ENTERING?
Let's go figure out how to close this up and keep them out of Gotham. We've had enough trouble.
WHERE'D SHE GO? THAT TRICKY...
STOP IT, JASON. REMEMBER ORACLE AND HOW YOU DEFEATED HER TOGETHER.
OKAY. THAT'S NEW.
WHAT THE...
WHAT HAVE WE HERE? AN INTERLOPER FROM ANOTHER WORLD.
IF YOU'RE LIKE THE LAST LOT THAT CAME HERE, YOU'LL MAKE A FINE CHAMPION FOR MY LORD.

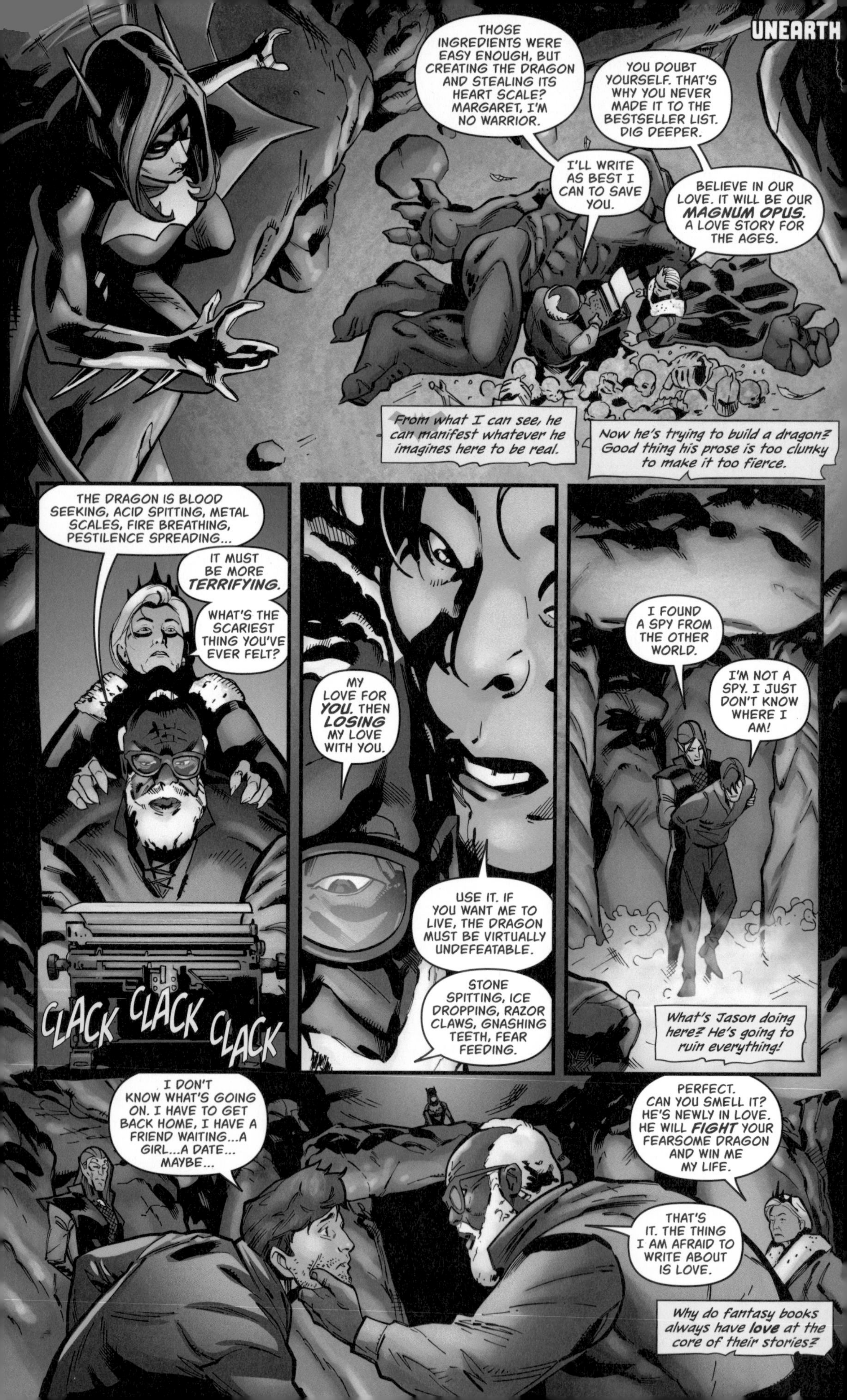
THOSE INGREDIENTS WERE EASY ENOUGH, BUT CREATING THE DRAGON AND STEALING ITS HEART SCALE? MARGARET, I'M NO WARRIOR.
YOU DOUBT YOURSELF. THAT'S WHY YOU NEVER MADE IT TO THE BESTSELLER LIST. DIG DEEPER.
I'LL WRITE AS BEST I CAN TO SAVE YOU.
BELIEVE IN OUR LOVE. IT WILL BE OUR MAGNUM OPUS. A LOVE STORY FOR THE AGES.
From what I can see, he can manifest whatever he imagines here to be real.
Now he's trying to build a dragon? Good thing his prose is too clunky to make it too fierce.
THE DRAGON IS BLOOD SEEKING, ACID SPITTING, METAL SCALES, FIRE BREATHING, PESTILENCE SPREADING...
IT MUST BE MORE TERRIFYING.
WHAT'S THE SCARIEST THING YOU'VE EVER FELT?
CLACK CLACK CLACK
MY LOVE FOR YOU. THEN LOSING MY LOVE WITH YOU.
USE IT. IF YOU WANT ME TO LIVE, THE DRAGON MUST BE VIRTUALLY UNDEFEATABLE.
STONE SPITTING, ICE DROPPING, RAZOR CLAWS, GNASHING TEETH, FEAR FEEDING.
I FOUND A SPY FROM THE OTHER WORLD.
I'M NOT A SPY. I JUST DON'T KNOW WHERE I AM!
What's Jason doing here? He's going to ruin everything!
I DON'T KNOW WHAT'S GOING ON. I HAVE TO GET BACK HOME, I HAVE A FRIEND WAITING...A GIRL...A DATE... MAYBE...
PERFECT. CAN YOU SMELL IT? HE'S NEWLY IN LOVE. HE WILL FIGHT YOUR FEARSOME DRAGON AND WIN ME MY LIFE.
THAT'S IT. THE THING I AM AFRAID TO WRITE ABOUT IS LOVE.
Why do fantasy books always have love at the core of their stories?

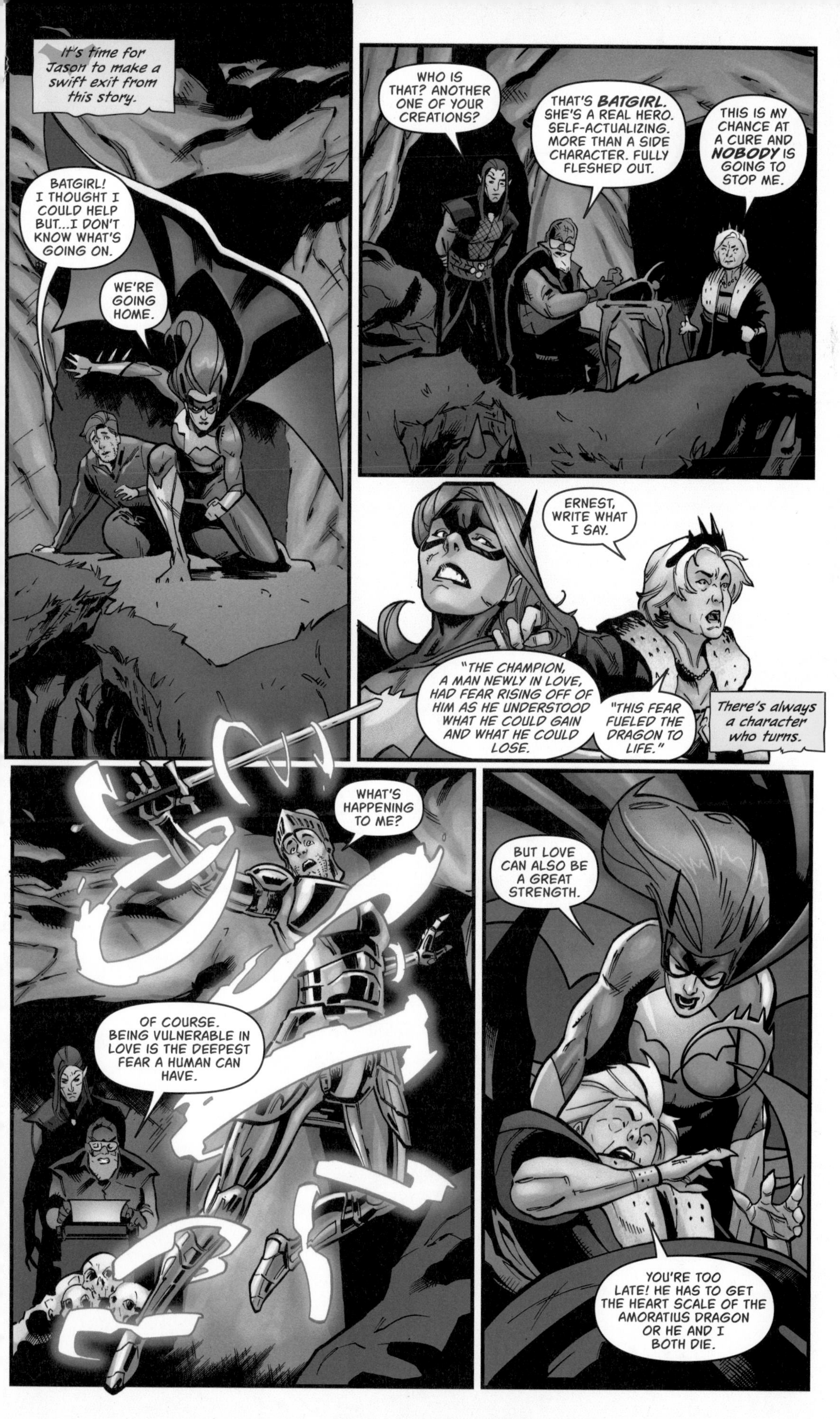
It's time for Jason to make a swift exit from this story.
BATGIRL! I THOUGHT I COULD HELP BUT...I DON'T KNOW WHAT'S GOING ON.
WE'RE GOING HOME.
WHO IS THAT? ANOTHER ONE OF YOUR CREATIONS?
THAT'S BATGIRL. SHE'S A REAL HERO. SELF-ACTUALIZING. MORE THAN A SIDE CHARACTER. FULLY FLESHED OUT.
THIS IS MY CHANCE AT A CURE AND NOBODY IS GOING TO STOP ME.
ERNEST, WRITE WHAT I SAY.
"THE CHAMPION, A MAN NEWLY IN LOVE, HAD FEAR RISING OFF OF HIM AS HE UNDERSTOOD WHAT HE COULD GAIN AND WHAT HE COULD LOSE.
"THIS FEAR FUELED THE DRAGON TO LIFE."
There's always a character who turns.
WHAT'S HAPPENING TO ME?
OF COURSE. BEING VULNERABLE IN LOVE IS THE DEEPEST FEAR A HUMAN CAN HAVE.
BUT LOVE CAN ALSO BE A GREAT STRENGTH.
YOU'RE TOO LATE! HE HAS TO GET THE HEART SCALE OF THE AMORATIUS DRAGON OR HE AND I BOTH DIE.

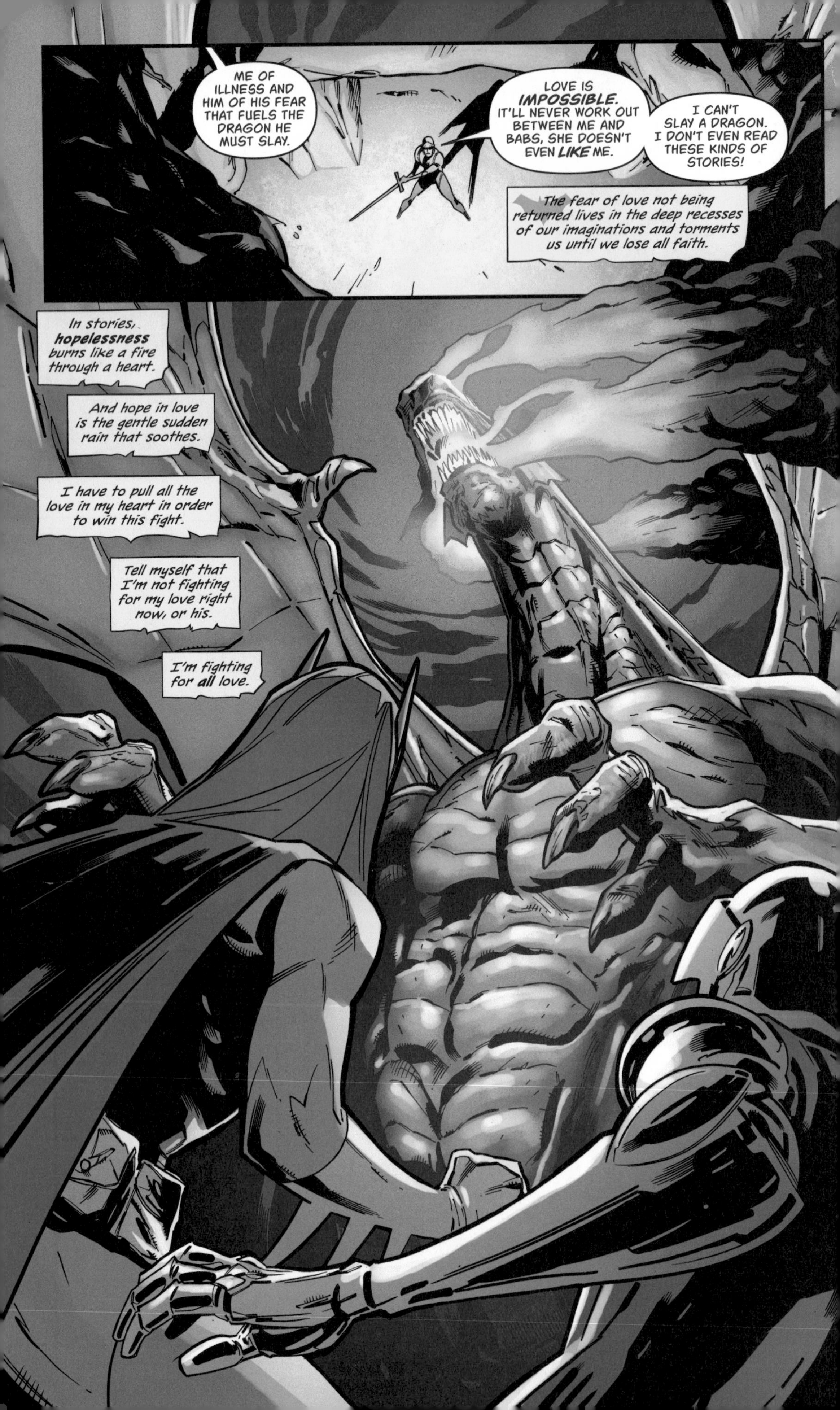

ME OF ILLNESS AND HIM OF HIS FEAR THAT FUELS THE DRAGON HE MUST SLAY.
LOVE IS *IMPOSSIBLE.* IT'LL NEVER WORK OUT BETWEEN ME AND BABS, SHE DOESN'T EVEN *LIKE* ME.
I CAN'T SLAY A DRAGON. I DON'T EVEN READ THESE KINDS OF STORIES!
The fear of love not being returned lives in the deep recesses of our imaginations and torments us until we lose all faith.
In stories, **hopelessness** burns like a fire through a heart.
And hope in love is the gentle sudden rain that soothes.
I have to pull all the love in my heart in order to win this fight.
Tell myself that I'm not fighting for my love right now, or his.
I'm fighting for **all** love.

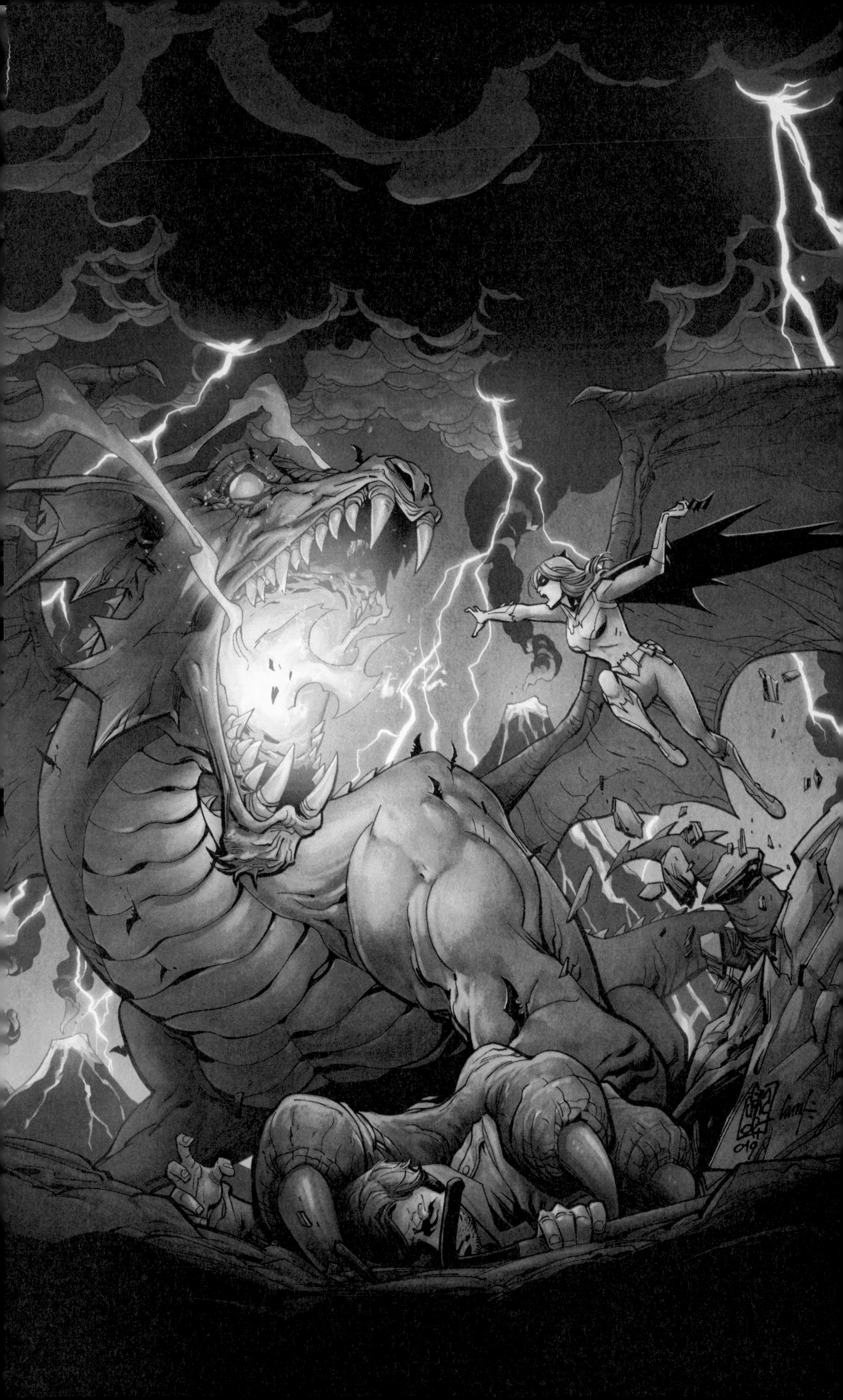

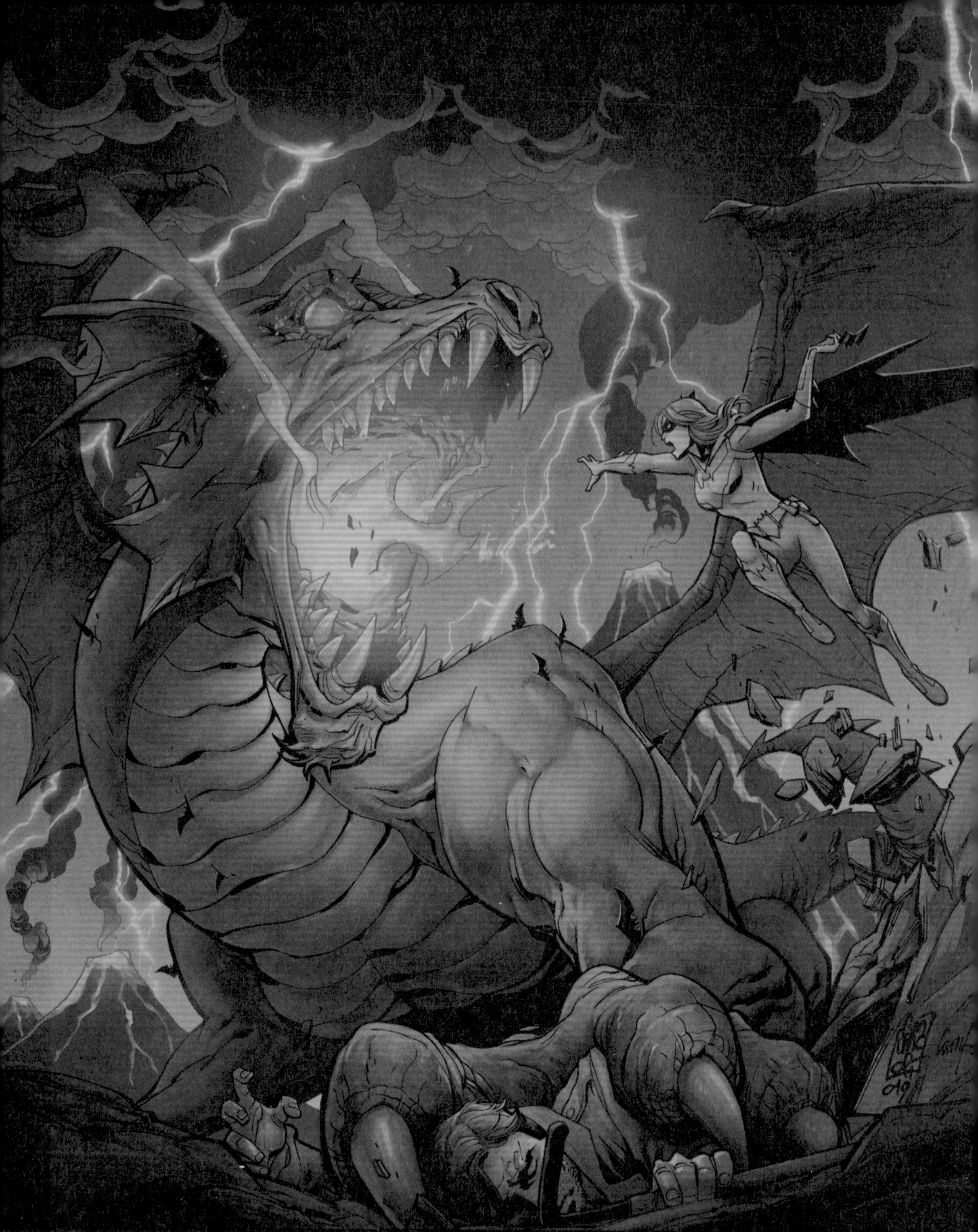

BATGIRL
#44

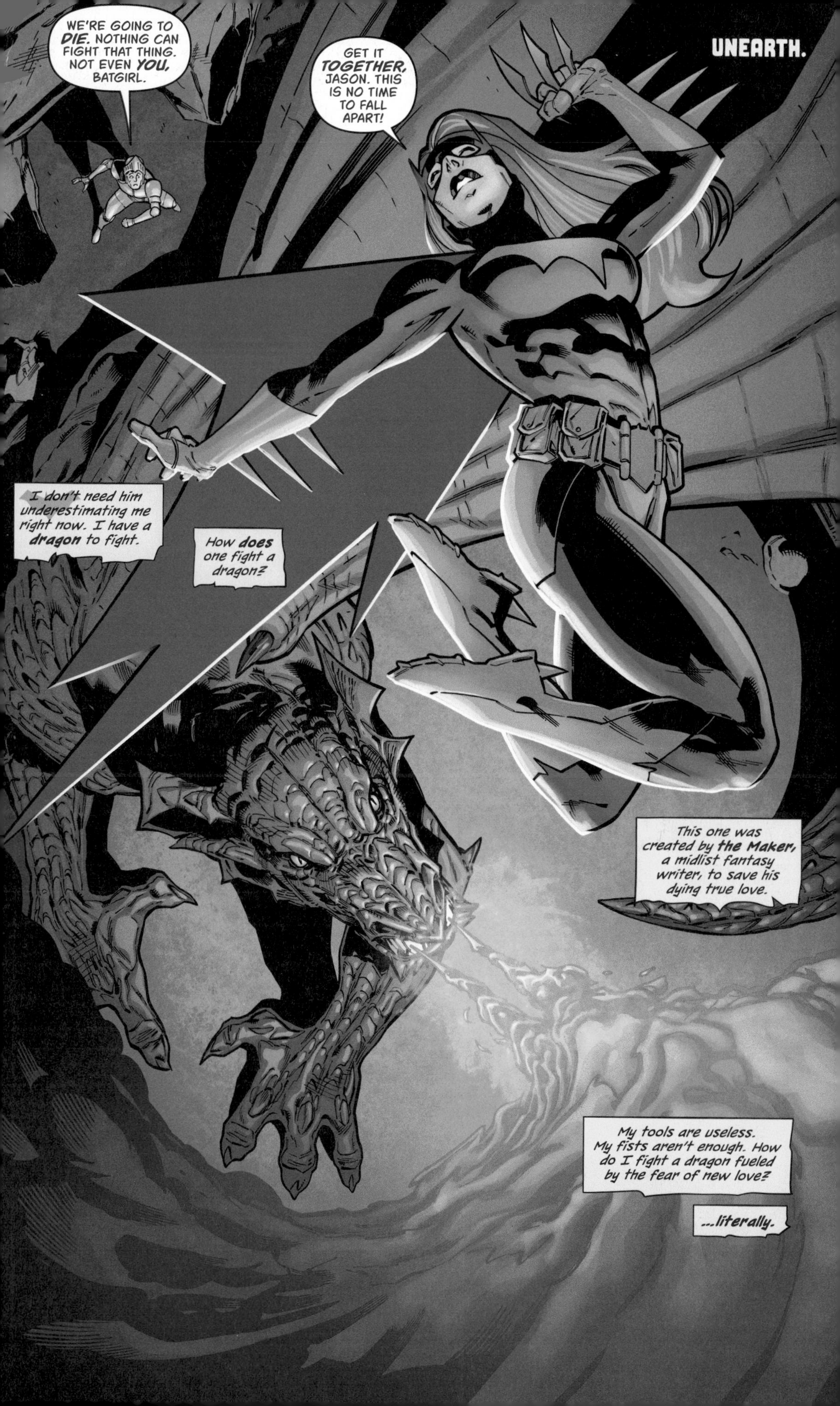
UNEARTH.
WE'RE GOING TO DIE. NOTHING CAN FIGHT THAT THING. NOT EVEN YOU, BATGIRL.
GET IT TOGETHER, JASON. THIS IS NO TIME TO FALL APART!
I don't need him underestimating me right now. I have a dragon to fight.
How does one fight a dragon?
This one was created by the Maker, a midlist fantasy writer, to save his dying true love.
My tools are useless. My fists aren't enough. How do I fight a dragon fueled by the fear of new love?
...literally.

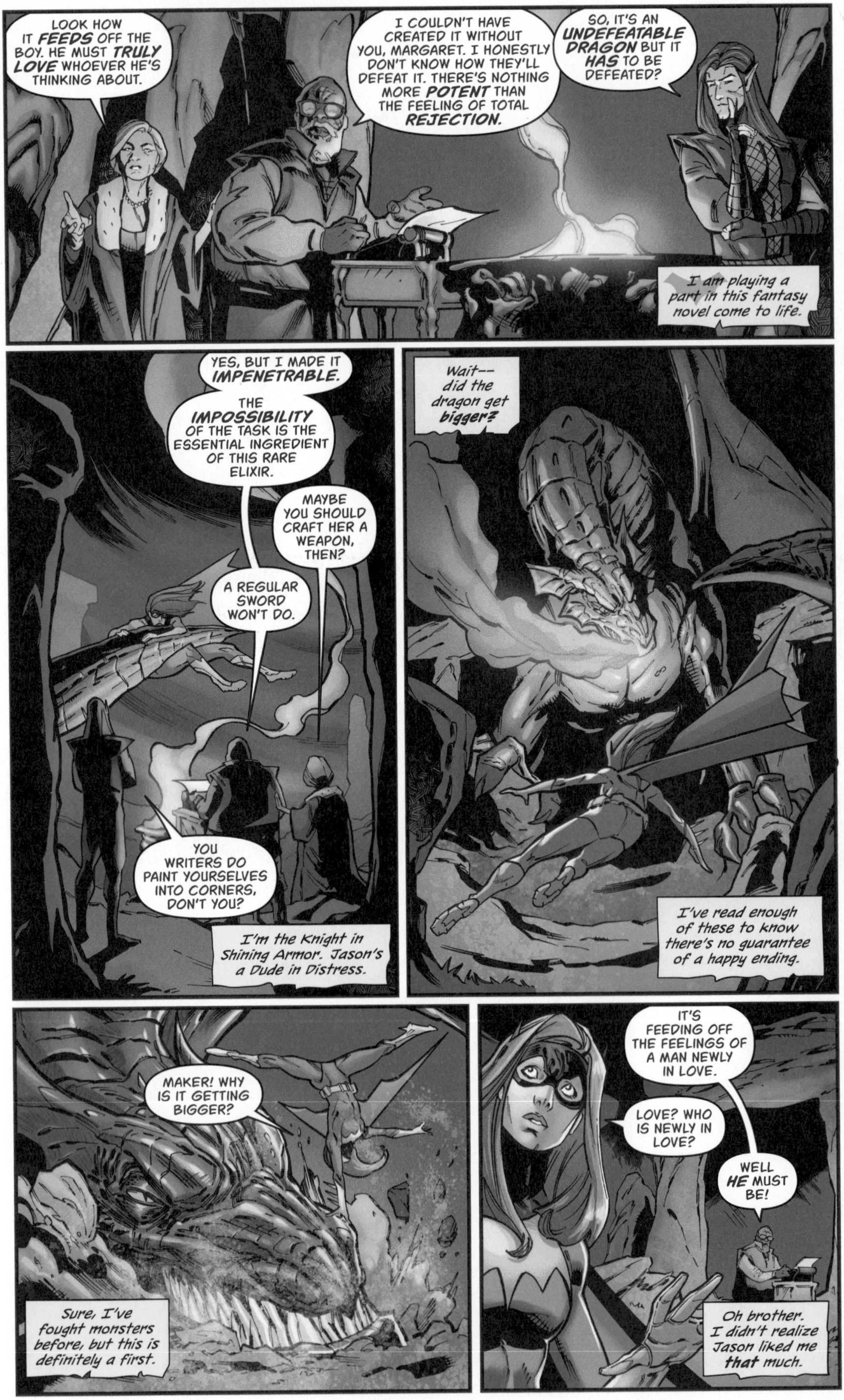

LOOK HOW IT FEEDS OFF THE BOY. HE MUST TRULY LOVE WHOEVER HE'S THINKING ABOUT.
I COULDN'T HAVE CREATED IT WITHOUT YOU, MARGARET. I HONESTLY DON'T KNOW HOW THEY'LL DEFEAT IT. THERE'S NOTHING MORE POTENT THAN THE FEELING OF TOTAL REJECTION.
SO, IT'S AN UNDEFEATABLE DRAGON BUT IT HAS TO BE DEFEATED?
I am playing a part in this fantasy novel come to life.
YES, BUT I MADE IT IMPENETRABLE.
THE IMPOSSIBILITY OF THE TASK IS THE ESSENTIAL INGREDIENT OF THIS RARE ELIXIR.
MAYBE YOU SHOULD CRAFT HER A WEAPON, THEN?
A REGULAR SWORD WON'T DO.
YOU WRITERS DO PAINT YOURSELVES INTO CORNERS, DON'T YOU?
I'm the Knight in Shining Armor. Jason's a Dude in Distress.
Wait-- did the dragon get bigger?
I've read enough of these to know there's no guarantee of a happy ending.
MAKER! WHY IS IT GETTING BIGGER?
Sure, I've fought monsters before, but this is definitely a first.
IT'S FEEDING OFF THE FEELINGS OF A MAN NEWLY IN LOVE.
LOVE? WHO IS NEWLY IN LOVE?
WELL HE MUST BE!
Oh brother. I didn't realize Jason liked me that much.

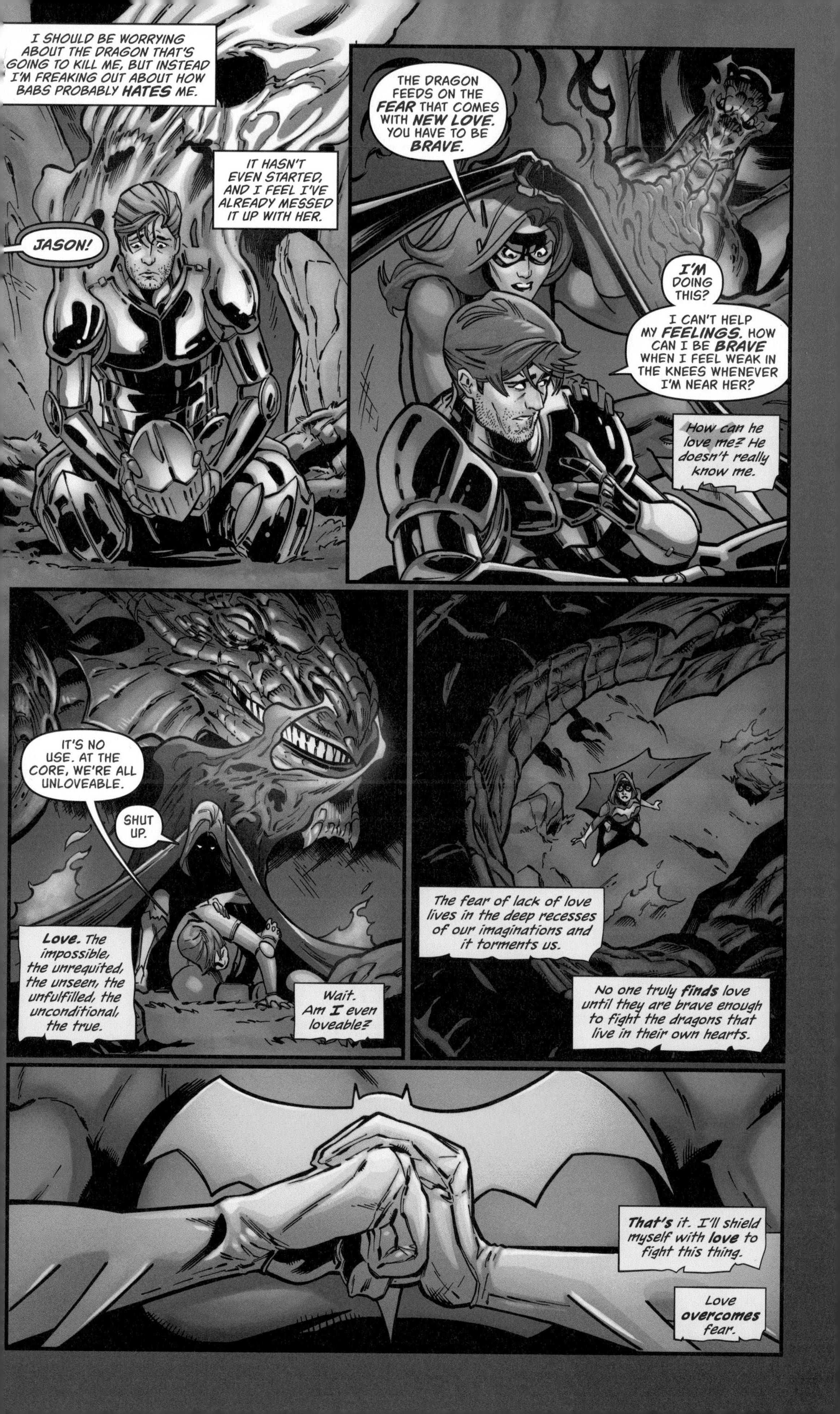

I SHOULD BE WORRYING ABOUT THE DRAGON THAT'S GOING TO KILL ME, BUT INSTEAD I'M FREAKING OUT ABOUT HOW BABS PROBABLY HATES ME.
IT HASN'T EVEN STARTED, AND I FEEL I'VE ALREADY MESSED IT UP WITH HER.
JASON!
THE DRAGON FEEDS ON THE FEAR THAT COMES WITH NEW LOVE. YOU HAVE TO BE BRAVE.
I'M DOING THIS?
I CAN'T HELP MY FEELINGS. HOW CAN I BE BRAVE WHEN I FEEL WEAK IN THE KNEES WHENEVER I'M NEAR HER?
How can he love me? He doesn't really know me.
IT'S NO USE. AT THE CORE, WE'RE ALL UNLOVEABLE.
SHUT UP.
Love. The impossible, the unrequited, the unseen, the unfulfilled, the unconditional, the true.
Wait. Am I even loveable?
The fear of lack of love lives in the deep recesses of our imaginations and it torments us.
No one truly finds love until they are brave enough to fight the dragons that live in their own hearts.
That's it. I'll shield myself with love to fight this thing.
Love overcomes fear.

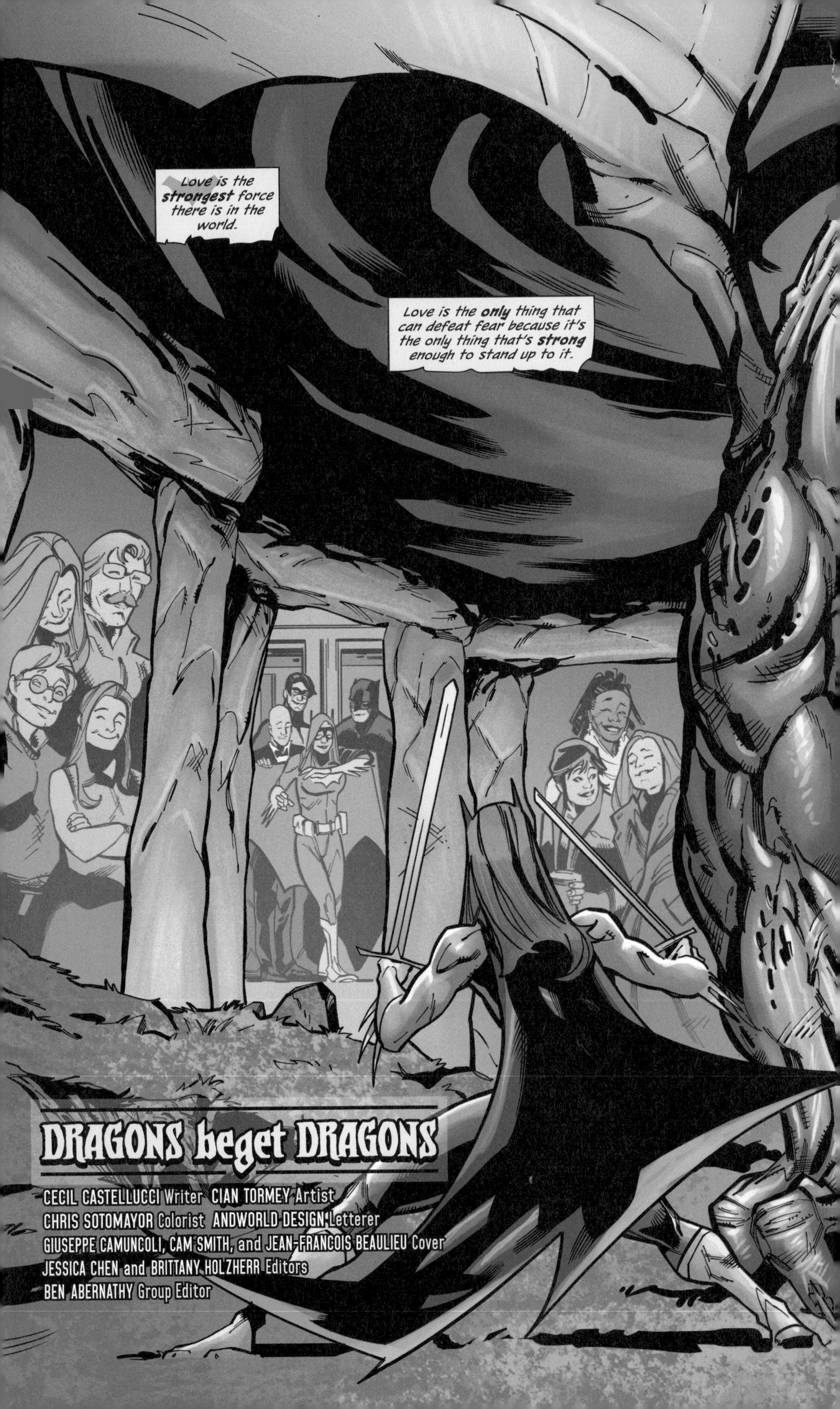

Love is the strongest force there is in the world.
Love is the only thing that can defeat fear because it's the only thing that's strong enough to stand up to it.
DRAGONS beget DRAGONS
CECIL CASTELLUCCI Writer CIAN TORMEY Artist
CHRIS SOTOMAYOR Colorist ANDWORLD DESIGN Letterer
GIUSEPPE CAMUNCOLI, CAM SMITH, and JEAN-FRANCOIS BEAULIEU Cover
JESSICA CHEN and BRITTANY HOLZHERR Editors
BEN ABERNATHY Group Editor

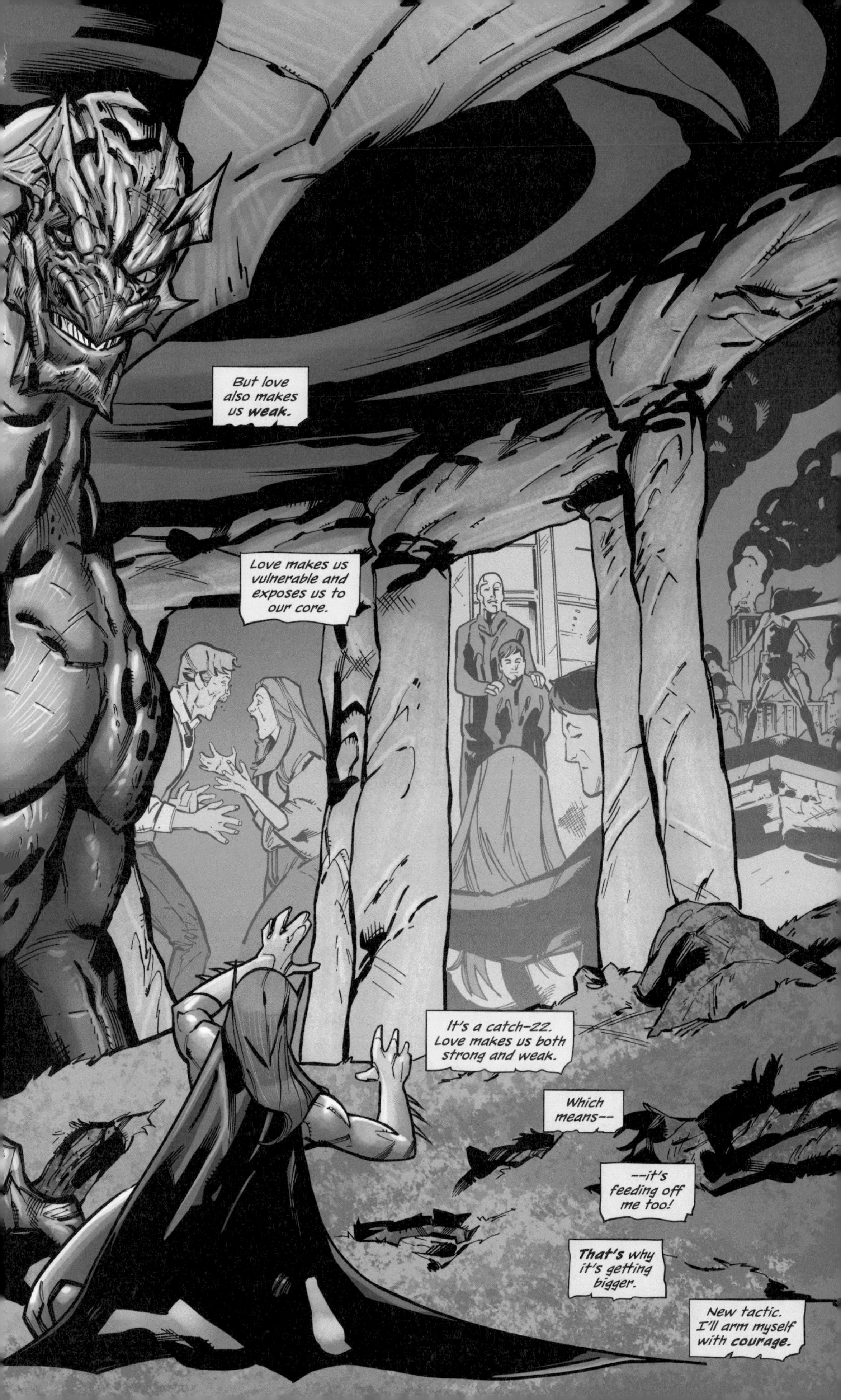
But love also makes us **weak.**
Love makes us vulnerable and exposes us to our core.
It's a catch-22. Love makes us both strong and weak.
Which means--
--it's feeding off me too!
That's why it's getting bigger.
New tactic. I'll arm myself with **courage.**

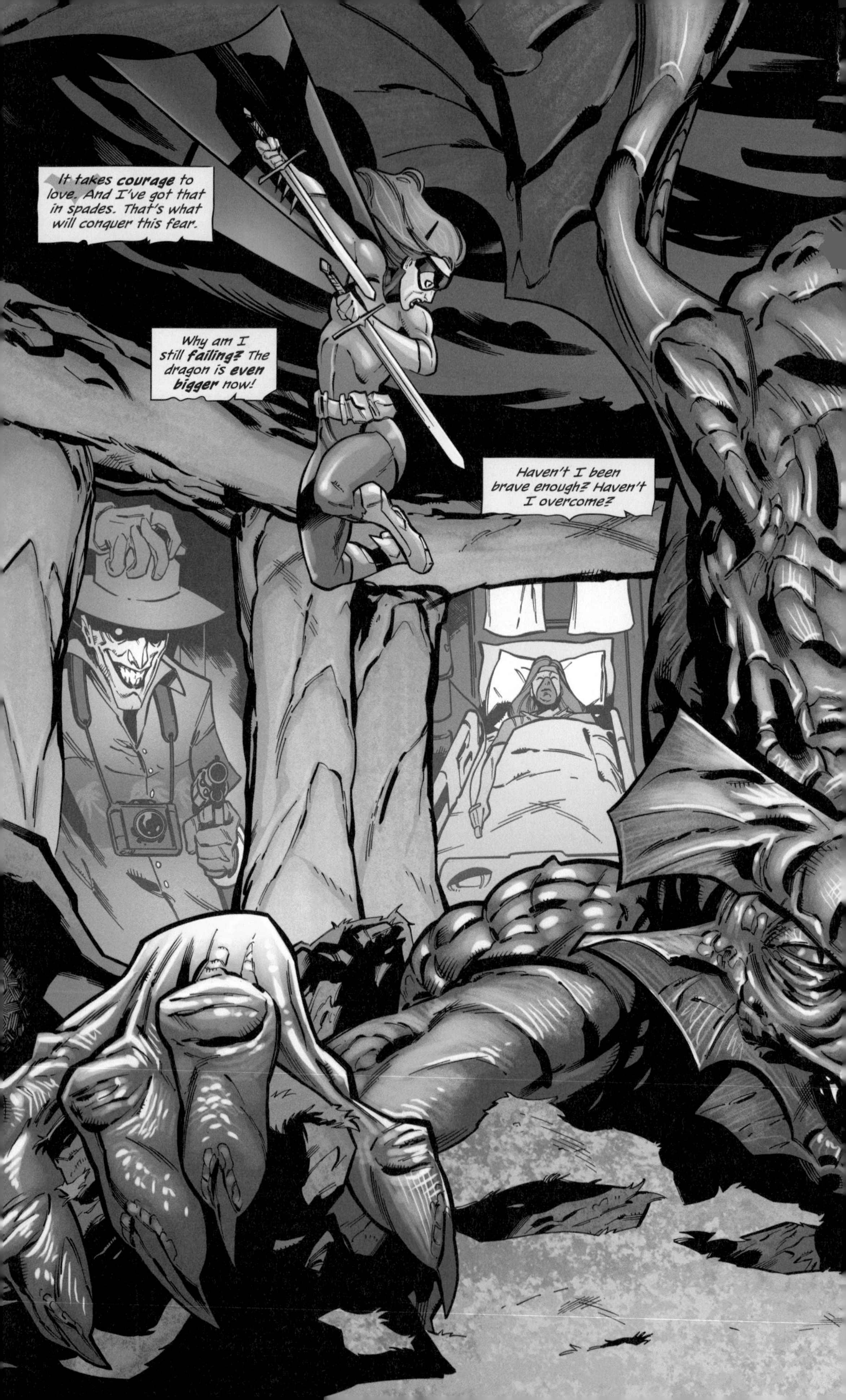
It takes **courage** to love. And I've got that in spades. That's what will conquer this fear.
Why am I still **failing?** The dragon is **even bigger** now!
Haven't I been brave enough? Haven't I overcome?

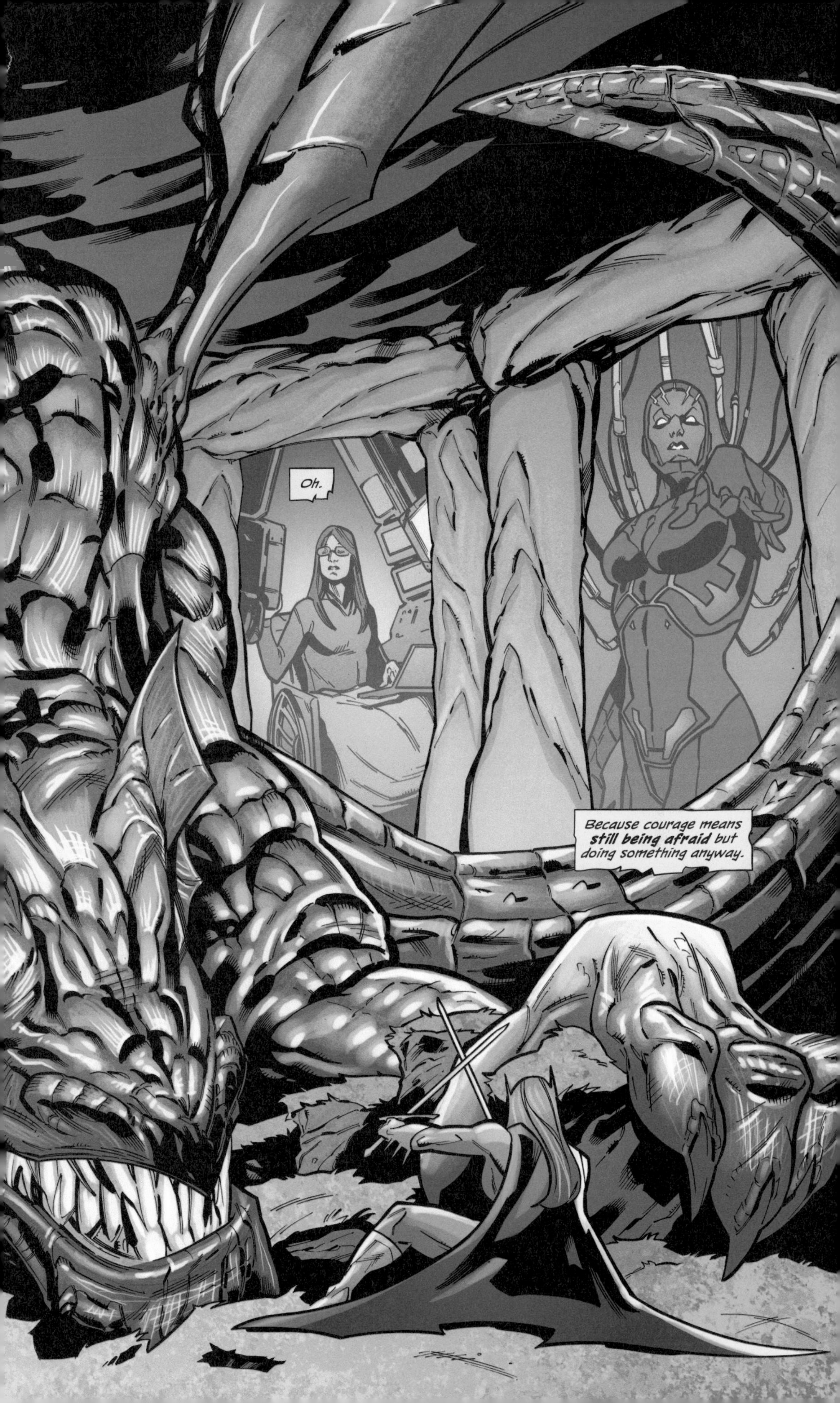

Oh.
Because courage means **still being afraid** but doing something anyway.

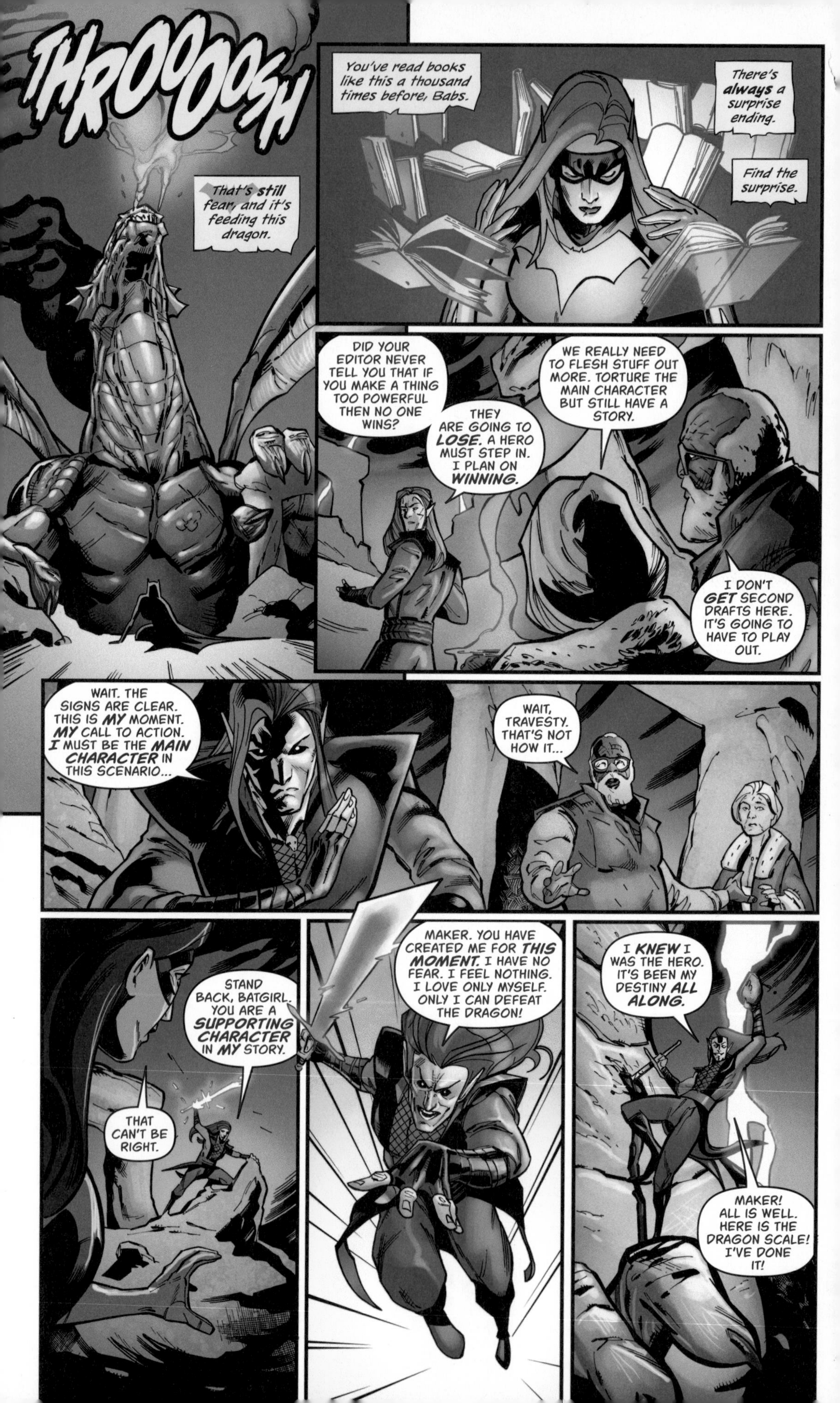

THROOOOOSH
That's still fear, and it's feeding this dragon.
You've read books like this a thousand times before, Babs.
There's always a surprise ending.
Find the surprise.
DID YOUR EDITOR NEVER TELL YOU THAT IF YOU MAKE A THING TOO POWERFUL THEN NO ONE WINS?
THEY ARE GOING TO LOSE. A HERO MUST STEP IN. I PLAN ON WINNING.
WE REALLY NEED TO FLESH STUFF OUT MORE. TORTURE THE MAIN CHARACTER BUT STILL HAVE A STORY.
I DON'T GET SECOND DRAFTS HERE. IT'S GOING TO HAVE TO PLAY OUT.
WAIT. THE SIGNS ARE CLEAR. THIS IS MY MOMENT. MY CALL TO ACTION. I MUST BE THE MAIN CHARACTER IN THIS SCENARIO...
WAIT, TRAVESTY. THAT'S NOT HOW IT...
STAND BACK, BATGIRL. YOU ARE A SUPPORTING CHARACTER IN MY STORY.
THAT CAN'T BE RIGHT.
MAKER. YOU HAVE CREATED ME FOR THIS MOMENT. I HAVE NO FEAR. I FEEL NOTHING. I LOVE ONLY MYSELF. ONLY I CAN DEFEAT THE DRAGON!
I KNEW I WAS THE HERO. IT'S BEEN MY DESTINY ALL ALONG.
MAKER! ALL IS WELL. HERE IS THE DRAGON SCALE! I'VE DONE IT!

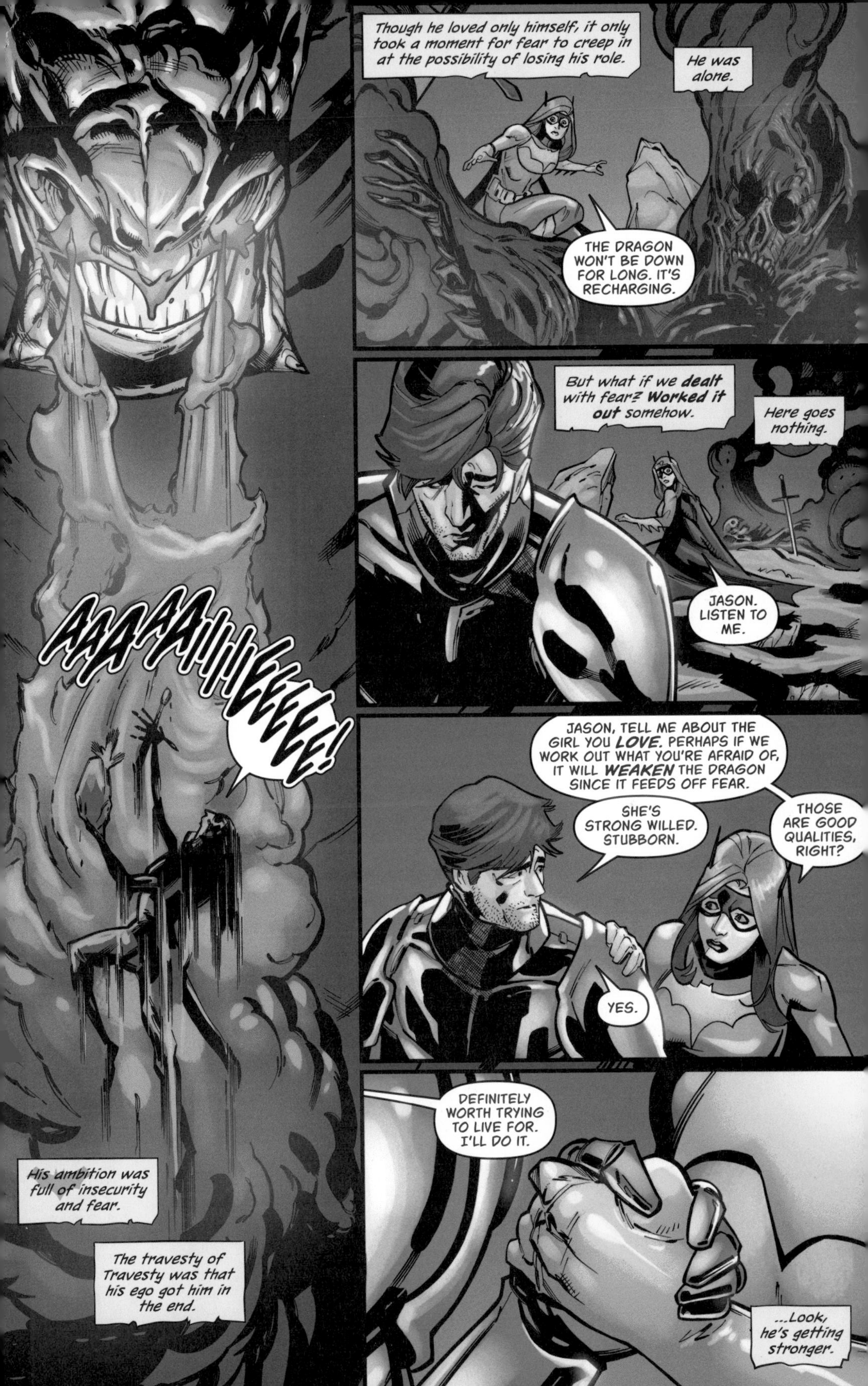
AAAAAIIIIEEEEE!
His ambition was full of insecurity and fear.
The travesty of Travesty was that his ego got him in the end.
Though he loved only himself, it only took a moment for fear to creep in at the possibility of losing his role.
He was alone.
THE DRAGON WON'T BE DOWN FOR LONG. IT'S RECHARGING.
But what if we dealt with fear? Worked it out somehow.
Here goes nothing.
JASON. LISTEN TO ME.
JASON, TELL ME ABOUT THE GIRL YOU LOVE. PERHAPS IF WE WORK OUT WHAT YOU'RE AFRAID OF, IT WILL WEAKEN THE DRAGON SINCE IT FEEDS OFF FEAR.
SHE'S STRONG WILLED. STUBBORN.
THOSE ARE GOOD QUALITIES, RIGHT?
YES.
DEFINITELY WORTH TRYING TO LIVE FOR. I'LL DO IT.
...Look, he's getting stronger.

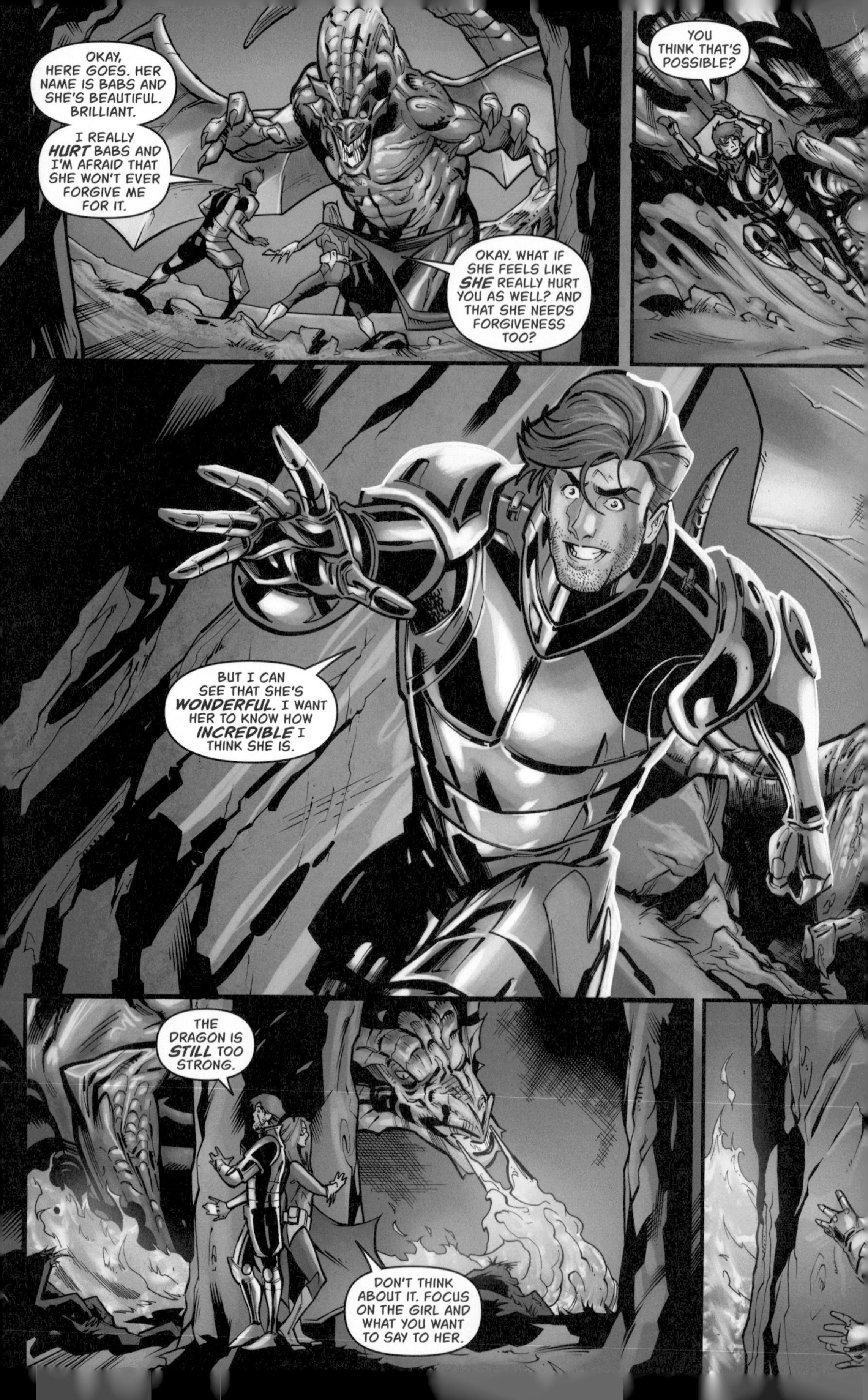
OKAY, HERE GOES. HER NAME IS BABS AND SHE'S BEAUTIFUL. BRILLIANT.
I REALLY HURT BABS AND I'M AFRAID THAT SHE WON'T EVER FORGIVE ME FOR IT.
OKAY. WHAT IF SHE FEELS LIKE SHE REALLY HURT YOU AS WELL? AND THAT SHE NEEDS FORGIVENESS TOO?
YOU THINK THAT'S POSSIBLE?
BUT I CAN SEE THAT SHE'S WONDERFUL. I WANT HER TO KNOW HOW INCREDIBLE I THINK SHE IS.
THE DRAGON IS STILL TOO STRONG.
DON'T THINK ABOUT IT. FOCUS ON THE GIRL AND WHAT YOU WANT TO SAY TO HER.

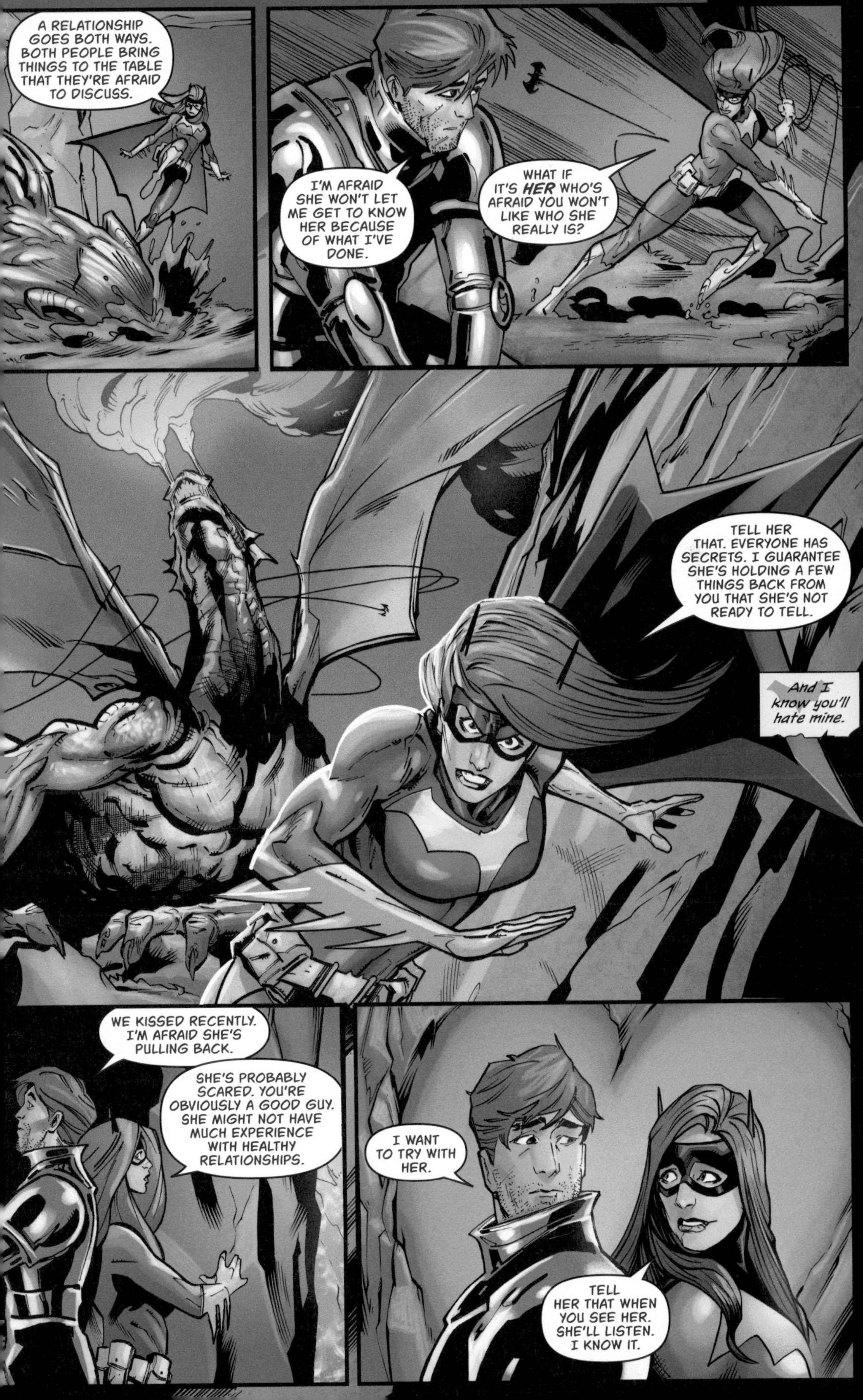
A RELATIONSHIP GOES BOTH WAYS. BOTH PEOPLE BRING THINGS TO THE TABLE THAT THEY'RE AFRAID TO DISCUSS.
I'M AFRAID SHE WON'T LET ME GET TO KNOW HER BECAUSE OF WHAT I'VE DONE.
WHAT IF IT'S HER WHO'S AFRAID YOU WON'T LIKE WHO SHE REALLY IS?
TELL HER THAT. EVERYONE HAS SECRETS. I GUARANTEE SHE'S HOLDING A FEW THINGS BACK FROM YOU THAT SHE'S NOT READY TO TELL.
And I know you'll hate mine.
WE KISSED RECENTLY. I'M AFRAID SHE'S PULLING BACK.
SHE'S PROBABLY SCARED. YOU'RE OBVIOUSLY A GOOD GUY. SHE MIGHT NOT HAVE MUCH EXPERIENCE WITH HEALTHY RELATIONSHIPS.
I WANT TO TRY WITH HER.
TELL HER THAT WHEN YOU SEE HER. SHE'LL LISTEN. I KNOW IT.

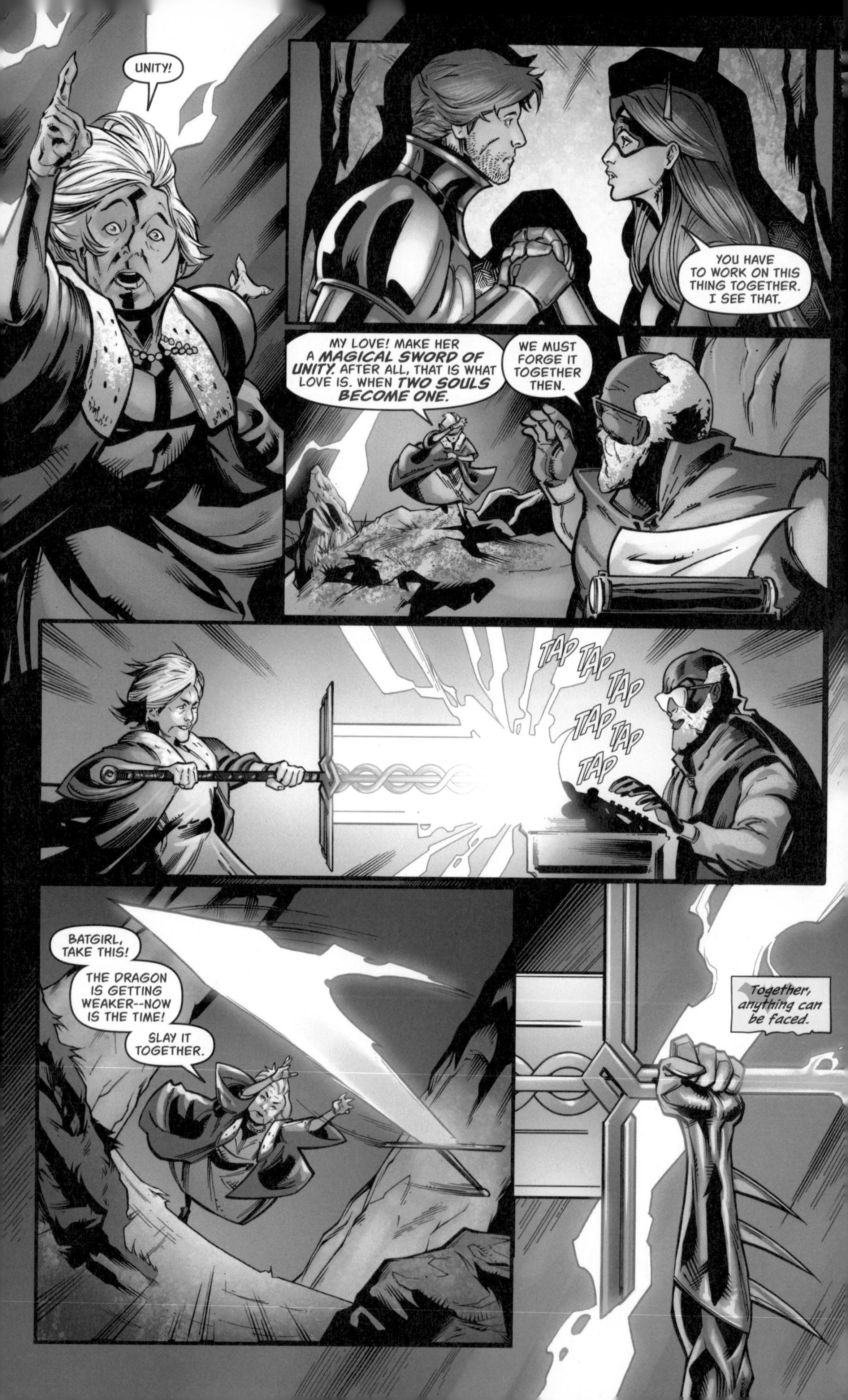
UNITY!
YOU HAVE TO WORK ON THIS THING TOGETHER. I SEE THAT.
MY LOVE! MAKE HER A MAGICAL SWORD OF UNITY. AFTER ALL, THAT IS WHAT LOVE IS. WHEN TWO SOULS BECOME ONE.
WE MUST FORGE IT TOGETHER THEN.
TAP TAP TAP TAP TAP TAP
BATGIRL, TAKE THIS!
THE DRAGON IS GETTING WEAKER--NOW IS THE TIME!
SLAY IT TOGETHER.
Together, anything can be faced.

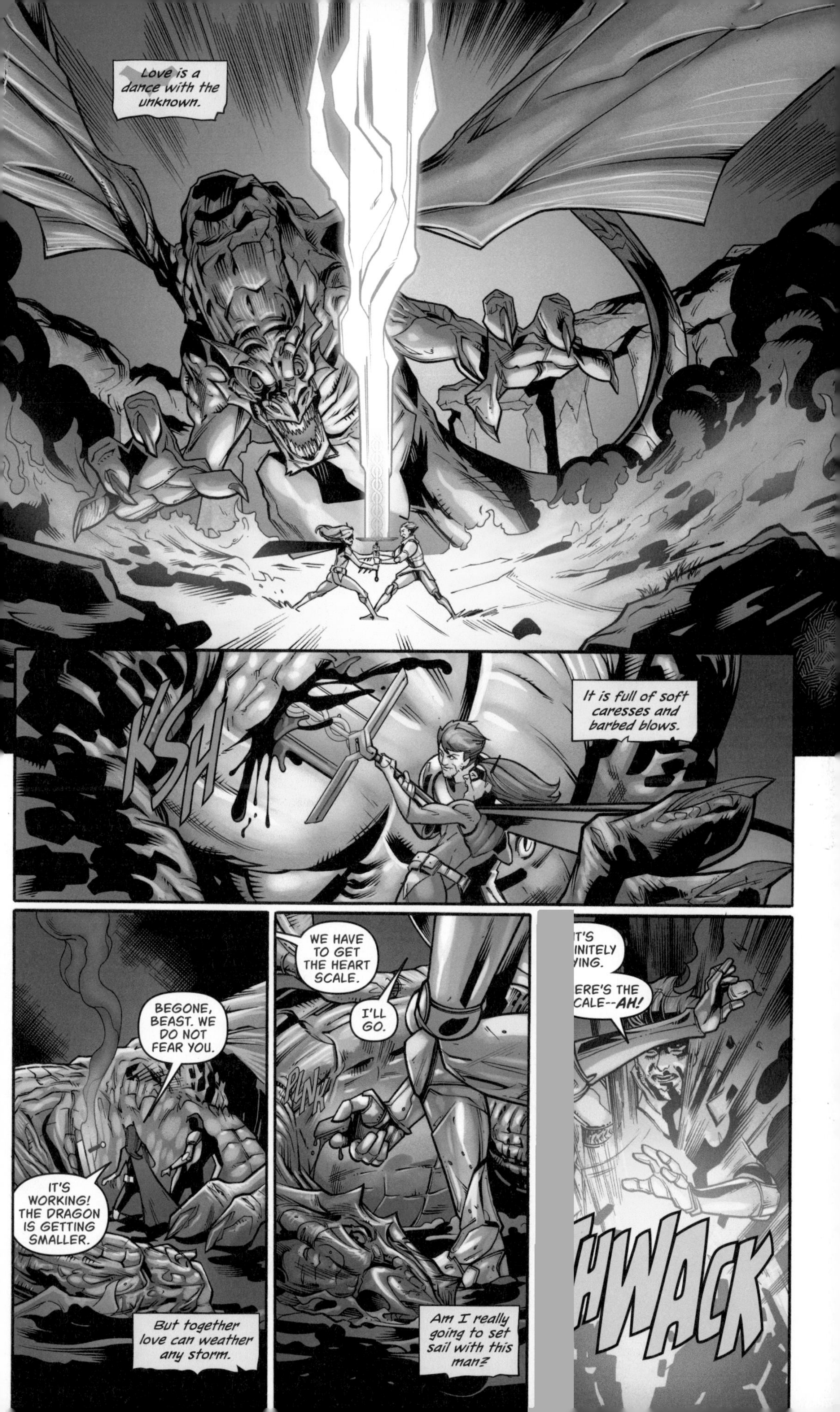
Love is a dance with the unknown.
KSH
It is full of soft caresses and barbed blows.
BEGONE, BEAST. WE DO NOT FEAR YOU.
IT'S WORKING! THE DRAGON IS GETTING SMALLER.
But together love can weather any storm.
WE HAVE TO GET THE HEART SCALE.
I'LL GO.
PLNK
Am I really going to set sail with this man?
T'S INITELY YING.
ERE'S THE CALE--AH!
HWACK

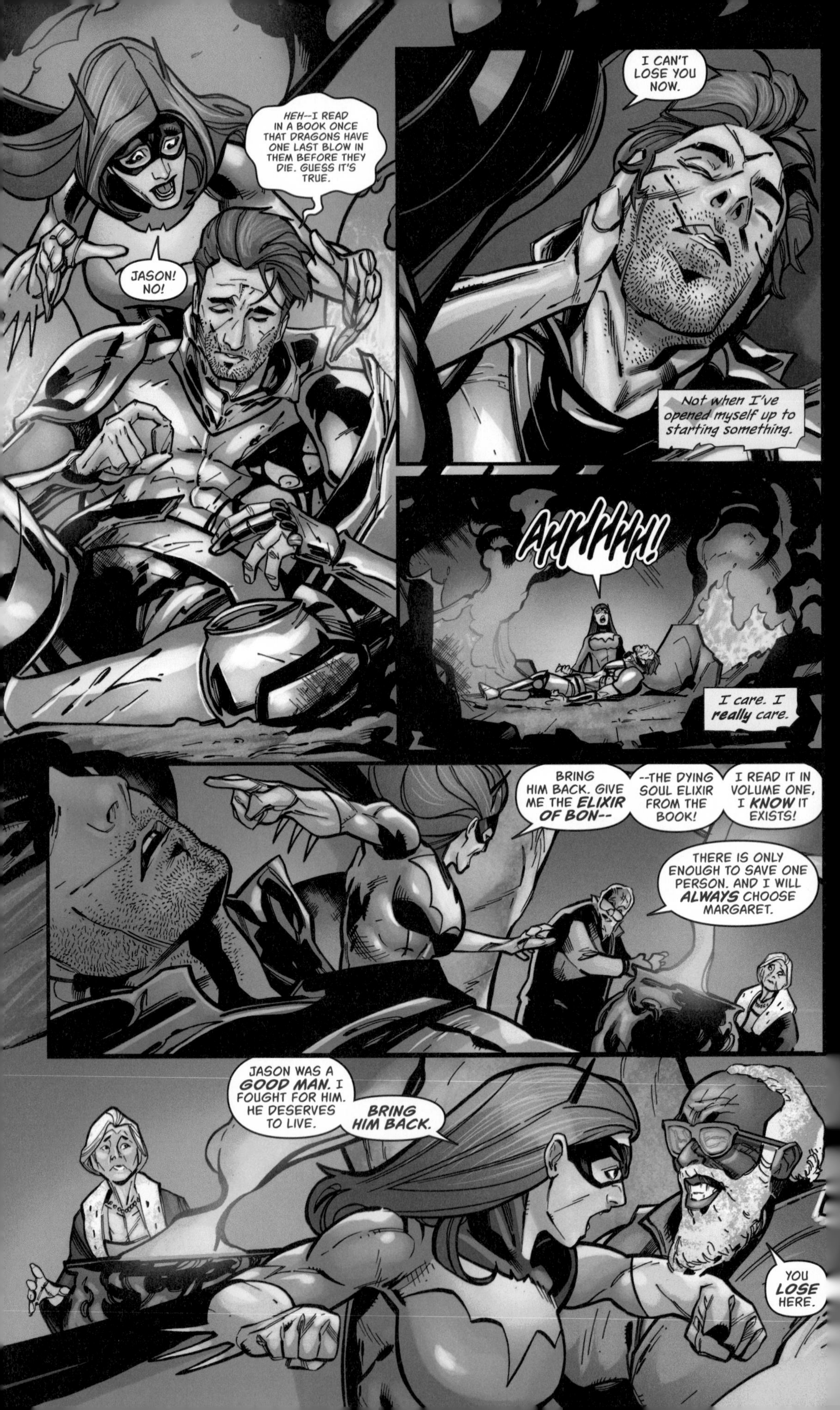
HEH--I READ IN A BOOK ONCE THAT DRAGONS HAVE ONE LAST BLOW IN THEM BEFORE THEY DIE. GUESS IT'S TRUE.
JASON! NO!
I CAN'T LOSE YOU NOW.
Not when I've opened myself up to starting something.
AHHHHH!
I care. I really care.
BRING HIM BACK. GIVE ME THE ELIXIR OF BON--
--THE DYING SOUL ELIXIR FROM THE BOOK!
I READ IT IN VOLUME ONE, I KNOW IT EXISTS!
THERE IS ONLY ENOUGH TO SAVE ONE PERSON. AND I WILL ALWAYS CHOOSE MARGARET.
JASON WAS A GOOD MAN. I FOUGHT FOR HIM. HE DESERVES TO LIVE.
BRING HIM BACK.
YOU LOSE HERE.

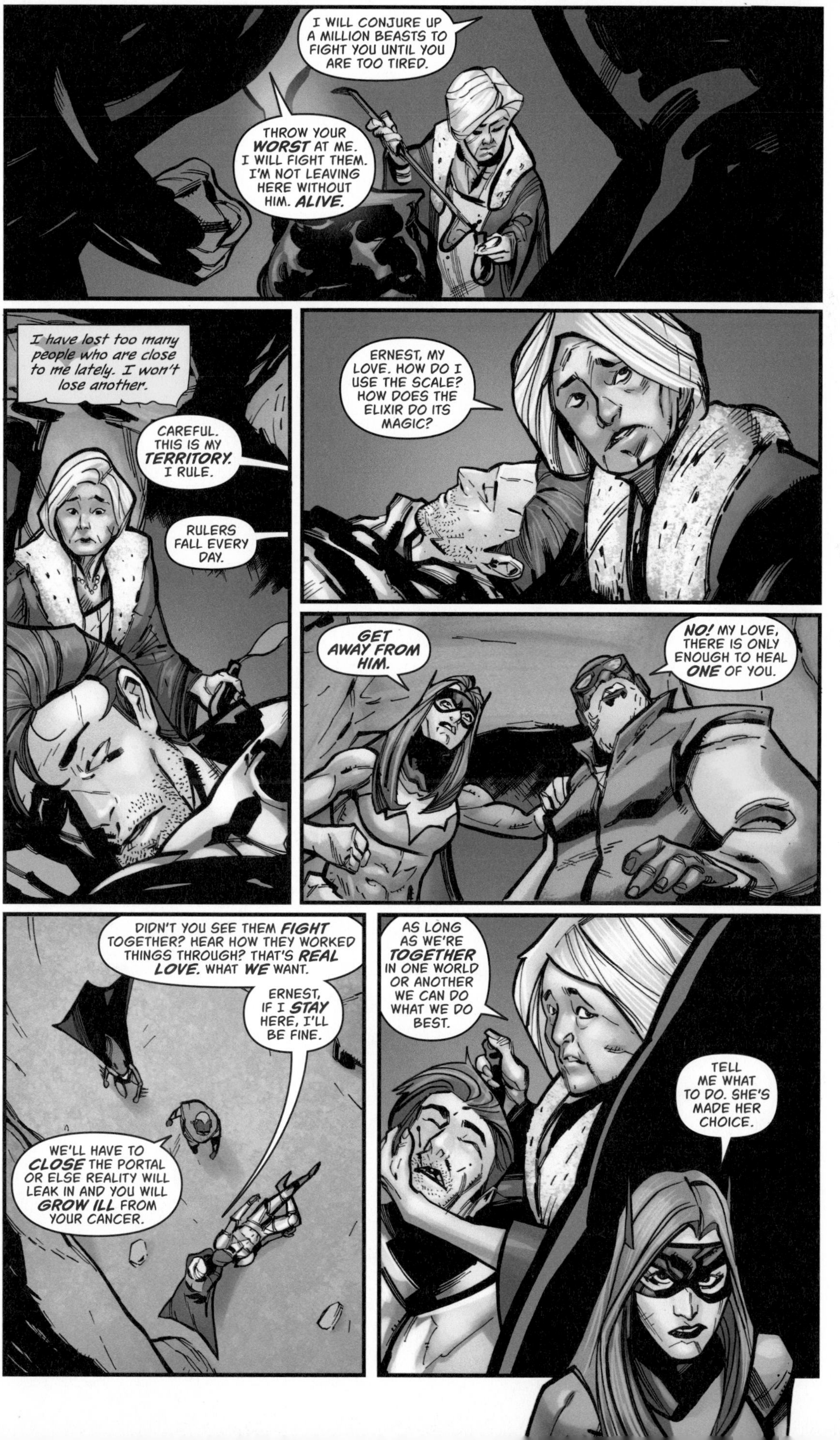
I WILL CONJURE UP A MILLION BEASTS TO FIGHT YOU UNTIL YOU ARE TOO TIRED.
THROW YOUR WORST AT ME. I WILL FIGHT THEM. I'M NOT LEAVING HERE WITHOUT HIM. ALIVE.
I have lost too many people who are close to me lately. I won't lose another.
CAREFUL. THIS IS MY TERRITORY. I RULE.
RULERS FALL EVERY DAY.
ERNEST, MY LOVE. HOW DO I USE THE SCALE? HOW DOES THE ELIXIR DO ITS MAGIC?
GET AWAY FROM HIM.
NO! MY LOVE, THERE IS ONLY ENOUGH TO HEAL ONE OF YOU.
DIDN'T YOU SEE THEM FIGHT TOGETHER? HEAR HOW THEY WORKED THINGS THROUGH? THAT'S REAL LOVE. WHAT WE WANT.
ERNEST, IF I STAY HERE, I'LL BE FINE.
WE'LL HAVE TO CLOSE THE PORTAL OR ELSE REALITY WILL LEAK IN AND YOU WILL GROW ILL FROM YOUR CANCER.
AS LONG AS WE'RE TOGETHER IN ONE WORLD OR ANOTHER WE CAN DO WHAT WE DO BEST.
TELL ME WHAT TO DO. SHE'S MADE HER CHOICE.

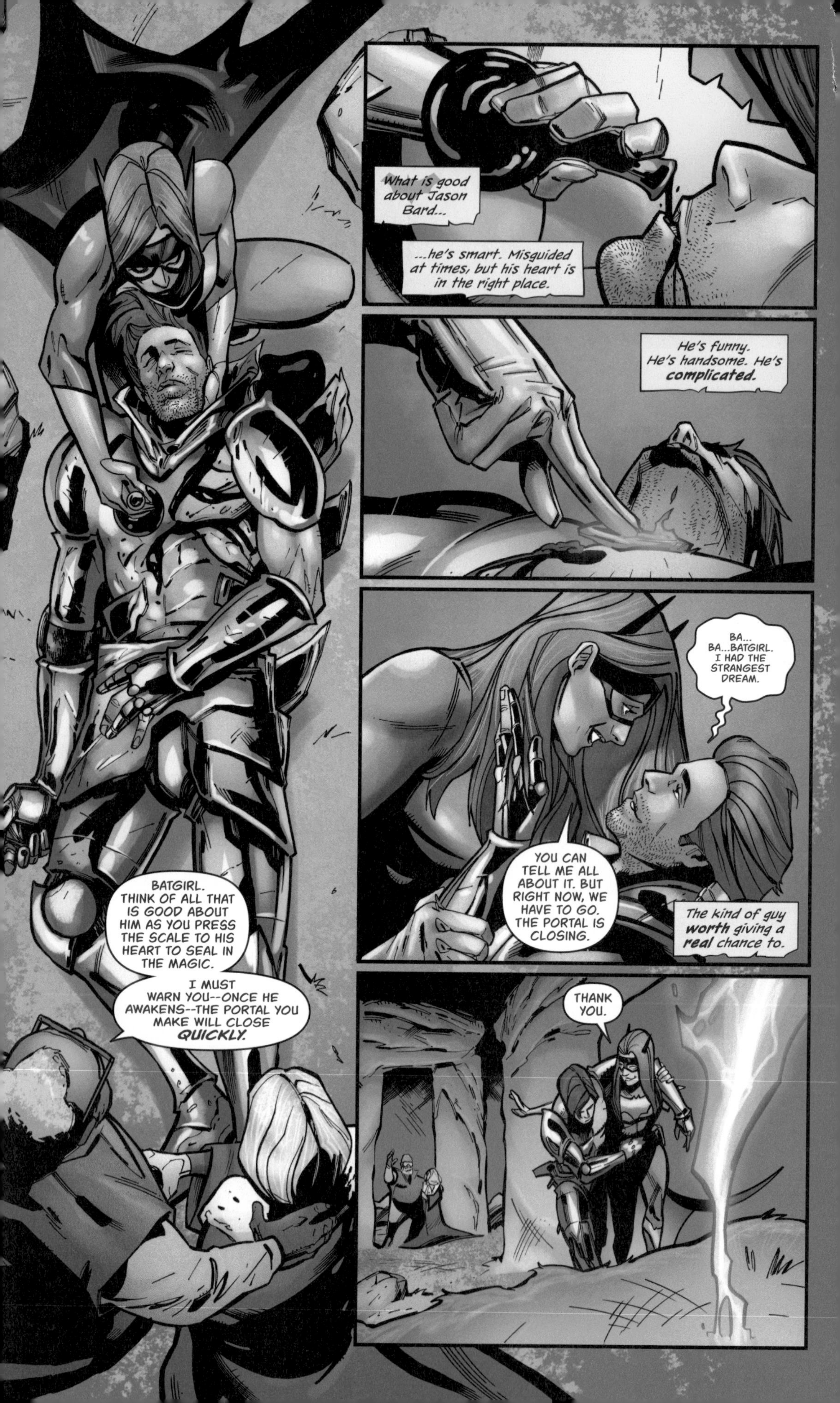

What is good about Jason Bard...
...he's smart. Misguided at times, but his heart is in the right place.
He's funny. He's handsome. He's **complicated.**
BATGIRL. THINK OF ALL THAT IS GOOD ABOUT HIM AS YOU PRESS THE SCALE TO HIS HEART TO SEAL IN THE MAGIC.
I MUST WARN YOU--ONCE HE AWAKENS--THE PORTAL YOU MAKE WILL CLOSE ***QUICKLY.***
BA... BA...BATGIRL. I HAD THE STRANGEST DREAM.
YOU CAN TELL ME ALL ABOUT IT. BUT RIGHT NOW, WE HAVE TO GO. THE PORTAL IS CLOSING.
The kind of guy **worth** giving a **real** chance to.
THANK YOU.

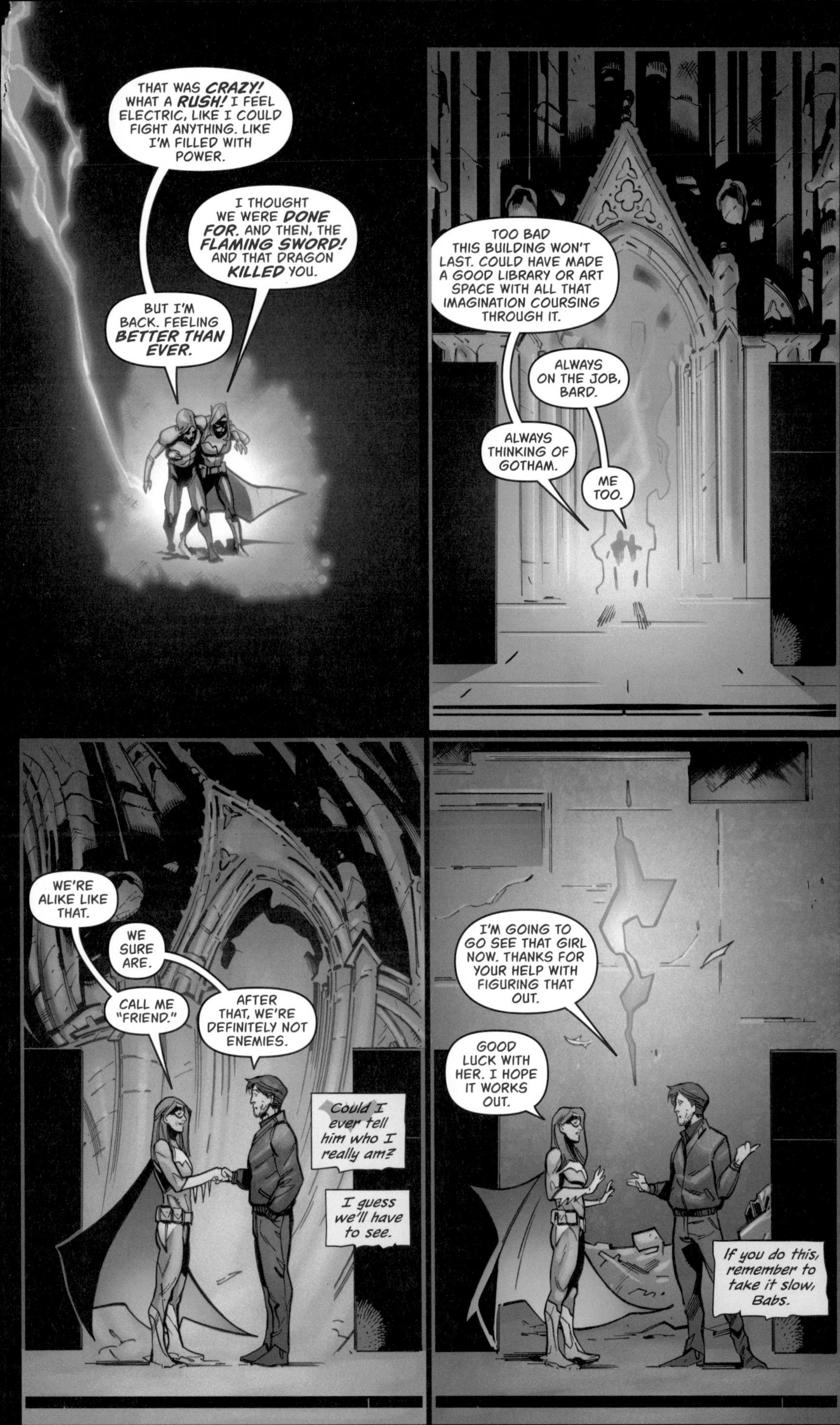
THAT WAS CRAZY! WHAT A RUSH! I FEEL ELECTRIC, LIKE I COULD FIGHT ANYTHING. LIKE I'M FILLED WITH POWER.
I THOUGHT WE WERE DONE FOR. AND THEN, THE FLAMING SWORD! AND THAT DRAGON KILLED YOU.
BUT I'M BACK. FEELING BETTER THAN EVER.
TOO BAD THIS BUILDING WON'T LAST. COULD HAVE MADE A GOOD LIBRARY OR ART SPACE WITH ALL THAT IMAGINATION COURSING THROUGH IT.
ALWAYS ON THE JOB, BARD.
ALWAYS THINKING OF GOTHAM.
ME TOO.
WE'RE ALIKE LIKE THAT.
WE SURE ARE.
CALL ME "FRIEND."
AFTER THAT, WE'RE DEFINITELY NOT ENEMIES.
Could I ever tell him who I really am?
I guess we'll have to see.
I'M GOING TO GO SEE THAT GIRL NOW. THANKS FOR YOUR HELP WITH FIGURING THAT OUT.
GOOD LUCK WITH HER. I HOPE IT WORKS OUT.
If you do this, remember to take it slow, Babs.

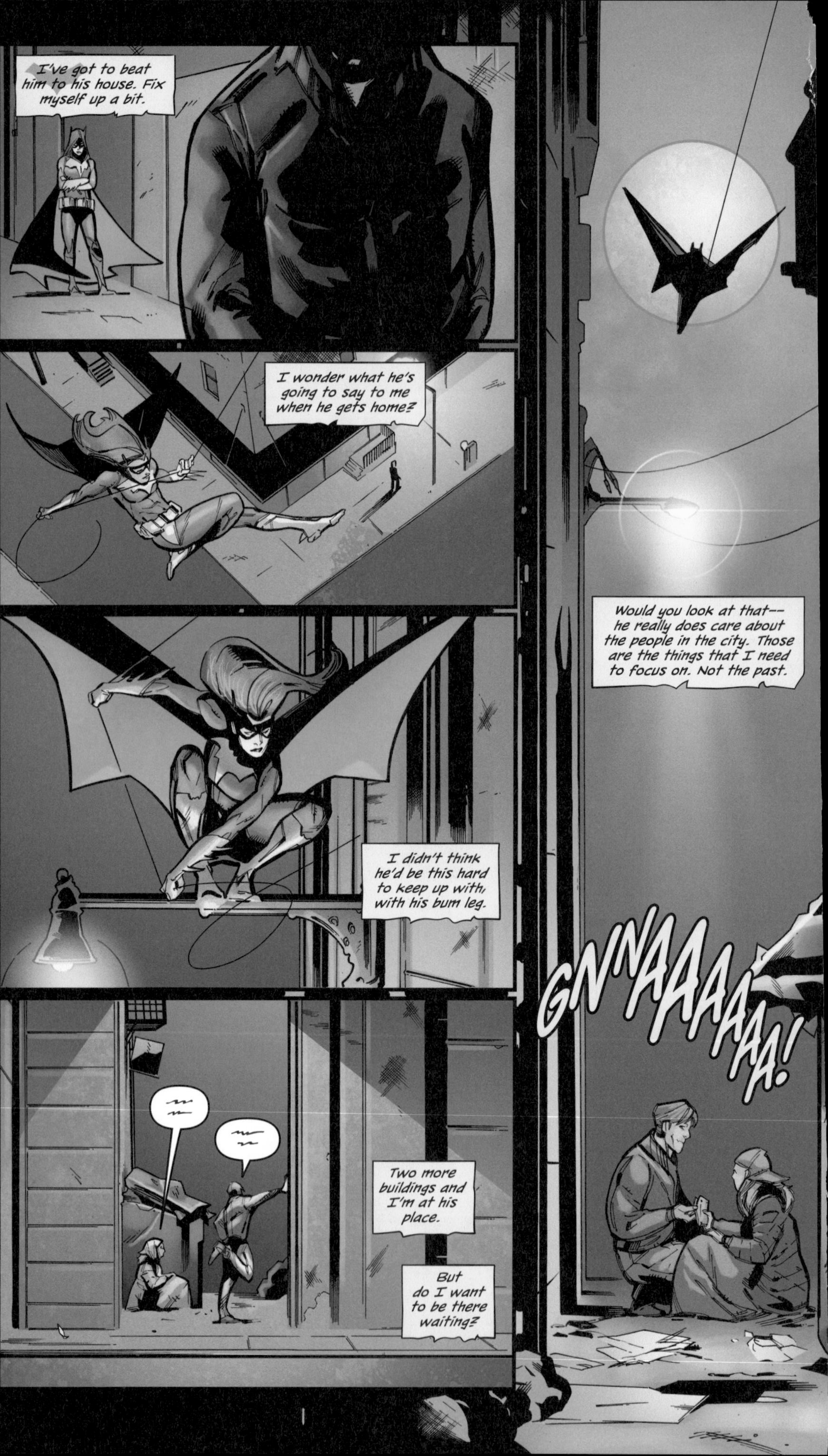
I've got to beat him to his house. Fix myself up a bit.
I wonder what he's going to say to me when he gets home?
I didn't think he'd be this hard to keep up with, with his bum leg.
Two more buildings and I'm at his place.
But do I want to be there waiting?
Would you look at that-- he really does care about the people in the city. Those are the things that I need to focus on. Not the past.
GNNAAAAAAA!

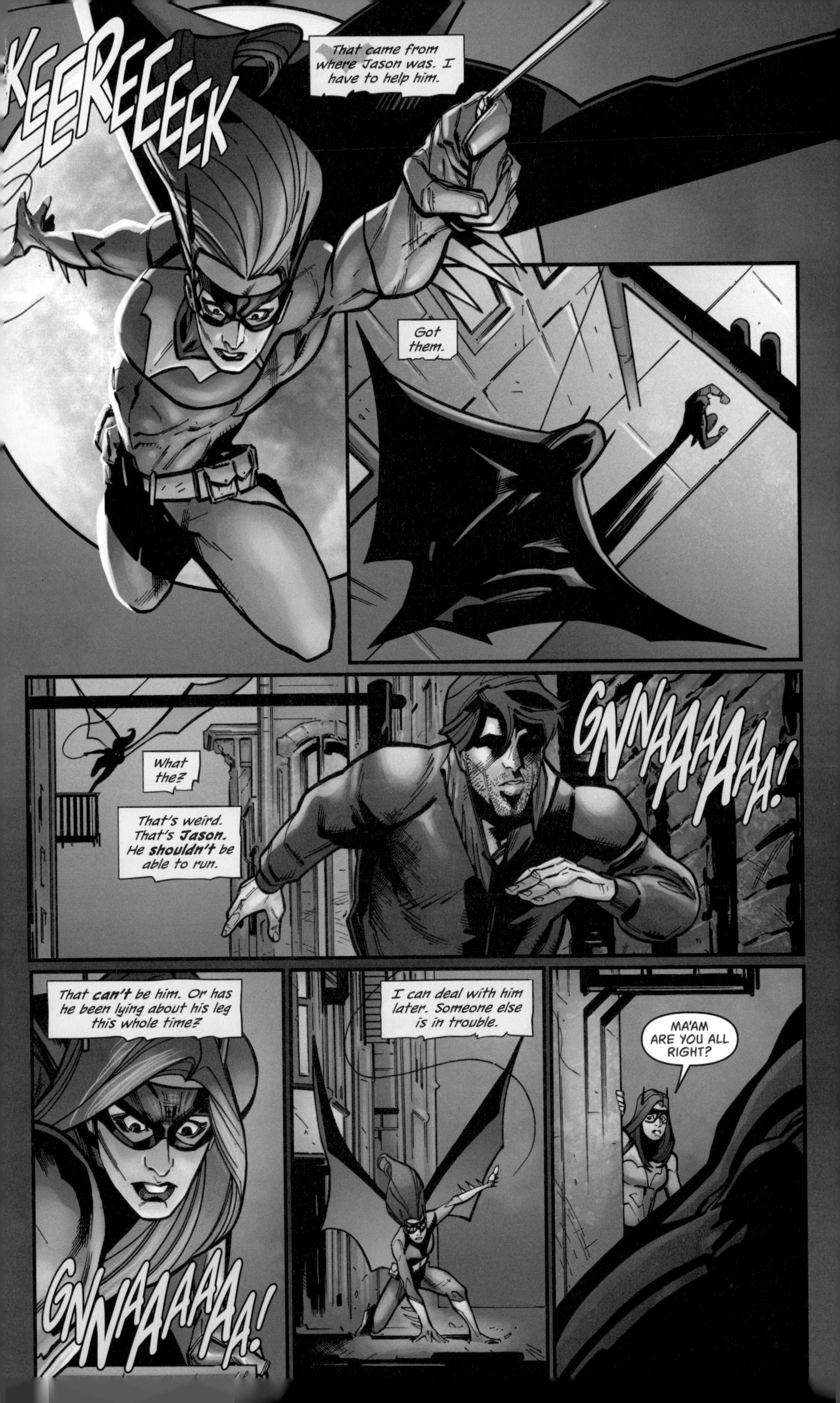
KEEREEEEK
That came from where Jason was. I have to help him.
Got them.
What the?
That's weird. That's Jason. He shouldn't be able to run.
GNNAAAAAAA!
That can't be him. Or has he been lying about his leg this whole time?
GNNAAAAAAA!
I can deal with him later. Someone else is in trouble.
MA'AM ARE YOU ALL RIGHT?

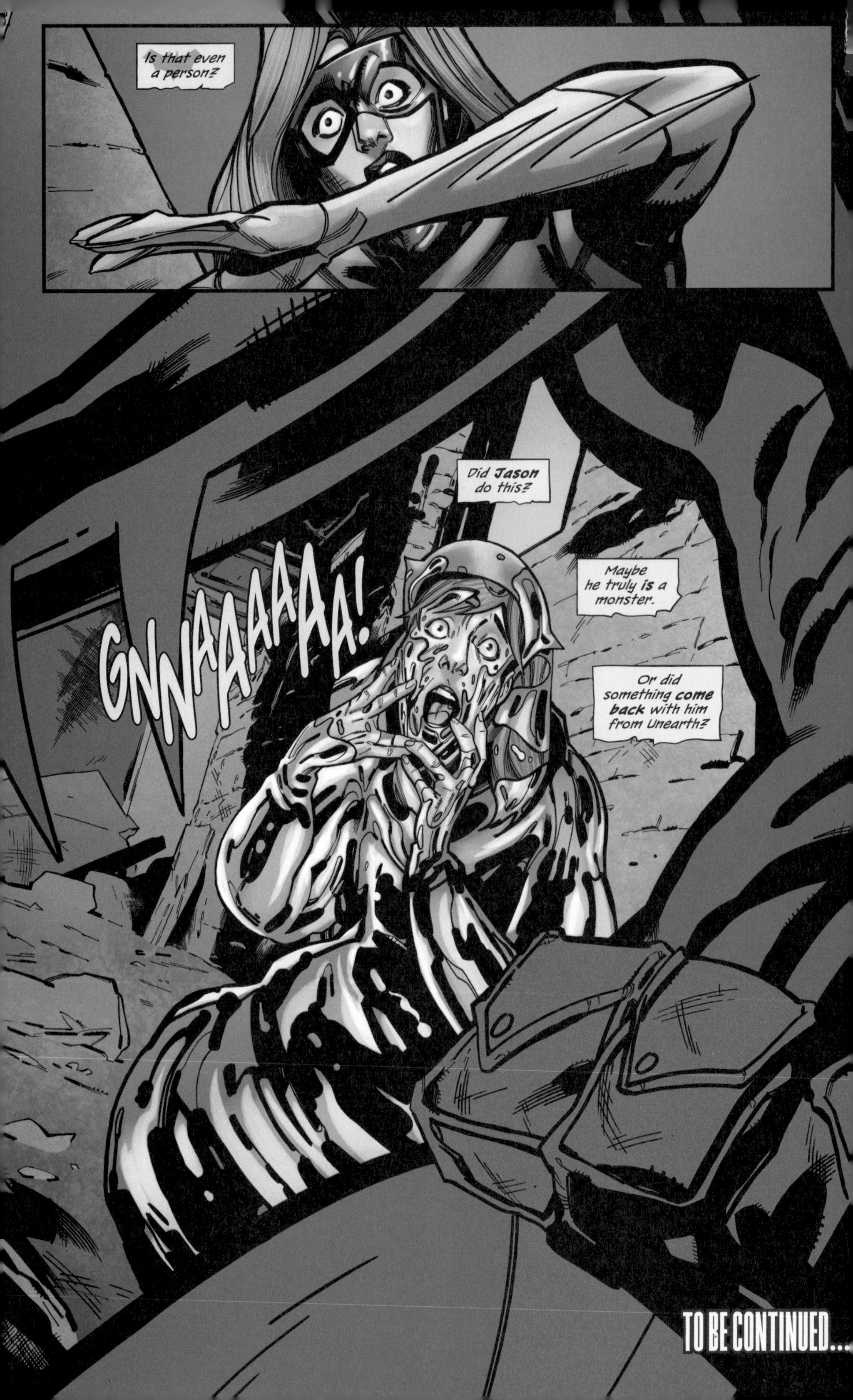
Is that even a person?
Did Jason do this?
GNAAAAAA!
Maybe he truly is a monster.
Or did something come back with him from Unearth?
TO BE CONTINUED...

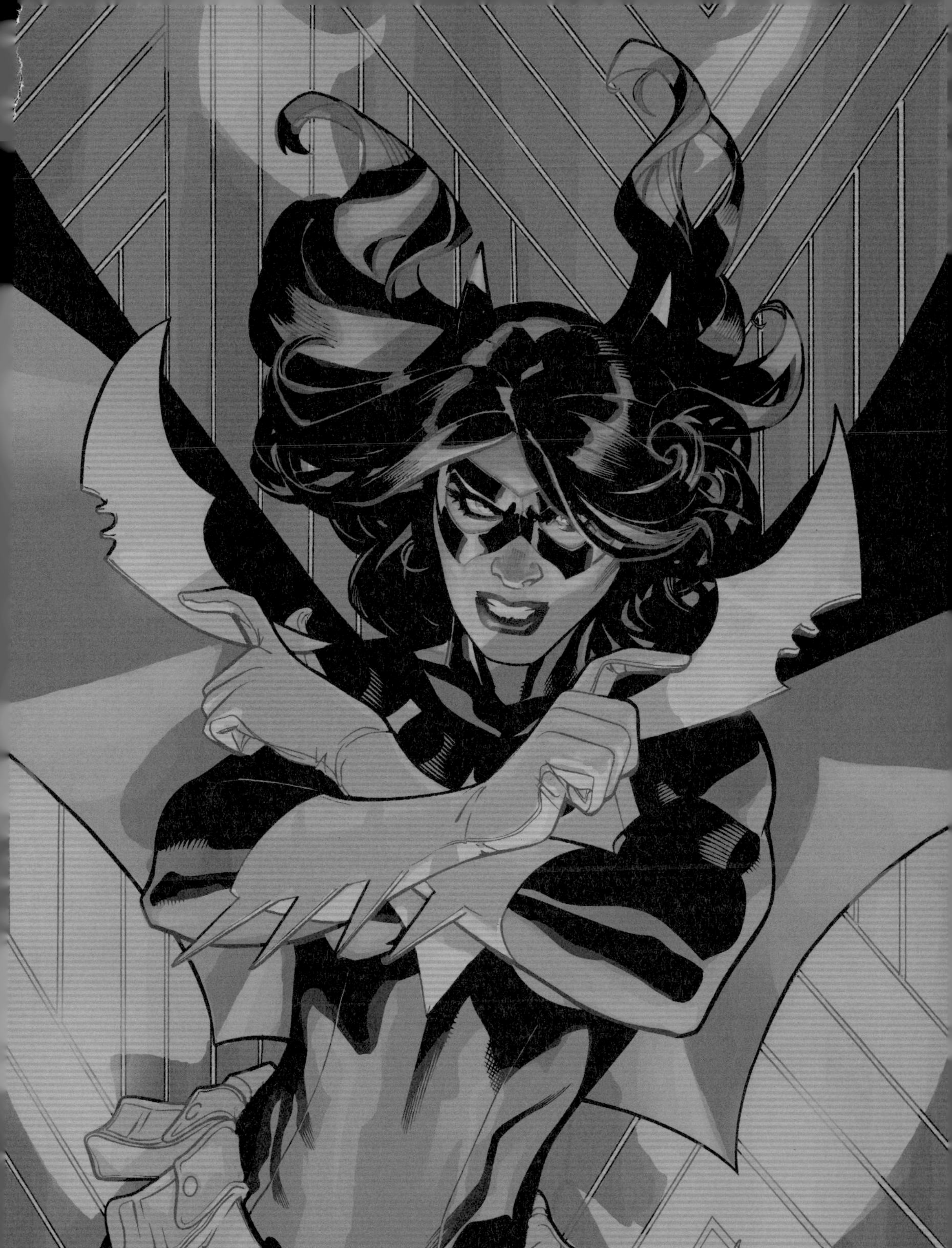

VARIANT COVER GALLERY

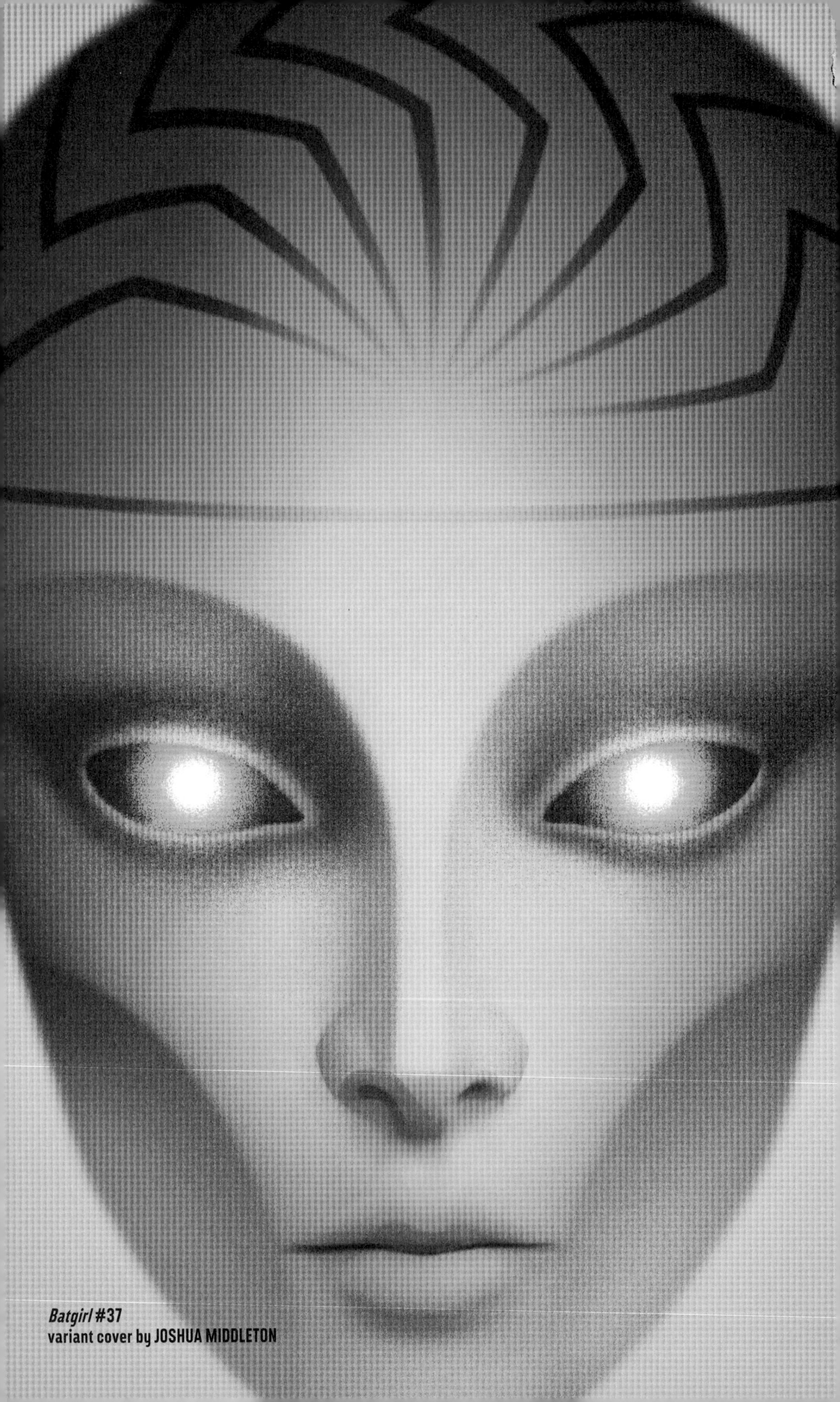

Batgirl #37
variant cover by JOSHUA MIDDLETON

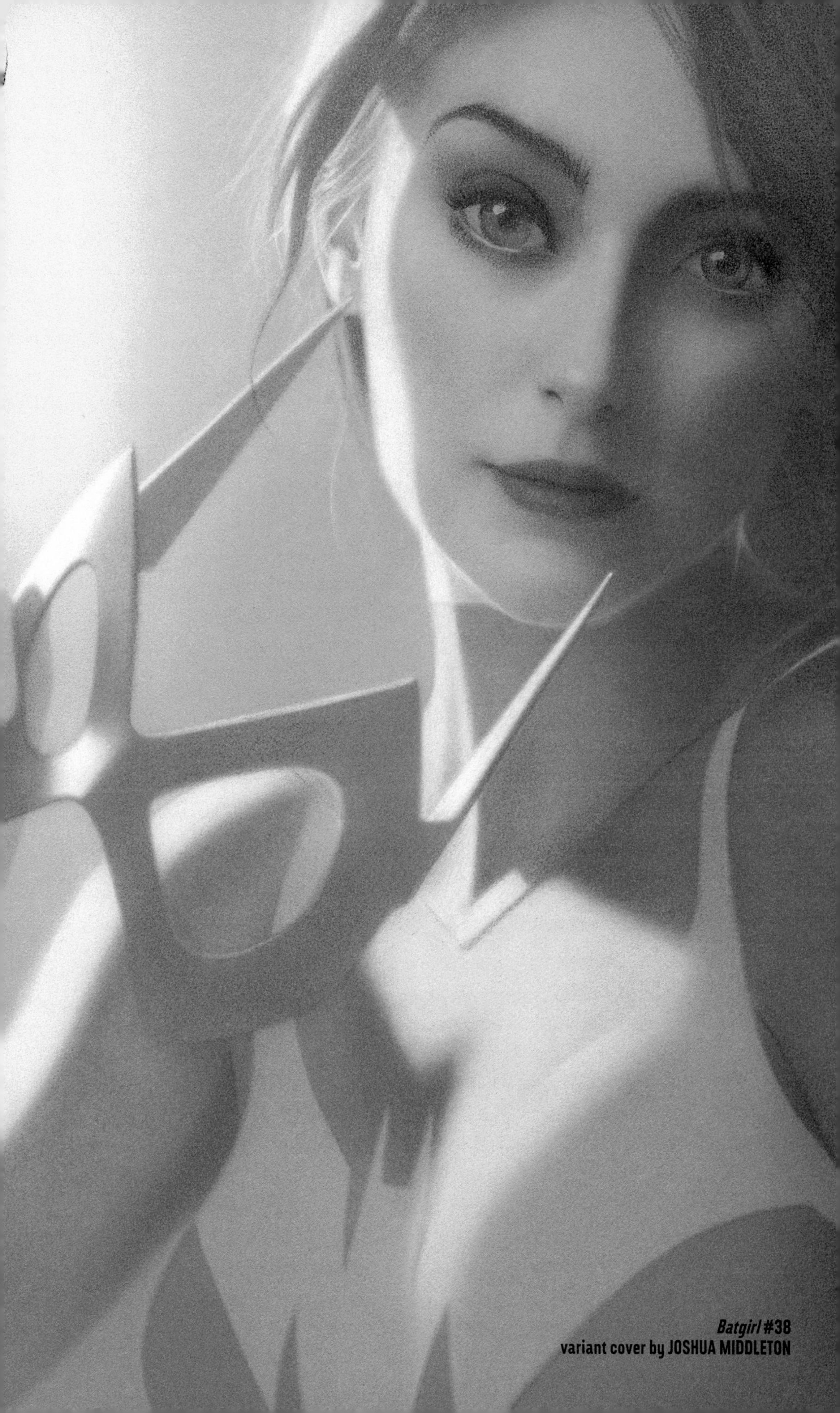

Batgirl #38
variant cover by JOSHUA MIDDLETON

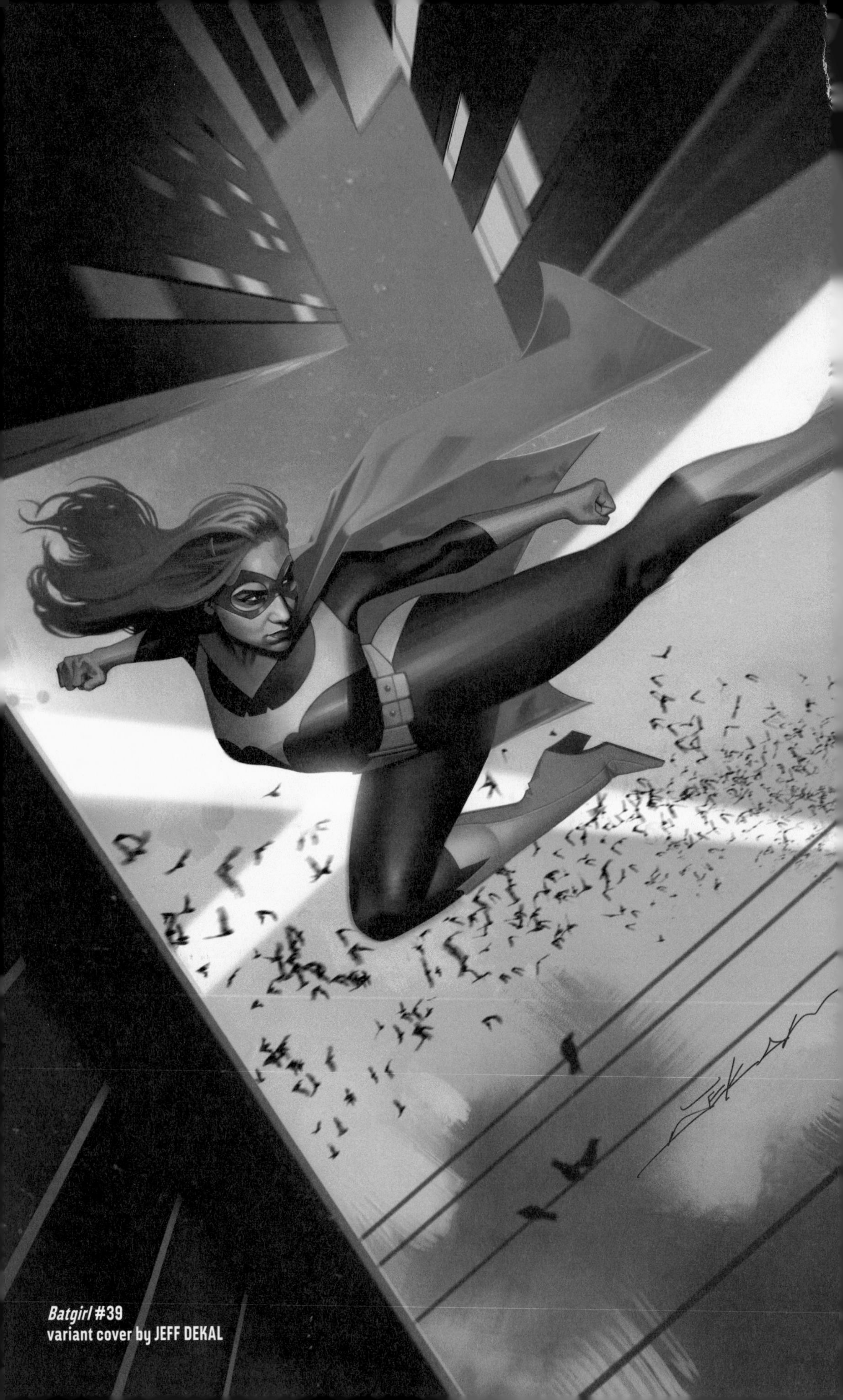

Batgirl #39
variant cover by JEFF DEKAL

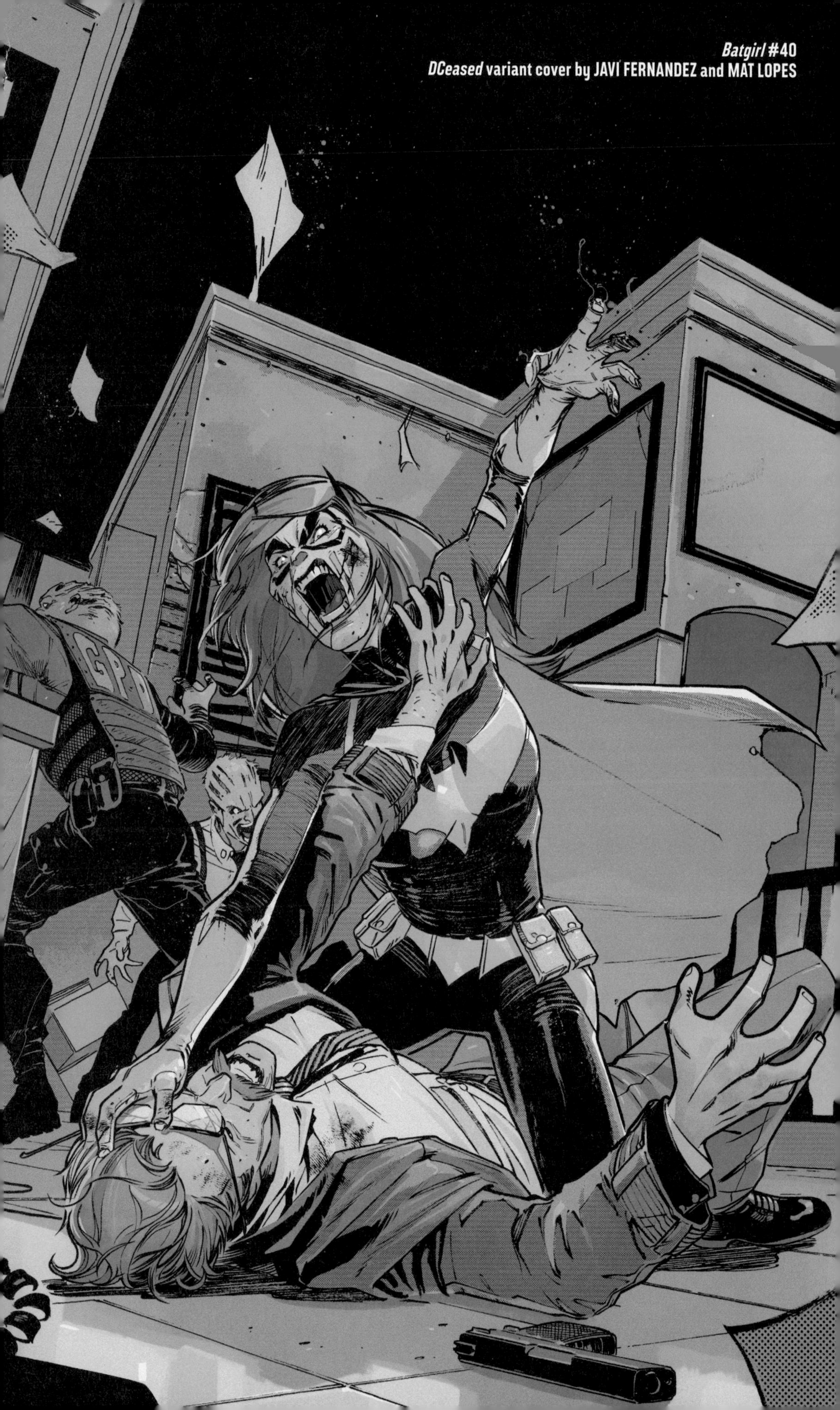
GPD

Batgirl #40
DCeased variant cover by JAVI FERNANDEZ and MAT LOPES

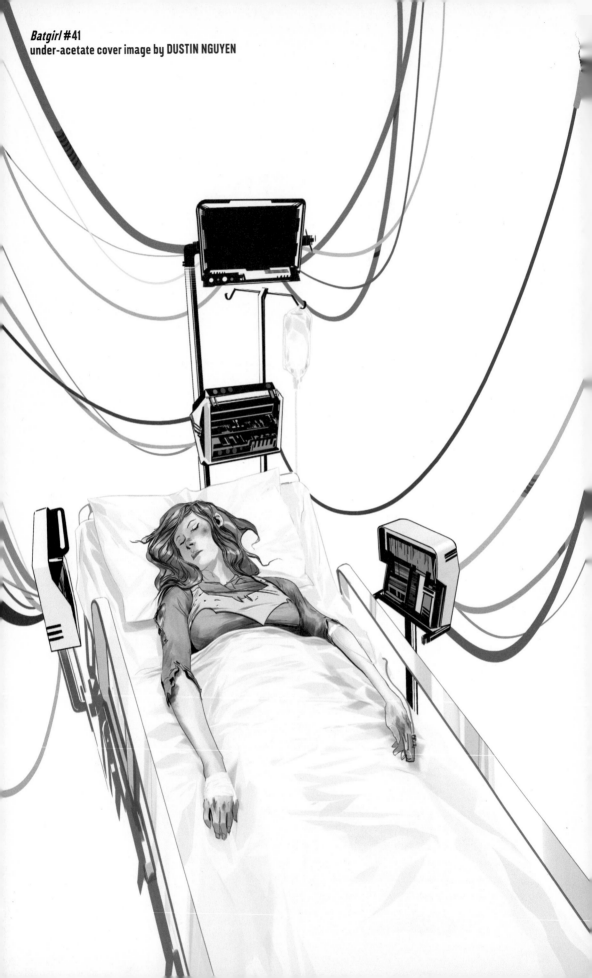

Batgirl #41
under-acetate cover image by DUSTIN NGUYEN

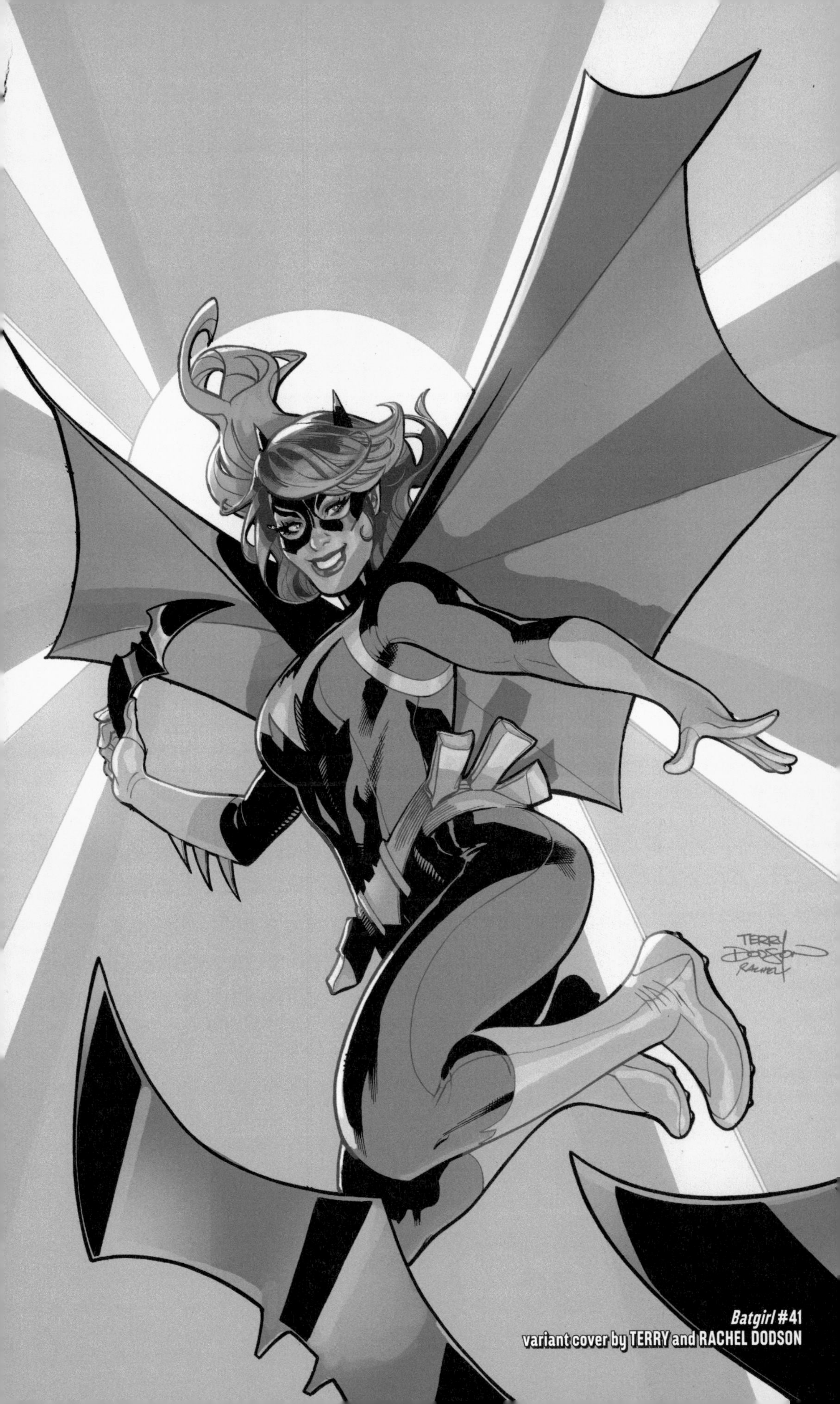
TERRY DODSON
RACHEL

Batgirl #41
variant cover by TERRY and RACHEL DODSON

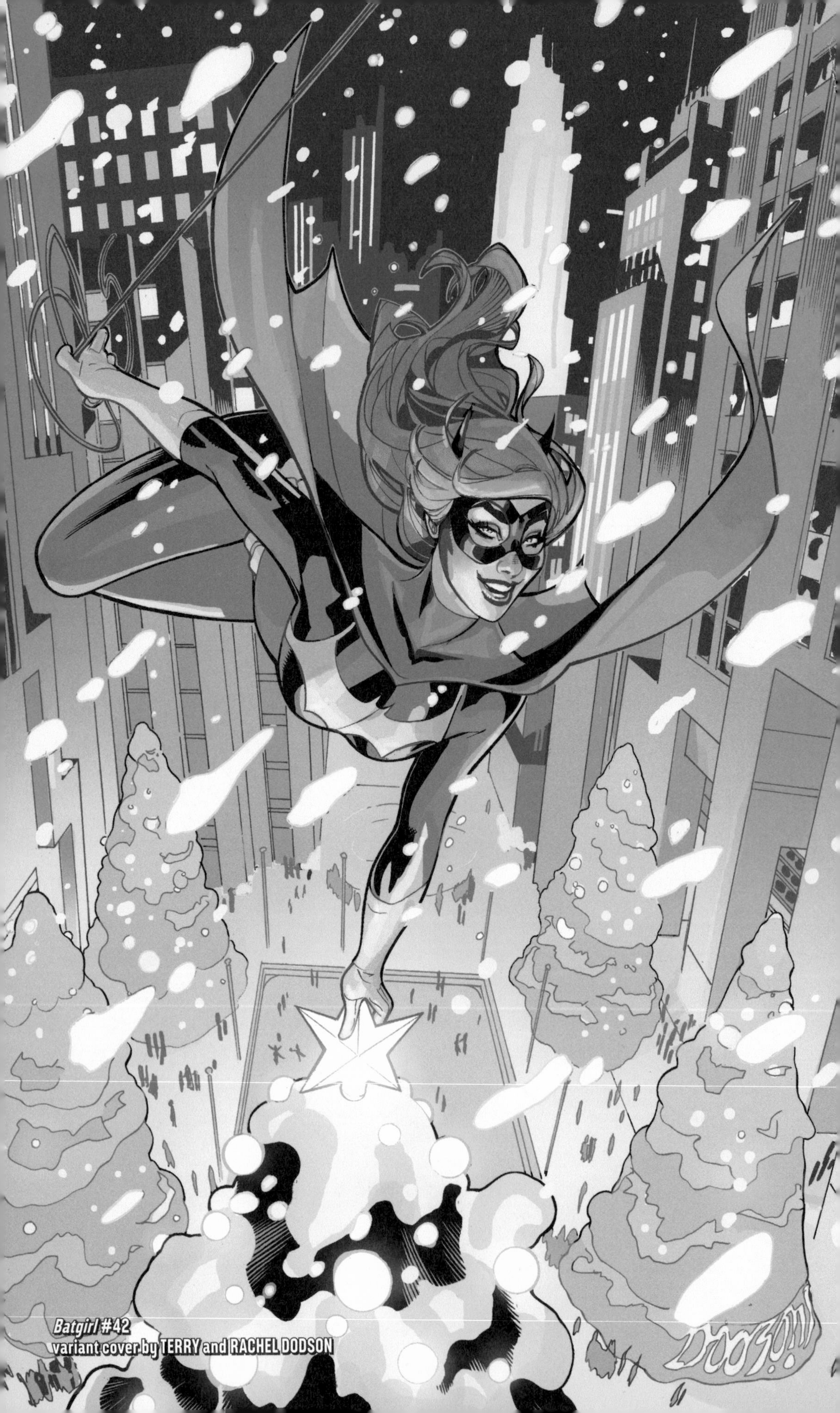

Batgirl #42
variant cover by TERRY and RACHEL DODSON

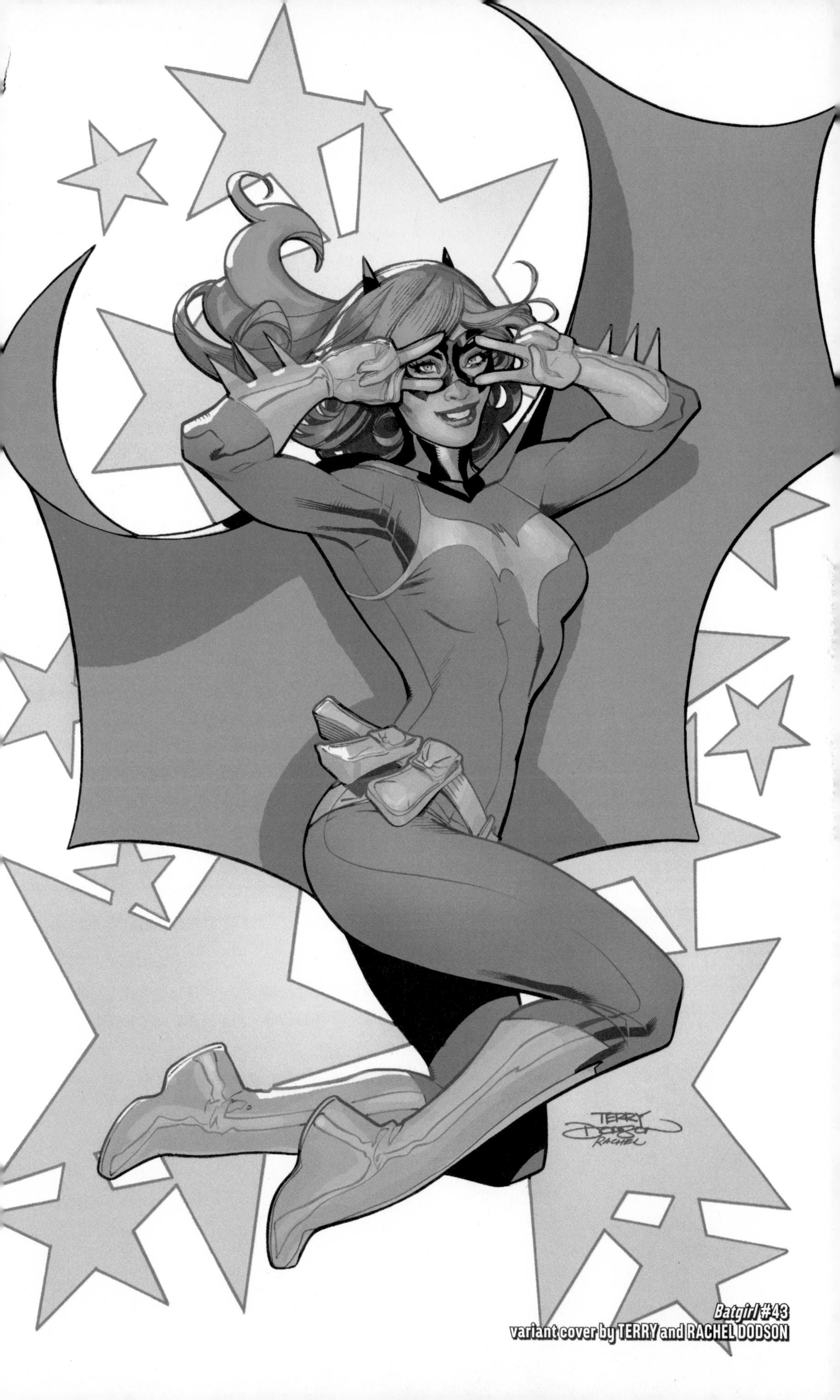
TERRY
DODSON
RACHEL

Batgirl #43
variant cover by TERRY and RACHEL DODSON

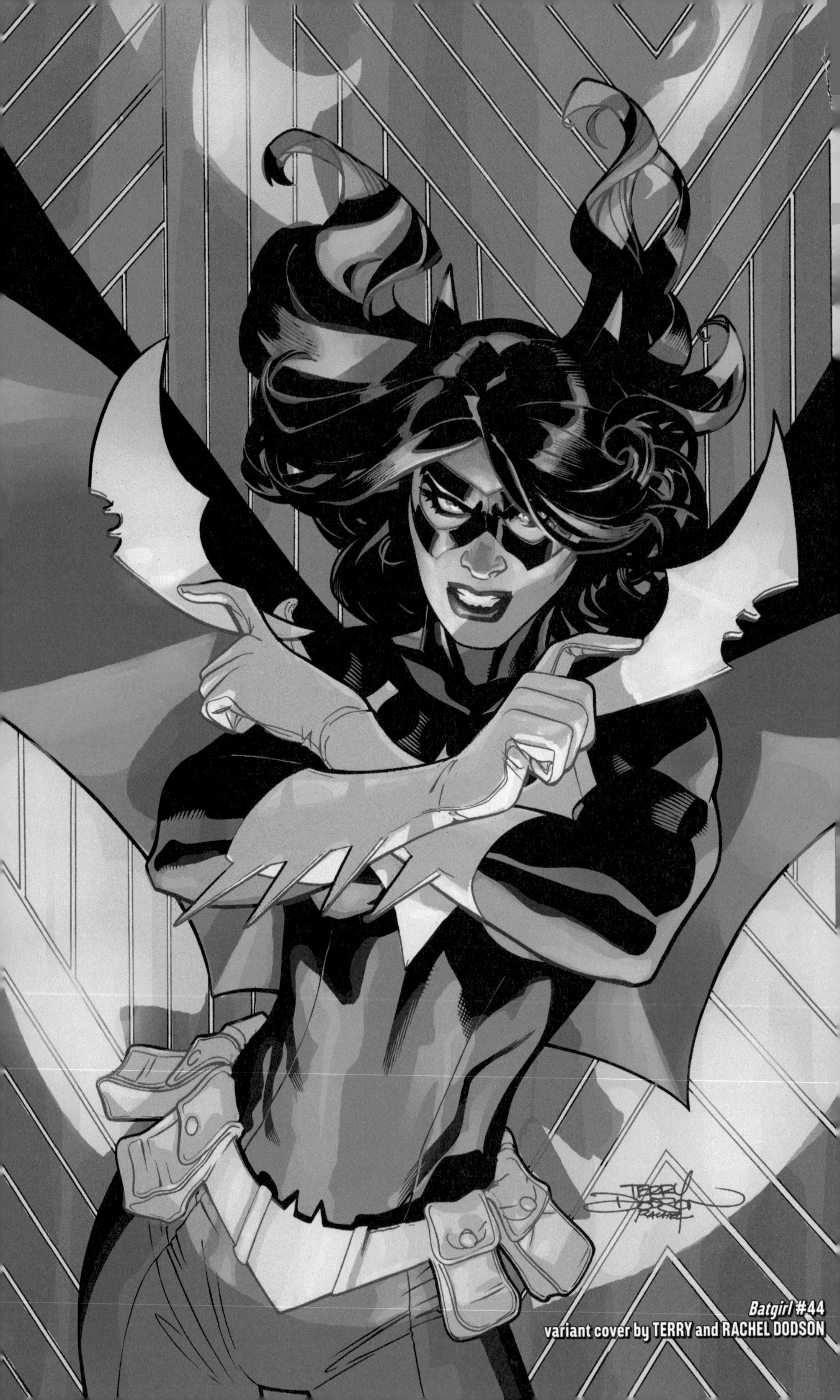

Batgirl #44
variant cover by TERRY and RACHEL DODSON

BATGIRL
VOL. 1: BATGIRL OF BURNSIDE
CAMERON STEWART & BRENDEN FLETCHER
with BABS TARR

BATGIRL VOL. 2:
FAMILY BUSINESS

BATGIRL VOL. 3:
MINDFIELDS

BLACK CANARY VOL. 1:
KICKING AND SCREAMING

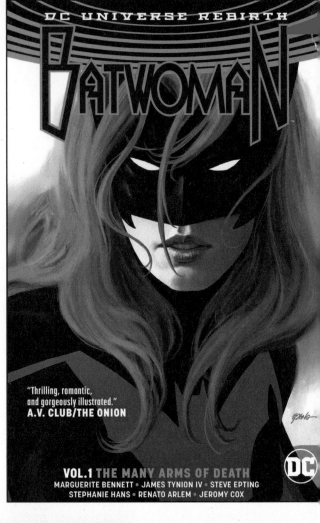